Tools of Transformation

The act of constructing a ritual object is an act of magic. The magician spends an extraordinary amount of time creating ritual objects, not because it is only through these objects that magic can rightly be performed, but because the act of creating is a magical process of growth. This process initiates the development of Will in accordance with Divine Intent or Purpose, and this in turn contributes to the success of the ritual.

The construction of a ritual object should be treated like any other magical operation. It should focus all parts of the magician's mind (intellect, creativity, imagination, spiritual self) into one purpose—to manifest an object which will be a receptacle for Higher Forces, in order that the magician too can become a worthy receptacle of that which is Divine.

With this book, clear instructions are finally available on how to create the wands and implements of the Golden Dawn, some of the most significant, profound, and beautiful of ritual tools in the Western Magical Tradition. With the materials available to the modern magician, these instruments can be created with stunning accuracy and magnificence. Learning to build and use your own magical tools is an essential step on the path of the magician. The tools you create will reinforce and enhance your magical abilities, and the act of creating them will trigger the transformation which brings spiritual growth.

About the Authors

Chic Cicero was born in Buffalo, New York. A former musician and businessman, Chic has been a practicing ceremonial magician for the past thirty years. He was a close personal friend of Israel Regardie. Having established a Golden Dawn temple in 1977, Chic was one of the key people who helped Regardie resurrect a legitimate branch of the Hermetic Order of the Golden Dawn in the early 1980s. Chic is a skilled craftsman who has personally created all of the implements shown in this book.

Sandra Tabatha Cicero was born in Soldiers Grove, Wisconsin. She graduated from the University of Wisconsin–Milwaukee, with a Bachelor's degree in the Fine Arts.

Both Chic and Tabatha are Senior Adepts of the Hermetic Order of the Golden Dawn and have several books published by Llewellyn. They share an enthusiasm for the esoteric sciences as well as a love of ritual, dance, music, and the creative arts. They live in Florida with their cat, Lealah, where they work and practice magic.

To Write to the Authors

If you wish to contact the authors or would like more information about this book, please write to the authors in care of Llewellyn Worldwide and we will forward your request. Both the authors and publisher appreciate hearing from you and learning of your enjoyment of this book and how it has helped you. Llewellyn Worldwide cannot guarantee that every letter written to the authors can be answered, but all will be forwarded. Please write to:

Chic Cicero and Sandra Tabatha Cicero
c/o Llewellyn Worldwide
P.O. Box 64383, Dept. K142-2
St. Paul, MN 55164-0383, U.S.A.

Please enclose a self-addressed, stamped envelope for reply, or $1.00 to cover costs.
If outside U.S.A., enclose international postal reply coupon.

The Magician's Craft

Creating Magical Tools

Chic Cicero
Sandra Tabatha Cicero

1999
Llewellyn Publications
St. Paul, Minnesota, 55164-0383, U.S.A.

SECOND EDITION
First Printing, 1999
(Formerly *Secrets of a Golden Dawn Temple*)

Cover design by Anne Marie Garrison
Cover art by Nybor/Nybor Mystical Art
Color plates, photos, and diagrams: Chic Cicero and Sandra Tabatha Cicero
Illustrations from *The Gods of the Egyptians, Egyptian Motifs*, and *The Complete Woodcuts of Albrecht Dürer* are courtesy of Dover Publications
Pillar Drawings copyright © Adam P. Forrest
Project management by Christine Snow
Book design by Sandra Tabatha Cicero

Library of Congress Cataloging-in-Publication Data
Cicero, Chic, 1936–
Creating magical tools : the magician's craft / Chic Cicero, Sandra Tabatha Cicero. -- 2nd ed.
p. cm.
Creating magical tools is based, in part, on Secrets of a Golden Dawn temple.
Includes bibliographical references and index.
ISBN 1-56718-142-2
1. Hermetic Order of the Golden Dawn--Rituals. I. Cicero, Sandra Tabatha, 1959– . II. Title.
BF1623.R7C48 1999b
135′.45--dc21 99-22890
CIP

Llewellyn Worldwide does not participate in, endorse, or have authority or responsibility concerning private business transactions between our authors and the public.

All mail addressed to the authors of this book is forwarded, but the publisher cannot, unless specifically instructed by the authors, give out an address or phone number.

Llewellyn Publications
A Division of Llewellyn Worldwide, Ltd.
P.O. Box 64383, St. Paul, MN 55164-0383
www.llewellyn.com

Printed in the United States of America

Dedication

This book is dedicated to the true Initiates of the Hidden Knowledge who work tirelessly and silently for the completion of the Great Work, without thought of monetary profit or personal glory. Without their careful nurturing, the special Light that remains to this day known as the Hermetic Order of the Golden Dawn would have certainly been extinguished.

We remain especially grateful to G. H. Frater E Cinere Phoenix for his devoted and firm commitment to the high ideals and original goals of the Golden Dawn.

We would also like to thank Carl and Sandra Weschcke for all that they have done to ensure that the teachings of the Golden Dawn have been readily available to students across the world.

Above all, we warmly thank Francis Israel Regardie, who held out the lamp of the Hidden Knowledge for all of us.

Acknowledgments

It gives us great pleasure to acknowledge the many people who contributed in some way to the completion of this book: Adam Forrest for his contribution of original artwork for the Pillar diagrams, the Foreword, much-needed corrections on the Coptic spellings and colorings of the various godforms of the Neophyte Hall, as well as his invaluable advice; Isidora Forrest for her work on robes, collars, and tabards, in addition to her photo of a stained glass Water Cup; Donald Michael Kraig for providing the Foreword; Ceil Thomas for providing the sections describing the Banners and the carrying case for the adept's magical implements; Bill Allen for his section on the Geomantic Divination Box; Anupassana and George Wilson who provided material on the nemyss and corrections for the Day/Night Houses of the planets in the section describing the Lotus Wand; Mitch and Gail Henson for their refinements of the nemyss pattern; V. H. Frater A. A. A. who pointed out corrections to the divine names on the Elemental Weapons; Bill and Judy Genaw for their new material on the Fire Wand; Harvey Newstrom for scanning in the text; Aaron Leitch for his work on the index; Kathi Reilly-Murphy for her insights into constructing the Lotus Wand; and finally Logan and Danaé Sullivan for their encouragement.

Other Books by the Ciceros

The Golden Dawn Magical System:
The New Golden Dawn Ritual Tarot Deck
The New Golden Dawn Ritual Tarot (book)
Secrets of a Golden Dawn Temple
Self-Initiation Into the Golden Dawn Tradition
The Golden Dawn Journal Series:
Book I: Divination
Book II: Qabalah: Theory and Magic
Book III: The Art of Hermes
The Magical Pantheons: A Golden Dawn Journal
Experiencing the Kabbalah

Forthcoming Books by the Ciceros

Ritual Use of Magical Tools: The Magician's Art
(*Secrets of a Golden Dawn Temple*, revised and expanded)
The Illustrated Tree of Life (tentative title)

Books edited by the Ciceros

The Middle Pillar: The Balance Between Mind and Magic by Israel Regardie
(3rd edition, edited and annotated with new material by the Ciceros)
A Garden of Pomegranates: Skrying on the Tree of Life by Israel Regardie
(3rd edition, edited and annotated with new material by the Ciceros)

I cannot now think symbols less than the greatest of all powers whether they are used consciously by the masters of magic, or half consciously by their successors, the poet, the musician, and the artist.

—W. B. Yeats (Frater D. E. D. I.) *Magic,* 1901

Contents

Illustrations

Color Plates

Diagrams and Charts

Foreword

Some people buy and read magical books without ever doing any real, practical magic. When you decide to use *this* book, however, you will truly take a step away from those dilettantes who claim to be magicians but who, in reality, are what Israel Regardie used to refer to as the "inepti."

To the best of my knowledge, two books were published over a decade ago which gave cursory (and sometimes incorrect) explanations on how to build a small selection of the tools described in this book, along with some generic magical tools. As of this writing neither of the two are in print. The book you hold in your hands, however, is quite different from them. They explained how to build objects; this explains how to use the tools you construct in the transformational alchemy which will lead to your further spiritual development. It is this growth which is the true goal of ceremonial magic and of groups such as the Hermetic Order of the Golden Dawn.

If you think that this is overstating the issue, good! You are on your way to becoming a true magician by not simply taking somebody's word for it. True magicians are thinkers and experimenters, not blind followers of personalities who died decades or centuries ago. But I am not overstating the issue. Building and working with the tools described in this book will make a difference in your life. The only way you will know this for sure, of course, is when you try them out for yourself.

Some people who are not ceremonial magicians have pointed out to me that the magical tools are only that—tools. A true magician, they claim, does not need to have daggers, wands, etc. They proudly say that they can do all the magic they desire with a few well-chosen words or a snap of the fingers.

While it is partly true that the tools are an extension of the magician (the proper consecration, charging and use of magical tools also makes them into powerful talismans of collected magical energy), such a claim misses the point. The various tools can be used as aids for learning how to direct magical energies, just as learning to read aloud precedes learning to read silently.

Any ritual can be successfully performed without tools and the understanding of the ritual and the proper visualizations and vocalizations. I have found, however, that the tools reinforce and enhance my own magical abilities. The tools do not give me added powers, but they do allow me to use my abilities to my fullest capacity. They enhance my ritual work and my life as a magician. They make every aspect of my life more magical. Let me describe some of my experiences in this.

The first tool I created and used was a robe. I owned a sewing machine—I used it primarily for patching up clothes—but I had never attempted a sewing project of this complexity. I had never even used a pattern.

I followed the instructions I had been given for making the robe to the letter. (I think I may have used too many pins to hold the material in place while I was sewing it, however. Dropped pins turned up in bare feet for months after I was finished!) Sometimes the pieces of cloth in front of me made no logical sense. Finally, it started to take shape. When it was finished I marveled at what I had created. The pieces of material had become a Tau robe. This certainly was an alchemical change.

No, there was no shaking of hands or tense anticipation as I put on the robe for the first time. It was, after all, just a piece of cloth. I knew that there would be no "poof" of smoke, leaving me surrounded by women, gold, and jewels, as a result of donning what I had made. I was wrong.

After I put it on I discovered that something did change—me. I had never worn a robe like this before. It felt good on me, like it was a part of me. I felt special. The first ritual I performed in it, the Lesser Banishing Ritual of the Pentagram, felt different—more effective, more powerful.

Perhaps it was a psychological lift, perhaps it was an objective change. I have no doubt, however, that when I wore the robe my rituals improved in quality, intensity, and effect. As a result of working with that one simple tool, I was accelerating my evolution into something more than I was—I was truly becoming a magician.

The next tool I made was an altar. I am not great with woodworking, but the design was simple. I spent a great deal of time getting a smooth coat of paint on the altar. As a finishing touch, I decoupaged a large painting of a pentagram (which I hand-colored) on the top and one of the Tree of Life on the front.

Using an altar—one specifically designed for doing ritual, not merely an extra table—made a difference in my rituals. The altar forms a central focal point around which the ritual circle is created. I discovered that it was an important addition to making a magical circle even though it was at the center and not the circumference.

As I slowly created or changed various items into magical tools, I found that my own abilities and spirituality were growing. Each new tool added to the power and effectiveness of my ritual work.

To my great surprise I discovered that when I was ready to use a tool which I did not have, it would either come to me or I would develop the skills to create it. I remember a "chance" occurrence which took place around 1980. I was walking around an area in San Diego where there were several used book stores, wondering how I would ever find a sword that I could adapt for magical use. I happened to walk past an Oriental herb store where martial arts classes were also taught. Something drew me inside and I saw a sword hanging on the wall which would have been perfect for my purposes. I asked if it was for sale and the one person in the store said I would have to ask the owner, as it was his personal sword. The owner, I was told, would be back in an hour.

During that hour I walked around with my head spinning. It was too perfect. It was the ideal shape. But had it been used for fighting? If so I would have to cleanse it very thoroughly. If it had ever drawn blood I didn't want it at all. Worst of all, I did not have a great deal of money. Going over my finances in my head I realized that I could only afford to pay $35.00 for any sword. I had already looked at many swords and most cost from $55.00 to many hundreds of dollars. Still, I knew I would never be content if I didn't find out the entire story of this sword.

After an hour had passed I went back into the store. The man whom I had talked with was gone and an older person was there. I asked him if he was the owner. When he told me he was, I asked how much he wanted for the sword.

He gazed up at the sword with a look in his eye as if he had forgotten about it entirely. "Gee," he explained, "I had never thought of selling it. I bought it from the maker when I was in Japan and I personally brought it over by boat. I was going to use it for [martial arts] practice but I never did. I'm sorry," he added, "but I couldn't sell it for less than $35.00."

Needless to say, after some minor physical alterations, appropriate painting, and magical consecration and charging, I still have it as one of my prime magical tools.

I think that using the tools of magic is important for practitioners. People in Western society today are different from those who lived 100 to 2,000 years ago. We now have blasting stereos and brilliant colors found on everything from television screens to shoelaces. Our lives are filled with an intensity of sensation—visual, aural, etc.—which might have inundated our predecessors. Those who have avoided society, who live in rural areas, and who have eliminated the intensity of city living from their lives, may find that a simple dagger and branch from a tree may be enough to use. I, however, grew up in a large city, and for many purposes find that I want more to help excite my senses and enhance my magic. For me there is a difference in performing rituals with specially created (or modified) and charged tools, as opposed to using no tools or items that are simply found. You will discover those differences, too.

I have worked with the Golden Dawn system of Magic, as outlined in Israel Regardie's *The Golden Dawn,* for many years and found my rituals to be enhanced by the tools I made and used. In turn, my work affected my psyche and helped to make me a more magical person. As I have written many times, "Magic is not something you do, magic is something you are."

I have spent thousands of hours over the last two-and-a-half decades in the trial and error of building tools. If I had possessed this book twenty-five years ago, I would have saved myself a great deal of time and effort. In a sense I envy those who are starting out in the study of ceremonial magic and the Golden Dawn system. Many of the things I had to learn through meditation, study of rare books, and trial-and-error are now easily available.

The magical current that is the source of the real power of the Golden Dawn can be tapped into by anyone. You do not need to be a member of any particular group. With diligence, practice, and the study of works such as this one and those of Israel Regardie, you can link with the Golden Dawn's magical current and become a magician in the Golden Dawn tradition.

Recently a person asked me, "If you were a member of a magical order, what grade would you be in?" "That's easy," I replied. "I'd be a neophyte. I'm still learning new things every day. Sometimes I find a teacher in the strangest places."

Yes, I do believe in the old statement that when the student is ready the teacher will appear.

This book can be your teacher if you are ready.

—Donald Michael Kraig

Preface

Man is a tool-using animal. . . . Without tools he is nothing, with tools he is all.
—Thomas Carlyle, *Sartor Resartus* (1833–34)

Whoever undertakes to create soon finds himself engaged in creating himself.
—Harold Rosenberg, *The Tradition of the New* (1960)

Some years back, when we first began making the various symbolic items, magical tools, temple furnishings, and ritual regalia that were needed to build a working temple in the Golden Dawn tradition, there were precious few published works that we could depend on for accurate resource material. Of these, Israel Regardie's *The Golden Dawn* and Robert Wang's *The Secret Temple* were paramount, and R. G. Torren's *The Secret Rituals of the Golden Dawn* was helpful as well. But these books, as rich as they were in their description of certain tools, rarely gave good, practical advice on the actual construction techniques for many of these implements. *The Secret Temple* was the lone exception, but even then, only a limited number of magical tools were discussed. Like generations of practicing magicians who came before us, we had to rely on our own creative abilities and ingenuity to devise ways of creating the necessary symbolism. Experimentation was the order of the day—some methods worked while others were retired to the scrap heap of "good but impractical ideas." By the time we had completed many of these items, we realized that we had enough material for a book, and *Secrets of a Golden Dawn Temple* was the result—a textbook which we hoped would make things easier for the next generation of temple-builders.

Secrets was an ambitious project. Not only did it include instructions on how to make over eighty magical implements, it also included rituals for consecrating and using these tools. In some ways the book was too ambitious, and we realized that we had probably included too much material for a single book. Some people thought it was simply a manual for creating magical tools, not realizing that it also contained nearly sixty separate rituals, meditations, and exercises.

Since 1992, when *Secrets of a Golden Dawn Temple* was first published, we have continued to find new ways of crafting magical implements. We have also found that many other magicians have come up with their own creative methods or helpful hints for making these items, and we wanted this material published as well. So when it came time to print a new edition of *Secrets,* we decided to rework the book into two volumes: *Creating Magical Tools* and *Ritual Use of Magical Tools*.

Creating Magical Tools describes all the symbolism and construction techniques of the implements that were previously included in *Secrets of a Golden Dawn Temple.* All of the consecration ceremonies and practical rituals are now contained in a companion volume, *Ritual Use of Magical Tools*. Both books have been updated with new material, endnotes, glossaries, and extensive indexes.

If man is indeed a tool-using creature engaged in the process of self-creation, then we offer this work to those who wish to build and use the symbols and tools of magic in the work of theurgy—in order to recreate within themselves a clearer reflection of the divine, in an effort to become more than human.

—Chic Cicero
Sandra Tabatha Cicero
Metatron House
Easter Sunday, 1999

Introduction

Magic is a spiritual science. It is a technical system of training with a divine rather than mundane objective. The goal of magic is to discipline and strengthen the will and the imagination. When you create something in your imagination, you are creating it in the subtle layers of the astral plane. All of the machines, music, books, inventions, and everyday objects that we use and take for granted began as blueprints in someone's mind. What was first imagined was then created. Bringing the astral image of something into manifestation, be it an object, event, circumstance, or spiritual state of mind, has always been one of the goals of magic. This is especially true when it comes to making magical or ritual objects.

The act of constructing a wand or other ritual object should be considered an act of magic. The magician spends an extraordinary amount of time creating ritual objects, not because it is only through these precious objects that magic can rightly be performed, but because the construction of these items is the catalyst for a magical process of growth, one which initiates the development of will in accordance with the divine intent or purpose. Israel Regardie, founder of the modern incarnation of the Golden Dawn, emphasized this point in regard to the fashioning of the magician's wand. This same principle may be applied to all of the magician's implements:

> *Since the Wand is the symbol of the Creative Will, its construction should be accompanied by a distinct exertion of that Will, and in this idea is the rational of many of the apparently far-fetched injunctions given by Theurgists in connection with the acquisition of suitable weapons....*
>
> *Were* [Eliphas] *Levi's advice to be followed, for instance, in connection with the Wand, then that instrument should be fashioned from a perfectly straight branch of the almond or hazel tree, cut without hacking or boggling with a single blow from the tree with a sharp knife before the sun rises, and at the season when the tree is about to blossom. It should be subjected to a process of meticulous preparation, stripping the branch of leaves and twigs, removing the bark, and neatly trimming the ends and smoothing down the knots, followed by other significant processes which can be ascertained by consulting Transcendental Magic. Underlying all these processes is the development of the Will. The Magician who has troubled himself to the extent of rising two or three times at midnight on behalf of his Wand and denied himself rest and sleep, will, by the very fact of his self-denial, have benefited considerable in Will. In such an instance, the Wand actually will be a dynamic symbol of the Creative Will, and it is such symbols and instruments as this which in Magic are required.*[1]

The elaborate preparation undertaken by the ceremonialist is necessary not for the performance of magic per se, but rather for the proper development of the mind and the creative will of the magician. This in turn contributes to the success of the ritual:

> [Wands and other Elemental weapons] *function as the visible embodiment of the Magician's own condition of soul and mind, without which they fail of effect as thaumaturgic symbols. If the Magician's mind, for instance, be not sharp and analytic, and if this quality of mind be not contributed to the making of the sword, how should the elemental spirits and the dog-faced demons obey his commands to get themselves gone from the circle of invocation? The chalice, too, as the symbol of the Intuition as well as of the divine Imagination, must likewise be fashioned in such a way and attended by high thoughts and great deeds as to embody some intuitional idea, either bearing on the exterior design or word of supreme significance, or exemplifying by the shape of the Cup alone a divine idea.*[2]

Constructing a ceremonial wand focuses all parts of the magician's mind (intellect, creativity, imagination, and spiritual self) into one purpose—to manifest an object which will be a receptacle for higher forces, in order that the magician, too, can become a worthy receptacle of that which is divine.

We have seen photographs of many elemental weapons constructed a century ago by some of the Golden Dawn's most prominent and brilliant members. Some of those implements seem very rough by our own standards, but achieving material perfection was never the point. What is important is that those members constructed their personal tools to the best of their abilities—putting their own creativity into action. A magician who works long and hard on a wand that looks crude will ultimately have more success than a person who purchases a ready-made wand that is flawless.

In writing this book we have tried to make available clear instructions on how to fabricate the wands and implements of the Golden Dawn, some of the most significant, profound, and beautiful of all the ritual tools that have ever been produced in the Western Magical Tradition. With the materials and tools available to the modern magician, these instruments can be recreated with stunning accuracy and magnificence. It is not our intention, however, to present merely a construction manual for the manufacture of magical implements. Granted, the main purpose of this book is to show how to produce the various items which are vital to a properly equipped Golden Dawn temple. More than that, we wish to give the student access to magical techniques which can be applied to those same implements, both in their construction, consecration, and their use. To that end we have provided consecration rituals and other ceremonies for these implements in the companion book *Ritual Use of Magical Tools: The Magician's Art.*

The construction of a ritual object should be treated like any other magical operation, and thus it is important to keep in mind the high purposes for which the objects are being made. You should not try gluing wand sections together or cutting out fabric for a robe if you are highly aggravated over something. The project can be put aside until things calm down.

An Overview

Chapter one of this book contains the bulk of information necessary for the construction of a Golden Dawn temple in the Outer Order—what is commonly known as the Neophyte Hall. Chapter two concentrates on the secondary props of the elemental halls and the Admission Badges for the various grades of the Outer Order.

In chapter three, the tools of the Portal grade are described, as well as the Enochian Tablets. The wands and some additional tools of the Second Order are examined in chapter four.

The adept's personal temple implements are given in chapter five. These include the four Elemental Weapons as well as the Magic Sword, Lotus Wand, and Rose Cross Lamen.

We have also included a section on the fabrication of new, non-traditional implements that are based on rituals inspired by the Golden Dawn system of magic. These are given in chapter six.

Safety

Many of the implements presented in this book require power tools or wood-carving instruments in their construction. If you are not skilled at working with these implements, then turn the job over to someone who is. Always use common sense when working with electrical tools or sharp cutting instruments. Never leave a power tool plugged in when not in use or when changing or removing saw blades or drill bits. If a power tool comes with a plastic or metal guard, use it. Use a vise attached to a sturdy work bench to secure your wooden project during construction. Always wear safety goggles and a mask when

Figure 1: Chic Cicero Constructing a Wand

woodworking to prevent dust or wood particles from getting into your eyes and nose. Always cut wood away from you, never toward you. By using the proper equipment and following standard safety precautions, the creation of the implements presented here will prove to be a rewarding, magical, and safe experience.

Color

Color is extremely important to the magician, because it is through the proper application of color, as well as through sound and symbol, that the ceremonialist is able to forge a magical link with the divine Intelligences. Thus color is of primary importance to the creation of virtually all of the implements discussed in this book. Because today pigments in paint are measured and standardized with a high degree of accuracy, students can paint their magical tools and be fairly certain that they have achieved the correct hue necessary to make the colors "flash" or complement each other. (Refer to the section on "Flashing Colors.")

Hue is that property of a color which gives it its name—red, blue, violet, and so on. It is the first thing we notice about a color (its redness, blueness, etc.). *Value* is the relative darkness or lightness of a color, such as in the distinction between "light green" and "dark green" or in "light blue" or "dark blue." *Chroma* (also called *intensity* or *saturation*) is the strength or purity of a color—its brightness or dullness.

The names given to pigments have always been a source of confusion to students exploring the color scales of the Golden Dawn. In this book, you will not find such nondescriptive titles as "butterfly blue" or "ultraviolet." Here, only the true or generic names of colors, as listed by color theorist Albert H. Munsell,[3] will be used.

Traditional Name	**Proper Name**
Scarlet	Red
Red Orange	Red-orange
Orange	Orange
Amber	Yellow-orange
Yellow or gold	Yellow
Greenish Yellow	Yellow-green
Emerald	Green
Greenish Blue	Blue-green
Blue or azure	Blue
Indigo	Blue-violet
Purple or puce	Violet
Ultraviolet or crimson	Red-violet

Since most of the implements are built from wood, any type of acrylic paint may be used to color them. However, since some brands do not have certain pigments required for making flashing colors, we recommend using Liquitex or Golden brand acrylic paints. The following list shows how the colors you will need are described by these two major brands of acrylic paint:

Color	Liquitex Acrylic Paint	Golden Acrylic Paint
Red	Naphthol Red Light Cadmium Red Medium	Cadmium Red Medium
Red-orange	Indo Orange Red	Vat Orange
Orange	Cadmium Orange Brilliant Orange	Cadmium Orange
Yellow-orange	Yellow Orange Azo	Cadmium Yellow Dark
Yellow	Cadmium Yellow Light Hansa Yellow Light	Cadmium Yellow Light
Yellow-green	Vivid Lime Green	Light Green (Yellow shade)
Green	Permanent Green Light	Light Green
Blue-green	Turquoise Green	Light Turquoise
Blue	Brilliant Blue Cerulean Blue	Cerulean Blue
Blue-violet	Cobalt Blue Brilliant Blue Purple	Cobalt Blue
Violet	Prism Violet	Medium Violet
Red-violet	Deep Magenta	Quinacridone Violet
Black	Mars Black	Mars Black
White	Titanium White	Titanium White
Gray	Neutral Gray	

You will also need to purchase Antique Gold and Iridescent White. If you do not have access to these brands of acrylic paint, find paints that have have the *nearest equivalent* in the Munsell system of hue specifications:[4]

Color	Munsell Hue	Value	Chroma
Naphthol Red Light	6.8 R	4.0	13
Cadmium Red Medium	5.6 R	3.9	12
Indo Orange Red	9.5 R	5.5	14
Cadmium Orange	3.6YR	7.0	14
Yellow Orange Azo	6.2YR	7.1	14
Cadmium Yellow Light	6.5Y	8.8	12.5
Vivid Lime Green	7.6YG	7.0	10
Permanent Green Light	1.2G	4.9	10
Turquoise Green	3.8BG	5.0	8
Brilliant Blue	8.0B	5.0	9
Cerulean Blue	2.7BP	4.0	9
Cobalt Blue	7.6BP	4.0	12
Prism Violet	5.0P	3.0	9
Mars Black	Black	1.5	0.1
Titanium White	White	9.6	0.1
Neutral Gray	Gray	5.0	0.1

Flashing Colors

Some items in this book are painted in what are referred to as "flashing colors." This means that certain implements are painted in complementary colors (two colors that are directly opposite each other on a color wheel). The pigment that covers the most area and portrays the overall color of the implement is known as the "ground" color. Symbols, names, or sigils are then painted on the ground in the appropriate flashing color, which is known as the "charge" color. When painting flashing colors, it is necessary to cover the implement with gesso, a white primer coat, first, then paint the ground color. When this is dry, paint the symbols and names first in white, and let the paint dry completely before painting the desired "charge" color over it. If you paint a charge color directly over a ground color, the ground will often absorb the charge rendering it dull and lifeless, negating its flash. By painting the names and sigils in white and then painting the pigment over this, the charge colors retain their vitality and the flashing colors remain true to their name and power.[5]

Color Scales

The teachings of the Golden Dawn encompass a great deal of material concerning the mystical Qabalah. An elaborate color scale system was devised by the Golden Dawn to depict the Sephiroth, the ten emanations of deity, in each of the four Qabalistic Worlds. The Qabalah teaches that the Sephiroth were created by the path of the Flaming Sword, which resulted in four worlds or realms, each evolving from the one before it, increasing in density as they near manifestation, descending from the spiritual to the physical. As an outcome of this, each Sephirah has four levels of existence attributed to it. The four worlds and their corresponding color scales are:

Name	Meaning	Scale	Letter	Element
Atziluth	World of Archetypes	King Scale	י	Fire
Briah	World of Creation	Queen Scale	ה	Water
Yetzirah	Astral World	Prince Scale	ו	Air
Assiah	Active World	Princess Scale	ה	Earth

The color scales have additional associations with the formula of the Tetragrammaton or "Four-lettered Name" of God. This in turn has correspondences with the four elements: King Scale—Fire, Queen Scale—Water, Prince Scale—Air, and Princess Scale—Earth. The King and Queen Scales, the fundamental scales of masculine (active) and feminine (passive) energies, are of primary importance to the construction of the many instruments in this book. By painting an implement with a passive Queen Scale color, the tool is rendered more open or receptive to the desired energies. On the other hand, if the King Scale color is used, the energy of the implement will be more outwardly forceful. On certain implements, both color scales will be represented to strike a balance between the active and passive energies. To learn more about these color scales, we suggest that the reader consult the Fifth Knowledge Lecture in Regardie's *The Golden Dawn,* as well as our first book, *The New Golden Dawn Ritual Tarot.*[6]

Endnotes

1. Regardie, *The Tree of Life,* 117.
2. Ibid., 117–8.
3. Munsell's system, introduced in 1913 with the publication of the Atlas of the Munsell Color System. Today, Munsell's system is used throughout the world.
4. The hue specifications listed here are for Liquitex brand acrylic paint.
5. Always use a good quality sealant on your magical implements to protect the painted surface and to prevent discoloration. Clear lacquer finish is the best sealant. Polyurethane and varnish tend to dry and age with a brownish tint that could discolor your ritual tools. For the various wands of the Golden Dawn, where color is a top priority, discoloration is certainly not desirable.
6. See Regardie, *The Golden Dawn*, 95–99, and *The New Golden Dawn Ritual Tarot* (book), 26–28.

CHAPTER ONE

Implements of the Neophyte Grade

During the process of initiation, the Neophyte encounters a temple filled with symbolism in the form of ritual implements and regalia possessed by officers who are the living personifications of the gods and goddesses of Egypt—the initiators into the higher mysteries. The hall of the Neophytes is the most important temple arrangement in all of the Outer Order rituals. Its composition is based primarily on the glyph of the Qabalistic Tree of Life. Within the Neophyte Ritual itself are hidden many formulæ of magic. The implements of the First Order are not present in the hall merely for theatrics and effect, but rather they are the visible emblems of invisible forces within the hall that are directed and orchestrated by the Hierophant and other Second Order members.

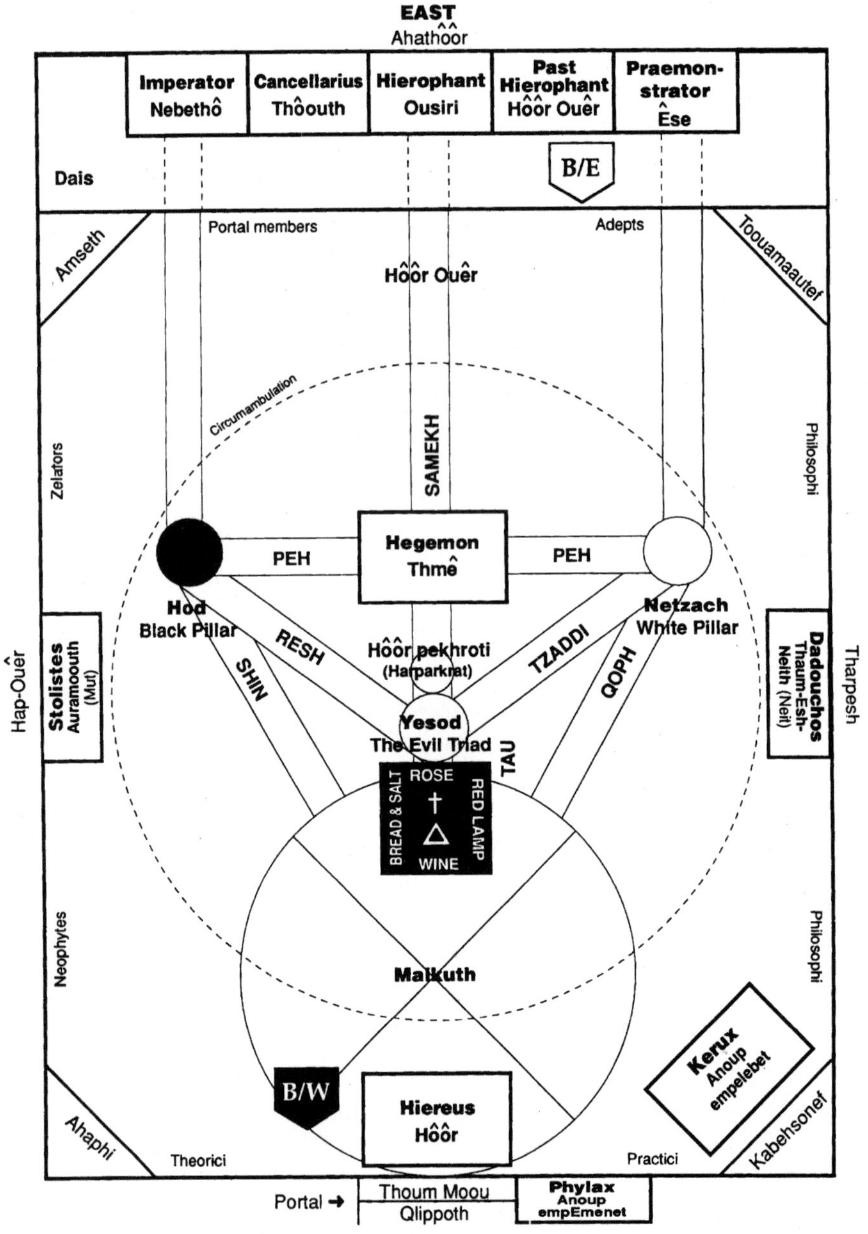

Figure 2: Temple Layout and Godforms of the Neophyte Hall

The Neophyte Hall

The ideal dimensions for an average temple should be approximately 20' by 16'. The Dais in the East should be about 4' in width, leaving the rest of the temple a 16' x 16' square. Of course, ideal conditions are not always available; at times a spare room or basement must serve as the Neophyte Hall, making the dimensions of the temple a non-negotiable issue. But if a large group of people is expected to work in the temple, bigger is better.

Ideally, the floor should be black or composed of black-and-white tiles. From the perspective of a new Neophyte undergoing initiation, (who is hoodwinked and sees little of the actual Neophyte Ritual), the entire room could be painted black. However, the temple is also used for elemental grade ceremonies, so it would be perfectly acceptable for the four walls to be painted in the four elemental colors: east—yellow, south—red, west—blue, north—black. The ceiling could be white. (In our first Neophyte Hall, constructed in 1977, the walls and the ceiling were completely draped in white silk fabric that was gathered at a point directly over the central and invisible station of Hôôr pe Khroti or Harparkrat.) Also, the Enochian Tablets, which are to be present in the Neophyte Hall but hidden from view, could be veiled with curtains in the appropriate elemental colors. (Information on the Enochian Tablets is provided in chapter three.) If at all possible, the room should be soundproof. We have often found that soft music, such as Tibetan Bells, playing faintly in the background (preferably on a tape deck with auto reverse), can noticeably enhance the psychic receptivity of all ritual participants. The lighting should be as dim as possible, with candlelight coming from each of the four quarters. In addition, there should be veiled lights atop the pillars, the red lamp on the altar, and the lamp of the Keryx. Ideally, these would be the only sources of light within the hall, although another light source could be placed in the eastern part of the hall, the direction of the dawning Sun. To the blindfolded candidate, who is groping in the darkness of the outer world, the main source of illumination is the lamp of the Keryx, which flickers dimly one step ahead at all times. The general atmosphere of the entire Neophyte Hall is one of solemn stillness, a darkness which is pregnant with power and hidden light.

The Altar

The altar is a point of focus in the Neophyte Hall of the Golden Dawn. Its black, closed shape is enigmatic, for it is an emblem of nature or the material universe, concealing the mysteries of all dimensions within, while revealing only the surface to the exterior senses. Its double cubical shape is derived from a passage taken from the Emerald Tablet of Hermes

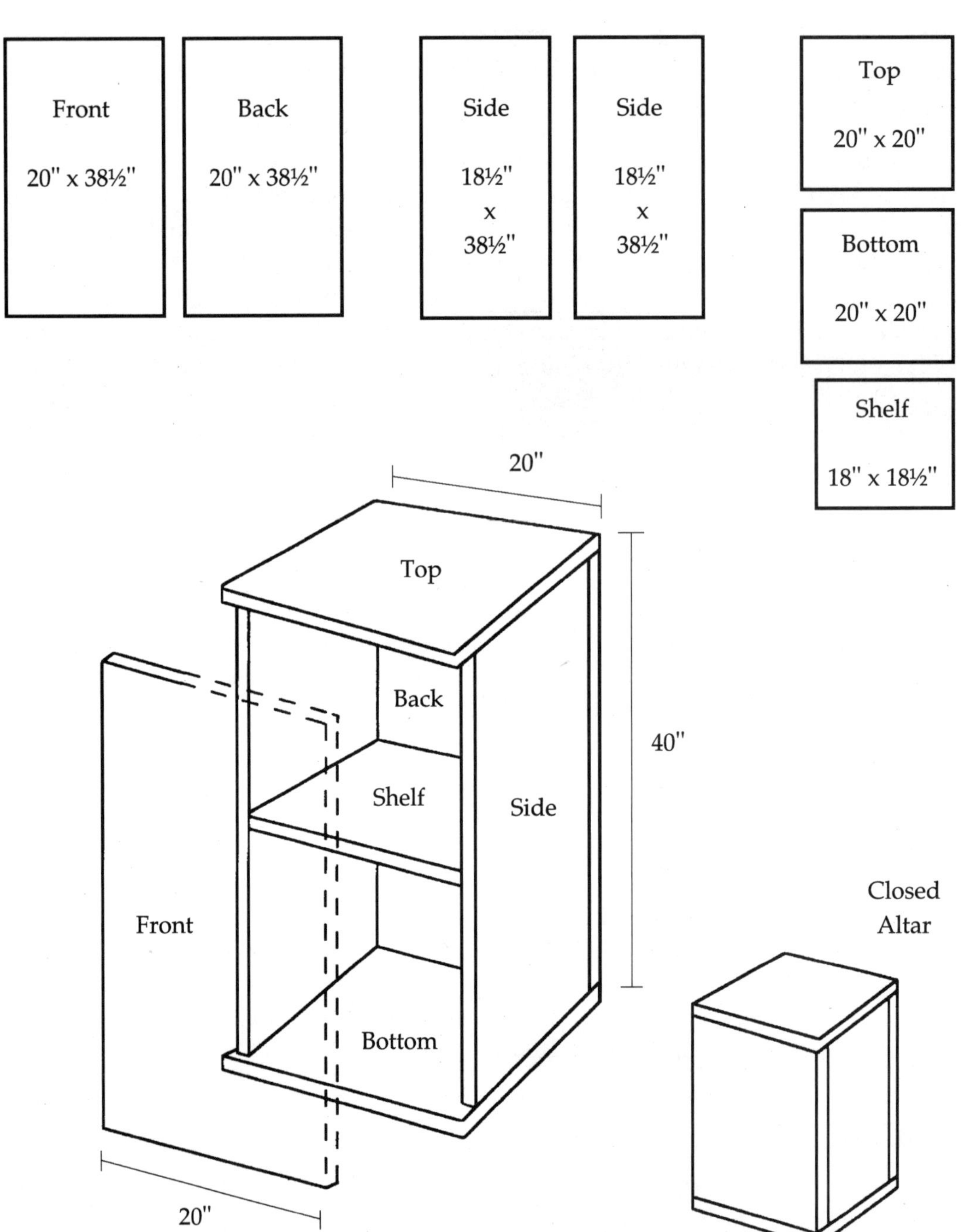

Figure 3: The Altar

which states, "Whatever is below is like that which is above, and whatever is above is like that which is below."[1] In the Neophyte Ritual, this idea is paraphrased as "The things that are below are a reflection of the things that are above."[2] The altar is black to symbolize the physical world in which we live...a world sometimes dark and obscure.

Placed in the eastern part of Malkuth (as far as the temple layout is concerned, see Figure 2, page 2), the altar is the core of the visible temple. It may be painted black, but to an adept its blackness will veil the colors of citrine on the east, olive on the south, and russet on the north. The west side alone and the base will be black, while the summit is of a brilliant whiteness.[3] All divine light brought into the temple through the Hierophant and circulated by the officers is eventually grounded within the symbols on the altar. Once the ceremony is ended, the supernal light is withdrawn from the symbols upon the altar so that it is not diminished by improper regard. In some ways the altar, like the individual, is a physical vessel which temporarily conceals and contains the spirit until it is withdrawn back into the godhead.

The altar is also an excellent container for ritual tools, candles, robes, and other implements. The double-cubical design provides plenty of space inside while the sliding front gives it the smooth appearance of a Chinese box.

Refer to Figure 3 on page 4 for construction diagrams.

Materials Needed

- 1½ sheets of ¾" plywood (pine or birch) in 4' x 8' sheets
- Yellow carpenter's glue
- 1½" brads (small nails)
- Wood putty
- Black polyurethane or acrylic enamel

Tools Needed

- Table saw or circular saw
- Hammer
- Nail punch
- L-square
- Putty knife
- Sandpaper (course, medium, and fine)
- Large paint brush
- Yard stick or tape measure

Construction

1. Lay out the 1½ sheets of plywood. Measure out and label clearly all the sections of the altar (front, back, etc.) as shown in Figure 3, page 4. (Front and back are each 20" x 38½", two sides are each 18½" x 38½", top and bottom are each 20" x 20", and the shelf is 18" x 18½".)
2. Cut apart all sections with the saw. Take one of the sections marked "side" and apply glue to one of the 38½" edges. Keep this edge facing up.
3. Line up the long edge of the "back" section perpendicular to the glued side and nail the two sections together. (Note: The edge of the back section will still be visible, while the glued side edge should not be.)
4. Take the remaining side panel and apply glue to one edge as in step 2. Nail this piece perpendicular to the remaining long edge of the back as in the previous step. (You should now have three sections nailed together which form an inverted U-shape.)
5. Lift the unfinished altar upright. Three edges (of the back and two sides) should now face the ceiling. Apply glue to all three edges. Take the top section and place it flush against these three edges. Nail into place.
6. Turn the altar upside-down and apply glue to the three edges as before. Nail the bottom panel flush against these three edges as in the previous step.
7. Lay the altar on its side. Measure to find the exact center of the back (both inside and out). With a pencil and ruler, draw a line parallel to the top and bottom which marks the center. Also find the center of the side panels and mark them.
8. Take the shelf and apply glue to one 18½" edge and both 18" edges. Slide the shelf inside the altar with the glued 18½" edge up against the center line drawn on the back. Make sure the shelf is straight. Nail the shelf into place from the outside (on all three sides).
9. The only remaining section is the front, which should fit snugly into place without the need for hinges. It can be pulled out or pushed into place, giving the altar a smooth, closed-cube appearance. (If too tight, the top and bottom edges may need some sanding.)

Finishing Steps

10. Using the nail punch and hammer, make sure no nail heads stick out from the wood. Fill any nail holes or cracks with wood putty and a putty knife. Let dry.

11. Sand off excess putty or any other rough areas remaining on the surface of the altar. Begin with course sandpaper, then go to a medium grade. Finish with fine sandpaper.
12. Paint the altar completely, inside and out, with black polyurethane or acrylic enamel. Allow to dry.

(Note: In the early Golden Dawn temples, the sides of the altar were often painted with flat black paint, while the top alone was coated with a glossy black. This made clean-up of accidental spills somewhat easier.) See our book *Ritual Use of Magical Tools*, chapter one, for "A Ritual Meditation on the Altar."

The Cross and Triangle

The cover of Israel Regardie's book *The Golden Dawn* has given many people the impression that the symbol of the Golden Dawn is the figure of the Sun within a Hexagram consisting of the two triangles of Fire and Water. However, the true symbol of the Order is the red cross above the white triangle. These emblems represent the forces and manifestation of the divine light, concentrated in the white triangle of the Supernals as the synthesis. The red cross of Tiphareth is placed above the white triangle, not to dominate it, but to cause it to descend and manifest into the Outer Order, as though the Christos, the slain and resurrected one, having raised the symbol of self-sacrifice, had thus touched and brought into action, in physical matter, the divine triad of light.[4] The cross and triangle represent life and light.[5]

Together, the cross and triangle act as receptacles of the divine light that is attracted into the temple by the Hierophant during the mystic circumambulation— symbolic of the rise of light. These sublime symbols also play an important role in the Neophyte Ceremony, especially when the new candidate is asked to take an oath. They remain a focal point for projected energy throughout the ritual. Whenever the Neophyte Hall is set up for personal magical work, such as charging a talisman, the cross and triangle should be on the altar, acting as a nucleus for the ceremony and attracting the divine forces into manifestation.

Of course one could make the cross and triangle out of cardboard, but they will not have nearly the same sturdiness and aesthetic appeal as the wooden cross and triangle described below. (See *Ritual Use of Magical Tools*, chapter one, for "A Meditation on the Cross and Triangle.")

Refer to Figure 4 on page 8 for construction diagrams.

Materials Needed

- One 5¼" square piece of soft wood (pine, bass, or balsa), ½" thick
- Gesso

- Acrylic paints: white and red
- Clear lacquer finish (spray or brush on)

Tools Needed

- Scroll saw or coping saw
- Electric drill with a bit that is wider than your saw blade
- Sandpaper (medium and fine grained)
- Artist's paint brushes

Construction

1. With the saw, cut a 5¼" equilateral triangle out of the piece of wood. (All three angles should be 60 degrees. See Figure 4.)
2. With a pencil, draw another equilateral triangle inside of the one you have just cut out. This one should be smaller on all sides by 2".
3. Drill a hole inside the pencil line of the smaller triangle. (Remember, it is important to use a drill bit that is wider than your saw blade. Try to drill the hole near one of the angled corners, not in the center of the triangle. This is because you will use the smaller triangular piece of wood to make the cross.)

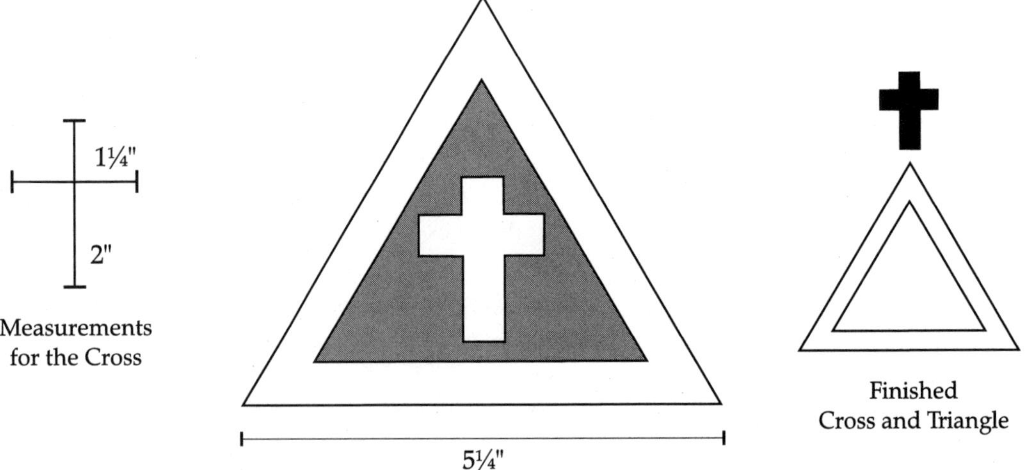

Figure 4: Construction of the Cross and Triangle

4. With your saw unplugged, detach the blade from the saw. Stick the blade through the hole you have drilled and reattach the blade to the saw. Plug the saw back in and begin cutting exactly on the penciled lines until you have completely cut out the inner triangle.
5. Unplug the saw. Detach the blade from the saw and remove the pieces of wood. You should now have a 5¼" equilateral triangle that is ½" thick on all sides of its three component lines. (The hollow space in the center should be 3¼" all around.)
6. Take the solid piece of wood you have cut from the center of the triangle and, with a pencil and a ruler, draw a Calvary cross of six squares, using ½" units of measure. (The shaft of the cross will be ½" wide and 2" long. The crossbeam will be ½" wide and 1½" long. The crossbeam should start ½" below the top of the shaft.)
7. Reattach the blade to the saw and plug the tool in. Cut the cross out of the wood.

Finishing Steps

8. Sand the entire surface of both the cross and the triangle. Start with the medium sandpaper and finish with the fine.
9. With a paint brush, cover both pieces with gesso. Let dry. Sand the gessoed pieces until smooth.
10. Paint the triangle with acrylic white. Paint the cross with red. Let both pieces dry thoroughly, then apply a sealant for protection.

The Banners of the East and West

The banners are the duality of light and dark working from east to west, where the pillars are duality of light and dark working from south to north, thus forming a cross within the Neophyte temple. They are not only barriers or signposts for the eastern and western parts of the hall, but they are also battery points along which the light-energy can travel from one end of the temple to the other and back again. (See Figure 5, page 10 and Color Plate 1.)

The Banner of the East is a representation of the initiate being transformed into the perfect knowledge of light. It is a symbol that can be used in meditation to help the student gain a greater understanding of what the Order is striving to teach. It is a symbol of the dawning Sun. The Banner of the East is described in the Portal initiation:

> *The field of the Banner of the East is White, the color of light and purity. As in the previous case, the Calvary Cross of six squares is the number of Tiphareth, the yellow Cross of Solar Gold, and the cubical stone, bearing in its center the sacred Tau of Life, and having*

> *bound together upon it the form of the macrocosmic Hexagram, the red Triangle of Fire and the blue Triangle of Water—the Ruach Elohim and the Waters of Creation.*[6]

It is the action of the Fire of the Spirit through the Waters of Creation under the harmony of the golden cross of the Reconciler.

> *Within the center of the Hexagram is a Tau-cross in white, to represent its action as a Triad; and the whole is placed on a white field representing the Ocean of Ain Soph Aur. The Banner is suspended from a gold colored bar by red cords, and the pole and base should be white. The base represents the purity of the foundation—the shaft, the Purified Will directed to the Higher. The golden cross-bar is that whereon the Manifest Law of Perfection rests; the Banner itself, the Perfect Law of the Universe, the red cords and tassels represent the Divine Self-renunciation, whose trials and sufferings form, as it were, the Ornament of the Completed Work.*[7]

This symbol can be also be likened to a shield that protects the student throughout the process of initiation from the forces of negativity. A greater knowledge of the Banner of the East will begin to unfold through meditation and Order work.

The Banner of the West is partly explained in the Zelator Initiation:

Figure 5: The Banners of the East and West

The White Triangle refers to the three Paths connecting Malkuth with the other Sephiroth; while the red cross is the Hidden Knowledge of the Divine Nature which is to be obtained through their aid. The Cross and Triangle together represent Life and Light.[8]

It can also represent the possibility of rescuing the evil; but it is the cross of Tiphareth that is placed within the triangle that represents the sacrifice that has to be made in order to reach the higher. The red cross may be bordered in gold to represent the metal obtained in and through the darkness of putrefaction. The Banner of the West is on a black field representing darkness or the ignorance of the outer world, the white triangle is the light shinning through the darkness but which is not comprehended. The Banner of the West is a symbol of twilight, the balance of light and darkness. The pole is black, also representing darkness, but the cross bar is gold and the tassels red for the same reasons as given for the Banner of the East.

The Banner of the East usually remains in the eastern portion of the hall while the Banner of the West is moved to many different positions. When used as a barrier, the Banner of the West is moved from place to place within the hall, in order to bar the way of the initiate. It makes a new demand on the candidate and requires a new sacrifice in order for the initiate to continue on the path leading to the higher.

It is preferable to always construct the banners in matching sets. These are tools that are always used together and should be created together. I always light a red candle and some incense before I begin working on any magical tool. While lighting the candle and incense I connect with the energies of Fire and Air, the creative and intellectual aspects of the work at hand. I ask the powers that be to guide my hands in this creation and bring me knowledge and wisdom through this work. I ask that the tool being created prove to be a valid instrument in my endeavors toward the Great Work.

Refer to Figure 6 on page 12 for construction diagrams.

Materials Needed

- ½ yard of white satin
- ½ yard of black satin
- ½ yard of gold (the new lamés work just fine)
- ⅓ yard of red satin
- ⅓ yard of blue satin
- 1 yard of iron-on interfacing (medium weight)
- 10 red tassels (short or long)
- 24" of red cord
- 24" of black cord

- 1 roll of bonding web
- Threads in the appropriate colors
- ¾" diameter dowels (2 pieces, 16" long)
- 4 screw-eyes (big enough for the cord to go through)
- Finial ends or wooden balls (to fit the end of the dowel)
- Wood glue
- Metallic gold paint
- Fine sandpaper

Tools Needed

- Sewing machine
- Scissors
- Needles and gold thread
- Iron and ironing board
- Measuring tape
- Access to a copy machine to enlarge the pattern pieces

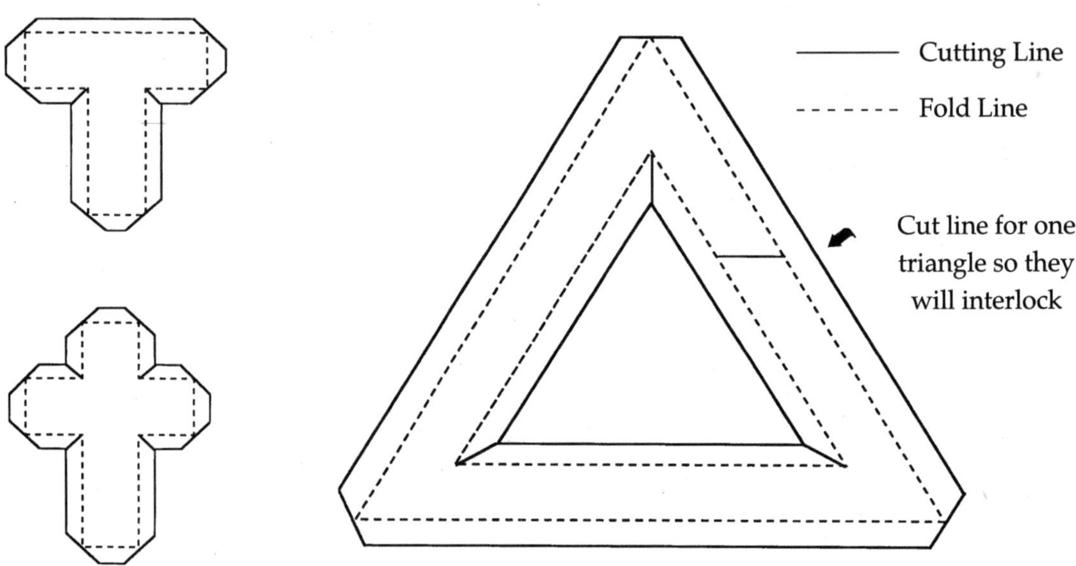

Figure 6: Banner Construction

Construction

1. Enlarge the banner patterns (shown in Figure 5, page 10) so that each banner is 15" wide. Make several copies so that you can use them as patterns to cut out and also as placement guides.
2. Begin with the banner field (the main part or background of the banner): cut two pieces for each banner (two pieces of white and two of black). The banner fields should have a ½" seam allowance all around, making the finished banner 16" wide. Do not sew the banner fields together at this time.
3. Cut out all the triangles and crosses to use as patterns. (For the *Banner of the East*— you will need one red triangle, one blue triangle, a large gold Calvary cross, and a small white Tau cross. For the *Banner of the West*—you will need one large white triangle and two small Calvary crosses—the smaller red cross lies on top of the slightly larger gold cross.) Cut pieces of iron-on interfacing slightly larger than the triangles and crosses.
4. Iron the largest triangle interfacing piece to the back of the white satin. Iron one of the smaller triangle pieces to the back of the blue satin and one to the back of the red satin. Iron the large cross piece and the middle-sized cross piece of interfacing to the back of the gold fabric. Next iron the smallest cross piece to the back of the red satin. Now iron the Tau cross piece of interfacing to the back of the white satin.
5. Lay the pattern pieces for each triangle and cross onto the back of each piece of fabric, and draw around each pattern piece, leaving a border of approximately ⅜".
6. Cut out the triangles and crosses, cutting the corners and central angles in as shown in Figure 6 on page 12. Pattern pieces are cut from the wrong side of fabric that has iron-on interfacing pressed on. Lay pattern piece on top of interfacing and trace around it. Cut approximately ⅜" for seam allowance. Trim outside corners and clip inside corners. Press along fold lines.

   (This technique is demonstrated with the large white triangle from the Banner of the West. After you have completed it you can move on to the other triangles and crosses and follow the same technique.)
7. Lay the paper pattern piece on the back of the cutout of the large triangle. Iron the seam allowance over the pattern piece forming a fold line. Remove the paper pattern and cut a strip of bonding web long enough to fit between the seam allowance and the triangle.
8. Press the seam allowance to the triangle. Repeat for the other arms of the triangle, being sure to do the inside of the triangle as well.

9. Press the points carefully so that you end up with a perfect triangle. Repeat this process with the other two triangles and the crosses.
10. After all the triangles and crosses are pressed flat (making sure the seam allowances are turned under and glued with the bonding web), then place the large white triangle on the right side of one of the black field pieces.
11. Use one of the extra enlargements of the Banner of the West to position it correctly. The lower points of the triangle should follow the line that is formed with the angles running downward to form the point of the banner.
12. Carefully pin the triangle in place and cut strips of bonding web for all three sides. Press the triangle in place, gluing it to the banner field piece. Next place the small gold cross within the triangle and follow the same procedure. Then glue the red cross on top of the gold cross and glue it down with bonding web.
13. Now that all the pieces are in place, stitch along all the edges to secure them to the field piece. This stitching will be seen on the banner so be sure to use the appropriate color thread with each item.
14. When you start to place the red and blue triangles on the gold cross on the Banner of the East, you must cut one of the triangles so that they interlock. There is a cutting line on the blue triangle showing where it needs to be cut. Interweave the triangles, pinning them in place as they move over each other.
15. After everything has been sewn to the front (of each separate banner), pin the back piece to the front, making sure the right sides (outsides) are facing each other. Be sure it is square and all the edges match.
16. Now stitch down one side, along the angle to the bottom point, up the other angle and then up the opposite side, making sure you leave a ½" seam allowance. Clip the corners and turn the banner inside out.
17. To make the corners square, take a pair of scissors and go inside the banner and push the corner seams outward. (Not too much that you push through, just enough to make them square.)
18. Press the banner so that the seams are flat. Next, fold and press a ½" seam along the top. Stitch this seam flat.
19. Now you are ready to hand-stitch the red tassels to each corner and the bottom point. To make the crossbars, sand the 16" long dowels smooth and attach the finials or 1" wooden balls to the ends.

20. Paint each crossbar with a metallic gold paint and let dry completely.
21. Place a screw-eye about ½" from the end of the dowel. Tie a knot in one end of the cord and thread it through one of the screw-eyes. Thread the other end of the cord through the other screw-eye and tie a knot.
22. Apply these same techniques to construct the Banner of the East. You can attach the banners to the golden cross bars with gold thread. The black cord is used to hang the Banner of the West and the red is for the Banner of the East. This forms a convenient suspension for the banners and makes it easy to remove them from the poles.

—Banner instructions contributed
by Ceil Thomas

The Banner Poles

Refer to Figure 7 on page 16 for construction diagrams.

Materials Needed

- Two 1¼" thick dowel poles, approximately 67" in length
- Two 4" x 4" thick pieces of wood, 6" in length
- One piece of ¾" thick plywood or pine, 8" x 16"
- One piece of ¾" thick plywood or pine, 6" x 12"
- Two finials (ornate wooden caps found in builder's supply stores)
- Two metal screw-in hooks
- Yellow carpenter's glue
- Wood putty
- White latex paint
- Black latex paint
- Box of 2" brads
- Sandpaper (course, medium, and fine grained)

Tools Needed

- Table or circular saw
- Hammer
- Awl
- Electric drill with a 1¼" spade bit

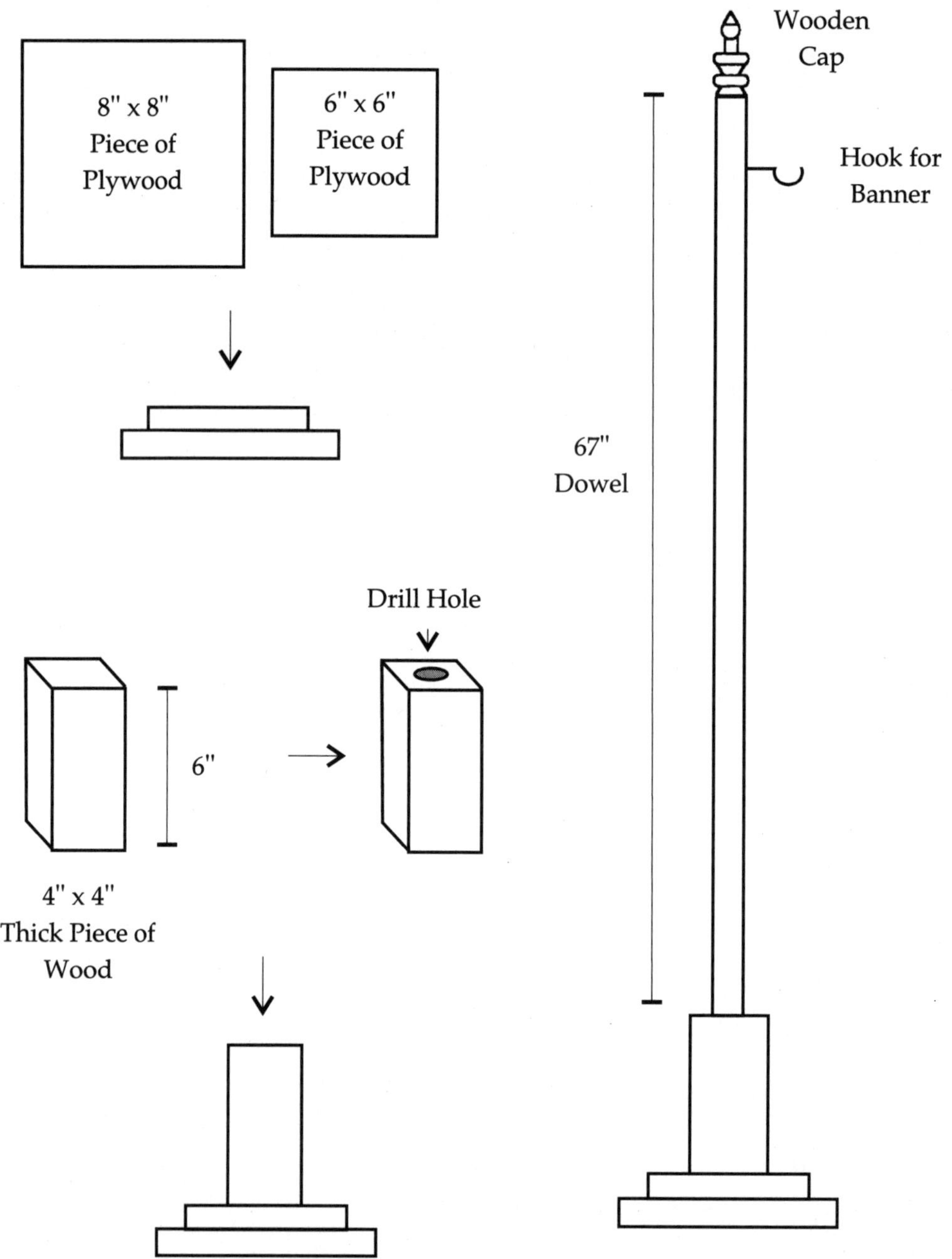

Figure 7: A Banner Pole

Construction

1. Take the 8" x 16" piece of plywood and cut it in half with the saw so that you are left with two 8" x 8" pieces of wood. Put one of the pieces aside.
2. Take the 6" x 12" piece of plywood and cut it in half, leaving you with two 6" x 6" pieces of wood. Put one of the pieces aside. Apply glue to the 6" x 6" piece of wood and center it on top of the 8" x 8" piece.
3. Take one of the 4" x 4" thick pieces of wood and drill a 1¼" wide hole into the center of one end. This hole should be at least 1½" deep. Glue and center the undrilled end of the 4" x 4" piece onto the top of the 6" x 6" plywood. Nail all three pieces together from the bottom.
4. Take the wooden finial and glue it to one end of the dowel pole. (Note: These wooden caps sometimes have a small dowel sticking out of the bottom. If this is the case, drill an appropriate sized hole into one end of the dowel and then glue the cap into place.) Glue the other end of the dowel into the hole drilled into the 4" x 4". Allow the glue to dry.
5. About 6" down from the top of the cap, make a small hole in the shaft with an awl. Screw the metal hook into the hole. (The banner will be suspended from this hook.) You should now have one completed banner pole. With the remaining materials, make a second banner pole in the same manner as the first.

Finishing Steps

6. Sand the pole. Begin with course grained sandpaper, continue with medium grained and finish with fine grained.
7. Paint one banner pole entirely white for the Banner of the East. The other pole used to support the Banner of the West should be painted completely black. (Note: It also is acceptable to paint the bottoms of the poles after the manner of the Pillars—with countercharged lotus petals.)

See *Ritual Use of Magical Tools*, chapter one, for "A Ritual Meditation on the Banners of the East and West."

The Pillars

The two pillars of the Neophyte Hall are referred to as the "the Pillars of Hermes" of "Shu" and of "Solomon." In the *Book of the Dead* they are called "The Pillars of Shu," the "Pillars of the Gods of the Dawning Light," and also as "the Northern and the Southern

Figure 8: Egyptian Pillars (Temple at Karnak)

Columns of the Gate of the Hall of Truth." The pillars represent the two columns in the temple of King Solomon and the two great contending forces of the manifest universe.

The Black Pillar on the left (north) side of the temple is called Boaz, and it represents the female or Yin principle. It is also known as the Pillar of Cloud and the negative polarity. The White Pillar on the right (south) side of the temple is called Jachin, and it represents the male or Yang principle. It is known as the Pillar of Light and Fire and the positive polarity. Dion Fortune called these columns the "Pillar of Force" (white) and the "Pillar of Form" (black).

In the ancient Egyptian texts, the pillars are represented by the sacred gateway, the door to which the aspirant is brought when he has completed the negative confession. (See Figure 8, page 18.) The two pillars of the Neophyte Hall are ornamented with symbolism consisting of Egyptian vignettes or drawings. (See Figure 9, page 20.) The archaic drawings on the one pillar are painted in black on a white ground, and those on the other in white on a black ground, in order to express the interchange and reconciliation of opposing forces and the eternal balance of light and darkness which gives force to the visible universe.

The black cubical bases represent darkness and matter wherein the Spirit, the Ruach Elohim, began to formulate the ineffable name, that name the ancient Rabbis have said "rushes through the universe"—that name before which the darkness rolled back at the birth of time. At the base of both pillars rise the lotus flowers, symbols of regeneration. (Note: These lotuses are to be painted just above the black cubical bases. The lotus on the White Pillar is painted black. Conversely, that on the Black Pillar is painted white.) The flaming red triangular capitals that crown the summit of the pillars represent the triune manifestation of the Spirit of Life, the Three Mother Letters of the *Sepher Yetzirah*, and the three alchemical principles of nature—sulfur, mercury, and salt.

In the Golden Dawn's Z–1 document, the Pillars are described as follows:

The Bases of the two Pillars are respectively in Netzach and Hod; the White Pillar being in Netzach and the Black Pillar in Hod. They represent the Two Pillars of Mercy and Severity. The bases are cubical and black to represent the Earth Element in Malkuth. The columns are respectively black and white to represent the manifestation of the Eternal Balance of the Scales of Justice. Upon them should be represented in counterchanged color any appropriate Egyptian designs, emblematic of the Soul.

The scarlet tetrahedronal capitals represent the Fire of Test and Trial; and between the Pillars is the porchway of the Region Immeasurable. The twin lights which burn upon their summits are "The Declarers of the Eternal Truth." The bases of the tetrahedra, being triangular, that on the White Pillar points East, while that on the Black points West. They

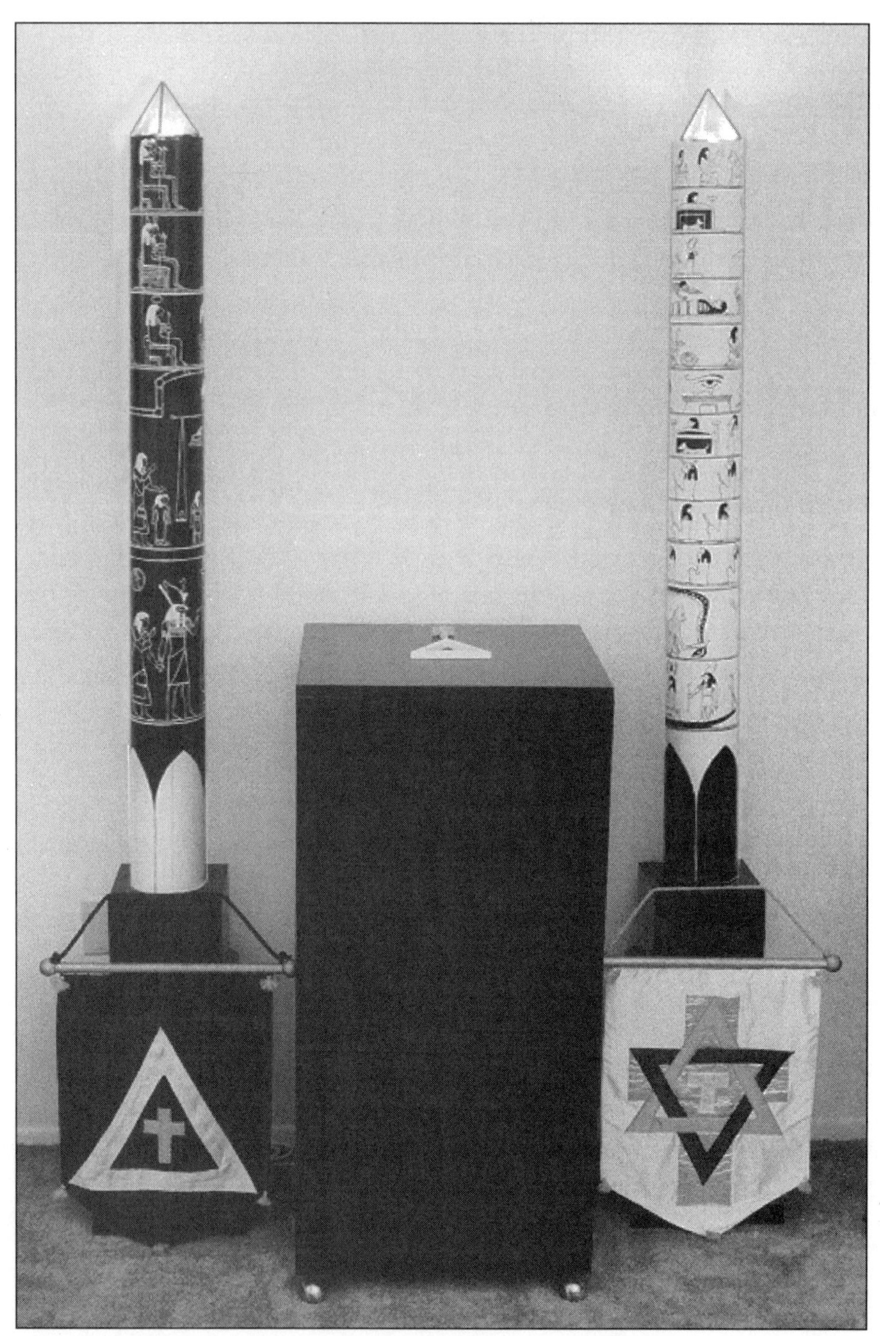

Figure 9: The Pillars, Banners, and Altar

thus complete the Hexagram of Tiphareth—though separate, as it is fitting in "The Hall of the Dual Manifestation of Truth."[9]

(Note: Some authors have interpreted the foregoing passage to mean that the capitals are four-sided pyramids which are attached to a flat triangular base. What the passage really implies is that the capitals themselves are triangular—having three sides that form a pyramid. The fourth side is actually the basal side that the pyramid rests on, as in the Admission Badge to the Thirty-first Path of Shin in the grade of Practicus.)

Construction of the black and white columns or pillars used in the Neophyte Hall (and throughout all the grades of the Outer Order) have resulted in some of the most creative designs imaginable. The two pillars, which rest on a square base and have a tetrahedron capital, can be built in a variety of ways.

One temple we know of uses massive wooden pillars that came from an old Victorian-style house. Columns like this can be found in salvage yards and used by the enterprising magician, so long as they are in good shape and not rotting away. (Be careful of rusty nails.) Once the old paint has been removed with solvent and any nail holes have been filled with wood putty, the columns can be set into wooden bases as described below and painted with black and white enamel. We must note that columns of this sort make the most impressive looking pillars that we have ever seen in any temple. (Pillars that are particularly heavy may require casters or wheels in order to be moved around the temple.

Long, thick lengths of PVC pipe, a sturdy plastic pipe used for plumbing and water drainage, can also be made into pillars and set into wooden bases. Stove pipe, which can be purchased at any home-builders supply store, also works. One initiate we know was able to procure interlocking, plastic trash cans which, when placed one on top of the other, made perfectly smooth, slender pillars. The outside of these pillars were then covered with self-adhesive black and white vinyl or contact paper.

Our own pillars were constructed from a ring of two-by-fours which were glued together and cut into circular form on a large lathe. (Definitely not the easiest way to make pillars.) Nowadays a number of companies specialize in making artificial stone and marble pillars, stands, and other decorative items, which are molded from new lightweight materials that resemble the real article. Although they can be costly, they could save the magician time and work.

One of the easiest ways to acquire a set of pillars is to use two heavy cardboard tubes which are found inside rolls of carpeting. (The local carpet store can usually provide these.)

Materials Needed

- Two 6' long cardboard tubes (from inside a carpet roll) approximately 6" to 8" thick
- One 4' x 8' sheet of ¾" plywood (pine or birch)
- Yellow carpenter's glue
- 1½" brads (small nails)
- Wood putty
- Black polyurethane or acrylic enamel
- White polyurethane or acrylic enamel

Tools Needed

- Table saw or circular saw
- Jigsaw or coping saw
- Electric drill with ¾" bit
- Vise
- Hammer
- Nail punch
- Putty knife
- Sandpaper (course, medium, and fine)
- Large paint brush
- Yard stick or tape measure

Construction

1. Cut the sheet of plywood cut into four pieces that are 13½" x 15". Cut out four more pieces that are 15" x 15". (These eight pieces are the *sides* of the two pillars' square bases.)
2. Cut two pieces of plywood that are 15" square. (These are the *tops* of the pillar bases.)
2. Draw a circle in the middle of both of the top pieces. Make sure the diameter of the circle is slightly larger than the diameter of the cardboard tubes.
3. Drill a hole in the center of the circle on both top pieces. Using the holes as a starting point, cut out the circles with the jig saw or coping saw.
4. Secure one of the 15" x 15" side pieces in the vise. Apply glue to the upright edge and nail one of the top pieces perpendicular to the glued edge. Remove from the vise.
5. Secure another of the 15" x 15" side pieces in the vise. Apply glue to the upright edge. Take the two pieces of wood that are already nailed together. Nail the opposite end of the top piece perpendicular to the glued edge. (You will end up with a top piece attached to two sides that are opposite each other.)

6. Take one of the 13½" x 15" side pieces and apply glue to three of its edges (the two long edges and one of the short edges.) Attach the piece to the three pieces already nailed together. The short edge will be against the top piece. Nail into place on three edges.
7. Take another of the 13½" x 15" side pieces and apply glue to three of its edges (the two long edges and one of the short edges.) Attach the piece to the four pieces already nailed together. The short edge will be against the top piece. Nail into place on three edges.
8. Cut two more 15" square pieces out of the plywood (These are the *bottoms*).
9. Glue and nail one of the bottoms to the open end of the base.
10. You now have a wooden box with a round hole in the top. Take the remaining six pieces of wood and create a second box.

Finishing Steps

11. Using the nail punch and hammer, make sure no nail heads stick out from the wood. Fill any nail holes or cracks with wood putty and a putty knife. Let dry.
12. Sand off excess putty or any other rough areas remaining on the surface of the wood. Begin with course sandpaper, then go to a medium grade. Finish with fine sandpaper.
13. Paint paint the two bases with black polyurethane or acrylic enamel. Paint the cardboard tubes—one black, the other white. Allow everything to dry.
14. Apply glue to the bottom edge of one of the cardboard tubes. Apply glue to the inside rim of the circle cut into one of the bases. (The circle you cut should be only wide enough to slip the pillar securely into the box.) Slide the glued end of the tube into the circular hole of the base. (Do the same with the other tube and base.) Allow to dry.

The two capitals surmounting the pillars are red tetrahedrons that can be fashioned out of cardboard. (See chapter two for the construction of a tetrahedron.) Ideally, the capitals should have some method of illumination from the inside, but this could result in a fire hazard, and, as always, safety should come before symbolism. A century ago, candles were placed on top of the pillars. Our own pillars are surmounted by red stained-glass capitals. A small light bulb can be placed inside the top of each hollow pillar by a metal bracket; the electrical cord runs down the hollow center of the pillar and out of a small hole drilled into the base. The lights to both pillars are connected to a rheostat so that the amount of light can be regulated and the heat it throws off kept to a minimum.

It is also possible to construct two tetrahedrons that can hold small battery-operated lights that are used to illuminate red stained glass or red transparency film.

Portable Pillars

A readily transportable and easily stored set of pillars can be made from cloth, which is then suspended from the ceiling or hung over any of a variety of portable supports, such as a microphone stand or patio umbrella stand.

You'll first need to obtain four urethane rings, such as those used to form the foundation for a seasonal wreath. Be sure to use urethane foam rather than styrofoam. Although the styrofoam will work, it tends to crumble, and small white flakes will adhere to the cloth as well as spread themselves around your temple space. The rings are available at most large craft stores and come in a variety of sizes.

The size ring you choose will determine the size of the columns. The height of the column should be proportional to the diameter of the ring; an aesthetic decision you will have to make. I have made 10' columns for use out of doors using 12" diameter rings and 8' columns for use indoors utilizing 10" rings. If you choose to set the columns on cube bases, you may wish to use smaller rings, 8" or 6" for instance.

The cloth that is used for the column itself should be a stretch-knit synthetic material rather than a broadcloth cotton. This is important since the stretching property of the knit cloth is necessary to wrap around the rings without folds or wrinkles.

Materials Needed

- Four urethane rings
- An ample amount of stretch-knit synthetic cloth
- Black and white thread
- Sturdy wire or string

Tools Needed

- Sewing machine
- Scissors and pins

Construction

1. The first step after obtaining the rings is to determine their inside circumference in order to know how wide to cut the material for the columns. Measure across the middle of the ring...you are measuring how wide the hole is at its widest point. In order to find out how big the hole is (its circumference), you will now need to multiply the width measurement across by 3.14 or 3 1/7, depending on whether you use a metric ruler or a traditional one. The resulting number plus 1" is the width the cloth must be. Its length should be one foot longer than the desired column height.

2. To create the columns, fold the cloth in half lengthwise. Remember, if the cloth has a grain or facing side, you will need to determine which end is up and which side is the outside. The right sides of the cloth (finished outside) should be facing each other at this point.

3. Sew a seam the length of the cloth ⅝" in from the cut edges, thus creating a long tube. Please note that the resulting tube will now be slightly smaller than the hole in the foam ring.

4. Turn the tube right side out and insert one end into the foam collar such that about 6" sticks through.

5. Opening the tube up, fold the excess material outside the foam ring and wrap it around the foam, tucking the excess material under what is now the bottom outside edge of the column. The material may now be fastened on the inside with pins. If you have measured everything correctly, the material should stretch nicely over the ring, leaving a tight, round column end with no wrinkles.

   (You may note that the seam will show where it wraps around the foam, but this is unnoticeable if its edges are folded back neatly, or you may choose to do some more involved sewing in order for the seam at this point to be hidden...that's up to you.)

6. Follow the same procedure for the other end of the column.

7. At this point the column is ready to be suspended in some manner. Wire or string can be attached to the top ring and the column hung from the ceiling or a doorway. Inspect the column to ensure that the rings are inserted evenly and do not hang at a strange angle. The column should hang in such a way that there are no wrinkles or folds; in fact, even from a short distance, the columns should look solid as if made of wood. If it does not, you have done something wrong.

8. The cloth can be painted or silk-screened with appropriate decoration, or left plain. This is more easily accomplished before it is sewn together, but you must be careful to leave room for the seam allowance and the material to be folded under at each end.

9. The finished columns can be hung over any sort of support, such as a microphone stand, or supports such as those on which the Banners hang. Since the columns are hollow tubes, the supports can be inside them, and thus not visible when the columns are in use. A more portable stand can be created using a telescope tripod, or fishing poles. Outdoors, poles can be driven into the ground and the column slipped over these. The column bottoms can be attached to the ground for more stability.

Another fairly simple column design for those with some carpentry experience is a *tapered square column*. Its advantage is that one side may be hinged and the interior used as storage space for the taller wands and staffs. The flat sides are also very easy to either paint with appropriate designs or to attach placards, tablets, photocopies or the like, as needed. The disadvantage is that they are a bit heavy, but the weight can be offset with the addition of casters or wheels built into the base.

1. The finished column is made in three pieces: a cube base, the tall tapered middle section, and the capital. The suggested size is an 18" cube with 5' columns and a 6" capital, creating an overall length of 7'. The cube bases are both painted black. One column will then be painted black, the other white, resulting in one entirely black structure and the other white standing on a black base.

2. Cut four pieces of 1" x 12" shelving board the desired column length minus the size of the cube base as the separate column capital. In the case of our example, this length would be 5'. Taper each of these pieces by cutting a triangular slice from both sides so that you wind up with four boards 5' long, 11¼" wide at one end and 8¼" wide at the other.

3. These four pieces are then nailed together such that they create a square column...you will need to overlap each piece correctly to avoid one width being wider than the other. The resulting column when viewed from the end will be a square tube and the overlapping edges will form a Fylfot cross, which you might take pains to orient appropriately for the column you are creating.

4. The capital for the columns is an 8" square with vertical corners, rather than tapered ones like the columns. Its top is a flat board, 11¼" x 11¼". Assembled, the capital looks sort of like a mortar board hat, but set atop the tapering column, it adds a finished proportion to the overall design. An improvement would be to use wide crown molding for the edges of the capital, which would present a curving, flared effect, thus lending more to the image of the papyrus style columns of ancient Egypt.

5. The three pieces are then fastened together, creating an impressively large column that leaves little doubt which way the path lies...just be careful moving these beacons, as their weight can pose somewhat of a challenge.

—Portable Pillar instructions contributed
by Frater R. H. K.

The Vignettes or Pillar Diagrams

The pillars of the Neophyte Hall are covered with Egyptian vignettes or diagrams. In the original pillar diagrams of the Golden Dawn in England, certain plates were left out of the vignettes from the Egyptian *Book of the Dead*. Regardie felt that this was because not all of the diagrams within those vignettes were essential to the Neophyte Hall as envisioned by MacGregor Mathers. The original art work of the pillar diagrams in this book were supplied by author, scholar, and magician Adam Forrest, and were based on descriptions from those earlier temples. However, as stated in the document known as Z–1, the pillars can be illustrated with any appropriate Egyptian designs, emblematic of the soul.

The Five Registers on the Black Pillar

For the pillar Boaz, the Order employs the symbolism of the vignette accompanying the 125th Formulæ of Coming Forth by Day. The 125th Formula is entitled "The Formula of Entering in the Hall of Two Truths; A Pæan to Osir, the Chief of Amentet." On the Black Pillar, the vignette is divided into five registers, which we shall call for the sake of this discussion B1 (the uppermost) through B5 (the lowest).

Register B1: (See Figure 10, page 28.) Registers B1–B3 depict a dozen deities who serve as witnesses to the Weighing of the Soul. Register B1 portrays the first four of the twelve gods: Sia, Hu, Hathor, and Hôr (Horus).

The first two deities occur most frequently as a pair. Sia and Hu are two aspects of the creative power of the high gods. The name of Sia means "mind" or "thought," equivalent to the Platonic Greek Nous. In Heliopolis, he was the mind of Rê, the source of life. In Memphis, he was identified with the heart of Ptah, the Creator. His intriguing name glyph, which he wears as a crown, has not yet been convincingly deciphered.

Register B2: (See Figure 10, page 28.) The next four deities are in Register B2: Iset (Isis), Nebethô (Nephthys), Nuet, and Geb. Iset and Nebethô are sisters, often referred to by many duel forms: e.g. the Yakhueti ("the Two Shining Ones"). Indeed it is impossible to understand Nebethô, who had no separate cult of her own, outside that relationship, for in truth she is an aspect of her sister; She is the Dark Iset. In the Greek Magical Papyri, we even find the compound form Isenephthys (i.e., Isis-Nephthys).

Register B3: (See Figure 10, page 28.)The last four of the twelve gods are illustrated in Register B3: Tefnut, Shu, Tum, Rê-Hôr-Akhuti. Rê-Hôr-Akhuti is the last of the twelve. His name means "The Sun, Hôr of the Two Horizons." (This is the deity whom Thelemites know from Crowley's simulated Coptic as Ra-Hoor-Khuit.)

B1

B2

B3

Figure 10: Golden Dawn Pillar Vignettes for the Black Pillar: B1, B2, B3

B4

B5

Figure 11: Golden Dawn Pillar Vignettes for the Black Pillar: B4, B5

Register B4: (See Figure 11, page 29.) This depicts the most famous tableau in the "Formulæ of Coming Forth by Day," and probably in all of Egyptian iconography: the Weighing of the Heart, or the Judgment Scene.

The initiate is separated into his many constituent parts. The tripartite monster with the head of a crocodile, the forequarters of a lion, and the hindquarters of a hippopotamus is named Ammut, literally "the Eater of the Dead." The candidate is finally either declared to be mêekheru (Egyptian for "justified, righteous"; literally "true of voice") or false. If false, his soul is devoured by the voracious Ammut.

Register B5: (See Figure 11, page 29.) The justified initiate, his heart having been found true in the Scales of Mêet, is led by Hôr, son of Iset, the archetype of the initiate in this world, into the presence of his father, Osir (Osiris), the archetype of the adept in the higher world.

Note that the initiate is now unified. The formula of *Solve et Coagula* is complete in him. Osir Onnofer (Egyptian for "Osiris the Beautiful One"), the Tipharetic god of rebirth and adeptship, is enthroned in a royal pavilion. The pavilion is flanked by the two sacred pillars, and its roof is topped with disk-crowned uraei, symbols of the power of the god.

Osir Onnofer is depicted in a balanced triple form. The two goddesses, Nebethô and Iset, who touch and support him are aspects of himself, as surely as the enthroned form of the king. The three deities represent the aspects of Osir Onnofer corresponding to the adept triad of Chesed, Gevurah, and Tiphareth. The three implements he bears represent the same triad of powers: the Nekhekh Scourge corresponds to Fire, Sulphur, and Nebethô; the Heka Crook to Water, Mercury, and Iset; and the Benu Phoenix Wand to Air, Salt, Osir, and the Middle Pillar.

The four Sons of Hôr are shown with the lotus.

The sacred Wadjet Eye, symbol of, in this case, the omniscience of the god, brings Osir the feather of Mêet, proof that the new adept is truly in equilibrium.

The adept is now identified with Osir the Beautiful and is even entitled to add the sacred name Osir to his own name.

The Vignettes of the White Pillar

For the Pillar Jakhin, the Order employs the symbolism of the vignette accompanying the 17th Formula of the "Formulæ of Coming Forth by Day." The 17th Formula bears the lengthy title "The Beginning of the Exaltations (and) Enlightenments, Coming Forth into Shining Nuterkheret (the divine underworld), into Beautiful Amentet (the west, where the Sun sets), Coming Forth by Day in All the Forms Which He Desireth, Playing Senet, Sitting in the Chamber, (and) Coming Forth as a Living Soul." On the White Pillar, the vignette is divided into twelve registers, which we shall call J1 (the uppermost) through J12 (the lowest).

Register J1: (See Figure 12, page 32.) This vignette shows the hieroglyphic emblem of Amentet, and the initiate in the *seh* hall playing senet. Senet is an ancient board game whose paradigm is the journey, unlike chess, whose paradigm is war. The Ba of the initiate on a shrine. The initiate in adoration before the Akoru (Sef and Duau), the twin lion gods of "yesterday" and "today."

Register J2: (See Figure 12, page 32.) Iset and Nebethô are depicted in adoration on either side of a chest from which the head of Rê arises.

Register J3: (See Figure 12, page 32.) The Initiate is seen in adoration before Osir and the Benu. A small votive altar is before him.

Register J4: (See Figure 13, page 33.) Iset and Nebethô as two hawks, and also as two uraeus cobras on two lotuses, flank the body of the initiate. The Ba brings *shen,* "infinity," to the initiate. (Note: The lotuses were mistakenly identified by Brodie-Innes as axes.)

Register J5: (See Figure 13, page 33.) The initiate is shown in adoration before two gods. The first is Hah, with his hand stretched forth over the Eye of Hôr. The second is Wadj-Wer, with his hands stretched out over two bodies of water.

Register J6: (See Figure 13, page 33.) Pylon of Rosetau is depicted with a seated god. The Wadjet Eye is over a pylon. The cow goddess Muhweret is also shown.

Register J7: (See Figure 14, page 34.) This vignette shows the four Sons of Hôr flanking a shrine from which the head of Rê rises.

Register J8: (See Figure 14, page 34.) Depicted here are four gods: Hôr Khant-Maati, Maa-Atefef, Kheribeqef, and Anup (Anubis).

Register J9: (See Figure 14, page 34.) Seven gods are shown: Nedjhah-Nedjhah, Aqedqed, Khantihehef, Imi-Onnutef, Teshermaa, Besmaa-em-Qereh, and Anemhur.

Register J10: (See Figure 15, page 35.) Initiate is seen in adoration before five ram-headed deities: Rê, Shu, Tefnut, Geb, Ba-Neb-Djedu.

Register J11: (See Figure 15, page 35.) Before the sacred Ished (the Greek Persea) tree, Rê in the form of Mau beheads Apop (Apophis). Ahathoor, the great goddess is also shown.

J1

J2

J3

Figure 12: Golden Dawn Pillar Vignettes for the White Pillar: J1, J2, J3

J4

J5

J6

Figure 13: Golden Dawn Pillar Vignettes for the White Pillar: J4, J5, J6

J7

J8

J9

Figure 14: Golden Dawn Pillar Vignettes for the White Pillar: J7, J8, J9

J10

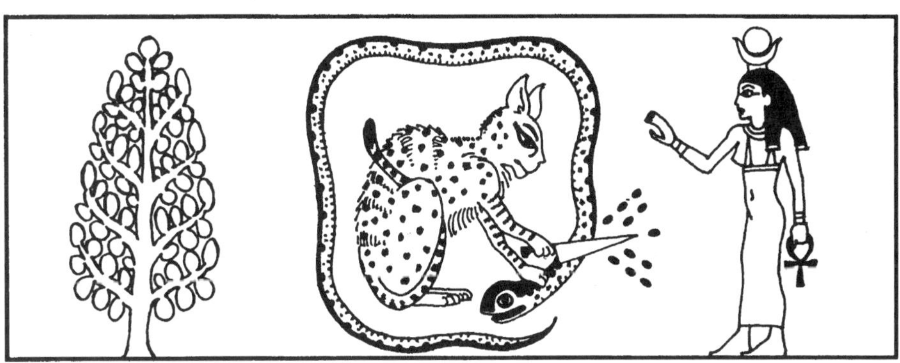

J11

J12

Figure 15: Golden Dawn Pillar Vignettes for the White Pillar: J10, J11, J12

Register J12: (See Figure 15, page 35.) This shows the Boat of Eternity, with Djehoti forward and Hôr aft, the goddess Ahathoor, and Khepri with the divine Scarab of the Dawn overhead.

—Pillar diagrams and explanations contributed by Adam Forrest

Concerning the Vignettes

(Note: This is an excerpt from a paper on "The Pillars"[10] by MacGregor Mathers.)

The archaic illustrations are taken from vignettes of the 17th and 125th chapter of the Ritual of the Dead, the Egyptian Book of the *Per-em-Hru* or the "Book of Coming Forth into the Day," the oldest book in the world as yet discovered. The Recension of the Priests of ON is to be found in the walls of the pyramids of the Kings of the 5th and 6th Dynasties at Sakarah, the recension of the 11th and 12th Dynasties on the sarcophagi of that period, and the Theban recension of the 18th Dynasty and onward is found on papyri, both plain and illuminated. No satisfactory translation of these books is available, none having been yet attempted by a scholar having the qualifications of mystic as well as Egyptologist.

The Ritual of the Dead, generally speaking, is a collection of hymns and prayers in the form of a series of ceremonial Rituals to enable the man to unite himself with Osiris the Redeemer. After this union he is no longer called the man, but Osiris, with whom he is now symbolically identified. "That they also may be One of us," said Christ of the New Testament. "I am Osiris," said the purified and justified man, his soul luminous and washed from sin in the immortal and uncreated light, united to Osiris, and thereby justified, and the son of God; purified by suffering, strengthened by opposition, regenerate through self-sacrifice. Such is the subject of the great Egyptian Ritual.

The 17th Chapter of the Theban recension consists of a very ancient text with several commentaries, also extremely old, and some prayers, none of which come into the scheme of the original text. It has, together with the scheme of the original chapter, been very carefully translated for the purpose of this lecture by the V. H. Frater M. W. T (Blackden), and V. H. Soror S. S. D. D. (Farr) has made many valuable suggestions with regard to the interpretation. The Title and Preface of the 17th Chapter reads:

Concerning the exaltation of the Glorified Ones, of Coming and Going forth in the Divine Domain, of the Genies of the Beautiful land of Amentet. Of Coming forth in the light of Day in any form desired, of Hearing the Forces of Nature by being enshrined as a living Bai.

And the rubric is:

The united with Osiris shall recite it when he has entered the Harbour. May glorious things be done thereby upon Earth. May all the words of the Adepti be fulfilled.

Owing to the complex use of symbols, the ritual translation of the Chapter can only be understood by perpetual reference to the ancient Egyptian commentaries, and therefore the following paraphrase has been put together to convey to modern minds as nearly as possible the ideas conceived by the old Egyptians in this glorious triumphal song of the Soul of Man made one with Osiris, the Redeemer.

I am TUM made One with all things.

I have become NU. I am RA in his rising ruling by right of his Power. I am the Great God self-begotten, even NU, who pronounced His Names, and thus the Circle of the Gods was created.

I am Yesterday and know the secret of Osiris, whose being is perpetually revered of RA. I have finished the work which was planned at the Beginning, I am the Spirit made manifest, and armed with two vast eagle's plumes. Isis and Nephthys are their names, made One with Osiris.

I claim my inheritance. My sins have been uprooted and my passions overcome. I am Pure White. I dwell in Time. I live through Eternity, when Initiates make offering to the Everlasting Gods. I have passed along the Pathway. I know the Northern and the Southern Pillars, the two Columns at the Gateway of the Hall of Truth.

Stretch unto me your hands, O ye Dwellers in the center. For I am transformed to a God in your midst. Made One with Osiris, I have filled the eye socket in the day of the morning when Good and Evil fought together.

I have lifted up the cloud-veil in the Sky of the Storm. Till I saw RA born again from out the Great Waters. His strength is my strength, and my strength in His strength. Homage to you, Lords of Truth, chiefs who Osiris rules. Granting release from Sin, Followers of Ma where rest is Glorious. Whose Throne Anubis built in the day when Osiris said:

"Lo, a man wins his way to Amentet. I come before you, to drive away my faults. As ye did to the Seven Glorious Ones who follow their Lord Osiris. I am that Spirit of Earth and Sun."

Between the Two Pillars of Flame. I am RA when he fought beneath the Ashad Tree, destroying the enemies of the Ancient of Days. I am the Dweller in the Egg. I am he who turns in the Disc. I shine forth from the Horizon, as the gold from the mine. I float through the Pillars of SHU in the ether. Without a peer among the Gods. The Breath of my mouth is as a flame. I light upon the Earth with my glory. Eye cannot gaze on my darting beams, as they reach through the Heavens and lick up the Nile with tongues of flame. I am strong upon Earth with the strength of RA. I have come into Harbour as Osiris made perfect. Let priestly offerings be made to me as one in the train of the Ancient of Days. I brood as the Divine Spirit. I move in the firmness of my Strength. I undulate as the Waves that vibrate through Eternity. Osiris has been claimed with acclamation, and ordained to rule among the Gods. Enthroned in the Domain of Horus where the Spirit and the Body are united in the presence of the Ancient of Days. Blotted out are the sins of his body in passion. He has passed the Eternal Gate, and has received the New Year Feast with Incense, at the marriage of Earth with Heaven.

TUM has built his Bridal Chamber. RURURET has founded his shrine. The Procession's completed. HORUS has purified, SET has consecrated, SHU made one with OSIRIS, has entered his heritage.

As TUM he has entered the Kingdom to complete union with the Invisible. Thy Bride, O Osiris, is Isis, who mourned Thee when she found Thee slain. In Isis, thou art born again. From Nephthys is thy nourishment. They cleansed thee in thy Heavenly Birth. Youth waits upon thee, ardour is ready at thy hand. And their arms shall uphold thee for millions of years. Initiates surround Thee and Thine enemies are cast down. The Powers of Darkness are destroyed. The Companions of Thy Joys are with Thee. Thy Victories in the Battle await their reward in the Pillar. The Forces of Nature obey Thee. Thy Power is exceeding great, The Gods curse him that curseth Thee. Thine Aspirations are fulfilled. Thou are destroyed who barred Thy way.

The 125th Chapter is concerned with the entry of an Initiate into the Hall of the Two Columns of Justice, and commenced with a most beautiful and symbolic description of Death, as a journey from the barren wilderness of Earth, to the Glorious Land which lies beyond. The literal translation of the opening lines is as follows:

I have come from afar to look upon thy beauties. My hands salute Thy Name of Justice. I have come from afar, where the Acacia Tree grew not. Where the tree thick with leaves is not born. Where there come not beams from herb or grass. I have entered the Place of Mystery. I have communed with Set. Sleep came upon me, I was wrapped therein, bowing down before the hidden things. I was ushered into the House of Osiris. I saw the marvels that were there. The Princes of the Gates in the Glory.

The illustrations in this chapter represent the Hall of Truth as seen through the open leaves of its door. The Hall is presided over by a God who holds his right hand over the cage of a hawk, and his left over the food of eternity. On each side of the God is a cornice crowned by a row of alternate feathers and Uraei symbolizing justice and fiery power. The door leaf which completes the right hand of a stall is called "Possessor of Truth controlling the Feet," while that on the left is "Possessor of strength binding the male and female animals." The 42 Judges of the Dead are represented as seated in a long row, and each of them has to be named, and the Sin over which he presided has been denied.

This chapter describes the introduction of the Initiate into the Hall of truth by Anubis, who, having questioned the aspirant, receives from him an account of his Initiation, and is satisfied by his right to enter. He states that he has been taken into the ante-chamber of the temple and there stripped and blindfolded, he had to grope for the entrance of the Hall, and having found it, he was reclothed and anointed in the presence of the Initiated. He is then asked for the Passwords and demands that his Soul should be weighed in the Great Balance of the Hall of Truth, whereupon ANUBIS again interrogates him concerning the symbolism of the door of the Hall, and his answers being found correct, ANUBIS says: "Pass on, thou knowest it."

Among other things the Initiate states that he has been purified four times, the same number of times that the Neophyte is purified and consecrated in the ceremony of the Neophyte. He then makes the long Negative Confession, stating to each Judge in turn that he is innocent of that form of Sin over which he judges. Then he invokes the Judges to do him justice, and afterwards describes how he had washed in the washing place of the South, and rested in the North, in the place called "Son of the Deliverers" and he becomes the Dweller under the Olive Tree of Peace, and how he was given a tall flame of Fire and a scepter of cloud which he preserved in the salting tank in which mummies were swathed. And he found there another scepter called "Giver of Breath" and with that he extinguished the flame and shattered the scepter of cloud, and made a lake of it. The Initiate is then brought to the actual Pillars, and has to name them and their parts under the symbol of the Scales of a Balance. He also has to name the Guardian of the Gateway, who prevents his passage, and when all these are propitiated, the plea of the Hall itself cries out against his steps, saying "Because I am silent, because I am pure," and it must know that his aspirations are pure enough and high enough for him to be allowed to tread upon it. He is then allowed to announce to Thoth that he is clean from all evil, and has overcome the influence of the planets, and THOTH says to him: "Who is He whose Pylons are of Flame, whose walls of living Uraei, and the flames of whose House are streams of Water?" And the Initiate replies "Osiris!"

And it is immediately proclaimed: "Thy meat shall be from the Infinite, and thy drink from the Infinite. Thou art able to go forth to the sepulchral feasts on Earth, for thou hast overcome."

Thus, these two chapters, which are represented by their illustrations upon the Pillars, represent the advance and purification of the Soul and its union with Osiris, the

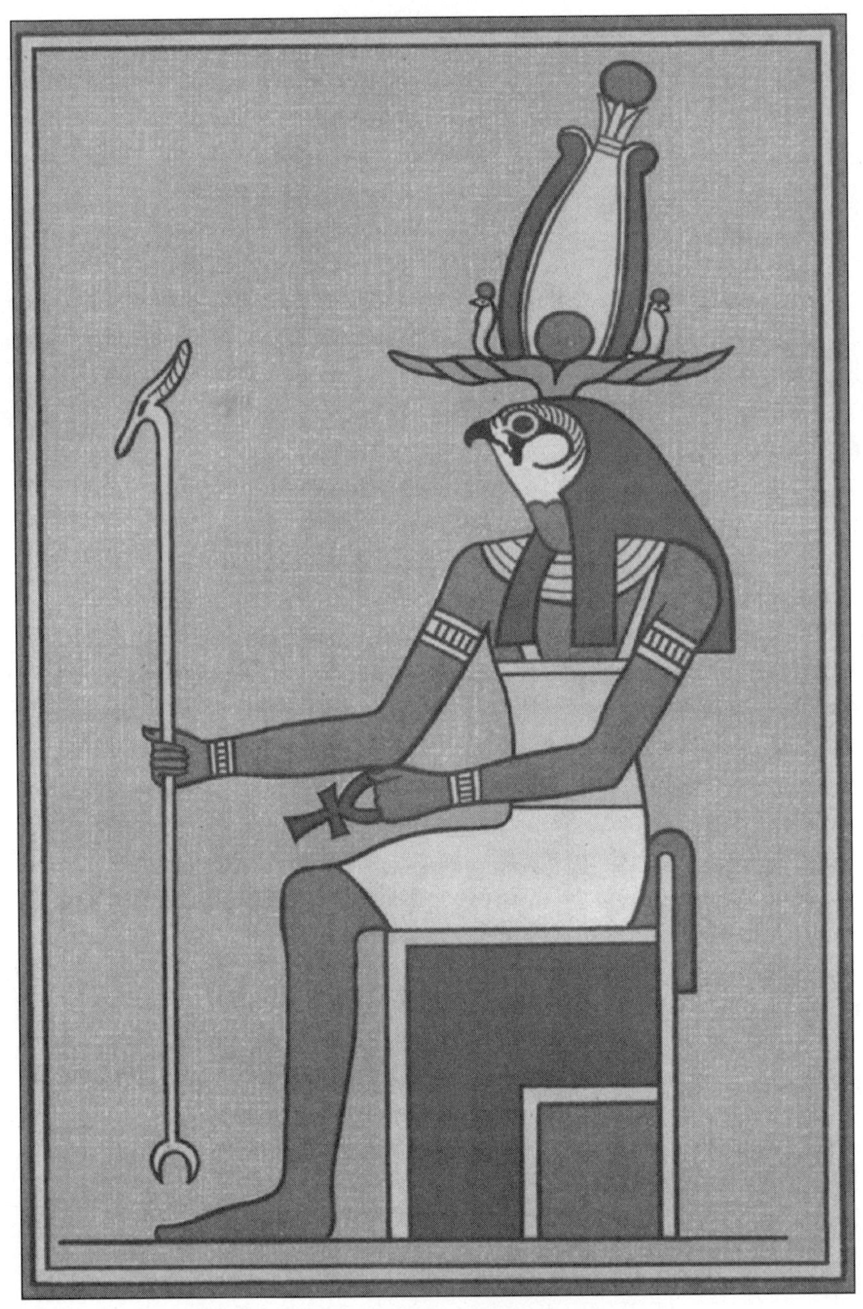

Figure 16: The God Hôôr-Ouêr Seated on an Iset

Redeemer, in the Golden Dawn of the Infinite Light, in which the Soul is transfigured, knows all, and can do all, for it is made One with the Eternal God.

KHABS AM PEKHT
KONX OM PAX
LIGHT IN EXTENSION

—"Concerning the Vignettes" is an excerpt from a paper on "The Pillars" [10] by MacGregor Mathers

The Iset or Temple Throne

The *iset* is one of our own contributions to the furnishings of a modern Golden Dawn temple. Its design is based on the traditional Egyptian throne seen in countless vignettes from the *Book of the Dead*. (See Figure 16, page 40 and Figure 17, page 42.)

In ancient times the throne represented the seat of divinity. Homage was paid to the throne in the absence of any human occupant. When a king spoke to the people from horseback, he did so as a king; but when he spoke from the throne, his words were considered the utterances of a god. The throne was regarded as a sacred dwelling-place that not only housed the divine spirit, but also acted as a container for spiritual energy, localizing it at certain times and places.

The throne, therefore, partakes of the same symbolism as a chalice; a receptacle of divine energies. It is thus a feminine symbol—the name "iset" is taken from the name of Isis (Êse or Iset), the Egyptian goddess whose name means "throne." This signifies her role as supporter or upholder of the universe. The sphere of Binah on the Tree of Life also has allusions to the throne; one of Binah's titles is Khorsia, meaning "throne," while the choir of angels associated with this Sephirah is the Aralim or "thrones." Binah is the reservoir of divine energy from the paternal Chokmah; she stabilizes and regulates it, eventually giving it form.

In the Neophyte Hall of the Golden Dawn, each throne is a seat of a particular godform, therefore, each is a reservoir for the energies that are attributed to a specific deity. A properly trained Hierophant creates the astral shells of each particular godform in the hall. On entering the temple and taking his or her station, each adept officer "steps into" and animates the particular godform and connects his or her Ruach with the godform "shell" located at the iset. At one point the Hierophant must leave the throne and take on a different godform, while leaving the original deity, in astral form, seated on the Dais. At certain times, if a temple is short on officers, it becomes necessary for a member to take on dual roles, moving around the temple as one godform, while building up the other form at its throne.[11]

The iset should not be considered as just another piece of furniture. Its design is based on that of a traditional Egyptian throne taken from ancient papyri, and it is intended to be a vessel for specific forces, which are built up by the Hierophant and employed in Golden Dawn ritual. The godform of each particular iset can be built up through a meditation designed to invoke it.

Refer to Figure 18, page 44 for construction diagrams.

Materials Needed

- One 4' x 4' sheet of ¾" plywood
- 12' to 13' of ¼" screen molding
- Yellow carpenter's glue
- 1½" brads
- Smaller brads (#6) for molding
- Wood putty
- Black polyurethane or acrylic enamel

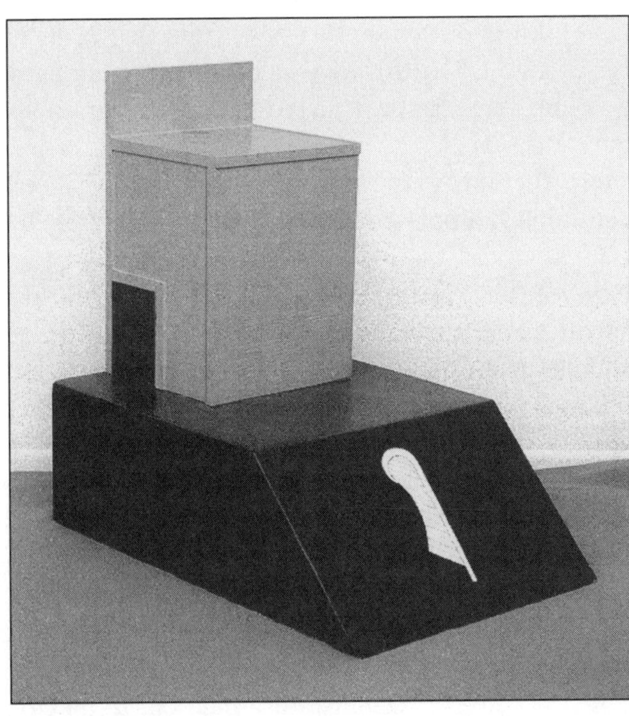

Figure 17: The Iset

Tools Needed

- Table or circular saw
- Hacksaw
- Miter box or simple protractor
- Hammer
- Nail punch
- Putty knife
- Sandpaper (course, medium, and fine grained)
- Large paint brush
- Yard stick or tape measure

Construction

1. Take the sheet of plywood and measure and label clearly all sections of the throne (see Figure 18, page 44). (The back is 12" x 20", the front is 12" x 15", the top is 11" x 12", and two sides are each 10½" x 15".) Cut all sections apart with the saw.
2. Take one side section and apply glue to one of the 15" edges. Keep this edge facing up. Take the front panel and line up one of its 15" edges perpendicular to the glued side edge. Nail the two pieces together. (Note: The edge of the front section should be visible, but not that of the side section.)
3. Take the remaining side panel and apply glue to one edge as before. Nail this piece perpendicular to the other 15" edge of the front as in the previous step. (Note: you should now have three sections nailed together which form the shape of an upside-down U.)
4. Place the throne on its front, so that the U-shape is upright. The two long edges of both side sections should be facing the ceiling. Apply glue to these two edges. Take the back panel and place it lengthwise over the glued side edges so that the top of the back section overhangs the 15" length of the sides and front by 5". Nail into place.
5. Stand the throne upright. Apply glue to the three flush edges of the front and two sides. (The back edge should be facing the ceiling, 5" above the glued edges.)
6. Take the top section and apply glue to one of its 12" edges. Place the top over the three glued edges of the front and sides, so that the glued 12" top edge is up against the back panel. Nail into place.

Finishing Steps

7. Take the screen molding and cut it with the hacksaw into the following lengths: two 20", two 15", two 11", and two 12¼" pieces.

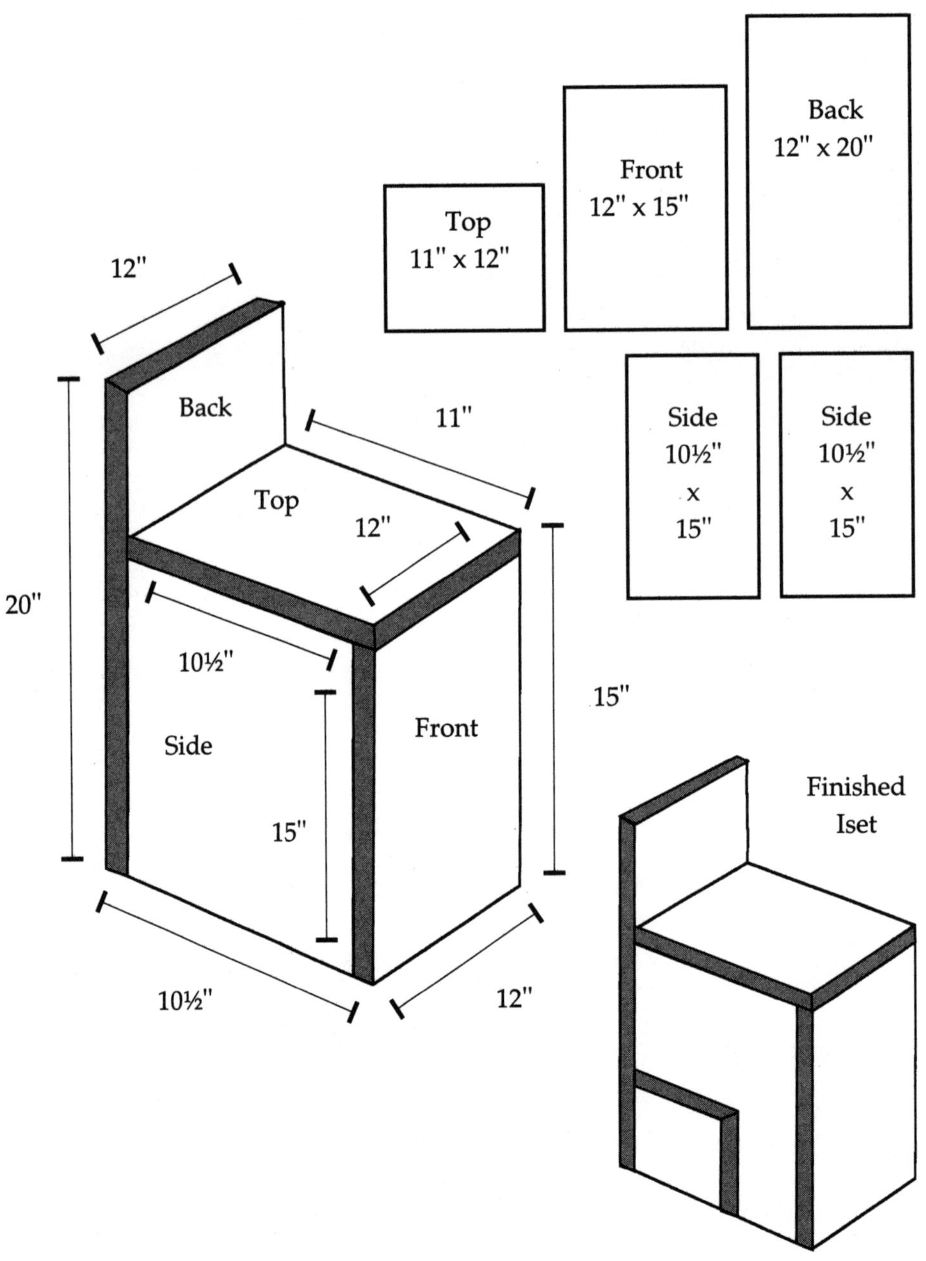

Figure 18: Construction of the Iset

8. With glue and small brads, attach molding to throne to give a recessed look as in the finished diagram.
9. You should be left with two pieces of 12¾" molding. Take one piece and measure off 7". With either a miter box or pencil and protractor, mark off and cut a 45-degree angle, so that you end up with two mitered pieces of molding (one 7" in length and the other 5¾"). Glue and nail into place on the throne as indicated by the diagram.
10. Use nail punch and hammer to make sure no nail heads stick out. Fill in nail holes and cracks with wood putty and putty knife. Allow to dry.
11. Sand off excess putty and rough areas. (Begin with course grained sandpaper, then switch to medium and fine.) Paint the entire throne with black polyurethane or acrylic enamel. Let dry.

In some cases, different officers will need thrones which are specifically colored to represent their particular office: for the Hierophant—red with inlaid green; Hegemon—white with inlaid black; and Hiereus—black with inlaid white. The rest of the thrones are to be all black. Each iset should be marked underneath so that they are always used by a specific officer.

The iset described here is light and can be easily moved around the temple. However, if larger isets are desired, simply increase the size of all construction measurements proportionally. Small cushions may be placed on the isets for added comfort.

The Primary Officers of the Neophyte Hall

The Officers and Their Godforms

(Note: The various Egyptian, Coptic, Graeco-Egyptian, and Greek versions of the godforms given here are from a paper titled "The Godforms of the Visible Stations," by Adam P. Forrest.)[12]

The Hierophant

Egyptian *Osir*, Coptic *Ousiri*, Graeco-Egyptian *Osiris*. Osiris in the Netherland. Expounder of the Mysteries in the Hall of the Dual Manifestation of the Goddess of Truth.

The Hierophant is the master of the hall, seated in the east of the temple, on the outer side of the Veil of Paroketh, to rule the temple under the presidency of the Greatly Honored Chiefs. There he or she fills the place of a Lord of the Paths of the Portal of the Vault of the Adepts, acting as inductor to the sacred mysteries. The Hierophant must be of the ⑤=⑥ grade and a Zelator Adeptus Minor. The office of Hierophant is represented by two godforms, the active and passive aspects of Osiris. Seated as Hierophant, he or she is clothed in the godform of Osiris, who never moves from the Dais. When the Hierophant has to move from the Dais, he or she is covered by the form of Osiris in action—Hôôr-Ouêr, Horus the Elder, which is built up by the Past Hierophant. If no one is seated as Past Hierophant, then Inner Order members help the Hierophant to formulate the second godform. The insignia and symbols of the Hierophant are:

- The throne of the east in the path of Samekh, outside the Veil of Paroketh
- The mantle (cloak or tabard) of bright flame scarlet, bearing a white cross on the left breast
- The lamen suspended from a white collar
- The Banner of the East
- The crown-headed scepter

The Hiereus

Egyptian *Hôr,* Coptic *Hôôr,* Graeco-Egyptian *Hôros,* Latinized Greek *Horus*. Horus in the Abode of Blindness unto and Ignorance of the Higher. Avenger of the Gods.

The station of Hiereus is at the extreme west of the temple and in the lowest point of Malkuth, where he is enthroned in its darkest part (in the quarter represented black in the Minutum Mundam diagram). Representing a terrible and avenging god at the confines of matter, at the borders of the Qlippoth, the Hiereus is enthroned upon matter and robed in darkness, and about his or her feet are thunder and lightning—the impact of the paths of Shin and Qoph—Fire and Water, terminating respectively in the russet and olive quarters of Malkuth. There the Hiereus is placed as a mighty and avenging guardian to the sacred mysteries. The symbols and insignia of the Hiereus are:

- The throne of the west in the black section of Malkuth, where it borders on the Kingdom of Shells
- The black mantle of darkness, bearing a white cross on the left breast
- The sword of strength and severity
- The lamen suspended from a scarlet collar
- The Banner of the West

The Hegemon

Egyptian *Mêet,* Coptic *Thmê,* Greek *Themis*. Before the Face of the Gods in the Place of the Threshold.

The station of Hegemon is between the two pillars whose bases are in Netzach and Hod, at the intersection of the paths of Peh and Samekh, in the symbolic gateway of occult science—as it were, at the beam of justice—at the point of intersection of the lowest reciprocal path with that of Samekh, which forms a part of the Middle Pillar. He or she is placed there as the Guardian of the Threshold of the Entrance and the Preparer of the Way for the Enterer—therefore the Reconciler between light and darkness, and the mediator between the stations of Hierophant and Hiereus. The symbols and insignia of Hegemon are:

- The mantle of pure whiteness, bearing on the left breast a red cross
- The miter-headed scepter
- The lamen suspended from a black collar

The Keryx

Egyptian *Anup em Yebet*, Coptic *Anoup-empelebet*, Graeco-Egyptian *Anoubis of the East*, Latinized Greek *Anubis*. Watcher for the Gods.

The Keryx is the Herald, the Guardian, and Watcher within the temple, as the Phylax is the Watcher without—and therefore the Keryx is in charge of the proper disposition of the furniture and stations of the temple. He or she is the guardian of the inner side of the portal—the sleepless Watcher of the Gods and the Preparer of the Pathway to divine wisdom. This officer is also the proclaimer. The Keryx's peculiar ensigns of office are:

- The red lamp to signify the hidden Fire over which he watches
- The magic staff of power to represent a ray of the divine light which kindles the hidden Fire
- Two potions whereby to produce the effect of blood

The Stolistes

Egyptian *Mut*, Coptic *Auramoouth*, Graeco-Egyptian *Mouthis*. The Light Shining through the Waters upon Earth. Goddess of the Scale of Balance at the Black Pillar.

The Stolistes is stationed in the northern part of the hall to the northwest of the Black Pillar whose base is in Hod, and is there as the affirmer of the powers of moisture, Water, reflected through the Tree into Hod. The cup is the receptacle of this, filled from Hod so as to transmit its forces into Malkuth, restoring and purifying the vital forces therein by cold and moisture. There is a connection between Auramoouth and the Aurim or Urim of the Hebrews. The Stolistes has the care of the robes and Insignia of the temple as symbolized by his or her cleansing and purification the purging away of the evil of Malkuth by the Waters of Spirit.

The Dadouchos

Egyptian *Neit,* Coptic *Thaum-Esh-Nêith,* Graeco-Egyptian *Neith.* Perfection through Fire manifesting on Earth. Goddess of the Scale of Balance at the White Pillar.

The Dadouchos is stationed towards the midst of the southern part of the hall, to the southwest of the White Pillar whose base is in Netzach and is there as the affirmer of the powers of Fire, reflecting down the Tree to Netzach. The censer is the receptacle thereof—the transmitter of the Fires of Netzach to Malkuth, restoring and purifying the vital force therein by heat and dryness. There is a connection between Thaum-Esh-Neith and the Thummim of the Hebrews.

The Dadouchos has charge of all lights, fires, and incense, as representing the purifying and purging of Malkuth by Fire and the light of Spirit. The Stolistes and the Dadouchos together also purify the temple, the members, and the candidate by Water and by Fire.

The Phylax (Sentinel)

Egyptian *Opowet,* Coptic *Ophooui,* Graeco-Egyptian *Ophois;* also Egyptian *Anu em Ament,* Coptic *Anoup emp Emenet,* Graeco-Egyptian *Anoubis of the West,* Latinized Greek *Anubis.*

The Watcher without. The Phylax sits outside of the hall to guard its outer perimeter. He or she has a sword in his hand to keep out intruders.

The Officers' Implements

All of the officers in the Neophyte Hall wield distinctive implements, each with its own distinctive symbology.

The Hierophant's Wand

The *Hierophant's Wand* (see Color Plate 2) is symbolically the most important wand in the Neophyte Hall and in all of the halls of the Outer Order. Known as the "Scepter of Power," this wand, when wielded by a duly initiated and trained Hierophant, is a powerful implement used to open or close the temple in any grade of the First Order. The wand represents the forces of the Middle Pillar on the Tree of Life. This fact reaffirms the Golden Dawn's emphasis that equilibrated forces (perfect balance of natural opposites) is the true source of life and light in the universe. The implements of the two contending forces, the Hiereus' Sword and the Hegemon's Wand, are also very powerful, but more limited in use. The Scepter of Power acts as a lightning rod which brings down the light from the Kether beyond the veil, and fuses the energies of the Tree together into a mighty triad of Severity, Mercy, and that which reconciles between them. This is especially apparent in the initiation ceremony of the Neophyte, when a triad of these same forces are formed over the head of the candidate on his or her reception into the Order.

The crown of the Hierophant's Wand naturally alludes to the Sephirah of Kether. If six crown points are used, the emphasis is on the Macrocosmic Hexagram; if ten are used, the totality of the Tree of Life is stressed. The three golden bands in descending order represent Daath, Tiphareth, and Yesod. The pommel or golden ball at the bottom of the wand refers to Malkuth. (Note: The topmost ring next to the crown is not properly a gold band like the others. It acts as a buttress and support for the wand head, giving it strength. This ring should be considered as part of the wand head itself. It thus partakes of the same symbolism as the crown and Kether.) The shaft represents the descending paths of Gimel, Samekh, and Tau. The Hierophant normally wields the implement by the path of Tau, the part of the shaft between the pommel and the third golden band. This symbolizes the active role he or she plays as a magnet for the divine light of Kether; attracting it through the Middle Pillar and bringing it into manifestation to Malkuth (the temple or the candidate). A true Hierophant who holds the title of "Expounder of the Mysteries" knows that he or she is ultimately a channel for the divine light, made worthy to do so through initiation, study, hard magical work, service to one's Fratres and Sorores, and selfless dedication to the Great Work. Ego should not play any role here. A Hierophant who lacks humility is not a true Hierophant.

Besides actual initiations, the Hierophant's Wand can be used for many magical purposes where the force of Kether and the Middle Pillar is desired, so long as it is used with the respect worthy of such a sublime and powerful implement. The wand can certainly be used to invoke or banish the elements with great effect, and this is precisely what the Hierophant does with it in the elemental grade ceremonies. (Note: In the original Order papers known as Z–1, there is a warning against misuse of the Hierophant's Wand. Many people have interpreted this to mean that this scepter is never to be used to invoke the elements in a ritual such as the SIRP. What Z–1 actually warns against is the use of the "Opening and Closing by Scepter" in a ritual where elemental spirits have been invoked. This method is only to be performed by the Hierophant when time is short, by simply declaring the temple open or closed by the power of the scepter. Once again this method is not to be used when the elements have been invoked—the proper Pentagrams must be drawn by the Hierophant in order to open or close the hall correctly.)

The Scepter of Power can also be employed to consecrate other implements or talismans with the particular energies of the spheres and paths of the Middle Pillar. See *Ritual Use of Magical Tools*, chapter one, "Consecration of a Tiphareth Talisman," employing the Scepter of Power.

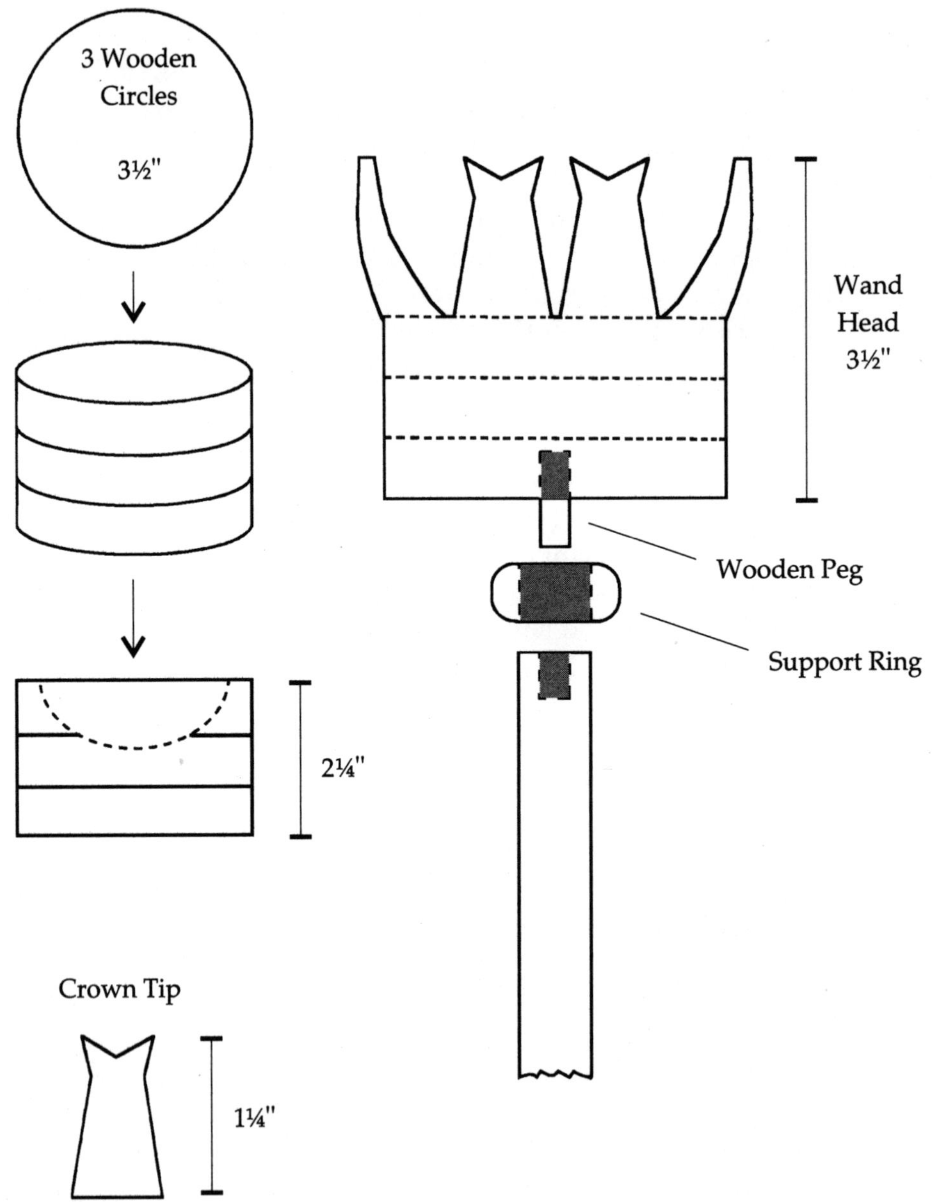

Figure 19: The Hierophant's Wand

A diagram showing the basic construction of a crown is shown in Figure 19, page 50, and of a wand in Figure 20, page 52.

Materials Needed

- One ¾" thick dowel approximately 36" long
- One 12" square piece of ¾" thick pine wood
- One 6" square piece of soft wood (balsa or bass), ¼" thick
- Two ¼" wooden dowels or pegs 1" in length
- One 1½" wooden ball
- Yellow carpenter's glue
- Gesso
- Acrylic paints: red and gold
- Clear lacquer finish (spray or brush on)
- Ruler or yard stick

Tools Needed

- Jigsaw or scroll saw
- Electric drill with ¼" and ¾" bits
- Sandpaper (medium and fine grained)
- Artist's paint brushes
- Rotary power tool with gouging bit

Construction: The Crown

(It is sometimes possible to find a metal candle holder or other decorative ornament in the shape of a crown. This is an acceptable alternative to making the crown out of wood in steps 1–5.)[13]

1. With the jigsaw, cut three 3½" diameter circles out of the ¾" thick piece of pine wood. (See Figure 19, page 50.)

2. Glue all three pieces together to make one solid circular piece of wood which is 2¼" in thickness and 3½" in diameter.

3. With rotary power tool and gouging bit, hollow out the top (flat) side of this circular piece of wood to form a concave or curved hollow space which is about ¾" to 1" deep. Sand smooth. (This step is optional.)

4. From the ¼" thick wood, cut out 6 to 10 crown tips. Taper the upper ends of the crown tips with sandpaper to form points. Angle the bottom ends of the crown tips

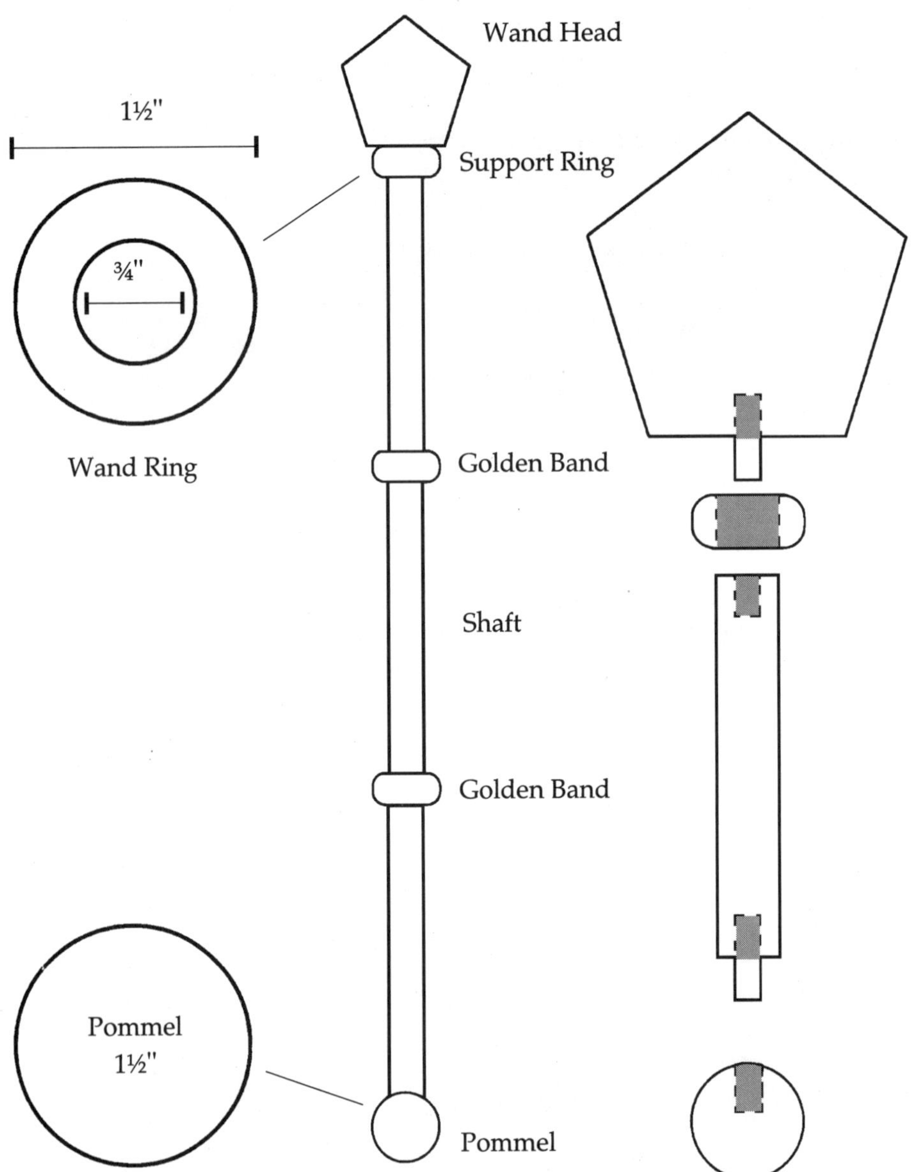

Figure 20: Basic Wand Construction

with sandpaper so that when glued to the main part of the crown, the tips will tilt outward slightly. Glue the tips around the edges of the top (hollowed-out) side of crown.

5. With rotary power tool, grind and sand out curves on sides of crown for a sculptural effect (as in diagram), or leave the curved sides smooth. Drill a hole ½" deep and ¼" wide in the center of the bottom of the crown.

Construction: The Shaft, Rings, and Pommel

(Note: For a easy alternative to making wooden rings, you may make rings out of strips of leather or double-stick foam tape that is 2" thick. Cut the strips of leather or tape into the appropriate lengths and glue or stick them to the wand shaft where needed. Otherwise, follow the instructions for making wooden rings below in step 6.)

See Figure 20, page 52 for construction diagrams.

6. Into the leftover piece of ¾" pine wood, drill a ¾" diameter hole. Around this hole, draw a 1½" diameter circle. Cut this circle out of the wood using the scroll saw. Repeat this same process three more times, so that you end up with four donut-shaped rings of wood.

7. Take the 36" long dowel (shaft) and drill a hole ½" deep and ¼" in diameter into one end of it. Do the same to the other end. Glue one of the 1" wooden pegs into one of the holes you have just drilled, so that half of the peg is embedded into the end of the dowel and half of it sticks out. Do the same at the other end of the shaft.

8. Apply glue to the inside of all four rings. Slide one of the rings over the top end of the shaft. Slide the remaining rings over the other end of the shaft and space all the rings evenly, approximately 9" apart, starting from the topmost ring. (Note: The rings should fit snugly. If they are too tight to slide into place, the inside hole may require some sanding.)

9. Take the 1½" wooden ball (pommel) and, with sandpaper, form a flattened area about ¾" wide. Into the center of this, drill a hole which is ½" deep and ¼" in diameter. Pour some glue into the hole you have just drilled and attach the ball to the bottom end of the shaft, over the wooden peg.

10. Finish assembling the wand by pouring some glue into the hole at the bottom of the crown and attaching it to the top of the shaft, over the wooden peg. (Note: The crown should fit snugly and butt up against the topmost ring.)

    Let the glue dry for a few hours.

Finishing Steps

11. Sand the entire surface of the scepter. (Begin using medium sandpaper, then switch to fine.) With a paint brush, cover the wand with a coat of gesso. Allow time to dry.
12. Sand the painted surface (especially the shaft) lightly with fine sandpaper until smooth. Paint the entire crown and shaft of the wand with acrylic red. Allow to dry.
13. Paint the four rings and pommel with antique gold. Allow to dry. Paint or spray on a sealant such as clear lacquer to protect the painted wand. Allow to dry.

The Hegemon's Wand

The miter-headed scepter (see Color Plate 2) is the distinctive ensign of the office of Hegemon. In the hands of a skilled initiate who holds the office of Hegemon, this wand is a powerful tool which attracts the forces of the Pillar of Mercy (the White Pillar) on the Tree of Life. This implement is the counterpart to the Sword of the Hiereus which represents the Pillar of Severity. Known also as the "Scepter of Wisdom," it is used by the Hegemon at all times when conducting the candidate throughout the hall. This is

Figure 21: The Headdress of the God Oannes / A Bishop's Miter

because it represents the attraction of the forces of the candidate's Higher Self which seek ever to aspire toward the forces of divine mercy and light. Outwardly, the wand is said to symbolize religion which guides and regulates life, but its occult meaning is far more complex than this. The wielder of the Scepter of Wisdom acts as the candidate's Higher Self which guides and protects him or her through the journey of initiation. The miter-head is split in two and not closed, to indicate the dual manifestation of wisdom and truth; and well as the two great contending forces of darkness and light. Above all, this wand symbolizes the goal of spiritual attainment—the marriage of opposites which results in ultimate union with the eternal.

The miter is the liturgical headdress worn by Catholic bishops as well as some Anglican and Lutheran bishops. It came into use in the eleventh century. According to Thomas Inman in *Ancient Pagan and Modern Christian Symbolism,* the shape of the miter was taken from the fish-skin headdresses of certain Assyro-Babylonian deities.[14] The sea god Oannes, who taught human beings the arts and sciences, is usually depicted with the body of a man underneath the body or skin of a fish. The open mouth of the fish resembles the two halves of the bishop's miter. (See Figure 21, page 54.) The fact that Christian symbolism often includes the image of a fish is certainly noteworthy in this regard.

As in the case of the Hierophant's Wand, this scepter has gold bands or rings which represent certain Sephiroth on the Tree of Life—in this case, the spheres of the right hand Pillar of Mercy. The miter-head, along with its supporting ring, represents Chokmah. The bands then symbolize in descending order the spheres of Chesed and Netzach. The sections of the shaft allude to the paths of Vav, Kaph, and Qoph. The grip by which the Hegemon normally holds the wand is by the path of Qoph (the path of the Moon, the forces of flux and reflux) between the last band and the pommel, which refers to Malkuth. The shaft is red to represent the primordial Fire of Yod energy—the first igniting spark of the Flaming Sword which formed the Tree of Life.

The split head of the miter is gold and, in some cases, the two tips each terminate in a ball. The miter is charged with a red Calvary cross of six squares. This represents the wisdom of Chokmah as a duplicated aspect of Kether, attracted by the symbol of self-sacrifice.

The Scepter of Wisdom can be employed to invoke the forces (Sephiroth and paths) of the Pillar of Mercy. Once again, such an implement must be handled with respect for its power and that which it symbolizes. It can be used for the consecration of talismans with the specific energies of the White Pillar in the same manner that the Hierophant's Scepter can be utilized for charging talismans with the forces of the Middle Pillar. One can also take advantage of the particular energies of the Hegemon's Wand which attract the forces of divine mercy and light. A ritual of this sort can greatly enhance spiritual development and eventually result in conversation with the Higher Self. See *Ritual Use of Magical Tools,* chapter one, for "A Spiritual Development Ritual."

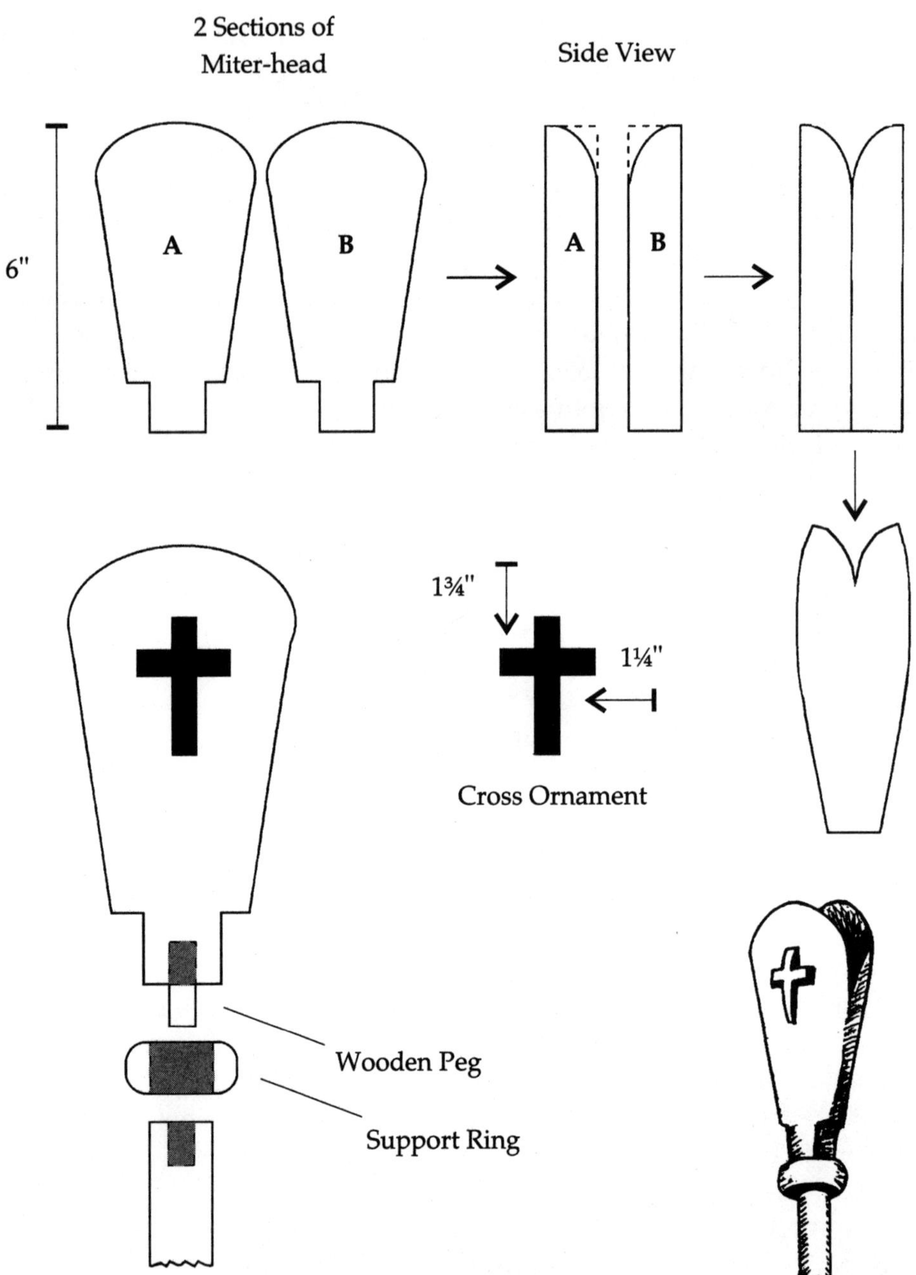

Figure 22: The Hegemon's Wand

Refer to Figure 22 on page 56 for construction diagrams.

Materials Needed

- One ¾" thick dowel approximately 36" long
- One 6" x 12" piece of ¾" soft wood (pine, balsa, or bass)
- One ¼" wide strip of balsa or basswood (found in most hobby shops)
- Two ¼" wooden dowels or pegs 1" in length
- One 1½" wooden ball
- Carpenter's wood glue
- Gesso
- Acrylic paints: red and gold
- Clear lacquer finish (spray or brush on)

Tools Needed

- Jigsaw
- Electric drill with ¼" and ¾" bits
- Sandpaper (medium and fine grained)
- Artist's paint brushes
- Rotary power tool with gouging bit

Construction: The Miter-head

1. With the jigsaw, cut out sections A and B from the 6" x 12" piece of wood as shown in Figure 22, page 56. (Both pieces are exactly the same—3" wide, 6" long.)

2. Lay section A flat on your table or work area. With a rotary power tool grind and sand down the curved edge of section A so that the curved part is thinnest at the very top of the miter, while the ends of the curve at the widest part of the miter are nearly their original width. (The result should be a piece of wood which at its widest point begins to taper down to a thin, curved edge at its top.) Repeat this procedure on section B.

3. Glue the ground-out sides of A and B together so that they lie one on top of the other. Viewed from the side, the top of the miter-head should show a hollowed-out V-shape.

4. Once the glue has dried, sand down the miter so that it tapers gracefully, getting thicker toward the bottom.

5. Drill a hole 2" deep and 4" wide in the center of the bottom side of the miter-head.

Construction: The Shaft, Rings, and Pommel

(Note: For an easy alternative to making wooden rings, you may make rings out of strips of leather or double-stick foam tape that is ½" thick. Cut the strips of leather or tape into the appropriate lengths and glue or stick them to the wand shaft where needed. Otherwise, follow the instructions for making wooden rings below in step 6.)

6. Into the leftover piece of ¾" thick pine wood, drill a ¾" diameter hole. Around this hole, draw a 1½" diameter circle. Cut this circle out of the wood using the scroll saw. Repeat this same process two more times, so that you end up with three donut-shaped rings of wood.
7. Take the 36" long dowel (shaft) and drill a hole ½" deep and ¼" in diameter into one end of it. Do the same to the other end. Glue one of the 1" wooden pegs into one of the holes you have just drilled so that half of the peg is embedded into the end of the dowel and half of it sticks out. Do the same at the other end of the shaft.
8. Apply glue to the inside of all three rings. Slide one of the rings over the top end of the shaft. Slide the remaining rings over the other end of the shaft and space all the rings evenly, approximately 11" apart, starting from the topmost ring. If the rings are too tight, sand inside the center hole. (Note: As with the preceding wand, the ring closest to the miter-head acts as a support and partakes of its symbolism. The remaining two rings are the proper gold bands.)
9. Take the 1½" wooden ball (pommel) and, with sandpaper, form a flattened area about ¾" wide. Into the center of this, drill a hole which is ½" deep and ¼" in diameter. Pour some glue into the hole you have just drilled and attach the ball to the bottom end of the shaft, over the wooden peg.
10. Finish assembling the wand by pouring some glue into the hole at the bottom of the miter-head and attaching it to the top of the shaft, over the wooden peg. (The miter-head should fit snugly against the support ring.) Let the glue dry.

Finishing Steps

11. Take the ¼" strip of balsa wood and cut it into six pieces: two 1¾" in length, and four ½" in length.
12. On the front of the miter-head, glue one larger and two smaller pieces of the wood so that they form the figure of a Calvary cross. Let dry. Sand down to smooth the edges of the four arms of the cross. With the remaining strips of wood, repeat this figure on the back of the miter-head.

13. Sand the entire surface of the scepter. (Begin using medium sandpaper, then switch to fine.) With a paint brush, cover the wand with a coat of gesso. Allow to dry.
14. Sand the painted surface (especially the shaft) lightly with fine sandpaper until smooth. Paint the shaft and two crosses with acrylic red. Allow to dry.
15. Paint the rings, pommel, and miter-head (except for the crosses) gold. Allow to dry. Paint or spray on a sealant such as clear lacquer to protect the painted wand. Allow to dry.

The Sword of the Hiereus

The sword is primarily comprised of a blade and a guard—it is thus an emblem of conjunction. During the Middle Ages, the sword often took on the form of a cross. Traditionally, the sword is the proper instrument of a knight, who is the defender of the forces of light against the forces of darkness. Its essential symbolic meaning is of the ability to wound and defend—attributes of strength and sovereignty. There is also a curious relationship between the words "sword" and "word."[15]

The Hiereus is the officer known as "the Avenger of the Gods" who guards the temple from the Qlippoth or evil demons that dwell beneath Malkuth in the Kingdom of Shells. This officer represents a terrible, avenging god at the confines of matter, who is enthroned upon matter and robed in darkness. The Hiereus' sword symbolizes the forces of the Pillar of Severity—Binah is at its tip, Geburah is at the midsection of the blade, and Hod is represented by the brass guard. The two paths of Cheth and Mem are attributed to the equal sections of the blade between Geburah and Binah, and between Geburah and Hod. The grip is red to represent the path of Shin—alluding to the universe governed by the flaming force of divine severity. Malkuth, although not a part of the Pillar of Severity, is represented by the black pommel, for, as is the case with the other scepters of the Outer Order, all the forces of the Tree of Life are grounded in Malkuth. The "Sword of Vengeance" is the name of this implement.

Because the sword of the Hiereus is used to guard the temple, its natural use, other than in Golden Dawn ceremonies, is for banishing and protection. At the beginning of the ceremony, or at any time during the ritual, the Hierophant may call upon the Hiereus to perform the Lesser Banishing Ritual of the Pentagram if needed.

Any convenient sword can be employed for the sword of the Hiereus. The best sword to obtain for this purpose would be a military or masonic sword with a brass guard. The grip should be painted red and the pommel should be black. It is also quite feasible for one to make a sword from an iron bar and a wooden handle (painted in the aforementioned colors.) For this task we suggest the reader refer to the section on construction of the Magic

Sword in chapter five. See *Ritual Use of Magical Tools*, chapter one, for "The Supreme Banishing Ritual of the Pentagram," employing the sword of the Hiereus.

The Caduceus Wand of the Keryx

The *Caduceus Wand of the Keryx* (see Color Plate 14) is a most impressive and complex implement. It is the wand of Hermes (also known as Thoth and Mercury), the god of wisdom, magic, and communication. Legend has it that Hermes intervened in a fight between two serpents who then curled themselves around his wand. An even older version of this dates back to ancient Mesopotamia, where the intertwining serpents were a symbol of the god who cures all illnesses, a meaning which was absorbed into Greek culture and is still preserved in the medical emblems of today. (See Figure 23.) Raphael, the healer of God and the archangel of elemental Air, also carries a caduceus.

Like the other wands thus far described, the symbolism of the caduceus is based upon the Tree of Life. The upper point of the wand rests on Kether, and the wings stretch out to Chokmah and Binah, thus comprehending the three Supernal Sephiroth. The lower seven are embraced by the serpents whose heads fall on Chesed and Geburah. These are the twin serpents of Egypt and the currents of the astral light. In addition to this, the wings and the top of the wand form the Hebrew letter Shin, the symbol of Fire. The heads and upper halves of the serpents form the letter Aleph while their tails enclose Mem, the symbol of Water—the Fire of Life above, the Waters of Creation below, and the Air as the Reconciler vibrating between Fire and Water.

Figure 23: Various Forms of the Caduceus

The rod of Hermes represents the balanced forces of eternal light working invisibly in the darkness. This wand, along with the Lamp of the Hidden Knowledge, is borne by the Keryx to lead the candidate who sees nothing but a dim hint of light through the hoodwink. The godform taken on by the Keryx is that of one of the Anubian Guards. (Anubis, god of the underworld, is considered a lower manifestation of Thoth.) The light he carries is the invisible divine force which guides the candidate, while the wand is that power which directs the flow of the divine current. The hidden energies of the wand may be revealed to the student through meditation.

The Caduceus Wand can be used in an invocation ritual of Hermes-Thoth to gain the magical knowledge necessary to become the archetypal magician. (See *Ritual Use of Magical Tools*, chapter one, for "An Invocation of Hermes-Thoth.") It could also be used to invoke the three ancient elements of Fire, Air and Water through the Three Mother Letters. Lastly, the wand could be employed in a healing ritual where the archangel Raphael would be invoked.

The method given below to make a Keryx Wand is complicated. We have seen adequate Caduceus Wands cut completely out of foam-core board, a piece of styrofoam that is approximately ¼" thick, covered on both sides with poster board. If the wand is not abused, it will hold up nicely. It is also possible to cut a flat Caduceus Wand completely out of one piece of pine or other soft wood that is ¾" thick (see Figure 25, page 62). One wand we've seen consisted of a 6" long metal caduceus glued onto the top of a staff that was painted in the colors of the Three Mother Letters.

Refer to Figure 24 on page 62 for construction diagrams.

Materials Needed

- One ¾" thick dowel approximately 31" long
- One pound box of oven-hardening clay
- One ¼" thick dowel 2¾" in length
- One 1⅝" wooden ball
- One ¾" thick dowel approximately 16" to 18" in length
- ¾" thick piece of soft wood approximately 4" x 14"
- Yellow carpenter's glue
- Wood putty
- Gesso
- Strong bonding glue such as epoxy
- Sheet of drawing paper at least 18" in length
- Aluminum foil
- Acrylic paints: red, yellow, blue, white, and black
- Sealant; clear lacquer finish (spray or brush on)

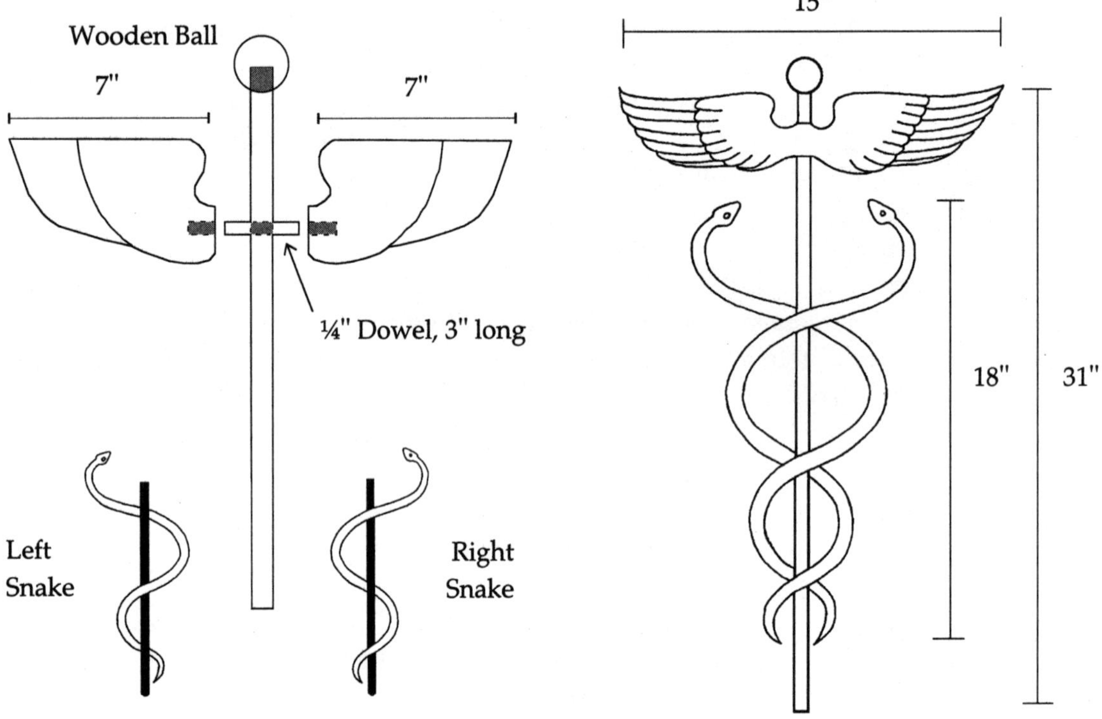

Figure 24: The Caduceus Wand of the Keryx

Figure 25: A Flat, Wooden Caduceus Wand

Tools Needed

- Jigsaw
- Electric drill with ¾" and ¼" bits
- Rotary power tool with gouging bit
- Sandpaper
- Artist's brushes
- Cookie sheet (used for baking)

Construction: The Wings

1. With the jigsaw, cut out two wing sections 7" long and approximately 4" wide as shown in Figure 24, page 62.
2. With a pencil, draw stylized feathers on both sides of both wings. Use the rotary power tool to gouge and grind the outline of the feathers, giving them a sculpted look. Sand the wings until they have a smooth, three-dimensional appearance.
3. At the part of each piece where the wing will be attached to the shaft of the wand, drill a hole that is ¼" wide and 1" deep. (Be sure both wings are drilled identically.)
4. Take the wooden ball and drill a hole into it that is ¾" wide and ¾" deep. Pour glue into the hole. Put one end of the 31" long dowel in the hole drilled into the wooden ball. Press in firmly and let the glue dry.
5. Approximately 3¾" down from the top of the ball, drill a ¼" hole completely through the shaft. Pour some glue into this hole. Take the thin 2¾" long dowel and run it through the hole so that 1" of the ¼" thick dowel sticks out on both sides of the shaft.
6. Pour glue in the holes previously drilled into both wing sections. Attach wings to the shaft by sliding them into place over the ¼" dowel on either side of the shaft. Let the glue dry firmly.
7. Where wings connect to the shaft, apply wood putty to fill in gaps and give a smooth, continuous appearance. Do the same where the shaft joins to the ball. Let the putty dry.
8. Sand the wand smooth and paint with gesso. Let dry. Sand the painted wand and put it aside.

Construction: The Serpents

9. On the sheet of drawing paper, draw the two serpents as depicted in Figure 24 on page 62, 18" in length. The widest part of the figure (just below the heads) should be approximately 9".

10. Take some of the clay and knead it by hand until it is soft and pliable. Then roll out a long coil or rope of clay. The coil should be about ⅝" thick and taper down to the serpent's tail. Check to see if the coil is nearing the proper dimensions of the serpent by and placing it in position over your drawing. Add some clay to the thick end of the coil, to give the serpent a diamond-shaped head. The mouth and eyes of the snake can be drawn into the clay with a toothpick or pin.

11. When you have one serpent that fits perfectly on your drawing, put it aside and get the cookie sheet and aluminum foil. Lay a piece of aluminum foil over the cookie sheet and wrap it firmly around the edges. Lay your drawing on top of the aluminum and, with a pencil, trace the pattern of the two serpents. (When you remove your drawing, the serpent pattern should be imprinted into the aluminum foil.) At this point you will refer to the diagram showing the Right Snake and the Left Snake. We will begin with the Right Snake. Place the clay snake onto the aluminum foil in the position of the Right Snake.

12. Take the 16" long dowel and position it onto the aluminum foil where the shaft of the wand would be according to the pattern. The Right Snake will touch this dowel in three places. The middle point where the serpent touches the dowel is the only one where the dowel is on top of the serpent. At the upper and lower points, drape the serpent on top of the dowel.

13. At the three points where the serpent joins the dowel, press the clay gently, so it will leave a slight indentation where the dowel touched it. (This will make it easier to attach the finished serpent to the real wand shaft later.)

14. Place the cookie sheet in the oven and follow the package directions for baking the clay. At this time, begin rolling out the second snake.

15. When finsihed baking, take the cookie sheet out of the oven and let the serpent cool before you touch it. After the serpent has cooled, remove it from the dowel and aluminum foil and set it aside. Get the second snake and place it onto the foil in the position of the Left Snake. As before, the snake will touch the dowel in three places. But this time at the middle point, the serpent will be on top of the dowel, while at the top and bottom points, the dowel will be on top of the serpent. Once again, press the clay gently so that the dowel will leave indentations. Bake the serpent as before.

Finishing Steps

16. Position the Right Snake into place on the winged shaft. Apply a strong glue such as epoxy to the three points where the serpent touches the shaft. Let dry. Position and glue the Left Snake into place on the wand. Let dry.

17. Paint the serpents with gesso. Allow to dry. Paint the top portion of the wand (which includes the ball and wings) with acrylic red. Paint the shaft yellow from the bottom of the wings to the second point where the serpents touch. Paint the remaining section of the shaft with brilliant blue. The Right Snake should be painted white, while the Left Snake is to be painted black. (Note: it is also acceptable to paint the serpents exactly as the shaft—yellow to the middle point and blue from the middle to the end of their tails.)

The Cup of Stolistes

The Stolistes is the officer responsible for purifying the hall and the members with the lustral Water. The *Cup of Stolistes* can be used to purify and purge any temple or sacred space from the influences of the mundane. The Water contained therein can be charged and employed in a ritual of self-purification as well. (See *Ritual Use of Magical Tools*, chapter one, for "The Rite of Self-Purification.") Any Water thus charged can be saved for use in later rites.

Construction

For the Cup of Stolistes, any brass chalice or metal goblet will suffice. However, if the reader truly wishes to have an authentic Stolistes implement, he or she should consult the section describing the Water Cup given in chapter five. This cup can be painted in the colors of blue and orange, but without the sigils or Hebrew names.

The Censer or Thurible of Dadouchos

The Dadouchos is the officer responsible for consecrating the hall and the members with Fire and incense. The censer can be used to consecrate, vitalize and devote any temple or sacred space to the workings of the divine spirit. In addition, the coals and incense contained therein can be charged and employed in a ritual of self-consecration. (See *Ritual Use of Magical Tools*, chapter one, for "The Rite of Self-Consecration.") Any ashes thus charged can be saved and used in later rites.

Construction

For the censer of Dadouchos, any metal brazier used for holding hot coals and incense will suffice. The best possible censer for this purpose will be suspended from a chain like the brazier used in many orthodox churches. This will enable the Dadouchos to swing the implement freely while consecrating the hall. However, the choice of a censer may well depend on what is available. (At certain times we have been forced to use a simple stick of incense as the implement of Dadouchos when certain important officers experienced allergic reactions to too much smoke.) The most significant aspect of this implement is that it contains the spark of the sacred flame.

The Sword of the Phylax (Sentinel)

The Phylax is the sentinel or guardian of the temple. Stationed just outside the temple, he guards against intruders with sword in hand. The most effective use of the Phylax's Sword, outside of a full Order ceremony, would involve a simple banishing ritual. (See *Ritual Use of Magical Tools*, chapter one, for "The Lesser Banishing Ritual of the Pentagram.")

Construction

Any convenient sword can be employed for the sword of the Phylax. As is the case with the Hiereus, the best sword to obtain would be a military sword with a brass guard. The grip should be painted black and the guard should be gold. One could also make a sword from an iron bar and a wooden handle to be painted in the aforementioned colors. We suggest that the reader refer to the section on construction of the Magic Sword in chapter five. (The Phylax's Sword would not have sigils or Hebrew names painted on it.)

The Implements of the Dais Officers

A Description of the Dais Officers

The Dais Officers include the Past Hierophant and either the Three Chiefs of the Outer Order or their local representatives, the Three Chiefs of the temple. The Three Chiefs are seated beside the Hierophant. The Imperator and Cancellarius are seated to the right of the Hierophant while the Praemonstrator and immediate Past Hierophant are to the left—the Cancellarius and immediate Past Hierophant being nearest to the Hierophant on their respective sides. The Chiefs stand before the veil in the east of the temple as the representatives of the Inner Order. Therefore, no meeting can be held without one of them present.

Preferably all Three Chiefs should be present (should a Chief be absent, it is well to have the station filled by another adept). The other officers of the temple exist only by their authority and permission.[16]

The Three Chiefs are in the temple and rule it, yet they are not comprehended in, nor understood by, the Outer Order. They represent, as it were, veiled divinities sending a form to sit before the Veil of Paroketh, and like the veils of Isis and Nephthys, they are impenetrable save to the initiate. The synthesis of the Three Chiefs may be said to be in the form of Thoth who comes from behind the Veil at the point of its rending. Yet separately, they may be thus referred to as follows.

The Imperator, from his or her relation to Geburah, may be referred to the goddess Nephthys[17] (Nebethô). On this officer the energy and stability of the temple depend; and if the Imperator has sub-officers to assist him or her, they partake of the same symbolism. The Imperator's mantle is the flame scarlet cloak of Fire and severity, and is thus the symbol of unflinching authority, compelling the obedience of the temple to all commands issued by the Second Order. The lamen is similar to that of the Hierophant, of the same colors, but depending from a green collar. The Imperator bears a sword similar to that of the Hiereus. The station of this officer in the temple is at the extreme right of the Dais, and at the Equinox the Imperator takes the throne of Hierophant when that office is vacated.[18]

The Praemonstrator, from his or her relation to Chesed, may be referred to the goddess Isis[19] (Êse). This officer's duty is that of teacher and instructor of the temple, always limited by the obligation to keep secret the knowledge of the Second Order from the Outer Order. The Praemonstrator superintends the working of the Outer Order, seeing that nothing in it is relaxed or profaned; and duly issues to the temple any instruction regarding the ritual received by him from the Greatly Honoured Chiefs of the Second Order. The Praemonstrator is therefore to the temple the reflector of the wisdom beyond. Any sub-officers partake of the same symbolism. The Praemonstrator wears a mantle which is the bright blue robe of Water, representing the reflection of the wisdom and knowledge of Chesed. He or she may wear a lamen like that of the Hierophant, but colored blue on an orange field and depending from a collar of orange. The Praemonstrator may bear a scepter surmounted by a Maltese cross in the elemental colors.[20]

The Cancellarius, from his or her property of recorder, may be referred to the god Thoth[21] (Thôouth). On this officer depends the records of the temple, the order of its working, the arrangement of its meetings, and the circulation of its manuscripts. The Cancellarius is the recorder and, more immediately than either of the preceding Chiefs, the representative of the executive authority of the Second Order over the Outer. The duty of the Cancellarius is to see that in no case knowledge of a grade be given to a member who has not properly attained to it. He or she is the immediate circulator of all communications from the Second Order. Any sub-officers partake of the same symbolism. The Cancellarius' mantle is the yellow cloak of Air. The Cancellarius may wear a lamen like that of Hierophant, but of yellow on a violet field, and depending from a purple collar; and he or she may bear a scepter surmounted by a Hexagram of amber and gold.[22]

The Past Hierophant, who served as Hierophant for the previous six months before the Equinox, also sits on the Dais and builds up the godform of Hôôr-Ouer (Horus the Elder). He or she wears the Hierophant's mantle as well as a smaller version of that officer's lamen. As already stated, the Past Hierophant's Scepter is the same as the Hierophant's, depicting the affinity which exists between these two Dais Officers. When the Hierophant moves off the Dais, he or she takes on the godform of Hôôr-Ouer built up by the Past Hierophant, who similarly assumes the godform of Osiris (Ousiri).

The scepters of the Chiefs should be of the same color as their mantles, with a gold band to represent Tiphareth, the first Sephirah of the Inner Order. The sword of Imperator should have a plain scarlet hilt, with gold or brass mountings, while the scepter of the Praemonstrator should be blue with a gold band.[23]

Of all the magical tools in the Neophyte Hall, the implements of the Dais Officers should be used only by the Chiefs of the Order or those temple Chiefs who represent them. They are designed to bring the energies of the spheres of Geburah, Chesed, and Tiphareth into the temple, grounding the current of the divine light in Malkuth. However, a magician would be well advised to set the wands in their proper stations in the east for all workings in the Neophyte Hall. A meditation on each of the Dais implements in turn will yield much valuable information concerning the workings of the triad of the Order.

The Imperator's Sword

The *Imperator's Sword* is a form of the sword of justice, a symbol assigned to the sphere of Geburah. This weapon implies governance and firmness; qualities necessary to the Chief who is symbolically seated in the sphere of Severity. The sword is associated with Fire and symbolizes purification. The steel of the sword alludes to toughness, and the all-conquering Spirit. This implement is used to bring the energies of Nephthys into the temple via the Black Pillar.

Any convenient sword can be employed for the sword of the Imperator. As is the case with the Hiereus, the best sword to acquire would be a military sword with a brass guard. The grip should be painted red and the guard should be yellow or gold. The magician could also make a sword after the manner of the adept's personal sword mentioned in chapter five, to be painted in the colors given here.

The Praemonstrator's Wand

The Maltese cross that crowns the wand of the Praemonstrator (see Color Plate 2) is described in the Portal Ritual thus:

> *The Cross of Four Triangles called the Maltese Cross, is a symbol of the Four Elements in balanced disposition. It is here given in the colors of the King's Scale, and is also assigned to the Four Sephiroth ruling the Grades of the Outer—Earth to Malkuth, Air to Yesod, Water to Hod, and Fire to Netzach.*
>
> *It is again, the Cross which heads the Praemonstrator's Wand, who represents the Sephirah Chesed, the Fourth Sephirah. Four is the number of Jupiter, whose Path unites Chesed to Netzach.*[24]

The Maltese cross, also known as the cross of four triangles and the pyramidal cross, represents the descent of the divine and angelic forces into the pyramid symbol. This implement is used to bring the energies of Isis into the temple via the White Pillar.

Refer to Figure 26 on page 70 for construction diagrams.

Materials Needed

- One ¾" thick dowel approximately 36" long
- One 5" x 9" piece of ¾" soft wood (pine, balsa or bass)
- Two ¼" wooden dowels or pegs 1" in length
- One 1½" wooden ball
- Yellow carpenter's glue
- Gesso
- Acrylic paints: red, yellow, blue, black, gold
- Clear lacquer finish (spray or brush on)

Tools Needed

- Scroll saw or jigsaw
- Electric drill with 4" and ¾" bits
- Sandpaper (coarse, medium, and fine)
- Artist's paint brushes (medium to large)

Construction: The Maltese Cross Head

1. Draw a 5" x 5" square on the piece of soft wood. Cut off the excess wood. Draw the shape of the Maltese Cross onto the piece of wood. (See Figure 26, page 70.) With the

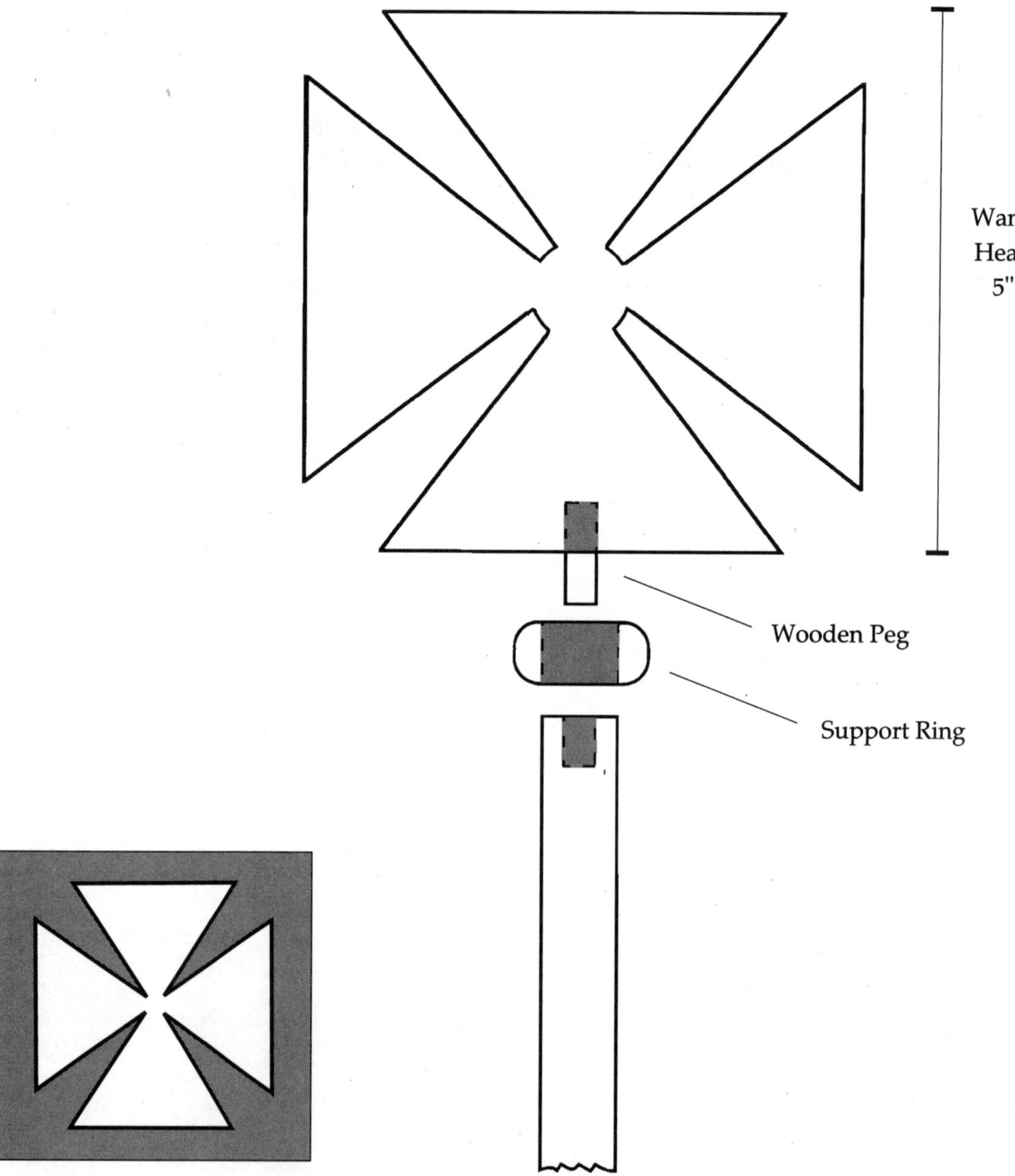

Figure 26: The Praemonstrator's Wand

saw, cut out the cross, removing the excess (shaded) area shown in the diagram. Sand smooth, starting with the course sandpaper and finishing with the medium and fine sandpaper .

2. Drill a hole ½" deep and ¼" wide in the center of the bottom side of the wand head.

Construction: The Shaft

3. Into the leftover piece of ¾" thick pine wood, drill a ¾" diameter hole. Around this hole, draw a 1½" diameter circle. Cut this circle out of the wood using the scroll saw. Repeat this same process once more, so that you end up with two donut-shaped rings of wood.

4. Take the 36" long dowel (shaft) and drill a hole ½" deep and ¼" in diameter into one end of it. Do the same to the other end. Glue one of the 1" wooden pegs into the hole you have just drilled, so that half of the peg is embedded into the end of the dowel and half of it sticks out.

5. Apply glue to the inside of one of the wooden rings. Slide it over the top end of the shaft. (Note: If the ring is too tight, sand inside its center hole.) Apply glue to the other wooden ring and slide it over the opposite end of the shaft to a point about at center of the dowel (approximately 17" up).

6. Pour some glue in the hole you drilled into the bottom end of the wand head and attach the Maltese cross to the wand shaft. The head of the wand should fit snugly against the supporting ring.

7. Take the 1½" wooden ball and, using sandpaper, form a flattened area about ¾" wide. Into the center of this, drill a hole which is ½" deep and ¼" in diameter.

8. Pour some glue into the hole you have just drilled and attach the ball to the bottom end of the shaft, over the wooden peg.

Finishing Steps

9. Sand the entire surface of the scepter so that it is smooth. With a paint brush, cover the wand with a coat of gesso. Allow to dry.

10. Sand the painted surface (especially the shaft) lightly until smooth. Apply a second coat if needed. Paint the head of the wand as follows:

    - Top quarter: Yellow
    - Bottom quarter: Black
    - Right quarter: Blue
    - Left quarter: Red

(Note: Both sides of the Maltese cross need to be painted; however the right and left quarters of both sides must be painted separately as described previously. You can't simply paint all the way around each arm. The front and back of the wand head should be separated by painting the side edges with gold.)

11. Paint the wand shaft completely blue. Paint the rings and pommel gold. Paint or spray on a sealant such as clear lacquer to protect the painted wand. Allow to dry.

The Cancellarius' Wand

The Hexagram that heads the wand of the Cancellarius (see Color Plate 2) is a symbol of perfection, of Tiphareth, and of the two great opposing forces, Fire and Water, or positive and negative, in balanced equilibrium. (See Figure 27 on page 73, and refer to the section on the Earth Pentacle in chapter five for more on the Hexagram.) This wand attracts the divine energy of Kether through the sphere of Tiphareth, bringing the energies of the Middle Pillar into the temple.

Refer to Figure 27, page 73 and Figure 28, page 74 for construction diagrams.

Materials Needed

- One ¾" thick dowel approximately 36" long
- One 7" x 9" piece of ¾" thick soft wood (pine, balsa, or bass)
- Two ¼" wooden dowels or pegs 1" long
- One 1½" diameter wooden ball
- Yellow carpenter's glue
- Wood putty
- Gesso
- Acrylic paints: yellow, orange, gold
- Clear lacquer finish (spray or brush on)

Tools Needed

- Scroll saw or coping saw
- Electric drill with ¼" and ¾" bits
- Sandpaper (coarse, medium, and fine)
- Artist's paint brushes (medium to large)

Construction: The Hexagram Head

1. Draw the Hexagram shown in Figure 28, page 74, with proper dimensions (4¼" x 6") on the 7" x 9" piece of wood. Figure 27 shows the degrees of the angles and size of the Hexagram.
2. With the saw, cut out the outer shape of the Hexagram and its supporting crescent shape.
3. Drill nine holes, one inside each of the shaded (negative space) areas of the wand head. (Remember: it is important to use a drill bit that is wider than your saw blade.)
4. With your saw unplugged, detach the blade from the saw. Stick the blade through one of the holes you have drilled and reattach the blade to the saw. Plug the saw back in and begin cutting out the shaded area of wood. Repeat this process for all nine drilled holes until all the waste area of wood has been cut out.
5. Drill a hole ½" deep and ¼" wide in the center of the bottom side of the wand head.

Construction: The Shaft

6. Into the leftover piece of ¾" thick soft wood, drill a ¾" diameter hole. Around this hole, draw a 1½" diameter circle. Cut this circle out of the wood using the scroll saw. Repeat this same process once more, so that you end up with two donut-shaped rings of wood.
7. Take the 36" long dowel (shaft) and drill a hole ½" deep and ¼" in diameter into one end of it. Do the same to the other end. Glue one of the 1" wooden pegs into the hole you have just drilled so that half of the peg is embedded into the end of the dowel and half of it sticks out.
8. Apply glue to the inside of the rings. Slide one ring over the top end of the shaft to a point at the center of the dowel (approximately 17" down). (If the ring is too tight, sand inside its center hole.) The other ring is the support for the wand head. Pour some glue in the hole you drilled into the bottom end of the wand head and attach the Hexagram to the wand shaft. Let dry.
9. Take the 1½" wooden ball and, using course sandpaper, form a flattened area about ¾" wide. Into the center of this, drill a hole that is ½" deep and ¼" in diameter. Pour glue into the hole you have just drilled and attach the ball to the bottom end of the shaft, over the wooden peg.

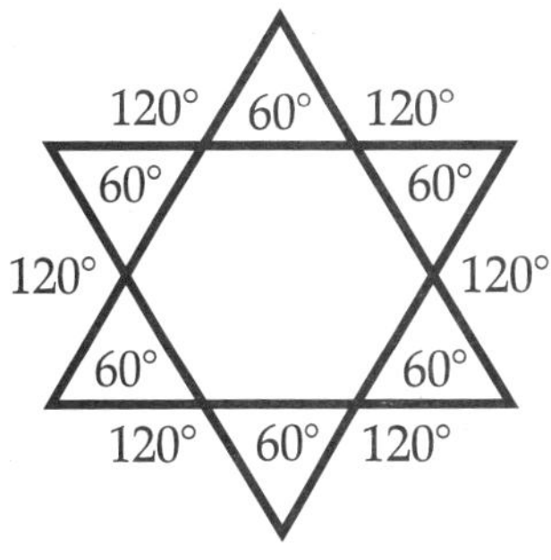

Figure 27: The Angles of a Hexagram

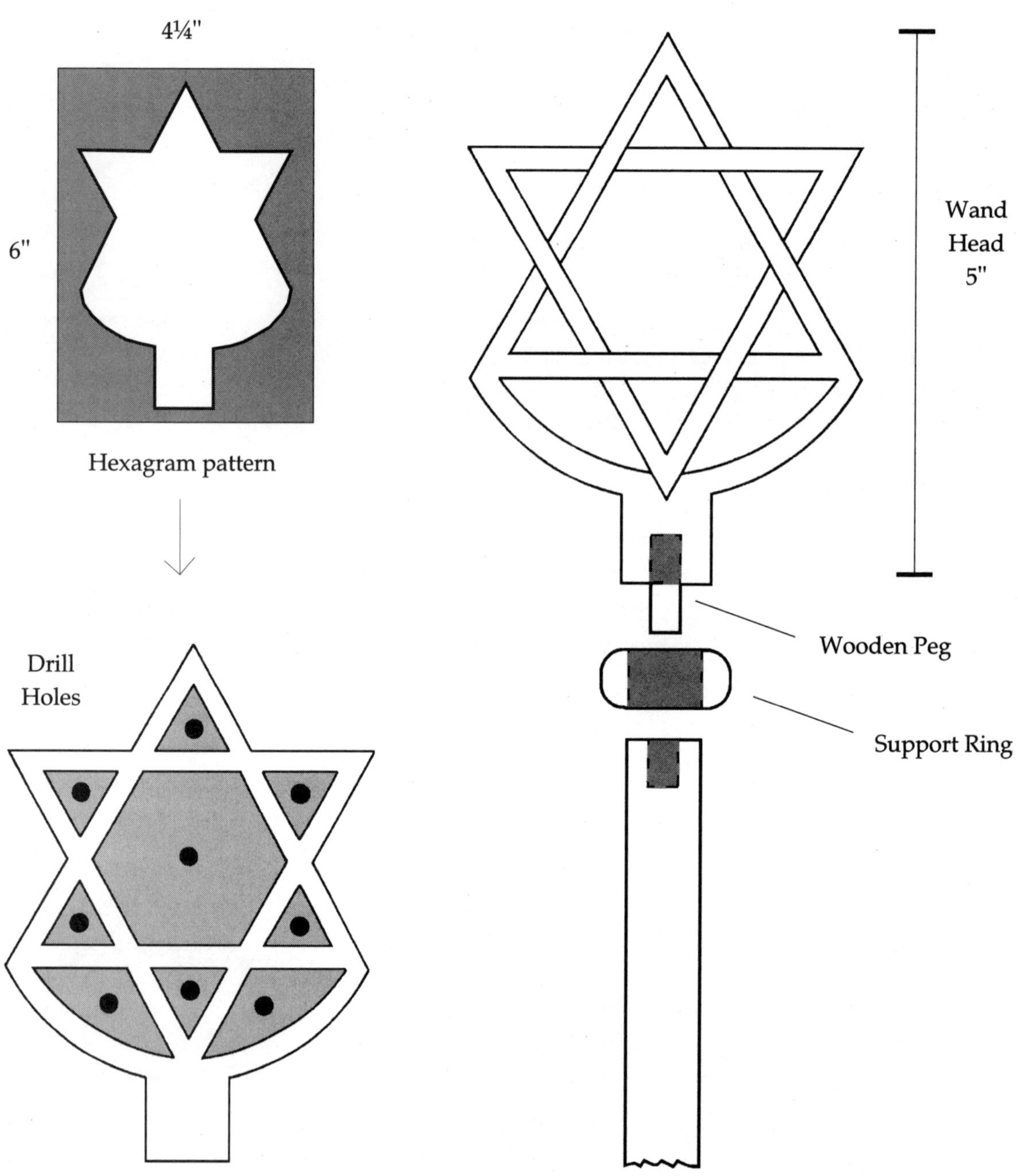

Figure 28: The Cancellarius' Wand

Finishing Steps

10. Sand the entire surface of the scepter so that it is smooth. (Begin with the course sandpaper, then switch to medium and fine.) With a paint brush, cover the wand with a coat of gesso. Allow to dry.

11. Sand the painted surface (especially the shaft) lightly with fine sandpaper until smooth. Apply a second coat if needed. Paint the wand as follows:

    - Shaft: Yellow
    - Ring and pommel: Gold
    - Wand head: Yellow

    (Note: The interlaced triangles forming the Hexagram should be differentiated somehow—either by painting gold lines to separate them, or by painting one triangle a slightly different shade of yellow (by adding some orange).

12. Paint or spray on a sealant such as clear lacquer to protect the painted wand. Allow to dry.

The Past Hierophant's Wand

The Past Hierophant's Wand is identical to that of the Hierophant. It might be desirable to make the Past Hierophant's Wand slightly smaller than that of the Hierophant.

The Lamens

A lamen is a symbol worn by an officer in a Golden Dawn temple. (See Color Plate 12.) Lamens are important tools which help officers focus on their assigned offices and the godforms they represent. The energy of a lamen is not unlike that of a talisman—built up by the group egregore and consecrated by initiates during numerous Order ceremonies and initiations. The lamens are usually placed at the officers' stations before the ceremony, to be worn only after entering the temple. Adept officers take on the godform previously built up by the Hierophant at the station. In a like manner, the lamens should be removed and left at the stations of the officers before exiting the temple at the closing. (For information concerning the lamens of the Dais Officers, review pages 66–68 for the descriptions of individual Dais Officers.)

The lamens are worn suspended from collars which vary in color, according to the office (see Figure 29). The collars of the Middle Pillar Officers are described below. The lesser officers wear lamens suspended from black collars. The designs are in white on a black field to show that they are administrators of the forces of light acting through the darkness, under the presidency of the superior officers.[25] (For instructions on how to make the collars, turn to page 81.)

The lamens can be used by the adept members of the temple to develop their skills at assuming godforms assigned to specific officers. The ritual "Assumption of Godforms: A Guided Meditation" in chapter one of *Ritual Use of Magical Tools* focuses on the various godforms of the Neophyte Hall. Immediately after this is a ritual called "The Rite of Assumption to the Godform of Thmê," describing how to use a lamen in the assumption of a godform.

The Hierophant's Lamen

The *Hierophant's Lamen* is partially explained in the Portal Ceremony as follows:

> *The Hierophant's Lamen is a synthesis of Tiphareth, to which the Calvary Cross of six squares, forming the cube opened out, is fitly referred. The two colors, red and green, the most active and the most passive, whose conjunction points out the practical application*

Figure 29: The Outer Order Lamens

of the knowledge of equilibrium, are symbolic of the reconciliation of the celestial essences of Fire and Water. For the reconciling yellow unites with blue in green, which is the complimentary color to red, and with red in orange which is the complimentary color to blue. The small inner circle placed upon the Cross alludes to the Rose that is conjoined therewith in the symbolism of the Rose and the Cross of our Order.

But in addition to this, it represents the blazing light of the Fire of the Sun bringing into being the green vegetation of the otherwise barren Earth. And also the power of self-sacrifice requisite in one who would essay to initiate into the Sacred Mysteries. So as the Scepter represents the Authority and Power of the Light, the lamen affirms the qualifications necessary to him who wields it, and therefore it is suspended from a white collar, to represent the Purity of the White Brilliance from Kether. Hence it should always be worn by the Hierophant.[26]

The Hiereus' Lamen

The *Hiereus' Lamen* is partially explained in the Portal as follows:

The Outer Circle includes the four Sephiroth, Tiphareth, Netzach, Hod and Yesod, of which the first three mark the angles of the triangle inscribed within, while the connecting Paths: Nun, Ayin, and Peh form its sides. In the extreme center is the Path Samekh through which is the passage for the Rending of the Veil. It is therefore a fitting lamen for Hiereus as representing the connecting link between the First and Second Orders, while the white triangle established in the surrounding Darkness is circumscribed in its turn by the circle of Light.

In addition to this explanation, this lamen represents "The Light that shineth in Darkness though the Darkness comprehendeth it not." It affirms the possibility of the Redemption from Evil and even that of Evil itself, through self-sacrifice. It is suspended from a scarlet collar as representing its dependence on the Force of Divine Severity over-awing Evil. It is a symbol of tremendous strength and fortitude, and is a synthesis of the office of Hiereus as regards the Temple, as opposed to his office as regards the outer world. For these reasons it should always be worn by Hiereus.[27]

The Hegemon's Lamen

The *Hegemon's Lamen* is explained in part in the grade of Philosophus as follows:

The peculiar emblem of the Hegemon is the Calvary Cross of Six Squares within a Circle. This Cross embraces Tiphareth, Netzach, Hod and Yesod, and rests upon Malkuth. Also the Calvary Cross of Six Squares forms the cube and is thus referred to the Six Sephiroth of Microprosopus which are Chesed, Geburah, Tiphareth, Netzach, Hod and Yesod. In addition to this, it represents the black Calvary Cross of Suffering as the Initiator by Trial and Self-Abnegation, and the Opener of the Way into the Comprehension of the Forces of the Divine Light. It is therefore suspended from a black collar to show that Suffering is the Purgation of Evil.[28]

The Keryx's Lamen

This lamen is explained in the grade of Theoricus as follows:

The Tree of Life and the Three Mother Letters are the Keys wherewith to unlock the Caduceus of Hermes. The upper point of the Wand rests on Kether and the Wings stretch out to Chokmah and Binah, thus comprehending the Three Supernal Sephiroth. The lower seven are embraced by the Serpents whose heads fall on Chesed and Geburah. They are the twin Serpents of Egypt and the currents of Astral Light. Furthermore, the Wings and top of the Wand form the letter Shin, the symbol of Fire; the Heads and the upper halves of the Serpents form Aleph, the symbol of Air as the Reconciler; while their tails enclose Mem, the symbol of Water—the Fire of Life above, the Waters of Creation below, and the Air symbol vibrating between them. [29]

The Stolistes' Lamen

This Stolistes' Lamen is explained in the grade of Practicus as follows:

The Cup of Stolistes partakes in part of the symbolism of the Laver of Brass and the Sea of Solomon. On the Tree of Life it embraces nine of the Sephiroth exclusive of Kether. Yesod and Malkuth form the triangle below, the former the apex, the latter the base. Like Caduceus, it further represents the three Elements of Water, Air, and Fire. The Crescent is the Water which is above the Firmament; the circle is the Firmament, and the triangle is the consuming Fire below, which is opposed to the Celestial Fire symbolized by the upper part of Caduceus.[30]

The Dadouchos' Lamen

This lamen is explained in the grade of Zelator as follows:

> *The Hermetic Cross, which is also know as Fylfot, Hammer of Thor, and Swastika, is formed of 17 squares taken from a square of 25 lesser squares. These 17 fitly represent the Sun, the Four Elements, and the Twelve Signs of the Zodiac. In addition to this, the lamen has a more extended meaning. The Hermetic Cross, the Bolt of Whirling Flame, which is represented by the cross of Four Axes whose heads may be either double or single and turned in either direction, is a symbol of terrific strength, and represents the Fire of Spirit, cleaving its way in all directions throughout the Darkness of Matter. Therefore it is borne on the Lamen of Dadouchos, whose office is that of Purification and Consecration by Fire, and from it also may be drawn by meditation several formulae of strength.*[31]

The Phylax's Lamen

An eye drawn in Egyptian style is the symbol on the lamen of the Sentinel. This signifies his role as the Watcher Without. It is the all-seeing eye which guards the temple. The "divine eye" of the Egyptians—a hieroglyphic called *Wadjet*, often called the Eye of Horus—was referred to "He who feeds the sacred Fire or the intelligence of man"... in other words, Osiris. The Egyptians also defined the eye (the circle of the iris with the pupil as its center) as the "Sun in the mouth," meaning "the creative word." The Phylax can be seen in this light as extending the "word" of Osiris beyond the borders of the temple, through the divine eye.

Lamens Construction

Refer to Figure 29 on page 76 for lamen designs.

Materials Needed

- One 10" x 20" piece of plywood, ¼" thick
- Wood putty
- Gesso
- Acrylic paints: black, white, red, green
- Sealant: such as clear lacquer finish

Tools Needed

- Electric jigsaw, scroll saw, or coping saw
- Compass, pencil, and straight edge
- File or rasp
- Artist's brushes (fine and medium sizes)
- Sandpaper (course, medium, and fine)

Construction

(Note: It is often possible to purchase pre-cut wooden disks at a craft store or hobby shop. These disks will save you time and labor, but they must be of comparable size and thickness to the ones described below.)

1. Using the compass, draw seven 4" circles on the piece of plywood. Cut out circles with a saw. (You may want to cut out seven square pieces of wood with a circle drawn on each piece, using a jigsaw. A scroll saw can then be used to cut out each circle from the separate squares.)
2. If the circle of wood has jagged edges, file them smooth. Any gaps in the wood can be filled in with wood putty. Sand the wood until it is smooth. Paint entirely with gesso. Let dry. Sand. Apply another coat if needed.
3. Draw the specific design shown for all seven officers' lamens—one on each of the seven disks.
4. Each lamen has a "ground" color and a "charge" color. The ground, also called the "field," refers to that area which serves as a foundation, base, or background. It is usually the largest area of color. The charge color is given to the sigil, "charging" the lamen with a specific symbol. In the officers' lamens, the charge color is also given to the outer circle that surrounds the field. The individual lamens should be painted as follows:
    - Hierophant: Ground color—green; charge color—red
    - Hegemon: Ground color—white; charge color—black
    - All Others: Ground color—black; charge color—white
5. After all the paint has dried, apply a coat of sealant for protection.

(Note: An extra length of plywood may be purchased and cut out for the lamens of the officers on the Dais. The four lamens are drawn exactly like the Hierophant's Lamen but painted thus: Imperator—ground color green and charge color red; Praemonstrator—ground color orange and charge color blue; Cancellarius—ground color violet and charge color yellow; Past Hierophant—ground color green and charge color red [lamen may be slightly smaller than the Hierophant's Lamen]).

The Collar

The primary symbolism of the collars has already been explained on pages 75–79. The lamens worn by the officers are suspended from collars that vary in color. Originally, the collar may have been merely a cord or a ribbon running through a hole in a "lip" created at the top of the lamen. In our opinion, such a hole drilled or cut into the lamen diminishes the integrity of its symbolism. It is aesthetically unacceptable as well. An eye-hook screwed into the top of a lamen is a better solution, but the lamen may be easily flipped over when worn. Both of these problems are solved by the construction of a proper fabric collar as given here.

Refer to Figure 30 on page 82 for construction diagrams.

Materials Needed

- One yard of sturdy, non-stretch fabric in the desired color
- One yard of fusible interfacing
- Thread in the desired color
- One 1" wide piece of self-adhesive hook and loop fasteners, 2" long
- Package of 1" wide hook and loop fasteners (not self-adhesive)

Tools Needed

- Sewing machine
- Scissors and pins
- Iron and ironing board

Construction

1. Cut out four identical collar shapes similar to that in Figure 30, page 82; two front pieces and two back pieces. (The collar pattern is 15" long.) Cut out two pieces of the fusible interfacing identical to the collar shape.
2. Iron and fuse the interfacing to the wrong side of both front pieces. (Follow manufacturer's directions for fusing the interfacing.)
3. Stitch the two front pieces together at the "V" (at the bottom). Stitch the two back pieces together in the same fashion. Stitch the front to the back, leaving one end open so you can turn it. (Be sure to clip around the curves.)
4. Turn the collar right side out. Iron flat and hand stitch the remaining open ends of the collar closed. Sew the two corresponding pieces of hook and loop fasteners to the two ends just stitched. Stitch another hook fastener tab to the back of the collar at the "V."

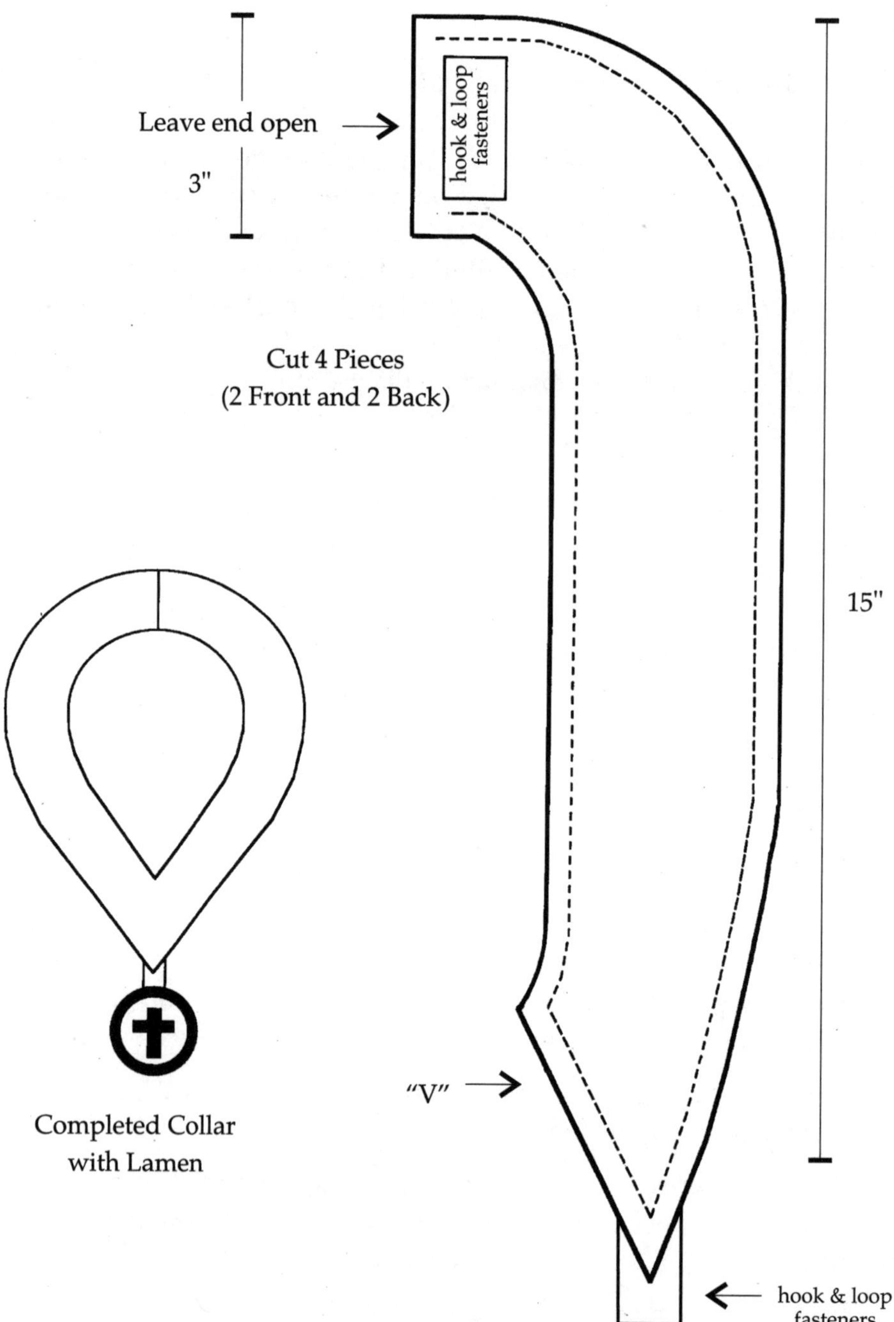

Figure 30: The Collar

5. Glue the corresponding loop fastener tab to the back of lamen. The lamen can now be attached to (or removed from) the collar at any time.

Apparel of the Outer Order Officers: The Cloak, Mantle, and Tabard

The *cloak* or *mantle* is a sleeveless, loose-fitting garment worn over the robe. In the Outer Order, the Dais Officers as well as the Middle Pillar Officers wear mantles emblazoned with certain symbols. The traditional form of the cloak seems very fitting for colder northern climates. However, we have often discovered that in subtropical environments, a cloak worn over a robe can be stifling and unconducive to magical work. Here we will describe how to construct both the cloak and the *tabard*—an acceptable alternative based on a garment worn by medieval knights over armor. (See Figure 31, page 84.)

Whether the cloak or the tabard is used, the symbolism remains essentially the same. The mantle or outer garment worn over the robe is a badge of authority. Its color and the color of the emblems attached to it signify energies specific to each officer. The mantles are always to be worn by the main officers in any hall of the Outer Order.

The Imperator's Mantle

The proper mantle of office of the Imperator is red—the flame scarlet cloak of Fire and severity, as on this officer do the energy and stability of the temple depend. This mantle is the symbol of unflinching authority, compelling the obedience of the temple to all commands issued by the Second Order; and upon the left breast thereof is the cross and triangle of the Golden Dawn, both white, presenting the purification of the temple in the Outer Order by Fire.[32]

The Praemonstrator's Mantle

The proper mantle of office of the Praemonstrator is the bright blue cloak of Water, representing the reflection of the wisdom and knowledge of Chesed. On the breast is the symbol of the Golden Dawn, the cross and triangle in white, representing the purification of the Outer Order by Water.[33]

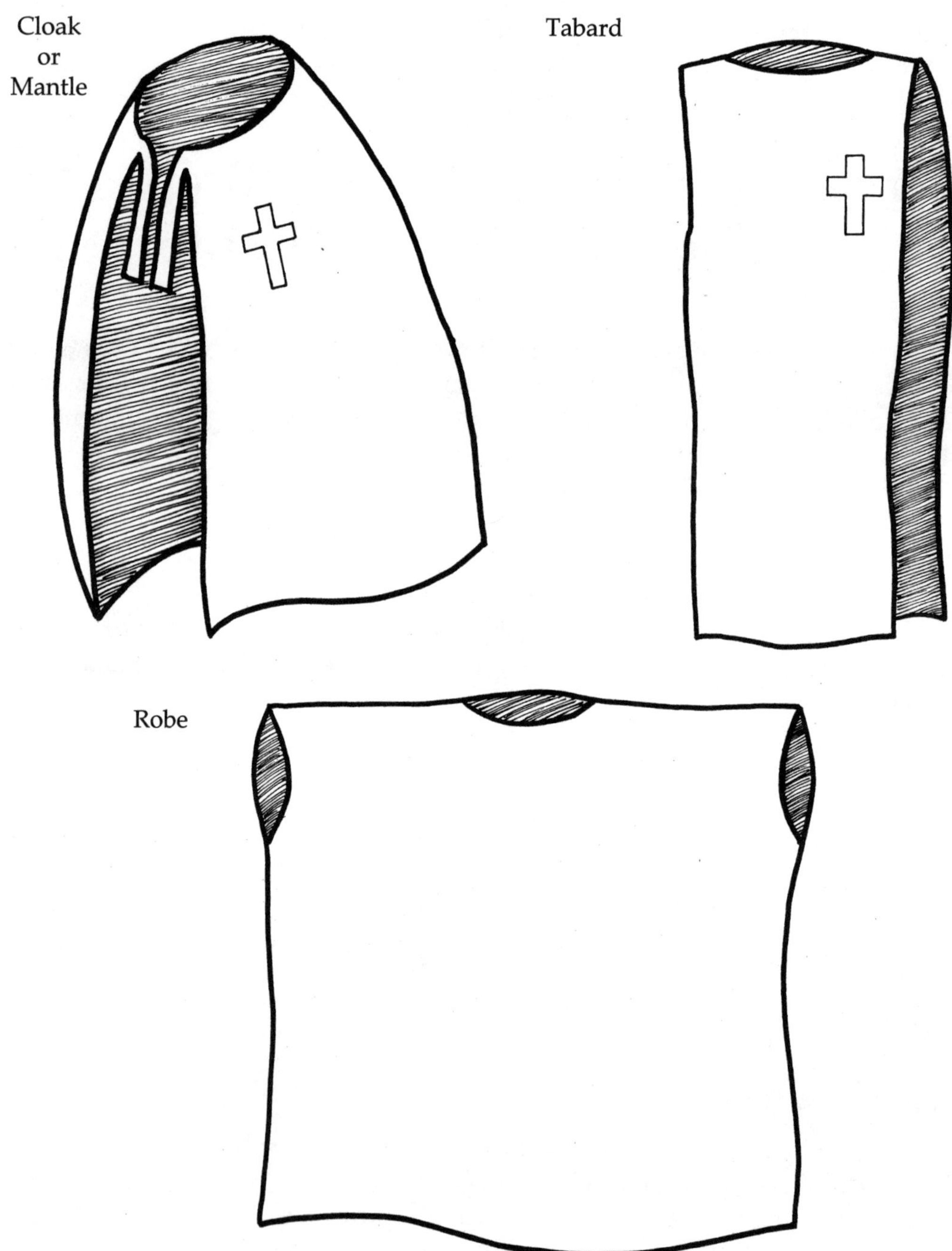

Figure 31: Cloak, Tabard, and Simple Robe

The Cancellarius' Mantle

The proper mantle of office of the Cancellarius is the yellow cloak of Air. On the breast is the Cross and Triangle of the Golden Dawn in white, representing the purification of the Outer Order by Air.[34]

The Hierophant's Mantle

The mantle of the Hierophant is bright red, representing the flaming energy of the divine light, shining into infinite Worlds. On the left breast is a white cross to represent purification unto the light, and this cross may be one of the following forms: Calvary, pyramidal, equilateral, or Maltese. It is indifferent which of the crosses be employed, seeing that each represents the operation of the light through the veil.[35] (Note: The mantles of the three Middle Pillar Officers should all bear the same style of cross, no matter which one is preferred. In the same manner, the Dais Officers should all bear the six-squared cross and the triangle—the symbol of the Hermetic Order of the Golden Dawn which they govern.)

The Hiereus' Mantle

The mantle of the Hiereus is the black cloak of darkness, threatening and terrible to the Outer, as concealing an avenging force ever ready to break forth against the evil ones. On the left breast is a white cross to represent the purification of matter into the light.[36]

The Hegemon's Mantle

The mantle of the Hegemon is the cloak of pure whiteness, representing the spiritual purity which is required in the aspirant to the mysteries and without which qualification none can pass between the eternal pillars. It represents the divine light which is attracted thereby and brought to the aid of the candidate. It symbolizes the self-sacrifice that is offered for another to aid him in the attainment of the light. It also signifies the atonement of error, the Preparer of the Pathway unto the divine. On the left breast is a cross of red, usually the Calvary form, to represent the energy of the lower will, purified and subjected to that which is higher—and thus is the office of Hegemon, especially that of the Reconciler.

The Cloak or Mantle Construction

Materials Needed

- Two yards of 45" wide non-stretch fabric in the desired color
- Thread in the desired color
- 6" square piece of felt in the appropriate color (white or red)
- Fabric cord or braid in the appropriate color (the same color as the cloak)
- Fabric glue or adhesive

Tools Needed

- Sewing machine
- Scissors and pins
- Dinner plate
- Pencil

Construction

1. Fold the 6' fabic in half lengthwise. The folded piece will be 3' in length.
2. Draw a half-circle at the center of the folded fabric. (A dinner plate makes an excellent pattern for a half-circle.) Cut out the half-circle so that when you unfold the material, a full circle hole is created at the center of the fabric. This is the neck line of the cloak.
3. Cut a line straight down the front from the neck.
4. Round off the corners and hem all edges.
5. Sew a cord to either side of the neck so that the wearer can tie a knot to secure the garment when in use.
6. Cut a 3" cross out of felt material and attach it to the left breast of the cloak with glue or fabric adhesive.

The Tabard Construction

Materials Needed

- Three yards of 45" wide non-stretch fabric in the desired color
- Thread in the desired color
- 6" square piece of felt in the appropriate color (white or red)
- Fabric glue or adhesive

Tools Needed

- Sewing machine
- Scissors and pins
- Dinner Plate
- Pencil

Construction

1. Cut out a piece of fabric that is 100" long and 16" wide.
2. Fold the fabric in half lengthwise, giving you 50" in the front and the back of the tabard.
3. Using a dinner plate as a pattern, draw a half-circle at the center of the folded fabric. Cut out the half-circle so that when you unfold the material, a full circle hole is created at the center of the fabric. This is the neck line of the tabard.
4. Hem all edges.
5. Cut a 3" cross out of felt material and attach it to the left breast of the tabard with glue or fabric adhesive.

The Magician's Basic Apparel

The Tau Robe

A black robe is part of the required clothing for all members of the Outer Order of the Golden Dawn. The Tau Cross, which looks like the letter "T," is the preferred form of this robe. This also refers to the Hebrew Tau, the last letter of the Hebrew alphabet. One theory states that this symbol originated among the Egyptians from the image of the wide rack of a bull's horns and the vertical line of the animal's face (Taurus).

By wearing the black Tau robe, the members of the Outer Order of the Golden Dawn affirm that their journey up the grades and toward the Light is one that begins in darkness—the darkness and ignorance of the outer, secular world. Only when the forces of the Black Pillar are rightly understood and balanced can the White Pillar be safely approached.

The robe should be worn whenever temple work is to be done. As part of the magician's total magical environment, the wearing of the robe helps to focus the mind on the ritual work at hand, putting the magician into a mystical state of consciousness which can

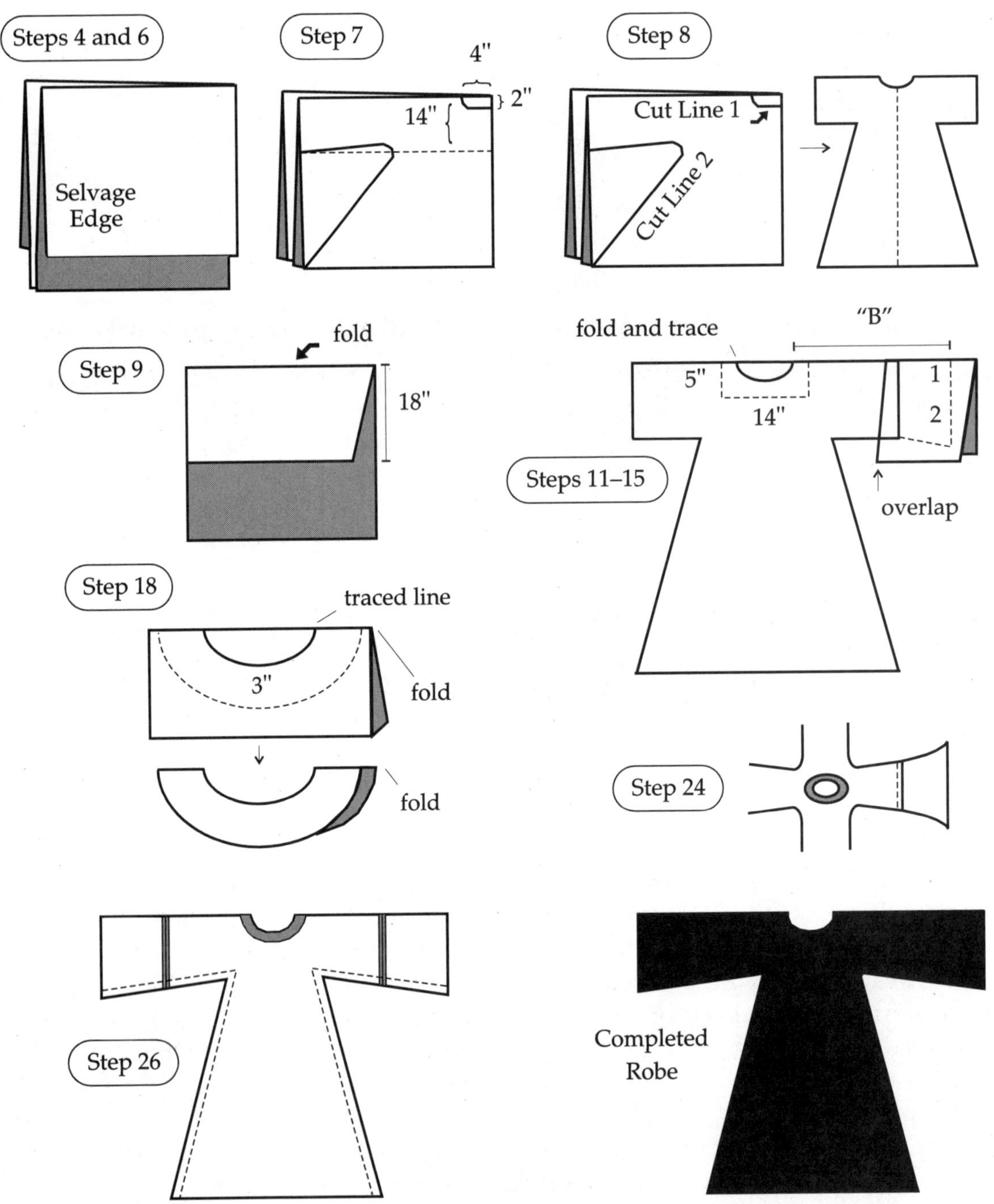

Figure 32: Tau Robe Construction

only aid in the success of the ceremony. See *Ritual Use of Magical Tools*, chapter one, for "A Ritual Meditation on the Tau Robe."

Refer to Figure 32 on page 88 for construction diagrams.

Materials Needed

- Black material (such as cotton, silk, doeskin, or crepe) 48" wide
- Black thread

Tools Needed

- Measuring tape
- Scissors and pins
- Sewing machine
- Iron and ironing board

Construction: Preparation of the Material

1. Measure yourself from your neck to the floor. This will be known as measurement "A." The material you buy should be twice the length of measurement "A," plus one yard.
2. Wash and dry the material in accordance with the manufacturer's directions. Iron the material if needed.

Preliminary Cutting

3. Lay the material out lengthwise with the right side up (the side which is to be the outside of the robe).
4. Fold a section over so that you have a doubled surface equal to "A," plus 4". (Note: there will be a single layer of fabric left over at the bottom.)
5. Cut off the single layer and put it aside for the time being.
6. Make a second fold lengthwise.

Marking the Material

7. With the tape measure, mark the fabric as follows:
    - 2" down from the top right-hand corner.
    - From the top right-hand corner, mark 4" across the top of the fabric.
    - 14" down from the top right-hand corner. (For a broad person, increase the measurement to 16".)

- From the last mark, draw a straight line across to the selvage edges.
- From the right-hand fold, measure along the marked line a length equal to ½ of your chest circumference.
- Connect the marks to make the following lines:
  - A semi-circular curve connecting the two marks at the top of the right-hand corner.
  - A diagonal line from the lower left-hand corner of the material to the ½ chest measurement mark.
  - A line that curves up 2" from the ½ chest measurement mark and connects with the chest measurement line at the selvage edge.

Cutting the Material

8. Cut through all layers of material (cutting lines 1 and 2 on the diagram). Unfold the material so that it looks more like the finished robe.

9. Take the single layer of material that was put aside earlier. Fold it widthwise with the inside out so that the doubled length is 18". (For broad persons, this measurement will be 20".) Cut off the single layer that remains at the bottom and put it aside.

10. Cut the remaining doubled portion in half.

The Sleeves

11. Take one of the two pieces just cut, and place it, with the fold on top, even with the fold at the top of the robe. Overlap the edges by 1" under the existing sleeve.

12. Measure from where your neck joins your shoulder, down the arm, to the tip of the middle finger. This is measurement "B."

13. Measure across the top of the robe from the right edge of the neck hole and mark off point "1" at a distance of measurement "B."

14. Draw a straight line down from the marked point "1" to point "2" in the diagram. From the corner of the robe sleeve draw an angled line to point "2."

15. Cut both lines which lead to point "2."

16. Do the other sleeve in the same manner.

Cutting the Facing

17. From the excess fabric, fold a piece of 10" x 14" material in half. Center the material under the neck hole of the robe. Trace the neck opening onto the fabric underneath.

18. Remove the marked piece of material and, using a tape measure, mark 3" away from the traced line in several places until you have a second curved line. Cut along both lines.
19. You should now have four pieces of fabric cut and ready to sew: the main part of the robe, two sleeves, and the neck facing.

Sewing the Neck Facing

20. Hem the outer edge of the neck facing ½" all around.
21. Lay the robe out flat, with the right side up. Pin the facing material around the robe's neck, placing the right sides of the fabric together. (Note: The hem of the fabric should be up.) Point the pins toward the center of the neck to make sewing over them easier.
22. Sew all around the neck, leaving a ⅝" seam. Clip all around the neck toward the seam, but take care not to cut the seam thread.
23. Turn the robe inside out. Pull the facing through the neck opening. Lay the robe out on its wrong side and tack.

Sewing the Sleeves and Sides

24. Lay the fabric out, wrong side up. Pin the right sides together (where sleeve extension meets the robe's sleeve. See the diagram). Sew along the dotted line, leaving ⅝" seam allowance. Iron the seams open.
25. Do the other arm the same way.

Sewing the Sides of the Robe

26. Fold the material over at the shoulders with the wrong side out. Pin under the arms and along the sides. Sew, leaving a ⅝" seam allowance. (See diagram.) Clip under the arm seam, toward the seam, but be careful not to cut the seam thread.

Finishing Steps

27. Hemming the sleeves: turn under ½" of the sleeve edge. Iron, pin, and sew. Try the robe on and turn the sleeve under so that the robe meets the first knuckle. Iron, pin, and sew.
28. Hemming the bottom: Turn the robe up ½". Iron, pin and sew. Try the robe on and turn up the bottom, so that the edge of the robe does not touch the floor. Pin, iron and sew.
29. Turn the robe right side out, try it on and check to make sure that it fits. Iron.

A Simple Robe

The Tau robe may seem too complex for magicians who lack sewing skills. A simple square robe can be manufactured quickly and easily. (See Figure 31, page 84.) Although it is not symbolically correct, the square robe is better than no robe at all, and it does have a very nice, spiritual feel to it.

Materials Needed

- 2½ to 3 yards of black material, 65" wide
- Black thread

Tools Needed

- Measuring tape
- Scissors and pins
- Sewing machine

Construction

1. Fold the material in half lengthwise.
2. At the center of the fabric, cut a circle for the neck.
3. Slip the material over your head though the hole just made and check the length of the robe, cuting off any excess material. (The robe should almost touch the floor.)
4. Sew up the sides of the robe, but leave 12" open at the top of both sides for arm holes. Hem around these arm openings.
5. Hem the bottom of the robe as well as the neck opening.

The Nemyss

The nemyss or Egyptian headdress is part of the traditional ceremonial garb of a Golden Dawn magician. It is shown in many ancient papyri as either flowing down the back of the neck or gathered—ending in a "tail." (See Figure 33, page 93.) We have chosen the gathered-style of nemyss as more truly representing the symbolism of eternal life, the ankh, which the nemyss is partly based on.

The ankh shape was supposedly based on the form of a sandal-strap. The contour of the ankh also resembles a device used in ancient Egypt to measure the depth of the river

Nile. Since the Egyptians depended heavily on this river for food and agriculture, the ankh-shape came to symbolize life itself.

The ankh cross is a sacred symbol which alludes to the manifestation of the divine life force. It also signifies the divine union of opposites; active and passive, male and female. The ankh combines the masculine Tau shape with the feminine oval, alluding to the powers of generation. The shape of the ankh expresses a profound idea—that of the circle of life spreading outward from its origin and manifesting into the four elements. From another point of view, the circle of the ankh alludes to the Sun, the horizontal line to the sky, and the vertical line to the Earth. As a microcosmic sign, the circle would represent the human head or reasoning powers (or the Sun, which gives man life), the horizontal line his arms, and the upright line his body. The ankh can also be interpreted as an early form of the emblem of Venus. In any case, the ankh, the sign of divine light and life, is the most sacred and enduring symbol of the ancient Egyptians.

The shape of the ankh is nearly the same as the symbol of Venus, the only planet whose sigil contains all the spheres of the Tree of Life. This, too, is symbolically very significant to the makeup of the nemyss. To wear an ankh in the form of a headdress signifies the striving for eternal life which only spiritual attainment can bring. In the mysteries of Egypt, the initiate encountered all varieties of actual and visualized dangers, holding above his head the Crux Ansata, before which the dark powers fled. In Hebrew tradition, the back of the head (Qoph) is covered during worship so that, symbolically, no impure or unbalanced energies or thoughts may "slip in." It is a symbol that one is in the presence of God. By covering one's head with the sacred emblem of the ankh, the Golden Dawn magician puts him or herself in a magical state of mind, and calls upon the forces of eternal life and light. But in addition to this, the initiate is covering the supernal Sephiroth in

Figure 33: Examples of the Egyptian Nemyss

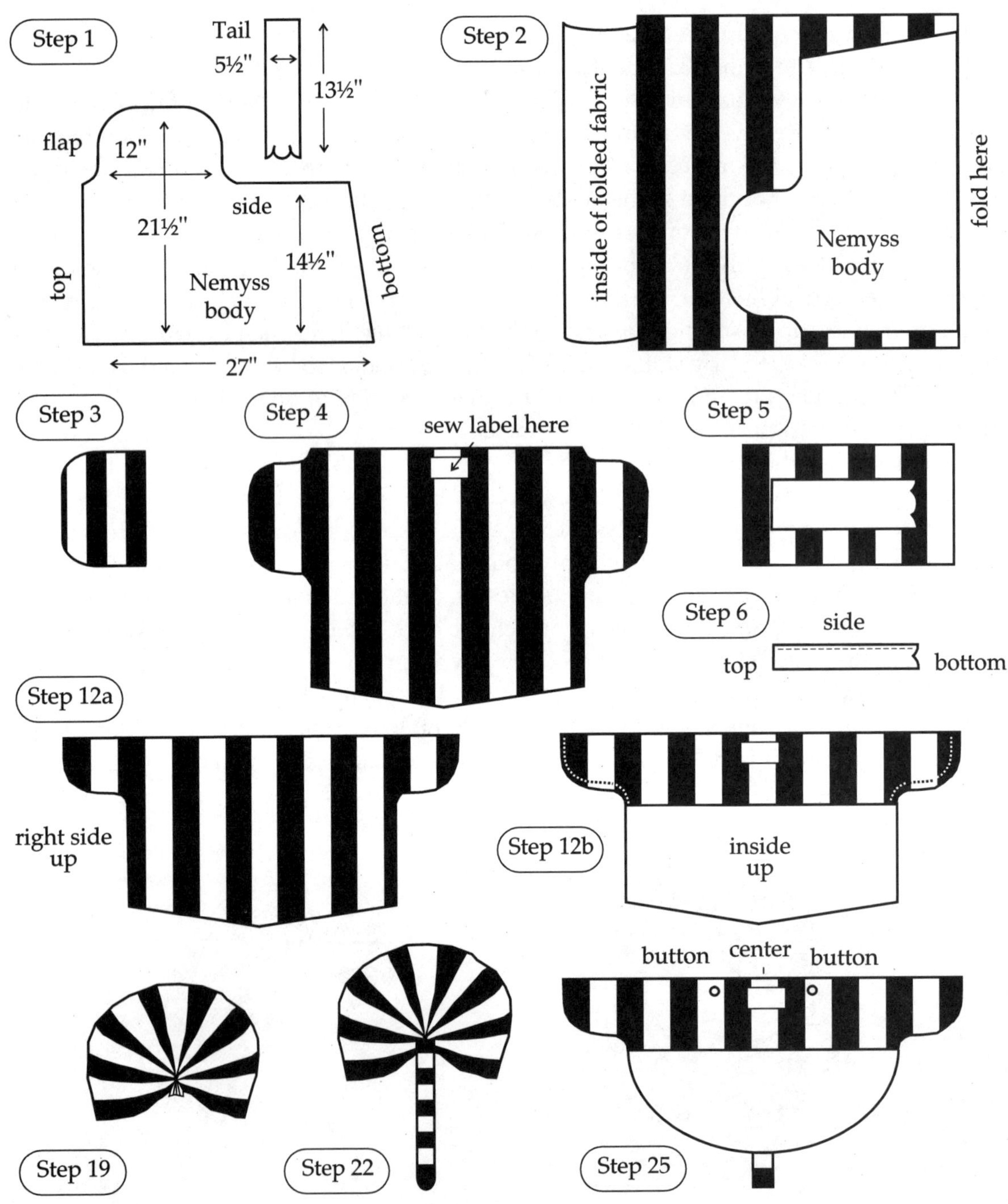

Figure 34: Nemyss Construction

his or her sphere of sensation for power and protection from all outside influences, including ones that might otherwise enter the subconscious through "the back of the head."

By wearing both the Tau robe and the nemyss together, the initiate truly becomes a complete and living symbol of the ankh. See *Ritual Use of Magical Tools,* chapter one, for "A Ritual Meditation on the Nemyss."

Refer to Figure 34 on page 94 for construction diagrams.

Materials Needed

- 1½ yards of black-and-white striped material (¾" or 1" wide stripes are best)
- White thread
- Package of polyester filling or similar stuffing material
- Buttonhole elastic
- Two clear stay buttons

Tools Needed

- Sewing machine
- Scissors and pins
- Measuring tape
- Straight edge and pencil
- Iron and ironing board

Preliminary Cutting

1. Create a paper pattern of the nemyss body and tail as shown in Step 1 in Figure 34, page 94. Fold your fabric lengthwise, making certain to leave enough material for the tail. The fold should be should be in the center of a white stripe. (This is so that the finished nemyss will be centered exactly in the middle of the forehead.)

2. Fold up the fabric so that enough of a single layer will remain for the tail. (See Step 2.) It is very important that the layers are exactly even, matching up the white stripes and black stripes. It may be necessary to hold the folded material up to the light to be certain. Place the pattern of the nemyss body onto the folded fabric as indicated.

3. Cut out the nemyss body. The rounded portion of the nemyss needs to be cut so that it will end in a white stripe. It may be necessary to slide the pattern so that when cutting you have about 8" of a black stripe showing. (See Step 3.)

4. The unfolded nemyss should look like Step4 in the diagram. Press it with an iron.

5. Now lay out the tail pattern on the single layer as shown in Step 5. Cut out the tail.

6. Pin the tail's right sides together as shown in Step 6. (The tail should now be inside out.)

Preparing the Tail

7. Sew the side seam of the tail about ¼"–¾". With an iron, press the seam just sewed. Be careful not to press the fold. Then press the seam open. (A broom handle can be inserted into the tail to make pressing the seam open a little easier.)
8. Pin the bottom of the tail. Sew the tail. With a scissors, trim close to the stitching you just made.
9. Turn the tail right-side out. Wiggle the bottom end to get rid of any puckering. Then stuff the tail with polyester filling or similar stuffing material. (Hint: Take a wooden chopstick and lightly tamp the fiberfill into the tail.) Don't overstuff.

Sewing the Nemyss

10. Go back to the main body of the nemyss. Finish the top and side edges by serging/pinking/zig-zagging the edge to prevent fraying during construction and future laundering. Press with the iron.
11. Find the center of the nemyss by folding it in half and putting a pin in the middle. If you have a personalized label for your nemyss, pin it here (see Step 4). Sew the label down.
12. Lay out the nemyss and fold back the top as shown in Step 12a. Pin the sides of the flaps together, making certain that the stripes are even. Sew the flaps using a ¼" seam allowance. Press the seams with an iron. (See Step 12b.)
13. Trim off excess leaving about ¼" seam showing. (This is where you can trim off most of the black stripe mentioned above in Step 2. This way you will not get a shadow effect of the little sliver of black stripe showing through.)
14. Clip the curved seams in little "V"-shapes to allow for turning, so that the nemyss will lie flat.
15. Now turn the nemyss right-side out. (A black lacquer chopstick or the slender end of an artist's paint brush can be used to carefully push the seams out. Be certain to push the corner out.) Then press the nemyss with an iron. Turn the nemyss wrong-side up on your work area.
16. Next, fold under a ¼"–⅜" hem on both sides, just below the two flaps. Press the folds with an iron to prepare the sides for being topstitched. Then topstitch the sides.
17. Serge/pink/zig-zag the bottom edge of the nemyss. Press it with the iron.

18. Thread a fairly large needle with some strong white thread and get ready to accordion pleat the bottom edge. Pick up the thread in the middle of each white stripe.

19. Pinch all the sewn/tacked stripes together neatly. Sew through all the layers many times to secure them. When finished, the back of the nemyss should fan out like an accordion. (See Step 19.)

20. Sew through all the layers many times to secure them.

Attaching the Tail

21. Fold under about ¼" of the top edge of the tail.

22. Put the tail on the nemyss, making sure that the side seam of the tail (that you sewed earlier) is on the underside of the nemyss. (See Step 22.) Then draw your running stitches tight, so that they are snug but not too tight around the pleated part of the nemyss. Tack the tail to the nemyss, going around it several times and distributing the gathers in the tail part evenly.

Finishing Steps

23. Cut out 8" of buttonhole elastic. Zig-zag or serge the edges so that they don't fray.

24. Turn the nemyss wrong-side up and find the center of the top edge. From the center point, measure off 5¾" from the right of the center mark and 5¾" from the left of the center mark. You should now have a total measurement of 11½" along the top edge of the nemyss. Mark off the ends of this area with a pencil, placing two dots there, about ½" up from the edge.

25. Sew two clear stay buttons on these penciled dots with a zig-zag stitch. Make sure that the buttons are sewn perpendicular to the bottom of the nemyss. (See Step 25.)

26. Attach the elastic. (Buttonhole elastic makes this simple because there is no need to sew the elastic on.)

27. Now try on your new nemyss.

—Nemyss construction contributed
by Gail Henson

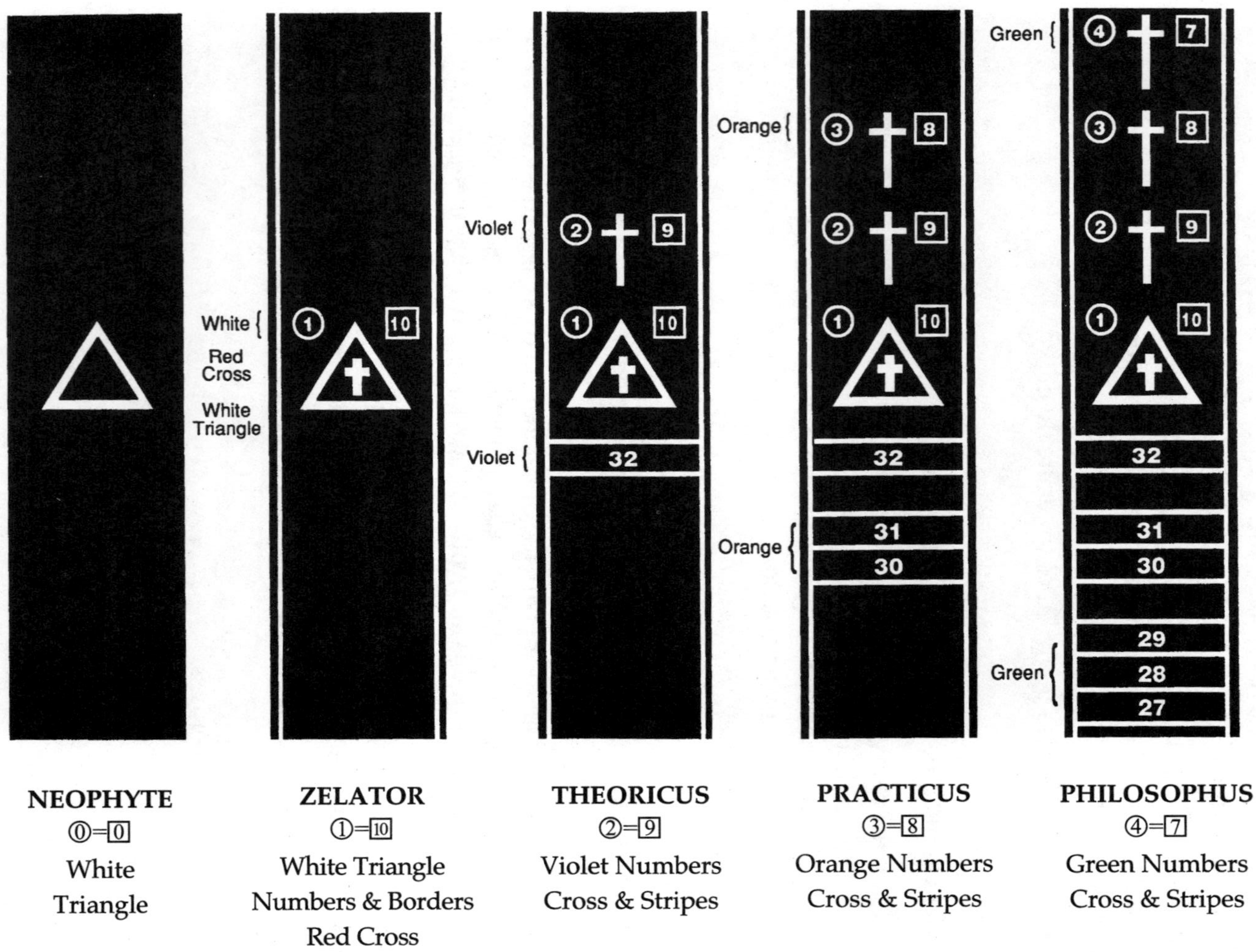

Figure 35: Outer Order Sashes

The Sash

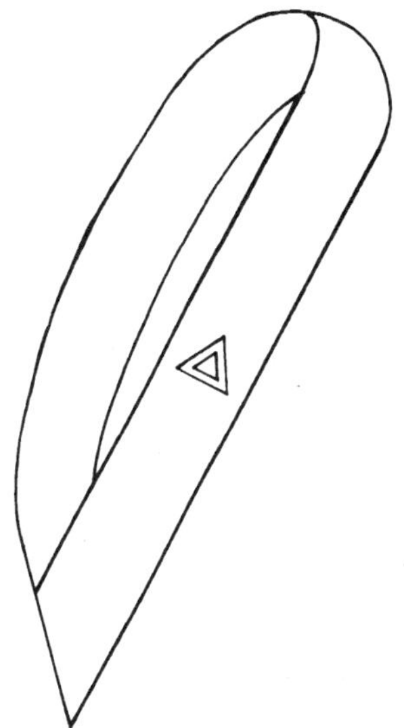

Figure 36: The Neophyte Sash

The *sash* is a long band of cloth worn over one shoulder as a symbol of rank. (See Figure 35 on page 98 and Figure 36.) It is to be constructed by the aspirant and embellished by him or her with symbols depicting the initiate's current status or grade.[37]

The sash of the First Order is black, to represent the Black Pillar, to which the Outer Order is referred. The sash fits over the initiate's left shoulder, running from the Chesed center to the Hod center (right hip). This also alludes to the watery and passive current of the Black Pillar.

The sash of a Neophyte is solid black with a white triangle to symbolize light dawning in darkness. In the grades that follow, additional emblems are added to the sash as shown in Figure 35.

Materials Needed

- 2½ yards of sturdy black material
- White ribbon or self-adhesive felt
- White thread and black thread

Tools Needed

- Sewing machine
- Scissors and pins
- Measuring tape
- Straight edge and pencil
- Iron and ironing board

Construction

1. To construct the sash, you will need 2½ yards of sturdy black material cut into a long strip that is 10" wide. Fold the material in half widthwise (not lengthwise), making the sash 5" wide. Iron the material flat.
2. Sew the lengthwise edges of the sash together, wrong side out. Turn the sash right side out. Iron flat.

3. Place the sash over your left shoulder and adjust it so that it crosses over your right hip. Pin the sash here to hold it in position. Trim off the excess material so that the ends of the sash form a point at the bottom of the piece. Hem up the ends of the sash and sew them together as pinned.[38]

4. For the white triangle, you may either glue on three strips of white ribbon or cut thin strips of white self-adhesive felt. (Additional grade symbols can be added employing these same materials, or by using fabric paint.)

Endnotes

1. Burckhardt, 196
2. Regardie, *The Golden Dawn*, 128.
3. Ibid., 333.
4. Ibid.
5. Ibid., 147.
6. Ibid., 219.
7. Ibid., 336.
8. Ibid., 147.
9. Ibid., 333.
10. Ibid., 55.
11. One of the Minutes books for the Paris Ahathoor temple of the Alpha et Omega confirms this practice. Ahathoor was always a small temple, with rarely more than a handful of initiates present at any given meeting. On some occasions a member had to pull "double duty" as two or more officers. In a Neophyte Ceremony on January 7, 1909, Mathers (V. H. Frater S. R. M. D.) was both Hiereus and Dadouchos, on July 28, 1914, he was Stolistes and Dadouchos for a 0=0 initiation, and for the Vernal Equinox Ceremony on March 19, 1921, Moina Mathers took the positions of Imperator and Hiereus.
12. The entire paper can be found on pages 6–17 of our book *Self-Initiation into the Golden Dawn Tradition.*
13. In large general merchandise stores, it is easy to find automobile air-fresheners in the form of a red and gold crown. They look quite nice and can be attached to the end of dowel for an easy-to-make Hierophant's Wand.
14. Inman, 21, 31–32.
15. Cirlot, 323–324.
16. Regardie, *The Golden Dawn*, 332.
17. Ibid., 342.
18. Ibid., 331.
19. Ibid., 342.
20. Ibid., 331.
21. Ibid., 342.
22. Ibid., 331.
23. Ibid., 332.
24. Ibid., 204.
25. Ibid., 339–310. The one exception is the Hierophant's Lamen, which is red and green.
26. Ibid., 336.
27. Ibid., 337–338.
28. Ibid., 339.
29. Ibid., 340.
30. Ibid.

31. Ibid.
32. Ibid., 331.
33. Ibid., 332.
34. Ibid.
35. Ibid., 335.
36. Ibid., 337.
37. In Regardie's *The Golden Dawn*, the sash emblems for the Theoricus Grade are listed as being white, while those for the Practicus Grade are said to be purple. The numbers given for the Zelator Grade are shown as red. The reasons for this particular color scheme have never been made clear. In fact the only colors given in the old Order papers that appeared appropriate were those for the Philosophus Grade—green for the Sephirah of Netzach. Consequently, current Order members are encouraged to use the colors of the Sephiroth for all of the elemental grades; violet for Yesod and the Theoricus Grade, orange for Hod and the Grade of Practicus. The flashing colors of the Sephiroth may also be used. The numbers 1 and 10 of the Zelator grade should be white, the color that flashes against the four-colored Sephirah of Malkuth.
38. Original Order sashes from a century ago where often constructed as long bands of cloth with buttons and button-holes at either end, rather than sewn together on the lower end of the sash.

CHAPTER TWO

Implements of the Elemental Grades

The basic implements and furnishings of a Golden Dawn temple have been thoroughly described in chapter one. However, there are still some First Order tools that have not yet been covered. These implements are not to be found in the Neophyte Hall but in halls pertaining to the four elemental grades between the Neophyte and the Portal. In addition to this, while the basic props and temple furnishings used throughout the Outer Order remain the same, the arrangement of the temple, or hall, varies with each grade. Sometimes the temple arrangement will change several times within a single grade ceremony. During the ceremony of the Philosophus, the temple furnishings change position four times.

What we are primarily discussing here are the halls of the implements belonging to the elemental grades of Zelator, Theoricus, Practicus, and Philosophus—including any additional props which need to be introduced. We will also be discussing the ten Admission Badges which are used in the elemental grade ceremonies. For additional information on the particular functions and attributions of the elemental grades, consult pages 28–33 of

Regardie's *The Golden Dawn*, or chapters two through five of our book *Self-Initiation into the Golden Dawn Tradition.*

The Elemental Halls

As mentioned in chapter one, the Neophyte Ritual is a preliminary ceremony that has hidden within it many magical formulae and techniques. It is a ritual designed to awaken the candidate to the divine light. After several purifications and consecrations, the candidate is placed between the two pillars, in the position of equilibrium and balance—on the path, so to speak, toward union with the Higher Self. The candidate has now been made aware of the divine light, but has yet to accomplish the task of divine union. This begins, in steps, through the elemental grades of the Outer Order.

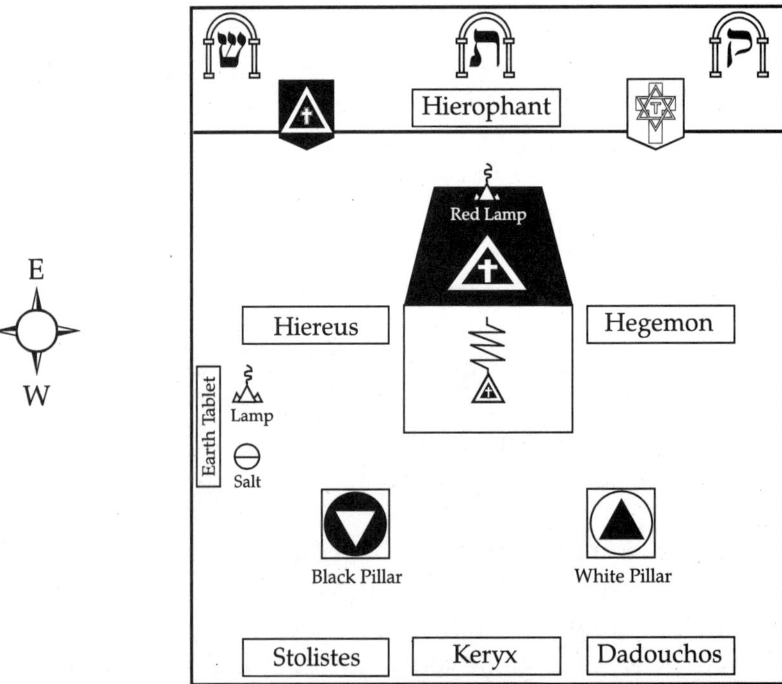

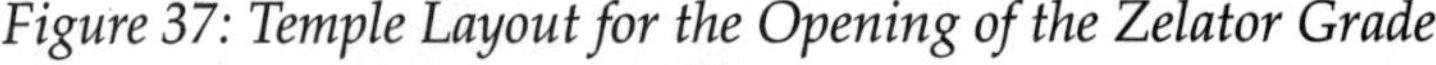
Figure 37: Temple Layout for the Opening of the Zelator Grade

The elemental grades, which are the four grades of the First Order, represent an awareness of the elements within the psychological make-up of the candidate. These "inner elements" can be described as different divisions of the subconscious. The process undertaken by an initiate advancing through the grades is truly an alchemical process, in which the psychic mechanism of the candidate undergoes a process of dissolution. During the ceremony of the Neophyte, the component elements are examined and purified through the elemental grade ceremonies, and finally all the base constituents are consecrated and integrated back into the psyche of the initiate. Thus aroused, the elemental portions of the mind become dedicated to divine union with the Higher Self, and ultimately to the completion of the Great Work. This process allows the initiate to bring unlimited energy and inspiration from the previously untapped subconscious depths into the realm of the conscious mind, where it can be employed for further spiritual growth.

The Ceremony of the Zelator ① = ⑩

The first elemental grade is that of Zelator, the grade which begins the alchemical metamorphosis of the candidate's psychic elements. The Zelator grade is attributed to the sphere of Malkuth, to the element of Earth, and to the earthy part of the candidate's inner being. During the Zelator Ceremony, god-names and spiritual entities connected with the element of Earth are invoked and the candidate is brought before three pathways: the Path of Evil, the Path of Good, and the Path of Balance. On the first two paths, the unprepared candidate is halted by guardians and forced to turn back. The candidate finally attempts to traverse the Middle Path and is barred again by the Kerubic guardians of good and evil, but the Hierophant, representing the eternal and the universal soul, intercedes and clears the path for safe passage. Access to the symbolic temple of Solomon is granted to the aspirant, who personifies a priest of the Hebrew mysteries entering the Tabernacle. The significance of certain symbols, such as the seven-branched candlestick, are explained to the candidate. At the end of the Zelator Ceremony, the Neophyte has become an initiate, and the element of Earth has been firmly established in his or her psyche.

Temple Set-up for the Zelator Hall

Here, the altar occupies a position much farther east that its previous position in the Neophyte Hall (see Figure 37, page 104). The pillars are moved well toward the west of the temple. The officers in the Zelator Hall are six in number: Hierophant, Hiereus, Hegemon, Keryx, Stolistes, and Dadouchos. (The Phylax remains outside the hall.) During the first part of the ceremony, the stations of the six officers form a triangle, the symbol of Supernal creation and divine revelation. The lesser three officers compose the base, the Hiereus and Hegemon, the representatives of the opposing forces of light and darkness, are next, and the Hierophant, who personifies the higher powers, is located at the apex. This triangle, apex upwards, is also a triangle of Fire, which points to a relationship that exists between the letters Yod (Fire) and Heh Final (Earth) of the Tetragrammaton. (Keep in mind that the choir of angels attributed to Malkuth is known as the *Ashim*, or the "Souls of Fire." The Admission Badge of this grade, the Fylfot Cross, holds another clue to this mystery, because it is formed of seventeen squares out of a square of twenty-five lesser squares. Twenty-five is also the number of squares attributed to the Qamea of Mars.) The initiation into the earthy Zelator grade and the sphere of Malkuth implies that a certain amount of Fire energy is involved. Since we have already shown that the elemental grades allude to an alchemical process of analysis and dissolution within the aspirant, it is only natural that we find a fiery undercurrent pervading this first step on to the Tree of Life.

At the second point in the ritual, a cross is formed by five of the officers, the shaft of the cross is created by the three Chief officers in alignment with the altar, while the Stolistes and Dadouchos compose the crossbar. This cross formation stresses the four elements as a balanced "whole" within the manifest universe, as well as the four subelements of Malkuth. The fact that it is composed of five officers and not six refers to the Pentagram, the number of man—the microcosm and the initiate. It also refers to the fifth element of Spirit, which surmounts and governs the other four.

The Ceremony of the Theoricus ② = 9

The next grade ceremony is that of Theoricus, which is attributed to the sphere of Yesod, the element of Air, and the Moon, the airy part of the initiate's psyche. In this ceremony, the initiate encounters the four *Kerubim*, the angelic choir referred to Yesod. As the presidents of the elemental forces, the four Kerubim are each assigned one of the letters of the divine name YHVH. The Kerubim operate in and through the four elements in Yesod—the astral matrix on which the manifest universe is formed. In the Theoricus temple, the initiate learns that the elemental Spirits are to be invoked through the power and the governance of the Kerubim and their zodiacal symbols. Between the spheres of Malkuth and Yesod lies the Thirty-second Path of Tau, a journey through the subconscious which the aspirant must undertake.

Temple Set-up for the Theoricus Hall

There are only four officers in the Theoricus Hall (see Figure 38, page 107). (All of the offices of the Neophyte Hall are held by Initiates who have attained to a certain grade. Since the offices of Stolistes and Dadouchos can be held by someone holding the grade of Zelator, these officers no longer appear in the grades beyond the 1=10.) The stations are symmetrically positioned, East, West, North, and South, with the pillars placed at the east end of the altar. This balanced arrangement suggests the reconciling element of Air mediating between all opposing energies within the hall, resulting in perfect equilibrium. The number four, with its correlation to Chesed (the first Sephirah to manifest below the Abyss) also alludes to the firm foundation or blueprint of the four elements inherent within the sphere of Yesod before they manifest in Malkuth.

The Ceremony of the Practicus ③ = 8

The third elemental grade is that of Practicus, which is assigned to the Sephirah of Hod, the element of Water, the planet of Mercury, and the watery part of the initiate's consciousness. During the ceremony, the aspirant is introduced to certain deities of the Samothracian Mysteries known as the *Kabiri*, "the Powerful." Three of the Kabiri, represented by the three Middle Pillar officers—the Hierophant, the Hiereus, and the Hegemon—are known as *Axieros, Axiokersos,* and *Axiokersa.* In this ceremony, they also represent

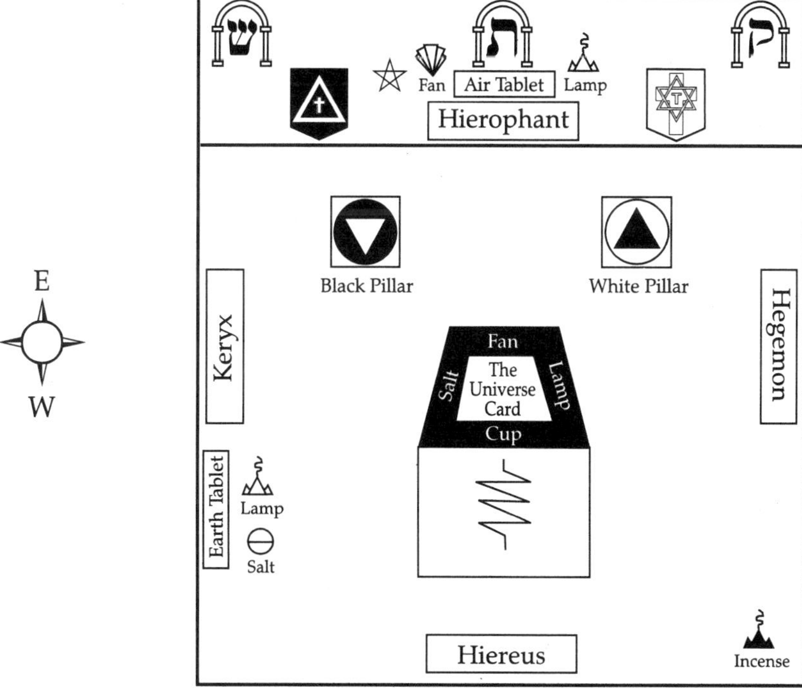

Figure 38: Temple Layout for the Opening of the Theoricus Grade

the various aspects of elemental Fire. The aspirant portrays the fourth Kabir, *Kasmillos*, brother of the other three, who is killed and resurrected in yet another allegory of the process of spiritual alchemy. The two paths which lead the candidate to the watery sphere of Hod are, in fact, fiery (the Thirtieth and the Thirty-first Paths of Resh and Shin). Water is nurturing and maternal, while Fire is productive and paternal; yet only from their union and perfect harmony can spiritual growth be attained. The two primary, parental elements of Fire and Water must always be held in balance. Thus, in this ritual the initiate's sphere of sensation, symbolized by stagnant Water, is vitalized by the fiery and solar paths, so that it becomes a worthy vessel for the divine light. The Waters of the intellect become a breeding ground for creativity and inspiration within the mind of the aspirant.

Temple Set-up for the Practicus Hall

As in the preceding ceremony, another officer is dropped from the ritual (see Figure 39). (The office of Keryx, which can be held by an initiate of the Theoricus grade, is no longer

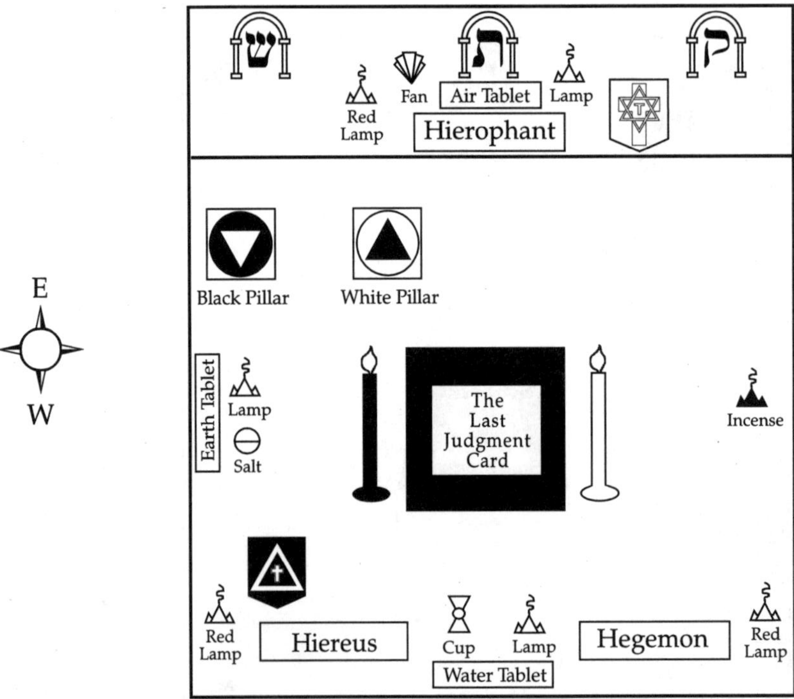

Figure 39: Temple Layout for the Opening of the Practicus Grade

required in the Practicus grade.) This leaves three officers who form an approximate equilateral triangle. The triangle, whose apex is again marked by the station of the Hierophant, refers to the Fire Triangle and the fiery nature of the Thirty-first and the Thirtieth Paths of Shin and Resh in relation to the Tree of Life diagram (as well as the relationship between the Tree of Life and the layout of the temple). For the later part of this ritual, when the temple is arranged in Hod, the Hierophant takes up a temporary position west of the altar, so that all three officers form the Water Triangle.

The Ceremony of the Philosophus ④ = 7

The fourth elemental grade, that of Philosophus, is attributed to the sphere of Netzach, the element of Fire, the planet Venus, and the fiery part of the initiate's psyche. In the Philosophus Ceremony, the aspirant encounters different deities from the Egyptian pantheon who represent the various aspects of Water. Just as in the preceding ceremony of Practicus, the two primary elements of Fire and Water must always be equilibrated. Therefore, two of the three paths traversed by the candidate in this grade are watery (the Twenty-eighth and the Twenty-ninth Paths of Tzaddi and Qoph). The third route, the Twenty-seventh Path of Peh, is a fiery path which joins Netzach to Hod on the Tree of Life. It is on this path that the candidate realizes the price of spiritual stagnation and ignorance. On this difficult route, the candidate must strive to rid himself or herself of all that is base and low, retaining only that which is true and divine. It is also on this path that the aspirant becomes suddenly aware of personal conflicts in his or her life, as well as various tests and trials of inner strength. This strenuous experience is one of the hallmarks of a successful initiation. As in alchemy, the process of analysis and dissolution must always precede assimilation. The task of Philosophus on the Twenty-seventh Path is to examine and balance the energies of Fire and Water, emotion and intellect.

Temple Set-up for the Philosophus Hall

The same three officers appear as before (see Figure 40, page 110). The office of Hegemon for this particular ceremony must be held by someone who has attained to the grade of Philosophus. (However in the other grade ceremonies, he or she need only be a Practicus.) In the 4=7 ritual, the officers form the Water Triangle with the station of the Hiereus marking the apex in the west. This alludes to the watery nature of the Twenty-ninth and the Twenty-eighth Paths of Qoph and Tzaddi, which the candidate traverses in this particular grade. The pillars are in the southeast, indicating the exact placement of the paths on the Tree, as before.

In the fourth part of the ceremony, which marks the candidate's entrance into the Twenty-seventh Path of Peh, all three officers are stationed in the east—the Hiereus and the Hegemon on either side of the Hierophant. This points out the placement of the Twenty-seventh Path on the Tree of Life as a reciprocal path—one which straddles all three columns on the Tree (the actual temple pillars are placed in the south). Finally, in the fifth segment of the ritual, the officers are positioned in the form of a Fire triangle, the symbol of the fiery nature of the Sephirah Netzach, into which the aspirant has achieved entry.

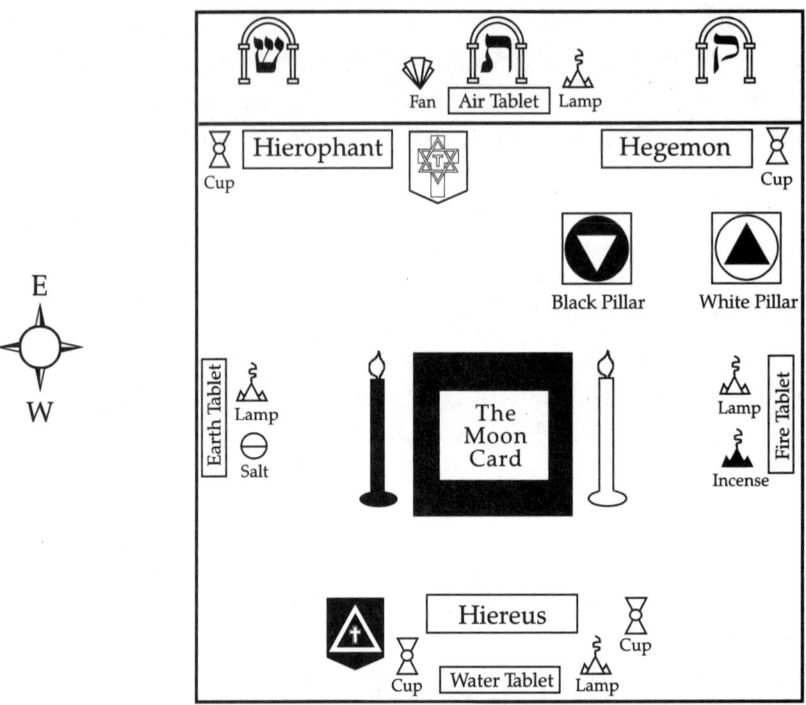

Figure 40: Temple Layout for the Opening of the Philosophus Grade

Admission Badges of the Elemental Grades

An *Admission Badge* is something that is given to a candidate at his or her initiation to ensure passage into the temple. It can be a solid geometric object, a diagram, or a lamen of one of the officers. The candidate is usually unaware of the significance of a particular badge until its symbolism is described within the ritual by the Hierophant or another officer.

We have always felt that an Admission Badge should be solid, even if described as a simple diagram. For this reason, many of our badges are constructed in the manner of a lamen, and indeed, a few of them are based on the actual lamens of particular officers. Some temples prefer to paint all of the badges white with black symbols, since traditionally the Outer Order members of the Golden Dawn were never taught the colors of the Minutum Mundum or the flashing colors. This is not so out-of-step with the times as it may appear on the surface; we have many times found that some students, who have committed to memory the color scales of other mystical/magical systems, become thoroughly confused when confronted with the King and Queen Scale colors of the Tree of Life. In these instances, the simple black and white badges are an aid to the student's ability to learn the correct symbolism without being bombarded by the advanced scales of color. However, we have chosen to incorporate the color scales into the badges, both for the richness of symbology as well as the beauty that the painted badges add to the ritual. This is a personal choice.

The Fylfot Cross

The *Fylfot Cross* is the Admission Badge to 1=10 grade of Zelator. It is also called the Hermetic Cross, the Hammer of Thor, the Gammadion, and the swastika. It is formed of seventeen squares out of a square of twenty-five lesser squares. These seventeen squares represent the Sun, the four elements, and the twelve signs of the zodiac.[1]

The Fylfot is an equilateral cross with arms bent at right angles, all in the same rotary direction, around a central axis. The Fylfot was widely known all over the ancient world as a symbol of prosperity and good fortune. (The word *swastika* is derived from the Sanskrit *svastika*, meaning "conducive to well-being.") The symbol was used extensively on ancient Mesopotamian coins. In Scandinavia it indicated the god Thor's hammer. The figure also appeared in early Christian and Byzantine art where it was called the *crux gammata* or gammadion cross, because it could be constructed from four Greek gammas. The swastika is still the most widely used beneficial symbol of Hindus and Buddhists in India. (It is very unfortunate that this ancient, sacred symbol was adopted by the Nazis in the early part of this century for their own corrupt, evil purposes.)

The symbol of the Sun is at the center of the cross at the point of stillness, while the zodiacal signs divided into the four triplicities make up the arms of the cross. The cardinal signs all begin at the center of the cross next to the solar symbol, followed by the fixed and mutable signs. The arms terminate with the elemental symbols of each triplicity. The whole cross represents the center of the universe giving rise to the celestial signs, which then formulate the elements of the physical world.

Since the Fylfot is originally formed out of twenty-five squares, this cross also has an affinity with Fire. (Twenty-five is the number of squares forming the Qamea or magical square of Mars.) According to Cirlot, all the words for "cross" (*crux, cruz, crowz, croaz, krois, krouz*) have a common etymological basis in *-ak, -ur,* or *-os,* signifying the "light of the Great Fire."[2] (This is also one reason why the lamen of the Dadouchos consists of this symbol.)

During the Iron Age, the swastika represented the supreme deity. In the Middle Ages, the general interpretation of the figure was that it symbolized movement and the power of the Sun. This cross also signifies the action of the origin on the universe.

In addition, the Fylfot is a symbol attributed to the first Sephirah, Kether. Here it represents the four latent (primal) elements whose energies are united in Kether, activated by the Primum Mobile or First Whirlings. These energies are finally differentiated into the four base elements of Fire, Water, Air, and Earth on reaching the level of Malkuth on the Tree. The Fylfot Cross, given to the candidate in the Zelator grade, points out a close relationship that exists between Kether and Malkuth.

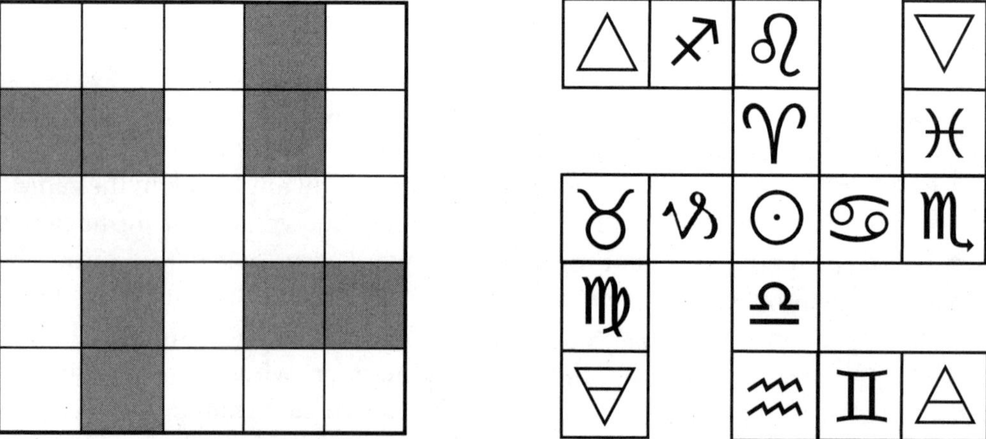

Figure 41: The Fylfot Cross

The Fylfot Cross, when painted black with white symbols, emphasizes the element of Earth, to which the Zelator grade is assigned. When painted in the four colors of Malkuth, it underscores the Sephirah which is attributed to the grade.

In addition to its employment in the 1=10 grade, the Fylfot Cross can be used by the Zelator in a ritual/meditation on the elemental make-up of Malkuth. (See *Ritual Use of Magical Tools*, chapter two).

Materials Needed

- One 5" x 5" piece of pine or bass wood, ½" thick
- Wood putty
- Gesso
- Liquitex acrylic paints: white, black, orange, violet, green
- Sealant such as clear lacquer finish

Tools Needed

- Scroll saw or jigsaw
- Pencil and straight edge
- Artist's brushes
- Sandpaper (medium and fine)

Construction

1. Take the 5" x 5" piece of wood and on one side, mark off five 1" squares (both vertically and horizontally). You will then have a piece of wood that has drawn on it a total of twenty-five 1" squares.
2. With a pencil, shade in the appropriate squares as shown in Figure 41, page 112. Cut out the shaded squares with the saw.
3. Fill in any gaps with wood putty. Sand with medium sandpaper until smooth.

Finishing Steps

4. Cover entirely with a coat of gesso. Let dry. Sand with fine sandpaper until smooth. Apply another coat if needed.
5. The finished cross may be painted in one of three ways:
    - White with black zodiacal and elemental symbols
    - Black with white zodiacal and elemental symbols

- Divided into the four colors of Malkuth: *citrine*—mixed from orange and green, *russet*—mixed from orange and violet, *olive*—mixed from green and violet, and *black*; the elemental and zodiacal symbols are to be painted on one side of the cross in white

6. Allow to dry. Spray or brush on a coat of sealant for protection. Let dry.

The Solid Greek Cubical Cross

A *Greek Cross* is a simple equal-armed cross.[3] (See Figure 42, page 116.) The Solid Greek Cubical Cross is the Admission Badge for the Path of Tau in the 2=9 grade of Theoricus. It is composed of twenty-two external squares which refer to the twenty-two letters that are placed thereon. The cross is an emblem of the equilibrated and balanced forces of the Elements.

On the front of the cross are the Hebrew letters which correspond to the four elements: Aleph–Air, Shin–Fire, Mem–Water, Tau–Earth. In the center is the letter Resh, which is attributed to the Sun.

On the back side of the cross are the letters that represent the remaining planets (minus Resh–Sol and Tau–Saturn): Beth–Mercury, Peh–Mars, Gimel–Moon, Daleth–Venus, with Kaph–Jupiter (the Wheel) in the center.

The remaining three sides of the Aleph (Air) arm are painted with the letters corresponding to Libra, Aquarius, and Gemini. The sides of the Shin (Fire) arm are covered by the letters which refer to Aries, Leo, and Sagittarius. The Mem (Water) arm includes the letters attributed to Cancer, Scorpio, and Pisces. The sides of the Tau (Earth) arm include the letters corresponding to Capricorn, Taurus, and Virgo.

The Cubical Cross combines the symbolism of the balanced elements with the twenty-two letters of the Hebrew alphabet to emphasize the eternal forces which lay behind the base elements of the physical universe. In the Theoricus Ceremony it is stated that:

> *Twenty-two are the letters of the Eternal Voice, in the Vault of Heaven; in the depth of the Earth; in the Abyss of Water; in the All-Presence of Fire. Heaven cannot speak their fullness—Earth cannot utter it. Yet hath the Creator bound them in all things. He hath mingled them in Water. He hath whirled them aloft in Fire. He hath distributed them through the planets. He hath assigned unto them the Twelve Constellations of the Universe.*[4]

It is for this reason that the *Cubical Cross* is the symbol which admits the candidate to the Thirty-second Path of Tau, from Malkuth to Yesod. It is called the Administrative Intelligence, which directs the seven planets in all their operations.[5] Symbolically, this path joins the Earth with the balanced powers of the seven planets (the microcosm portrayed by the hexagram). It is the first path leading out of the material state of Malkuth toward a comprehension of the personality, formed by the Higher Self to function in a particular incarnation. On this path, the initiate encounters his or her own individual consciousness. This includes a descent into the subconscious with its hidden fears and self-made demons, as well as an ascent into a new life of higher consciousness. In addition to its use in the 2=9 grade, the solid Cubical Cross may be utilized by the Theoricus in a ritual/meditation on the Thirty-second Path (see *Ritual Use of Magical Tools*, chapter two).

Refer to Figure 42 on page 116 for construction diagrams.

Materials Needed

- One 1' piece of 1½" x 1½" stock wood
- Wood putty
- Yellow carpenter's glue
- Gesso
- Acrylic paints: blue-violet, yellow, and orange
- Clear lacquer finish

Tools Needed

- Table saw or hack saw
- Craft knife
- Sandpaper (course, medium, and fine)
- Artist's brushes

Construction

1. Take the piece of wood and mark off the following lengths: one 4½" long piece, two 1½" long pieces. (See Figure 42, page 116.) Cut the marked sections apart with the saw.
2. Smooth each piece with sandpaper and fill in any gaps with wood putty. (Begin with course sandpaper, followed by medium sandpaper.)
3. Glue the two smaller pieces to the center of the length of the larger section, one on either side, as shown in the diagram.
4. After the glue has dried, take the knife and score both the front and back of the long section with two notched lines, so that the cross has the illusion of being constructed from five separate 1½" cubes.

Finishing Steps

5. Cover entirely with a coat of gesso. Let dry. Sand with fine sandpaper until smooth. Apply another coat if needed.

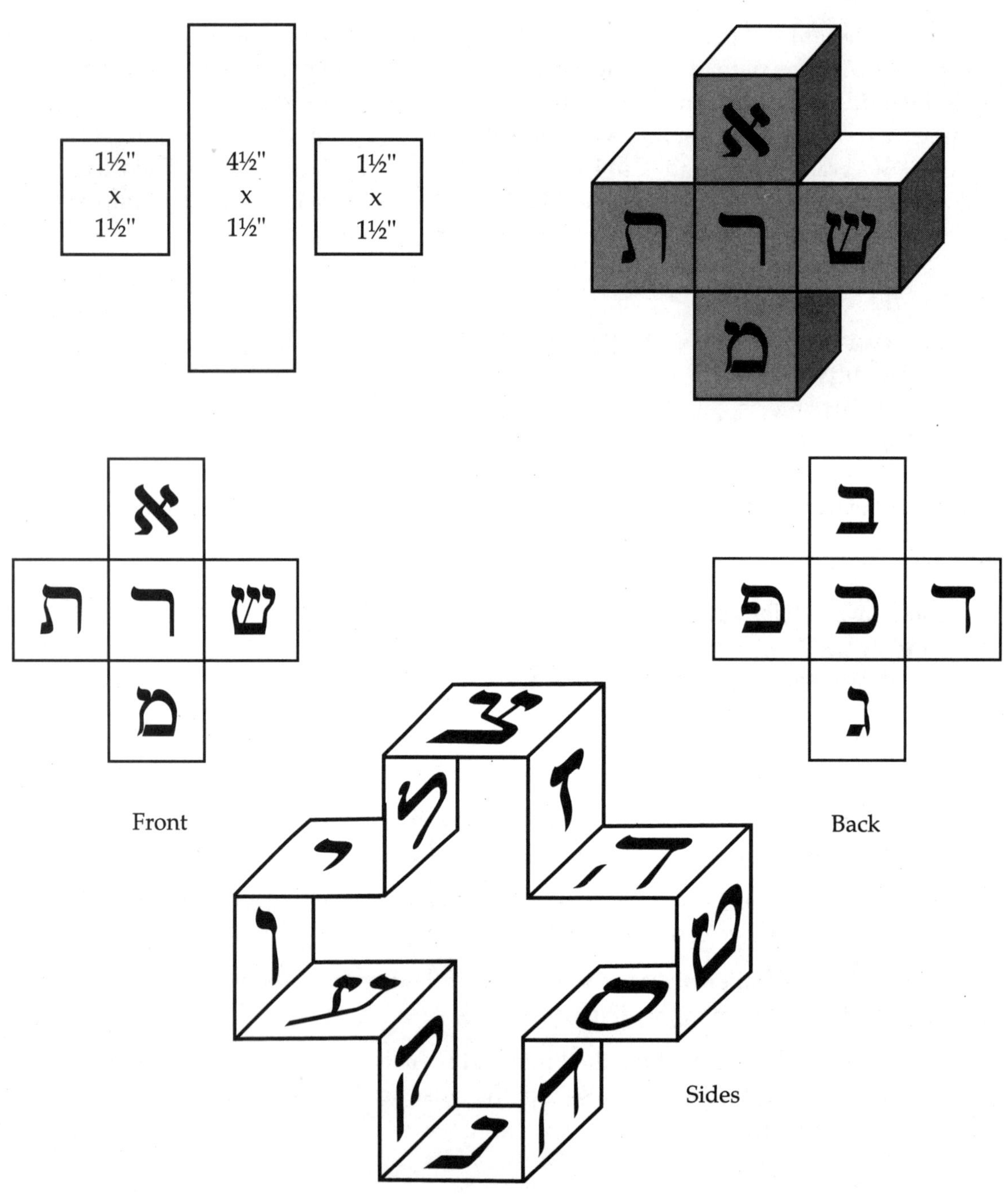

Figure 42: The Solid Greek Cubical Cross

6. The cross can be painted either white with black letters or blue-violet with orange-yellow letters (for the Path of Tau). On the front side of the cross the Hebrew letters are to be arranged as follows:

   - Top square: Aleph א
   - Bottom square: Mem מ
   - Middle square: Resh ר
   - Right square: Shin ש
   - Left square: Tau ת

   On the back side of the cross the following letters are to be painted:

   - Top square: Beth ב
   - Bottom square: Gimel ג
   - Middle square: Kaph כ
   - Right square: Daleth ד
   - Left square: Peh פ

   On the three remaining sides of the Aleph-Beth arm, the letters Lamed ל, Tzaddi צ, and Zayin ז should be painted, in that order—with Lamed on the left side of the Aleph, and Zayin to the right. On the three remaining sides of the Mem-Gimel arm, the letters Cheth ח, Nun נ, and Qoph ק should be painted in the same way, with Cheth to the right of Mem, and Pisces on the left. (Note: The Kerubic Sign is always on the outermost side of the arm.) On the sides of the Shin-Peh arm, the letters Heh ה, Teth ט, and Samekh ס should be painted, with Heh on the side above Shin, and Samekh on the bottom side. On the three sides of the Tau-Daleth arm, the letters Ayin ע, Vav ו, and Yod י should be painted, with Ayin on the bottom side and Yod on the top (etc.). (Note: The letters should be painted so that at any given angle that the viewer is looking, all the letters on that side appear to be upright. Example: If the cross is placed standing on its Mem-arm, the viewer looking straight down on the top of the cross will see the letters Yod, Tzaddi, and Heh all upright—the bottoms of all the letters point toward the front side of the cross. A view of the left side of this cross in this position will reveal the letters Lamed, Vav, and Qoph, one above the other, their bottoms all toward the Mem-arm.)

7. When all the paint is dry, apply sealant for protection.

The Caduceus Badge

The *Caduceus Admission Badge* grants the candidate entry into the temple of Yesod. It is an explicit representation of the same energies found hidden in the wand and lamen of the Keryx. On the front of the badge, the caduceus is shown against the glyph of the Tree of

Life. On the reverse side, the staff is displayed with the Three Mother letters of the Hebrew alphabet. (This symbolism has been thoroughly discussed in chapter one. See the Wand of the Keryx, page 60.) The caduceus is also a symbol of precise symmetry. The winged sphere and intertwined serpents also suggest the tri-unity of heraldry (a shield between two supporters), always expressive of the idea of active equilibrium, of opposing forces balancing one another in such a way as to create a higher, static form. It is this equilibriating and reconciling aspect of the caduceus which allies it to the element of Air.

If the badge is painted primarily yellow, it emphasizes the element of Air, to which the grade of 2=9 is attributed. If the badge is painted primarily violet, it underscores the Sephirah of Yesod, which is also assigned to the Theoricus grade.

Materials Needed

- 5" x 5" piece of plywood, ¼" thick
- Wood putty
- Gesso
- Acrylic paints: yellow, violet, red, orange, green, blue, blue-violet, white, black, neutral gray
- Clear lacquer finish

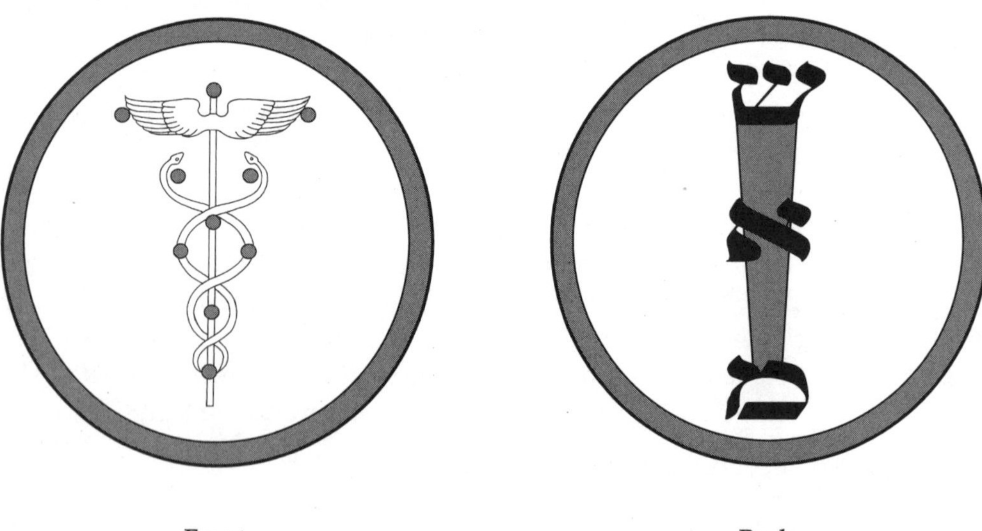

Front Back

Figure 43: The Caduceus Badge

Tools Needed

- Electric jigsaw or coping saw
- Compass, pencil, and straight edge
- File or rasp
- Artist's brushes (fine and medium sizes)
- Sandpaper (medium and fine)

Construction

(Note: Just as with the officer's lamens in chapter one, it may be possible to purchase precut wooden disks at a craft store or hobby shop, so long as they are of comparable size and thickness.)

1. Using the compass, draw a 4" circle on the piece of wood. (See Figure 43, page 118.) Cut out the circle with the saw.
2. If the circle of wood has jagged edges, file them smooth. Any gaps in the wood can be filled in with wood putty. Sand the wood with until it is smooth. (Begin with medium sandpaper and finish with fine.)
3. Paint entirely with gesso. Let dry. Sand. Apply another coat if needed.

Finishing Steps

4. The badge may be painted in one of three ways:
   - White with black diagrams
   - Primarily yellow with violet diagrams
   - Primarily violet with yellow diagrams
5. When the ground color is dry on both sides of the badge, the two different forms of the caduceus may be drawn on it (one on either side). (See Figure 43, page 118.) Both staffs should be primarily painted in the corresponding "flash" color of the "ground" color. If the base color of the badge is yellow, the caduceus will be violet (or vice versa).
6. On the drawing of the caduceus encompassing the Tree of Life, the Sephiroth should be painted in their usual Queen Scale colors. (A thin, white line should be painted around the spheres of Tiphareth and Yesod.)
7. On the reverse side of the badge, the Hebrew letters should be painted as follows: Shin—red, Aleph—yellow, Mem—blue. After all the paint has dried, apply a sealant for protection.

The Tetrahedron

The *Solid Triangle, Pyramid of Flame,* or *Tetrahedron* is the Admission Badge for the Thirty-first Path of Shin in the 3=8 grade of Practicus. It is an appropriate hieroglyph of Fire, representing the simple Fire of nature and the hidden or latent Fire.[6] It is formed of four triangles, three visible and one concealed, which yet is the synthesis of the rest. The three visible triangles represent Solar Fire, Volcanic Fire, and Astral Fire, while the fourth and basal triangle represents latent heat. Active Fire is *Aud,* passive Fire is *Aub,* equilibrated Fire is *Aur,* while the Hebrew name of Fire itself is *Asch.*[7]

The *Sepher Yetzirah* calls the Thirty-first Path (from Malkuth to Hod) the Perpetual Intelligence, because it regulates the motions of the Sun and Moon in their proper order, each in an orbit convenient for it.[8] For the initiate traveling this path, the key is "perpetual." This is the persistent regulation of the progress of the initiate's personality toward the cosmic consciousness. The angelic powers, called forth by the student journeying upon the Tree, determine what aspects of the initiate are unsuitable for his or her spiritual growth. These undesirable qualities are slowly burned away by the purging Fire of Shin. This permits the "Sun and Moon" of the initiate (i.e. the positive and negative sides of the student) to work "each in their proper order."

In addition to its use in the 3=8 grade, the Tetrahedron may be used by the Practicus in a ritual/meditation on the Thirty-first Path. (See *Ritual Use of Magical Tools,* chapter two.)

Refer to Figure 44 for construction diagrams.

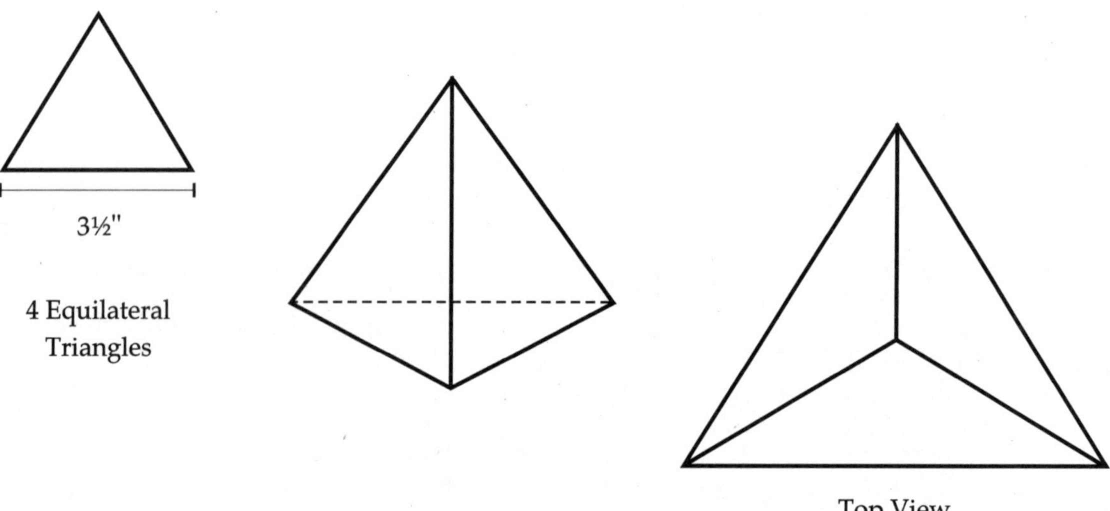

Figure 44: The Tetrahedron

Materials Needed

- One 12" x 6" piece of heavy cardboard (such as matte board or thick poster board)
- White glue
- Gesso
- Acrylic paint: red
- Clear lacquer finish

Tools Needed

- Craft knife or matte-cutter
- Medium-sized artist's brush

Construction

1. Draw four equilateral triangles on the cardboard that are 3½" long on each side (see Figure 44 on page 120).
2. Using the matte-cutter or craft knife and straight edge, cut all the triangles out so that all of them have beveled edges. This means that you should adjust your cutting tool so that it slants and cuts the cardboard at an angle. The beveled edges should all slant toward the inside of each triangle, so that when you fit all the triangles together, the outside edges will fit precisely, leaving a barely noticeable seam.
3. Glue all four triangles together so that they fit perfectly together into a four-sided pyramid, including the bottom. (Note: you may have to trim some of the triangles for this to happen.) Allow glue to dry thoroughly. Cover the pyramid entirely with gesso. Let dry. Add a second coat if needed.
4. The Tetrahedron can be painted in one of two ways:
    - entirely white
    - entirely red
5. When the paint has dried, spray or brush on a coat of sealant to protect the paint.

The Solar Greek Cross of Thirteen Squares

The *Solar Greek Cross of Thirteen Squares* is the Admission Badge to the Path of Resh in the 3=8 grade of Practicus. It is formed of thirteen squares which refer to the Sun's motion through the zodiac. The zodiacal signs are further arranged in the arms of the cross according to the four elements, with the Sun in the center, and representing that luminary as the center of the whole figure.[9] (See Figure 45, page 122.)

The Thirtieth Path of Resh is called "the Collecting Intelligence," because from it astrologers deduce the judgment of the stars, the celestial signs, and the perfections of their science according to the rules of their resolutions. It is, therefore, the reflection of the Sphere of Sun and the Path connecting Yesod with Hod, Foundation with Splendor.[10]

This path, which connects the sphere of Yesod to that of Hod, is described as the "Collecting Intelligence," because it governs many integral factors in the make-up of the individual personality...specifically, the signs of the zodiac, which are vessels of planetary influence. A person's sun sign is central to both his or her present and past incarnations. The Thirtieth Path signifies a collecting of knowledge on every level. On this path, the "collected" parts of the student's personality are given an infusion of the Sun's intellectual qualities of warmth and light. Here the student also begins to perceive the higher forces which have formed his or her own personality.

In addition to its role as Admission Badge in the initiation ceremony of the Practicus grade, the Solar Greek Cross can be employed by the Practicus in a ritual/meditation on the Thirtieth Path (see *Ritual Use of Magical Tools*, chapter two).

Refer to Figure 45 for construction diagrams.

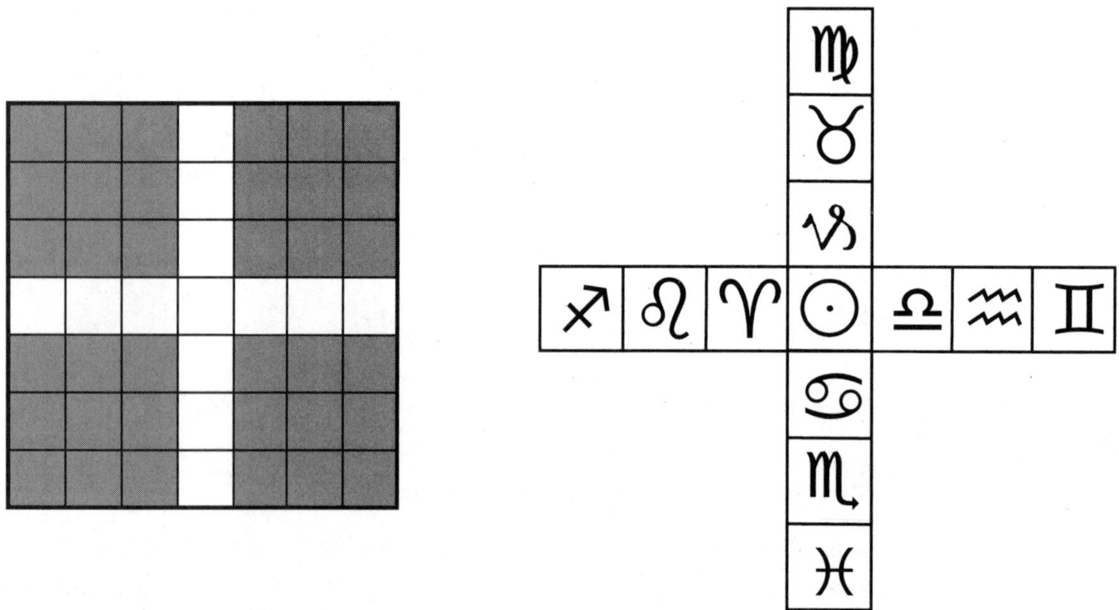

Figure 45: The Solar Greek Cross of Thirteen Squares

Materials Needed

- One 5¼" x 5¼" piece of pine or bass wood, ½" or ¾" thick
- Wood putty
- Gesso
- Acrylic paints: orange, blue
- Clear lacquer finish

Tools Needed

- Scroll saw or jigsaw
- Artist's brushes
- Sandpaper (medium and fine)

Construction

1. Take the 5¼" square piece of wood and on one side, mark off (both vertically and horizontally) a series of ¾" squares. You will then have a piece of wood that has drawn on it a total of forty-nine squares.
2. With a pencil, shade in the appropriate squares as shown in Figure 45, page 122. Cut out the shaded squares with the saw.
3. Fill in any gaps with wood putty. Sand with medium sandpaper until smooth.

Finishing Steps

4. Cover entirely with a coat of gesso. Let dry. Sand with fine sandpaper until smooth. Apply another coat if needed.
5. The finished cross can be painted in one of two ways:
    - White with black sigils
    - Orange with blue sigils
6. Spray or brush on a coat of sealant for protection. Let dry.

The Stolistes Cup Admission Badge

The *Stolistes Cup Admission Badge* grants the candidate entry into the Water temple of Hod. It is an explicit representation of the same energies found within the lamen and implement of the Stolistes (see Figure 46, page 124). This badge partakes in part of the symbolism of the Laver of Moses and the Sea of Solomon.

On the Tree of life, it embraces nine of the Sephiroth, exclusive of Kether. Yesod and Malkuth form the triangle below, the former the apex, the latter the base. Like the caduceus, it further represents the three elements of Water, Air, and Fire. The crescent is the Water which is above the firmament, the circle is the firmament, and the triangle the consuming Fire below, which is opposed to the celestial Fire symbolized by the upper part of the caduceus.[11] The cup is a symbol of spiritual receptiveness.

If the badge is painted primarily blue, it emphasizes the element of Water, to which the grade of 3=8 is attributed. If the badge is painted primarily orange, it underscores the Sephirah of Hod, which is also assigned to the Practicus grade.

Materials Needed

- One 5" x 5" piece of plywood, ¼" thick
- Wood putty
- Gesso
- Acrylic paints: yellow, violet, red, orange, green, blue, blue-violet, white, black, gray
- Clear lacquer finish

Tools Needed

- Electric jigsaw or coping saw
- Compass, pencil, and straight edge
- File or rasp

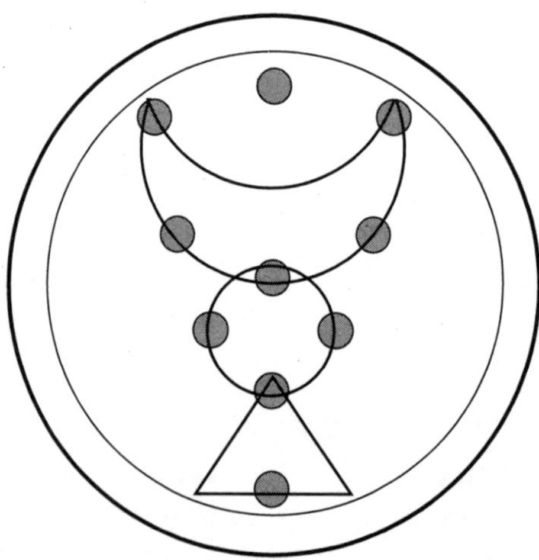

Figure 46: The Stolistes Cup Admission Badge

- Artist's brushes (fine and medium sizes)
- Sandpaper (medium and fine)

Construction

Follow steps 1–3 for the Caduceus Badge construction on page 119.

Finishing Steps

4. The badge may be painted in one of three ways:
    - White with black outline
    - Primarily blue with an orange chalice
    - Primarily orange with a blue chalice
5. On the drawing of the Stolistes Cup encompassing the Tree of Life, the Sephiroth can be painted in their usual Queen Scale colors. (A thin, white line should be painted around the spheres of Chesed and Hod, to make them stand out.)
6. After all the paint has dried, apply a sealant for protection.

The Calvary Cross of Twelve Squares

The symbol of the *Calvary Cross* is based on the shape of the cross that Christ was crucified on at Mount Calvary. The Calvary Cross of Twelve Squares encompasses symbolism of the Garden of Eden and of the zodiacal signs. (See Figure 47, page 126.)

> *The Calvary Cross of Twelve Squares is the Admission Badge to the Path of Qoph in the 4=7 grade of Philosophus. It is formed of twelve squares which fitly represent the Zodiac which embraces the Waters of Nu as the ancient Egyptians called the Heavens, the Waters which are above the Firmament. It also alludes to the Eternal River of Eden, divided into four heads which find their correlations in the four triplicities of the Zodiac.*[12]

The great river is called *Naher*, which flows out of Eden, namely from the Supernal triad. At Daath, it is divided into four heads. The first river is called *Pison*, the river of Fire, which flows into Geburah. Second is the river *Gihon*, the river of the Waters which flow into Chesed. The third is *Hiddekel*, the river of Air, flowing into Tiphareth, and the fourth, which receives the virtues of the other three, is *Phrath* (Euphrates), which flows down upon the Earth.[13]

Cancer, the cardinal sign of Water, is placed at the junction of the cross (and of the four rivers). All the cardinal and mutable signs are shown in alternating positions on the central shaft of the cross, while the cross bar is composed of the fixed or Kerubic signs.

The Twenty-ninth Path of Qoph from Malkuth to Netzach is called the Corporeal Intelligence, because it forms the very body which is so formed beneath the whole order of the Worlds and the increment of them. It is, therefore, a reflection of the watery sign of Pisces and the path connecting the material universe as depicted in Malkuth, with the Pillar of Mercy and the side of Chesed, through the Sephirah Netzach, and through it do the waters of Chesed flow down.[14]

Paul Foster Case describes the "Corporeal Intelligence" as "body consciousness" representing that stage of incarnation in which the physical body is organized into a form that the soul may inhabit.[15] This path is concerned with the acts of reproduction and physical evolution. In addition, this is also a path of the lower astral, where the student must face and overcome the phantoms and illusions reflected from the material plane. This probationary path of Water is also sexual—full of passions, reflexes, and instincts. On this sometimes harsh path, the initiate learns not to fear the dark, but to accept it as the counterpart of the light; examine it carefully and wait for the Sun to rise again.

In addition to its role as Admission Badge in the initiation ceremony of the Philosophus grade, the Calvary Cross of Twelve Squares may be employed by the Philosophus in a ritual/meditation on the Twenty-ninth Path (see *Ritual Use of Magical Tools*, chapter two).

Refer to Figure 47 for construction diagrams.

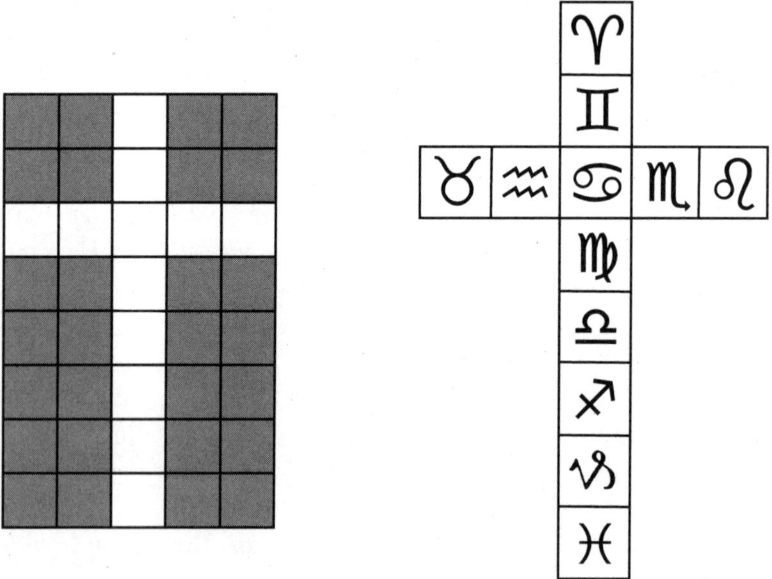

Figure 47: The Calvary Cross of Twelve Squares

Materials Needed

- One 3¾" x 6" piece of pine or basswood, ½" or ¾" thick
- Wood putty
- Gesso
- Acrylic paints: red-violet, yellow, green
- Clear lacquer finish

Tools Needed

- Scroll saw or jigsaw
- Artist's brushes
- Sandpaper (medium and fine)

Construction:

1. Take the piece of wood and, on one side, mark off (both vertically and horizontally) a series of ¾" squares. You will then have a piece of wood that has drawn on it a total of forty squares.
2. With a pencil, shade in the appropriate squares as shown in Figure 47, page 126. Cut out the shaded squares with the saw.
3. Fill in any gaps with wood putty. Sand with medium sandpaper until smooth.

Finishing Steps

4. Cover entirely with a coat of gesso. Let dry. Sand with fine sandpaper until smooth. Apply another coat if needed.
5. The finished cross can be painted in one of two ways:
   - White with black sigils
   - Red-violet with yellow-green sigils
6. Spray or brush on a coat of sealant for protection. Let dry.

The Pyramid of the Four Elements

The *Pyramid of the Four Elements* is the Admission Badge for the Twenty-eighth Path of Tzaddi in the 4=7 grade of Philosophus. On the four triangles are the Hebrew names of the four Elements: *Ash* אש—Fire, *Maim* מים—Water, *Ruach* רוח—Air, and *Aretz* ארץ—Earth. On the apex is the word *Eth,* composed of the first and last letters of the Hebrew alphabet את and implying essence or Spirit. The square base represents the material universe and on it is the word *Olam* עולם meaning "World."[16]

The word *pyramid* is derived from a root word that means "Fire," signifying that it is the symbolic representation of the one divine flame. A pyramid can easily be likened to the "Mountain of God," which was believed to stand in the center of the Earth. The four sides of the pyramid are triangular to represent the three-fold aspect of the divine enthroned within every aspect of the four-fold universe.[17] The square base is a reminder that the structure is firmly based on the immutable laws of nature. The truncated pyramid shows the essence of the divine firmly planted at the top of the design. It, too, is a square to indicate that the four-fold model of the cosmos begins with the Tetragrammaton.

The *Sepher Yetzirah* calls the Twenty-eighth Path the "Natural Intelligence"; through it is consummated and perfected the nature of every existing thing beneath the Sun. It is, therefore, a reflection of the airy sign Aquarius, the Water-bearer, unto which is attributed the countenance of man, the *Adam* who restored the world.[18] For the initiate, this path that runs between Yesod and Netzach represents the hope of rebuilding the Garden of Eden by the deliberate changing of consciousness through the act of mediation; a combination of knowledge and imagination. Case describes meditation as "an unbroken flow of knowledge in a particular object."[19] The fish-hook of Tzaddi is cast into the ocean of subconscious mentality to catch a bit of divine truth. It is a period of inner quest and search. The process of meditation is both the procedure and the goal of spiritual attainment, for the act itself results in a change of energy from one form to another. The student on this upper astral path is exploring the very basic mysteries behind creation, life, and death. However, the initiate on the Twenty-eighth Path must take care not to become bewitched by the glamours and illusions which start in the sphere of Yesod. This is the path of the hopes, dreams, and visions of mankind infused with the fertile life-force of Netzach. The way back to Eden is this—learn to function in accordance with the universal will.

In addition to its use in the 4=7 grade, the Pyramid of the Elements may be used by the Philosophus in a ritual/meditation on the Twenty-eighth Path (see *Ritual Use of Magical Tools*, chapter two).

(Note: The pyramid, based on a drawing in the Fifth Knowledge Lecture of Regardie's *The Golden Dawn*, page 79, is shown formed from a single piece of cardboard that can be folded into the pyramid shape. In actual practice, however, we have never found this pattern adequate given the proportions seen in the drawing.

If an easy method of making the pyramid out of paper or cardboard is desired, then we suggest using the pattern shown in Figure 48, page 129. After cutting out the pattern, fold side A in first, then fold sides B and C over side A. (Be sure to tuck in A's side flaps.) Tape or glue the cover flaps of B and C in place over the cover flap of A. Finally fold in side D, making sure that both side flaps are tucked inside, while D's cover flap is taped or glued in place over the cover flaps of the other sides.)

For a more sturdy pyramid, follow the directions given below, referring to the diagrams in Figure 49 on page 130.

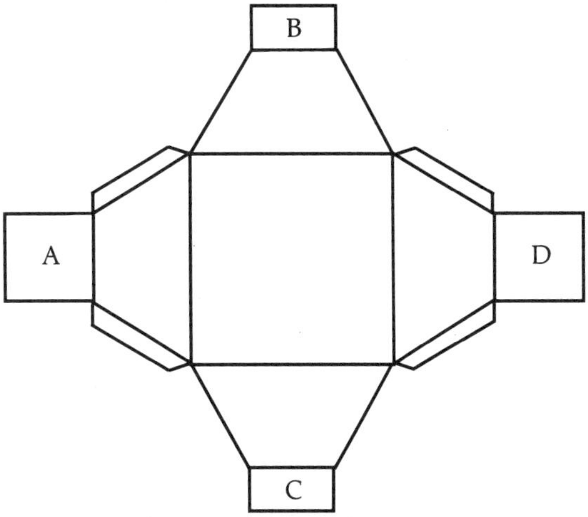

Figure 48: The Paper Pyramid

Materials Needed

- One 12" square piece of heavy cardboard (such as matte board or thick poster board)
- White glue
- Gesso
- Acrylic paint: violet, yellow
- Clear lacquer finish

Tools Needed

- Craft knife or matte-cutter
- Medium-sized artists' brush

Construction

1. Draw four equilateral triangles on the cardboard that are 3¼" long on each side. (See Figure 49 on page 130.)
2. Draw one 3¼" square that will be the bottom of the pyramid. Draw a smaller version for the top that is ½" square.
3. Using the matte-cutter or knife and straight edge, cut the four triangles and the two squares so that all of them have beveled edges that slant toward the inside of each piece.
4. Cut ½" off the top angle of all four triangles. (This will give the pyramid its "truncated" look.)
5. Glue all four triangles together so that they fit perfectly together onto the base square. Glue the base and the top to the triangles so that they also fit perfectly together. (Note: You may have to trim some of the triangles for this to happen.) Allow glue to dry thoroughly.

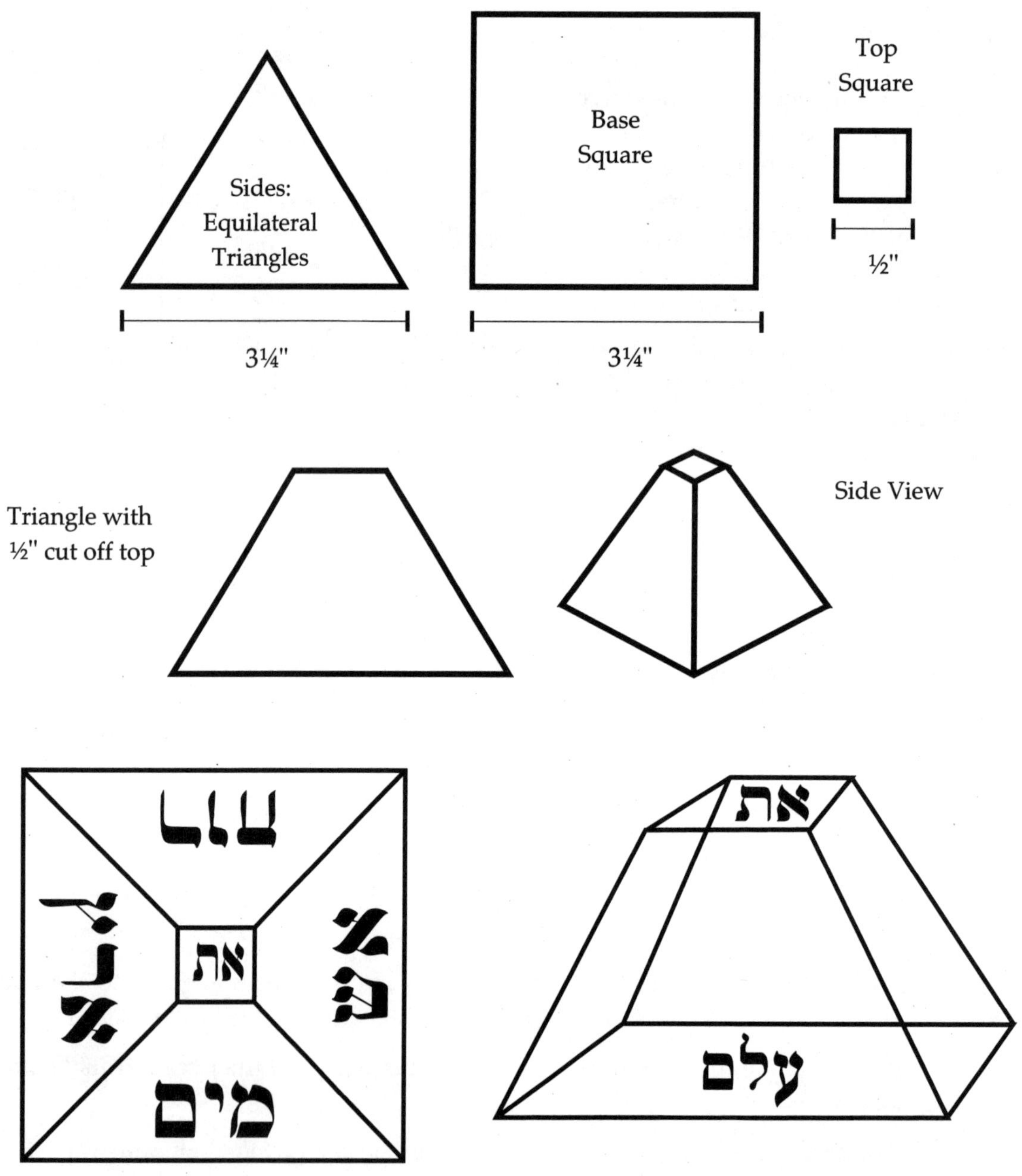

Figure 49: The Pyramid of the Four Elements

6. Cover the pyramid entirely with gesso. Let dry. Add a second coat if needed.
7. The truncated pyramid can be painted in one of three ways:
   - Entirely white with black letters
   - Entirely violet with yellow letters
   - With the sides, top, and bottom colored in the elemental hues: Spirit apex white with black letters, Fire side red with green letters, Water side blue with orange letters, Air side yellow with violet letters, Earth side black with white letters, base colored in the four Malkuth colors with white letters[20]
8. When the paint is dry, spray or brush on a coat of sealant to protect the paint.

The Calvary Cross of Ten Squares

The *Calvary Cross of Ten Squares* is the Admission Badge to the Path of Peh in the 4=7 grade of Philosophus. It is formed of ten squares which represent the ten Sephiroth in balanced disposition, before which the formless and the void rolled back. It is also the opened out form of the double cube and of the Altar of Incense.[21] (The Altar of Incense before the Veil of the Holy of Holies, was overlaid with gold to represent the highest degree of purity.) This alludes to the Path of Peh as a vehicle of purification…where the microcosm of man (represented by the ten Sephiroth) learns to separate the pure from the impure…to become a perfect mirror of the greater Tree, the Macrocosm of the universe.

The *Sepher Yetzirah* calls the Twenty-seventh Path the "Exciting Intelligence" because by it is created the Intellect of all created beings under the highest heaven. It is, therefore, a reflection of the sphere of Mars, and the reciprocal path connecting Netzach with Hod, Victory with Splendor. It is the lowermost of the reciprocal paths, straddling all three pillars on the Tree.[22] To the initiate, this is one of the most difficult paths on the Tree because it involves the sudden and complete destruction (or purification) of old "realities." However, the destruction of the tower as portrayed in the Sixteenth Key of the tarot is followed by a process of rebuilding, which balances the eternal conflict within all humans—the battle between intellect (Hod) and desire (Netzach). The balance between logic and emotion must be accomplished before any real spiritual progress can take place. The tower of old beliefs, prejudices, and habits, formed by parents, teachers, institutions, and peers, must be blasted and reexamined. Some remnants of the tower may then be reintegrated, others discarded. It is up to the initiate to decide.

The names of the Sephiroth in Hebrew are painted on the ten squares of the badge: 1—Kether כתר, 2—Chokmah חכמה, 3—Binah בינה, 4—Chesed חסד, 5—Geburah גבורה, 6—Tiphareth תפארת, 7—Netzach נצח, 8—Hod הוד, 9—Yesod יסוד, 10—Malkuth מלכות. (See Figure 50.)

In addition to its role as Admission Badge in the initiation ceremony of the Philosophus grade, the Calvary Cross of Ten Squares may be employed by the Philosophus in a ritual/meditation on the Twenty-seventh Path (see *Ritual Use of Magical Tools*, chapter two).

Refer to Figure 50 for construction diagrams.

Materials Needed

- One 3¾" x 4½" piece of pine or basswood, ½" or ¾" thick
- Wood putty
- Gesso
- Acrylic paints: red, green
- Clear lacquer finish

Tools Needed

- Scroll saw or jigsaw
- Artist's brushes
- Sandpaper (medium and fine)

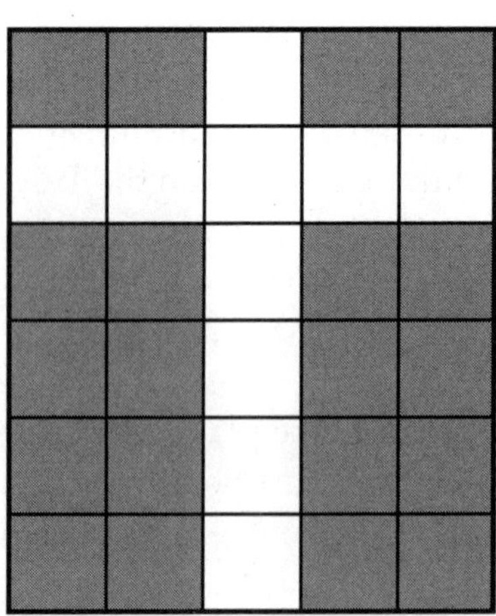

		1 כתר		
3 בינה	5 גבורה	6 תפארת	4 חסד	2 חכמה
		7 נצח		
		8 הוד		
		9 יסוד		
		10 מלכות		

Figure 50: The Calvary Cross of Ten Squares

Construction

1. Take the piece of wood and, on one side, mark off (both vertically and horizontally) a series of ¾" squares. You will then have a piece of wood that has drawn on it a total of thirty squares.
2. With a pencil, shade in the appropriate squares as shown in Figure 50 on page 132. Cut out the shaded squares with the saw.
3. Fill in any gaps with wood putty. Sand until smooth with medium sandpaper.

Finishing Steps

4. Cover with a coat of gesso. Let dry. Sand with fine sandpaper until smooth. Apply another coat if needed.
5. The finished cross can be painted in one of two ways:
   - White with black sigils
   - Red with green sigils
6. Spray or brush on a coat of sealant for protection. Let dry.

The Hegemon's Cross Admission Badge

The *Hegemon's Cross Admission Badge* grants the candidate entry into the grade of Philosophus. This badge is based on the Calvary Cross of Six Squares which embraces Tiphareth, Netzach, Hod, and Yesod, and rests upon Malkuth. Also, the Calvary Cross of Six Squares is the opened-out form of the cube, and is thus referred to the six Sephiroth of Microprosopus, which are Chesed, Geburah, Tiphareth, Netzach, Hod, and Yesod.[23] (See Figure 51, page 134.)

This badge is given to the Philosophus to emphasize the balance that must be attained in the 4=7 grade between Water and Fire, emotions and intellect. The Calvary Cross of Six Squares underscores the reconciling sphere of Tiphareth, tempering and equilibriating between the opposing energies which meet head-to-head in this harsh grade.

If the badge is painted primarily red, it emphasizes the element of Fire, to which the grade of 4=7 is attributed. If the badge is painted primarily green, it underscores the Sephirah of Netzach, which is also assigned to the Philosophus grade.

Materials Needed

- 5" x 5" piece of plywood, ¼" thick
- Wood putty
- Gesso

- Acrylic paints: red, green
- Clear lacquer finish

Tools Needed

- Electric jigsaw or coping saw
- Compass, pencil, and straight edge
- File or rasp
- Artist's brushes (fine and medium sizes)
- Sandpaper (medium and fine)

Construction

Follow steps 1–3 for the Caduceus Badge construction on page 119.

Finishing Steps

4. The badge may be painted in one of three ways:
    - Black outer circle and cross against a white field with white circles (for the Sephiroth)
    - Red outer circle and cross with a green inner field
    - Green outer circle and cross with a red inner field
5. The Sephiroth can be painted in their usual Queen Scale colors if so desired. After all paint has dried, apply a sealant for protection.

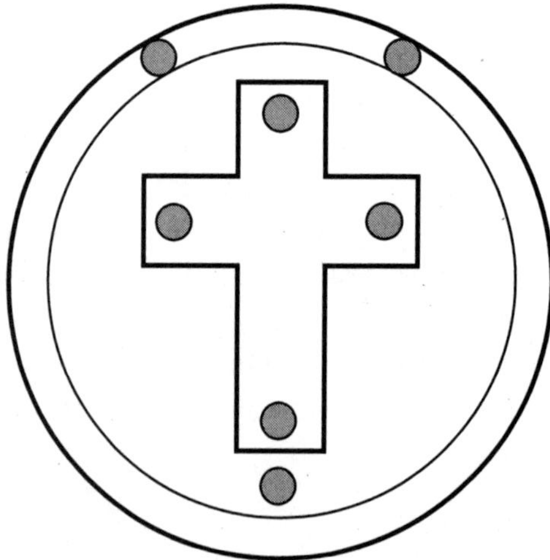

Figure 51: The Hegemon's Cross Admission Badge

Endnotes

1. Regardie, *The Golden Dawn*, 148.
2. Cirlot, *A Dictionary of Symbols*, 70.
3. A floor plan design in the form of a Greek cross, with four arms or wings of equal length projecting from a square central mass, was widely used in Byzantine church architecture.
4. Regardie, *The Golden Dawn*, 159.
5. Ibid., 159.
6. Ibid., 70.
7. Ibid., 172.
8. Ibid.
9. Ibid., 175.
10. Ibid.
11. Ibid., 71.
12. Ibid., 185.
13. Ibid., 177.
14. Ibid., 185.
15. Case, *The Tarot*, 177.
16. Ibid., 187.
17. Cirlot, 268.
18. Regardie, *The Golden Dawn*, 188.
19. Case, *The Tarot*, 167.
20. The sides of the Pyramid of the Four Elements were traditionally portrayed in a different manner: the side of Air was opposite that of Fire, while the side of Water was opposite that of Earth. However, this arrangement is based on Enochian work that is taught in the grade of Zelator Adeptus Minor. We see no reason to confuse the Philosophus with this arrangement only to inform him that the key to the puzzle is "beyond his grade," a phrase that is often misused by some esoteric teachers as a tool of the ego or a mask for their own lack of knowledge. The arrangement of the elements given here is appropriate for all Outer Order teachings.
21. Regardie, *The Golden Dawn*, 191.
22. Ibid., 191.
23. Ibid., 193.

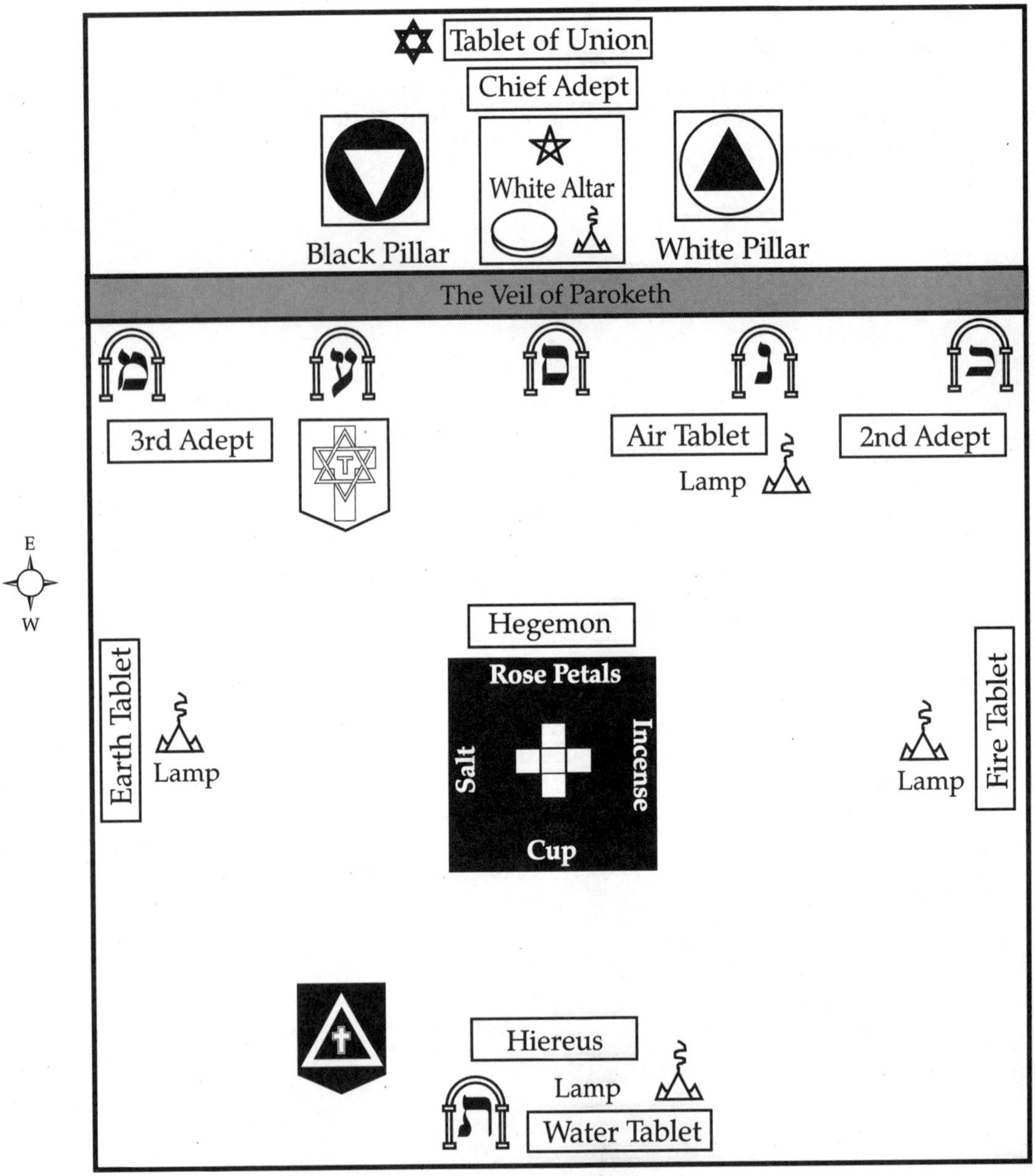

Tablet of Union

Chief Adept

White Altar

Black Pillar

White Pillar

The Veil of Paroketh

מ ע ס נ כ

3rd Adept

Air Tablet

2nd Adept

Lamp

Hegemon

Rose Petals

Salt

Incense

Cup

Earth Tablet

Lamp

Lamp

Fire Tablet

Hiereus

Lamp

ת

Water Tablet

Figure 52: The Portal Hall

CHAPTER THREE

Implements of the Portal Grade

The Portal grade of the Golden Dawn is an intermediary stage between the First and Second Orders (also called the Outer and Inner Orders—specifically, the Golden Dawn and the R. R. et A. C.). The Portal initiate (*Dominus Liminis*) is in a unique position of not belonging to either Order. The aspirant has completed the curriculum of the Golden Dawn after leaving the Philosophus grade, but is not yet a member of the *R. R. et A. C.* (the *Ordo Rosae Rubeae et Aureae Crucis*). The candidate is thus in a period of probation to determine his or her possibility of admittance to the R. R. et A. C., for it is truly a separate Order from that of the Golden Dawn.

Admission to the Second Order requires that the candidate aspire to create a sense of inner balance within, not merely to strive to attain the title of a high degree in order to flaunt the ego. Advancement to the Portal grade does not guarantee admission to the Second Order. As it states in the Portal ceremony: "Admission further can be earned no more by excellence in intellectual learning alone, though that also is required of you. In token that all true knowledge cometh of grace, not upon demand. . . ."[1]

Whereas the entire Outer Order represents what in the strict interpretation of the Golden Dawn calls the "First Degree," the Portal is referred to the "Second Degree." (An initiation into the R. R. et A. C. would be the "Third Degree.") This is also the first time throughout all the initiations that the candidate is formally presented with the White Pillar. Until now the initiate has been working with the Black Pillar which represents the Outer Order, as stated several times in the Portal ritual:

> *...take in your right hand the Banner of the West and place your left hand in that of the Very Honored 3rd Adept, who is the living Symbol of the Black Pillar which ruleth in the Outer Order...*[2]

A primary theme in the Portal ceremony is the candidate's coming out of darkness and into the light. Only after the darkness of the Black Pillar (i.e., the initiate's lower personality symbolized by the elemental grades of the Outer Order) has been explored and dealt with can the White Pillar be safely approached:

> *Having traversed the Path of Tau, the darkness of the Astral Plane and of the Black Pillar, stand firm in Yesod, that the Black Pillar may become the White...*[3]
>
> *...Stretch out your hand to touch the Black Pillar, the Pillar of the First Degree, wherein all was as yet in the darkness of the Path Tau. This was a period of restriction and of groping, as was shown by the black sash, the Sign of the First Degree. Among its symbols were the Cross, upon which meditate, the mysteries of growth and change may become revealed.*
>
> *Stretch out now your right hand to touch the White Pillar, the Pillar of the Second Degree, wherein is the Fire of the Path Samekh. Its token in our Order, is the White Sash.*[4]

The white sash is given to the initiate as a token of his or her attainment to the Portal or Second Degree. The Portal sash is completely white, with no numbers or decorations of any kind, and it fits over the candidate's right shoulder instead of the left shoulder. Just as the black sash alluded to the watery current of the Black Pillar, the white sash leads from Geburah to Netzach (right shoulder to left hip), indicating the fiery current of the White Pillar.

In the Portal grade there is a curious mixture of both Outer Order officers and Inner Order adepts. The Hiereus and the Hegemon of the Outer Order are in charge of the secondary elements of Earth and Air, while the Second and Third Adepts of the Inner Order are in charge of the primary elements of Fire and Water. However, the Portal grade is especially referred to the fifth element of Spirit or *eth* (embodied by the Chief Adept), which crowns the four elemental grades of the Outer Order just as the Spirit point crowns the Pentagram. This grade in particular is concerned with the process of inner alchemy—

of separating and examining the parts of one's own psychological and spiritual workings—in order to balance and merge them again into a more unified whole, which makes true spiritual attainment possible.

This chapter contains instructions on how to construct the temple furnishings and the wands and lamens that are unique to this grade and found nowhere else in either the First or Second Orders. We have included all of the Enochian Tablets here, for although they are introduced to the candidate one by one in each of the four grades of the Outer Order, they are not presented as a unified system of magic under the presidency of the Tablet of Union (Spirit) until the Portal grade. (The tablets are present in the Outer Order Hall, but they are, for the most part, behind veils until required for specific grade ceremonies.)

The Temple Furnishings of the Portal Grade

In the Portal Hall, the Chief Adept sits in the eastern-most part of the temple behind the white altar. (See Figure 52, page 136.) Above his or her throne is placed the Tablet of Union. Flanking the white altar are the two pillars. This entire portion of the hall is concealed behind the Veil of Paroketh, a physical curtain that represents an etheric boundary which lies before the Sephirah of Tiphareth on the path of Samekh leading from Yesod. Just west of the veil are placed the Hebrew letters Mem, Ayin, Samekh, Nun, and Kaph—corresponding to further paths on the Tree of Life. The Second and Third Adepts are seated in the southeast and the northeast respectively. The black altar is located just west of the center of the hall. The Hegemon sits east of the altar, and the Hiereus is stationed in the west. The Enochian Tablets are placed in their respective quarters: Air—east, Fire—south, Water—west, and Earth—north.

The Veil of Paroketh

The *Veil of Paroketh,* in addition to being an actual physical prop in the Portal Hall, is a symbol of an astral veil that exists on the glyph of the Tree of Life. It is described in the Portal grade as the Veil of the Tabernacle, before the Holy of Holies: the Inner Sanctum of the temple. The veil is a demarcator which separates the four lowest Sephiroth on the Tree of Life from the rest of the Tree. Situated on the Twenty-fifth Path of Samekh, the veil is the boundary between Tiphareth, the seat of the Higher Self, and the seventh, eighth, and ninth spheres which make up the triad of the lower personality.[5] To truly "rend the veil" means to evolve beyond the needs and wants of the lower personality and take a conscious

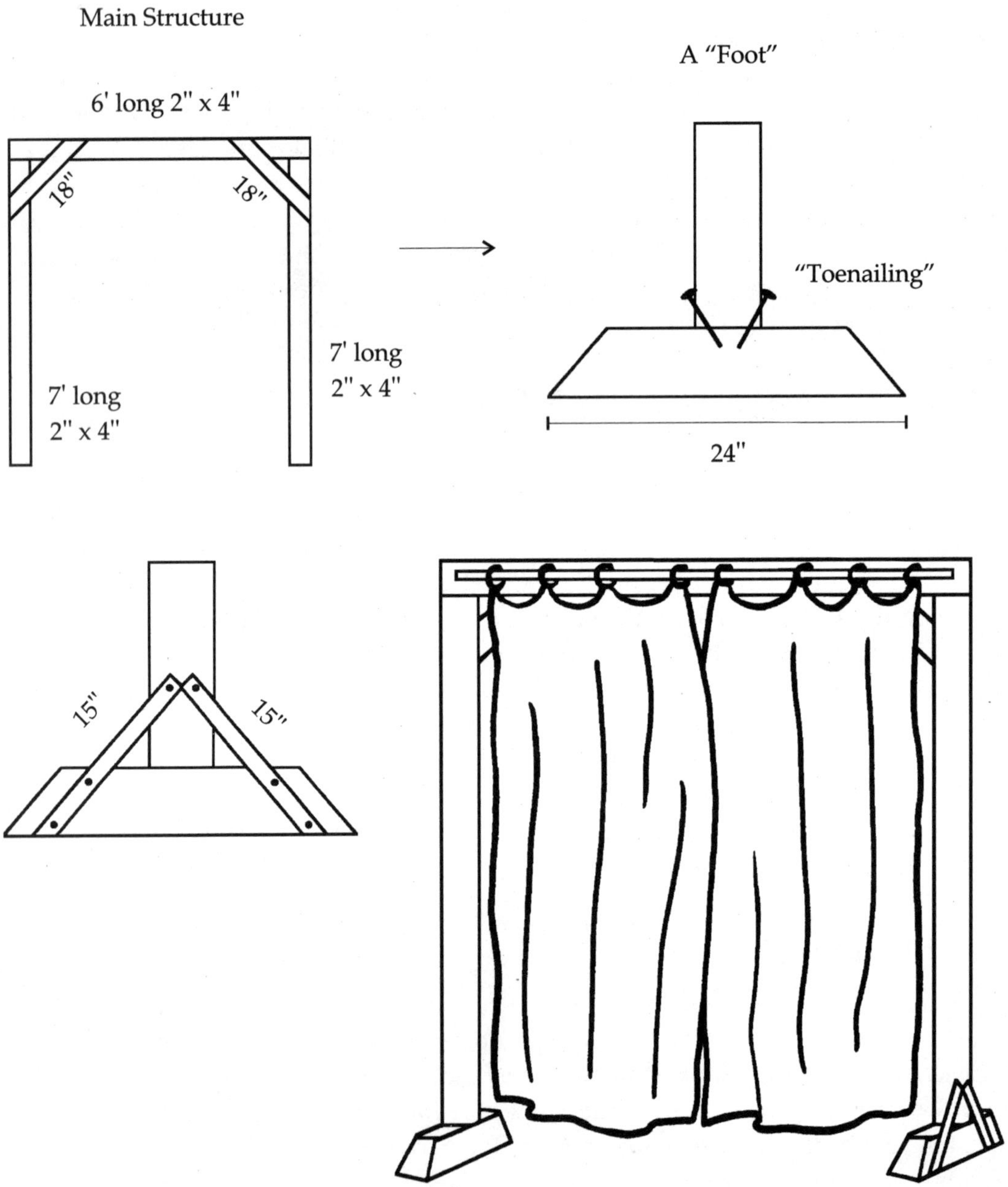

Main Structure

6' long 2" x 4"

18"

18"

7' long
2" x 4"

7' long
2" x 4"

A "Foot"

"Toenailing"

24"

15"

15"

Figure 53: The Veil of Paroketh

step toward union with the Higher Self. This conscious act of aspiration implies both a willingness to become a true initiate of the mysteries, as well as the willingness to undergo the sacrifice that is necessary to achieve this goal. Paroketh is also described as the "Veil of the Four Elements of the Body of Man (i.e., humanity), which was offered on the Cross for the service of man."[6] The veil is that which divides the apparent "separateness" of the world below from the "wholeness" of the world above, through self-sacrifice or self-denial. (Perhaps a more appropriate term would be "limit-denial.") The four separate elements which make up the personality of the initiate must be purified by an infusion of Spirit before the domain of the Higher Self can be approached in any way. Only in this manner, can the Initiate become greater than the sum of his or her parts.

The Hebrew letters which make up the word Paroketh are Peh פ, Resh ר, Kaph כ, and Tau ת; four letters which have additional correspondences to the four elements in the Portal ceremony. Beyond the veil of the four elements lies the fifth element—Spirit.

The Veil of Paroketh is also the symbol of the division that exists between the First and Second Orders.

Refer to Figure 53 on page 140 for construction diagrams.

Materials Needed

- Two 7' long 2" x 4" boards
- One 6' long 2" x 4" board
- One 4' long 2" x 4" board
- Two 6' long 1" x 2" boards
- 2" nails
- 2½" nails
- Adjustable curtain rod and attachments
- Two 65" x 90" pieces of fabric (white, gold, or violet; two bed sheets in any of the above colors may be used)
- Sheer fabric 65" x 90" (may also be either white, gold, or violet)
- Flat latex paint in the same color as the chosen fabric

Tools Needed

- Table saw, miter saw, or circular saw (or hand saw and miter box)
- Hammer
- Sewing machine
- Scissors

Construction

1. Take the two 7' long 2" x 4"s and nail them to either end of the 6' long 2" x 4", as shown in Figure 53, page 140. Take one of the 1" x 2"s and cut off two 18" lengths from it.
2. Using a miter saw or a hand saw and miter box, miter all four ends of the 18" pieces, so that they are all angled at 45 degrees.
3. Nail the two 18" lengths to the 2" x 4"s, to act as corner braces of the main structure, as shown in the diagram.
4. Take the 4' long 2" x 4" and cut it in half. (These pieces are to be the "feet" which support the whole structure.) Miter all four ends of the feet as before (optional).
5. Nail one of the feet perpendicular to the remaining (bottom) end of one of the 7' long boards. Do this by "toe-nailing." (Using the longer 2½" nails, pound the nails at an angle through the sides of the 7' board into the foot. See diagram.)
6. Cut the remaining 1" x 2" board into four 15" lengths. Miter one end of all four boards.
7. Nail all of these 15" long boards to the outside of the structure to act as braces for the feet. (One pair per foot as shown in the diagram. The mitered ends will be closest to the floor.)

Finishing Steps

8. Paint the entire structure with latex paint in one of the colors described earlier. Allow to dry.
9. Using screws or nails, attach the adjustable curtain rod to the 7' length of the top board.
10. Attach the fabric to the rod as you would a normal curtain. (The sheer material goes over the heavier fabric on the front side.) You may wish to sew a large hem in the top of the material and thread the curtain rod through it, or simply push the round drapery pins directly through the fabric and hang them on the rod. Trim off any excess material and hem the bottom.

The White Altar

This altar is used by the Chief Adept behind the Veil of Paroketh. It is a reflection of the black altar of the Outer Order, but on a higher plane of working. Follow the instructions given in chapter one, pages 3–7, on the construction of the double cubical altar, but use white paint instead of black.

The Implements of the Officers

The Third Adept's Wand

The salt-headed wand is the scepter of the Third Adept in the Portal temple of the Order. (See Color Plate 10.) The Third Adept in this particular ceremony represents the feminine qualities of moisture and receptability. There is valid speculation within the Order as to the correctness of the symbolism concerning this particular wand—whether or not the symbol of mercury should actually replace the salt symbol as the wand-head. However we shall not enter into this discussion here. What we have provided is a description of the Third Adept's wand as portrayed in the original Order documents.

Of the three alchemic essentials, salt is the physical vehicle of manifestation for the other two. (The phrase "salt of the Earth" takes on new meaning in this regard.) Sulfur characterizes each thing in a particular way—mercury gives animation—but salt provides the matrix. Salt is the receptive body, the material substance. Salt is in a continual state of evolution, taking on a new body as the old body is steadily cast away. This is a process of purification that arises out of separation. To cleanse is to purify, but the work of purification is more than a degree of cleansing. That which is pure is freed from that which is impure. The purification of the body, soul, and Spirit, is an important step in the initiate's spiritual evolution.

The symbol of salt on the Tree of Life embraces all the Sephiroth except Malkuth, and is as it were, the Reconciler between sulfur and mercury. The horizontal dividing line in the sigil implies the precept of Hermes, "as above so below."[7] (See *Ritual Use of Magical Tools*, chapter three, for a ritual titled "The Rite of Self-purification through Salt.")

Refer to Figure 54 on page 144 for construction diagrams.

Materials Needed

- One ¾" thick dowel approximately 36" long
- One 6" x 6" piece of ¾" soft wood (pine, balsa, or bass)
- One ¼" wooden dowel or peg 1" in length
- Yellow carpenter's glue
- Gesso
- Acrylic paint: blue
- Clear lacquer finish (spray or brush on)

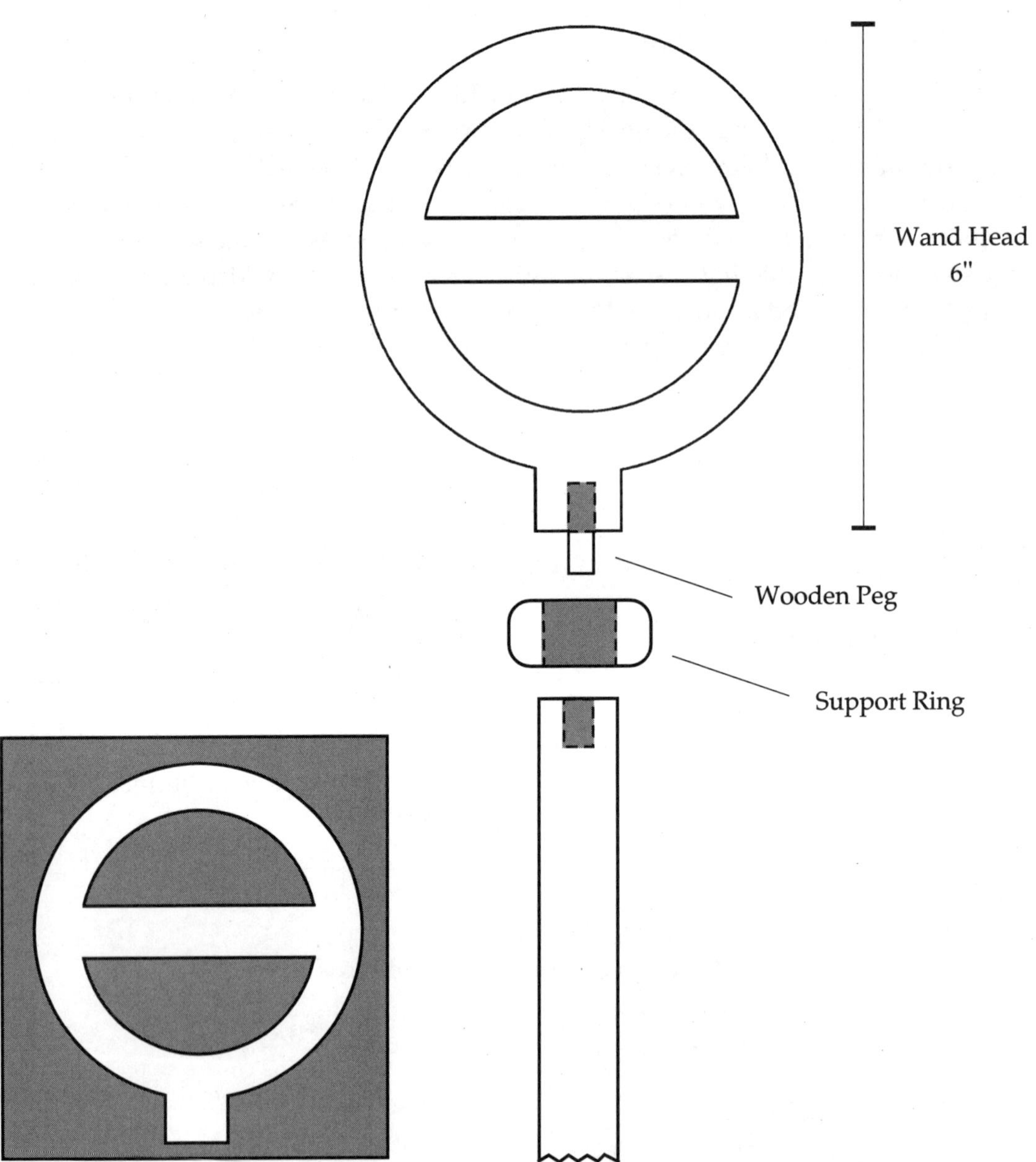

Figure 54: The Third Adept's Wand in the Portal

Tools Needed

- Scroll saw or coping saw
- Electric drill with ¼" and ¾" bits
- Sandpaper (coarse, medium, and fine)
- Artist's paint brushes (medium to large)

Construction: The Head

1. Draw the sigil of salt ⊖ shown in Figure 54, page 144, on the 6" x 6" piece of wood. With the saw, cut out the outer shape of the symbol.
2. Drill two holes inside the shaded half-circle areas of the wand head. (Remember: it is important to use a drill bit that is wider than your saw blade.)
3. With your saw unplugged, detach the blade from the saw. Stick the blade through one of the holes you have drilled and reattach the blade to the saw. Plug the saw back in and cut out the shaded area of wood.
4. Drill a hole ½" deep and ¼" wide in the center of the bottom side of the wand head.

Construction: The Shaft

5. Into the leftover piece of ¾" thick wood, drill a ¾" diameter hole. Around this hole, draw a 1½" diameter circle. Cut this circle out of the wood using the scroll saw. You will end up with a donut-shaped ring of wood.
6. Take the 36" long dowel (shaft) and drill a hole ½" deep and ¼" in diameter into one end of it. Glue the 1" wooden peg into the hole you have just drilled so that half of the peg is embedded into the end of the dowel and half of it sticks out.
7. Apply glue to the inside of the ring. Slide it over the top end of the shaft. (If the ring is too tight, sand inside its center hole.)
8. Pour some glue into the hole you drilled into the bottom end of the wand head and attach the salt sigil to the wand shaft. The head of the wand should fit snugly against the supporting ring. (Note: You may wish to add a middle band and a pommel to the wand for aesthetic purposes.)

Finishing Steps

9. Sand the entire surface of the scepter so that it is smooth. (Begin with course sandpaper and finish with medium sandpaper.) With a paint brush, cover the wand with a coat of gesso. Allow to dry.

10. Sand the painted surface (especially the shaft) lightly with fine sandpaper until smooth. Apply a second coat if needed.
11. Paint the wand entirely blue. Paint or spray on a sealant to protect the painted wand. Allow to dry.

The Second Adept's Wand

The sulfur-headed wand is the scepter of the Second Adept in the Portal temple of the Order. (See Color Plate 10.) The Second Adept in this ceremony represents the qualities of heat and the active male principle. That is why the most fiery of the *three alchemic principles* is attributed to this particular officer.

Sulfur is that which gathers together and fashions all that is of the Earth. The nature of sulfur is both tangible and intangible. Within its tangible aspects, it is an oil and is to be found in all substances. Its intangible aspect is that of consciousness, which is found in all substances in varying degrees. Sulfur corresponds to the superconscious or cosmic consciousness.

J. E. Cirlot described sulfur as symbolic of the desire for positive action and of vital heat. In the complicated symbolism of alchemy, sulfur represents one of the stages of the evolution of matter (and of the human psyche). Cirlot also reviewed the ideas of Rene Alleau, who said that the various stages, from the lowest to the highest, can be classified as follows: *prior elements*, denoting the inherent possibilities of the cosmos, or of man; *prime matter,* or the elementary organization of inherent possibilities, equivalent perhaps to the unconscious or the instincts; *mercury*, or the first purification, feelings, imagination, the dominant feminine principle; *sulfur,* or more profound and intensive purification, reason, and intuition, the masculine principle; and the *Great Work*, or transcendence.[8]

The symbol of sulfur on the Tree of Life does not touch the four lowest Sephiroth. The cross terminates in Tiphareth, whereby, as it were, the supernal triangle is to be grasped, and Tiphareth is the purified human being.[9]

The sulfur-headed wand could be used by the magician in a work of inner alchemy; that is, as part of a consecration rite designed to elevate the individual mind toward the cosmic consciousness. This process of self-evolution uses the heat and activity of alchemic sulfur to expand one's spiritual awareness. (See *Ritual Use of Magical Tools*, chapter three, for a ritual titled "The Rite of Self-consecration through Sulfur.")

Refer to Figure 55 on page 147 for construction diagrams.

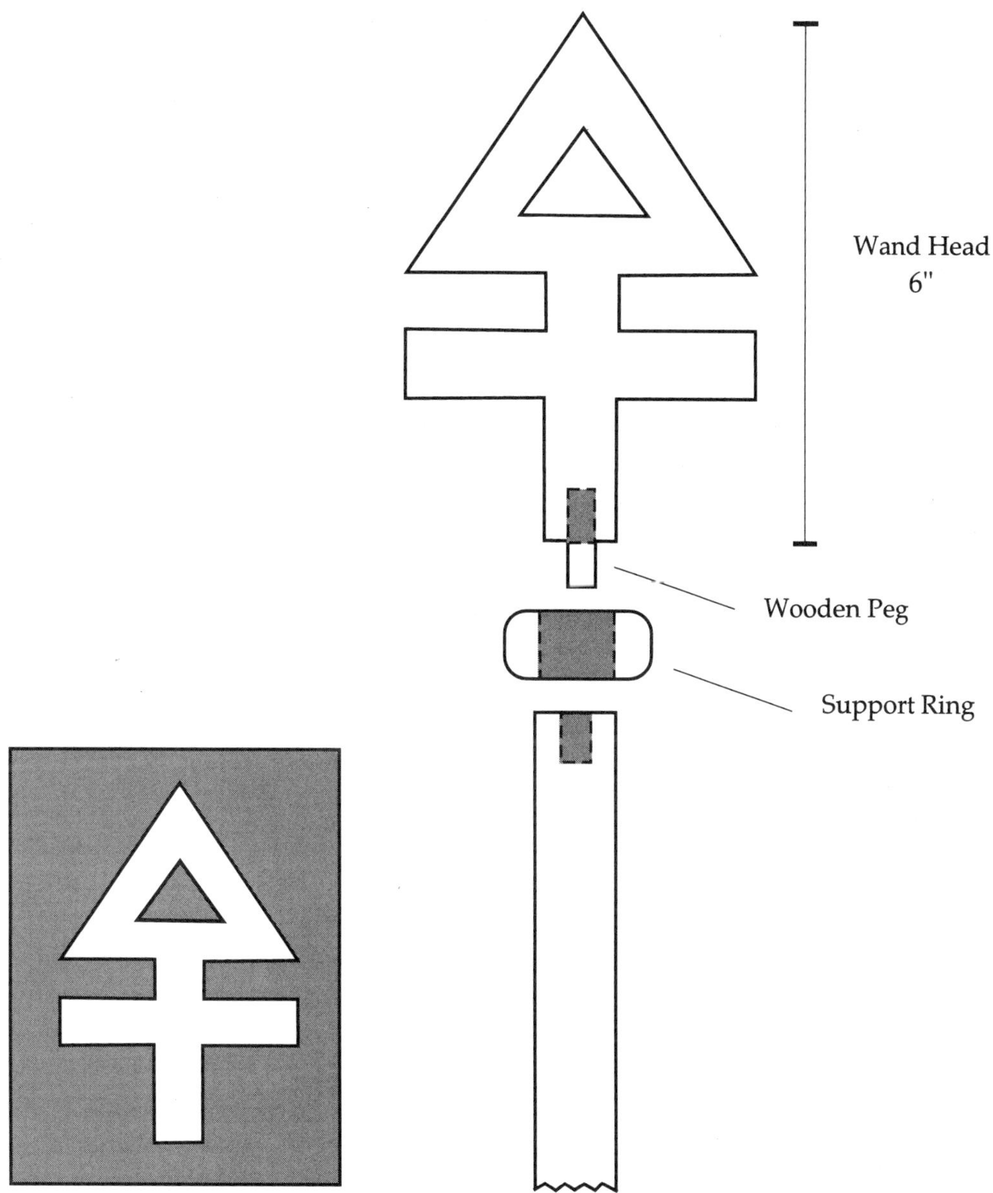

Figure 55: The Second Adept's Wand in the Portal

Materials Needed

- One ¾" thick dowel approximately 36" long
- One 4" x 7" piece of ¾" soft wood (pine, balsa, or bass)
- One ¼" wooden dowel or peg 1" long
- Yellow carpenter's glue
- Gesso
- Acrylic paint: red
- Clear lacquer finish (spray or brush on)

Tools Needed

- Scroll saw or coping saw
- Electric drill with ¼" and ¾" bits
- Sandpaper (coarse, medium, and fine)
- Artist's paint brushes (medium to large)

Construction: The Head

1. Draw the sigil of sulfur 🜍 shown in Figure 55, page 147, on the 4" x 7" piece of wood. With the saw, cut out the outer shape of the symbol.
2. Drill one hole inside the central shaded area of the triangular section of the wand head. (Remember: it is important to use a drill bit that is wider than your saw blade.)
3. With your saw unplugged, detach the blade from the saw. Stick the blade through one of the holes you have drilled and reattach the blade to the saw. Plug the saw back in and cut out the shaded area of wood.
4. Drill a hole ½" deep and ¼" wide in the center of the bottom side of the wand head.

Construction: The Shaft

Follow steps 5–8 as given for the construction of the Third Adept's Wand on page 145.

Finishing Steps

9. Sand the entire surface of the scepter so that it is smooth. (Begin with coarse sandpaper, finish with medium.) With a paint brush, cover the wand with a coat of gesso. Allow to dry.
10. Sand the painted surface (especially the shaft) lightly with fine sandpaper until smooth. Apply a second coat if needed.

11. Paint the wand entirely red. Paint or spray on a sealant to protect the painted wand. Allow to dry.

The Chief Adept's Wand

The Pentagram-headed wand is the scepter of the Chief Adept in the Portal temple of the Order. (See Color Plate 10.) The Pentagram represents the four elements of nature crowned and united by the fifth—Spirit. To the Egyptians, the five-pointed star signified "rising upward towards the point of origin."[10] For centuries the five-pointed star has been used as a symbol of protection, and an amulet for health and well-being. It was popular among the Babylonians, Egyptians, Assyrians, and Hebrews. According to Eliphas Levi, the man most responsible for the occult revival of the nineteenth century, magicians of old used to draw the symbol on their doorsteps to keep malevolent spirits out and beneficent spirits in. And as early as the sixth century B.C.E., Pythagoras, the Greek philosopher-mystic, used the Pentagram as a holy symbol for his followers.

The fifth element of Spirit, also called the *quintessence,* crowns and connects the other four. It is Spirit which transcends the others and makes the whole of the Pentagram greater than the sum of its parts. Spirit is the divine and guiding principle. This is one reason magicians stress that it is important to keep the Spirit point of the Pentagram upward.

Five, the number of points on a Pentagram, was a number peculiarly associated with the ideas of marriage and union, as it is the first number beyond the monad formed from the union of the first odd and even numbers, male and female. Thus, it is an appropriate symbol for the Chief Adept to wield in a ritual where the four elements of the candidate's psyche are united and equilibrated in a type of "alchemical wedding."

The Pentagram is wielded by the Chief Adept to instill these ideas deeply within the psyche of the candidate, whom in this ritual symbolically receives the fifth and final element.

The shaft of the scepter is also painted in the five elemental colors of the Pentagram: Spirit—white (the longest section on the wand), Fire—red, Air—yellow, Water—blue, and Earth—black.

The Pentagram-headed scepter can be employed to invoke any or all of the five elements including Spirit. An Adept could certainly use this wand in a ritual where the Enochian tablets, including the Tablet of Union, are also present. (A ritual employing this wand is given in *Ritual Use of Magical Tools* in chapter three.)

Refer to Figure 56 on page 150 and Figure 57 on page 151 for construction diagrams.

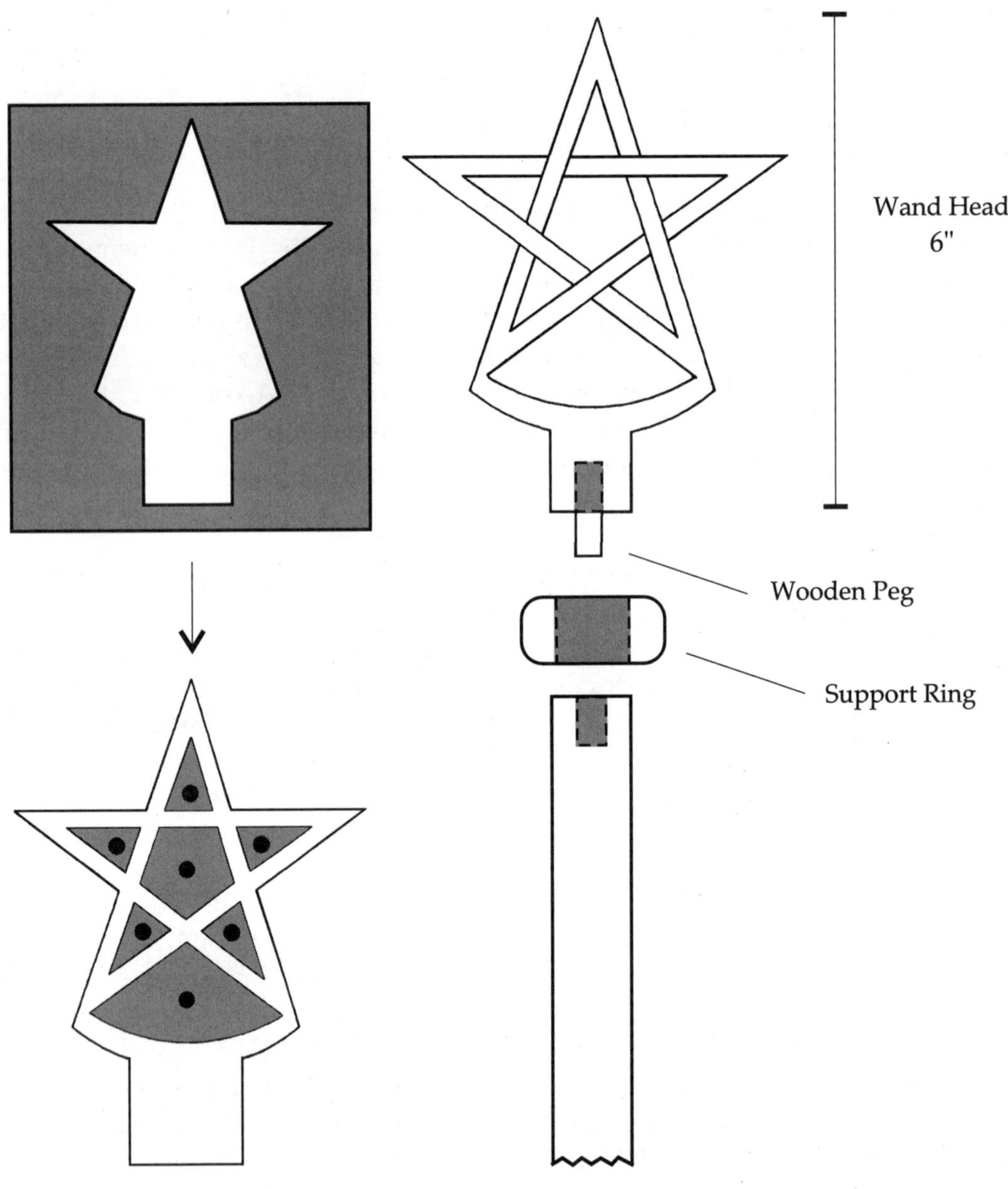

Figure 56: The Chief Adept's Wand in the Portal

Materials Needed

- One ¾" thick dowel approximately 36" long
- One 6½" x 6" piece of ¾" soft wood (pine, balsa, or bass)
- One ¼" wooden dowel or peg 1" in length
- Yellow carpenter's glue
- Gesso
- Acrylic paints: red, yellow, blue, black, and white
- Clear lacquer finish (spray or brush on)

Tools Needed

- Scroll saw or coping saw
- Electric drill with ¼" and ¾" bits
- Sandpaper (course, medium, and fine)
- Artist's paint brushes (medium to large)

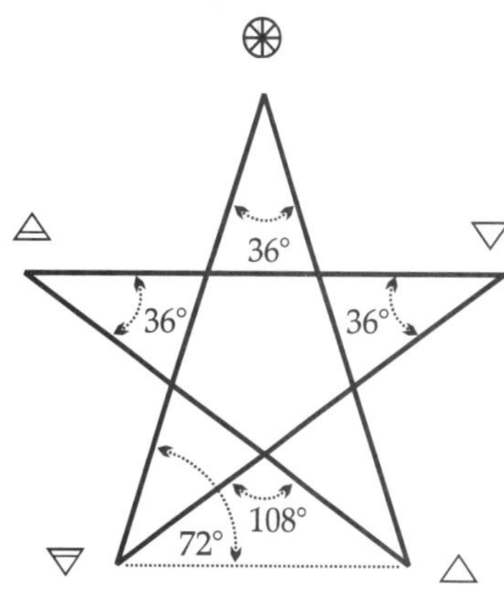

Figure 57: Angles and Elemental Attributions of the Pentagram

Construction: The Pentagram Head

1. Draw the Pentagram shown in Figure 56 on the 6½" x 6" piece of wood. (See Figure 57, showing the degrees of the angles and size of the Pentagram.) With the saw, cut out the outer shape of the Pentagram.

2. Drill seven holes, one inside each of the shaded (negative space) areas of the wand head. (Remember: it is important to use a drill bit that is wider than your saw blade.)

3. With your saw unplugged, detach the blade from the saw. Stick the blade through one of the holes you have drilled and reattach the blade to the saw. Plug the saw back in and begin cutting out the shaded area of wood. Repeat this process for all seven drilled holes until all the waste areas of wood are cut out.

4. Drill a hole ½" deep and ¼" wide in the center of the bottom side of the wand head.

Follow steps 5–8 as given for the construction of the Third Adept's Wand on page 145.

Finishing Steps

9. Beginning with course sandpaper and finishing with medium sandpaper, sand the entire surface of the scepter so that it is smooth. With a paint brush, cover the wand with a coat of gesso. Allow to dry.

10. Sand the painted surface (especially the shaft) lightly with fine sandpaper until smooth. Apply a second coat if needed.
11. With a pencil mark the shaft into five sections: the top section under the wand head will be 10" in length, this includes the support ring; the next three sections will all be 6" in length; the final section will be 8" in length.
12. Paint the head of the wand and the first section white. Paint the second section red. Paint the third section yellow. Paint the fourth section blue. Paint the last section black. Paint or spray on a sealant such as clear lacquer to protect the painted wand. Allow to dry.

The Lamens

The lamens belonging to the officers in the Portal differ from those lamens attributed to the same officers in the First Order. The reason for this is that the Portal Hall is the first temple yet encountered where all the officer's lamens have changed. Even the Hiereus and the Hegemon, the only officers remaining from the Outer Order, wear emblems completely different from the ones they wore in the Neophyte Hall. In fact, all of the officers in the Portal, with the exception of the Chief Adept, wear symbols that are unique to this particular hall. The Second and Third Adepts wear lamens that symbolize their specific elemental affiliation. The Hiereus and the Hegemon both wear lamens that are adorned with hexagrams—references to the macrocosm and to the perfected human being.

The Hegemon's Lamen

In the Portal Hall, the Hegemon reveals his or her important duties as the keeper of the balance within the temple. The lamen depicts the opposing triangles of Fire and Water interlocked and conjoined and in perfect equilibrium...the Macrocosmic Hexagram.

The Hexagram is commonly known to many people as the Star of David. Magicians also know it as the Seal of Solomon and the Star of the Macrocosm. In ancient times, it was a popular amulet used to guard it's owner against fire and enemies. To Jews, it is the symbol of their faith, which represents the union of Spirit and matter. In biblical times, King David used it to symbolize his ability to unite the twelve tribes of Israel into a single, powerful kingdom. When placed on the Tree of Life, the six points of the Hexagram are aligned with Daath, Chesed, Geburah, Netzach, Hod, and Yesod, while the center is the Sephirah of Tiphareth, to which this symbol especially refers. Unlike the Pentagram, the

Hexagram cannot be inverted, so if the Pentagram can be said to represent man (humanity), then the Hexagram represents perfected man (enlightened humanity).[11]

This lamen is not unlike a simplified version of the Banner of the East, minus the central crosses, showing the Hegemon's importance in bringing the candidate throughout all the grades to the antechamber of the light of L. V. X. In the Portal ritual, she is also the officer who performs all of the workings of elemental Air (after the Chief Adept has invoked all of the elements). She therefore indicates that Air is the Reconciler between the forces of Fire and Water, and that only through perfect balance of these two extremes is the Portal to the light traversed.

The Hiereus' Lamen

The Hiereus' Portal Lamen is identical to one of the diagrams shown to the candidate in this grade:

> *Below, is shown the Occult Symbol of Malkuth, the Tenth Sephirah. It is in four parts, corresponding to the Maltese Cross. They are Fire of Earth, Water of Earth, Air of Earth, Earth of Earth, as indicated by the Symbol. They correspond to the four grade of the First Order, which in one sense, quitteth not Malkuth, being the Grades of the four lowest Sephiroth of Malkuth in Assiah. Upon them is surcharged a white Hexagram in a circle. The 6 and the 4 make 10, the number of Malkuth on the Tree.*[12] *The Hexagram is also the Sign of the Macrocosm—of Tiphareth, and of the Six Upper Sephiroth, wherefore it is white—Spirit ruling over matter. Six is a perfect number, for its whole equals the sum of its parts...Remember that the whole number of Malkuth is 496—which again is a perfect number. Malkuth must then be equated and perfected by the 6 ruling the 4: and the link between 6 and 4 is the number of the Pentagram.*[13]

The Hiereus is the officer who sits in the lowest point of Malkuth in the hall at the border of the Qlippotic Realm, enthroned on matter and robed in darkness. In the Portal, this officer is in charge of the workings of elemental Earth. The Hiereus' Lamen in this grade primarily shows that Spirit must always govern matter (represented by the four subelements). If Spirit does not crown matter (as in the figure of the upright Pentagram), the result is chaos and evil, symbolized by the Qlippoth.

The Third Adept's Lamen

The Third Adept portrays the forces of Water. This officer oversees all the workings of Water in the Portal grade and represents the powers of the feminine and the Black Pillar. The Third

Adept's Lamen is painted in the flashing colors of elemental Water, blue and orange. The lamen shows an octogram in the center of which is a Water Cup drawn in the style of the Stolistes Admission Badge of the Practicus ceremony. The octogram is formed from two squares superimposed one over the other at an angle. It thus refers not only to the sphere of Hod, but also to that of Chesed (i.e., the two watery Sephiroth).

The Second Adept's Lamen

The Second Adept depicts the powers of Fire and is in charge of all the workings of Fire in the Portal grade. This officer represents the powers of the masculine and the White Pillar in the Portal ceremony. The Second Adept's Lamen is painted in the flashing colors of elemental Fire. On it are shown an upright Fire triangle within a Pentagram. The Pentagram refers to the sphere of Geburah, the fiery Sephirah.

(Note: The Chief Adept's Lamen differs from the others in that it is in the shape of the Rose Cross, a purely Second Order emblem. This lamen is worn by the Chief Adept in the Portal grade to give the candidate a glimpse of the *Rosicrucian* symbolism of the Second Order. Because it is not like the other Portal lamens, its use and symbolism is discussed separately and in greater detail on page 157.)

The lamens are hung from collars in the specific elemental colors. Although these lamens officially occur only in the Portal ceremony, they may be utilized by an Adept in any ceremony invoking elemental energies. A magician of the Portal grade can use them in a ritual/meditation designed to visually explore their colors and symbolism (see *Ritual Use of Magical Tools*, chapter three).

Refer to Color Plate 10 and Figure 58 for diagrams of the lamens.

Figure 58: The Officers' Lamens in the Portal

Materials Needed

- One 12" x 12" piece of plywood, ¼" thick
- Wood putty
- Gesso
- Acrylic paints: black, white, red, green, blue, orange, violet
- Clear lacquer finish

Tools Needed

- Electric jigsaw, scroll saw, or coping saw
- Compass, pencil, and straight edge
- Protractor
- File or rasp
- Artist's brushes (fine and medium sizes)
- Sandpaper (medium and fine)

Construction

(As noted in chapter one, pre-cut wooden disks may be purchased at a craft store or hobby shop. If these are not available, continue as indicated below.)

1. Using the compass, draw four 4" circles on the piece of wood. Cut out circles with saw. (See Figure 58, page 154.)
2. If the circle of wood has jagged edges, file them smooth. Any gaps in the wood can be filled in with wood putty. Sand the wood with medium sandpaper until it is smooth.
3. Paint with gesso. Let dry. Sand with fine sandpaper. Apply another coat if needed.

The Hegemon's Lamen

1. This lamen requires that you draw a perfect Hexagram within a circle. This is done as follows: find the center hole created by the compass point and draw a second, smaller circle ½" inside the edge of the disk.
2. Lightly draw a cross from the center of the circle which divides it into four equal portions.
3. Divide the circle into six equal parts beginning at the intersection of the top of the circle and the vertical line of the cross.
4. Draw lines which connect these points, forming the Hexagram. Draw a second set of lines approximately ¼" inside the first, giving the Hexagram its thickness.

5. The lamen is to be painted as follows: the Fire triangle is red, and the Water triangle is blue. (Be sure to make the triangles interlock.) They are painted against a white "ground." Apply sealant for protection.

The Hiereus' Lamen

1. Follow steps 1–4 for the Hegemon's Lamen (page 155.)
2. The Hexagram is to be painted white against a ground composed of the four colors of Malkuth surrounded by a white outer circle. (Note: This lamen looks identical to the Earth Pentacle of the Zelator Adeptus Minor, except for the absence of sigils and Divine names around the white outer edge. See chapter five, page 252.) The inner ground is a circular section divided into the colors of citrine (top quarter), russet (left quarter), olive (right quarter), and black (bottom quarter). When paint is dry, apply sealant.

The Third Adept's Lamen

1. On this lamen, an octogram is to be drawn: find the center hole created by the compass point and draw a second, smaller circle ½" inside the edge of the disk.
2. Lightly draw a cross from the center of the circle which divides it into four equal portions. Connect the points of the cross to form a square.
3. Find the center of each side of the square and draw a second cross from the center of the circle to the edge of the outer circle.
4. Connect the points of the cross to form a second square, which overlaps the first. Both squares together form the octogram.
5. A cup shaped like that of the Stolistes is to be drawn in the center of the lamen.
6. The octogram is to be painted completely orange. The cup and the small ground area behind the octogram should be painted blue. The outer circle should also be painted orange. Apply sealant for protection.

The Second Adept's Lamen

The Second Adept's Lamen requires that you draw a perfect Pentagram within a circle. This is done as follows:

1. Find the center hole created by the compass point and draw a second, smaller circle ½" inside the edge of the disk. Draw one line through the center point to the circle just drawn.

2. Using a protractor, draw two lines from the top point of the first line to the edge of the circle. These two lines should be at an angle of 18 degrees on either side of the original line. (The same lines will form a 36-degree angle with each other.)
3. From the bottom points of the two lines, draw two more lines, both at angles of 36 degrees from the first pair of lines. Connect the remaining ends of the last pair of lines, forming the Pentagram.
4. Paint the Pentagram entirely, filling in its form with green paint. A red Fire triangle should be painted at the center of the figure. The ground area behind the Pentagram should also be painted red. The outer circle should be green. When all paint is dry, apply sealant for protection.

The Chief Adept's Lamen

This outer form of the *Rose Cross Lamen* is revealed to the candidate, as described in the Portal ceremony, as a symbol which unites the numbers four, five, and six. (The four arms of the cross, six the number of Tiphareth, to which the Rose Cross is attributed, and the five elements represented by the four arms of the cross plus the circle of Spirit.)

The cross is a complex symbol whose main meanings include that of "conjunction" of opposing forces. The cross represents the mystic center of the cosmos...the place of junction for the forces of the universe. Consequently, the cross affirms the primary relationship between the two worlds of the celestial and the Earth-bound (Spirit and matter). It represents the Spirit or divine light, brought into the physical world of manifestation—life (the human body) symbolized by the four elements which are the components of life.[14]

The rose is primarily a symbol of completion, total achievement and perfection. It also alludes to the mystic center and the heart.[15] The rose is a yonic symbol associated with regeneration, productivity and purity. Because the flower unfolds when it blossoms, it is a worthy symbol of spiritual growth. To the Greeks it was a symbol of sunrise. The rose is the sacred flower of Venus, goddess of love, attributed to the seventh Sephirah. (Seven is described as the most blessed of all the numbers...and it is also the number assigned to the act of initiation into the mysteries.)

The cross and rose together refer to the synthesis of all these ideas. The red rose also alludes to the compassion and sacrifice of the Christos, the Slain and Resurrected One. The golden cross alludes to the spiritual gold concealed within human nature.

This type of lamen can also be worn in general ritual work by a Neophyte Adeptus Minor (N. A. M.) who has not yet constructed a personal Rose Cross Lamen as described in chapter five.

Refer to Figure 59 on page 158 for construction diagram.

Materials Needed

- One 6" square piece of pine, bass, or plywood, ½" or ⅜" thick
- One small piece of ⅛" thick basswood
- Yellow carpenter's glue
- Wood putty
- Gesso
- Acrylic paints: red, white, gold
- Sealant

Figure 59: The Chief Adept's Lamen in the Portal

The Banners

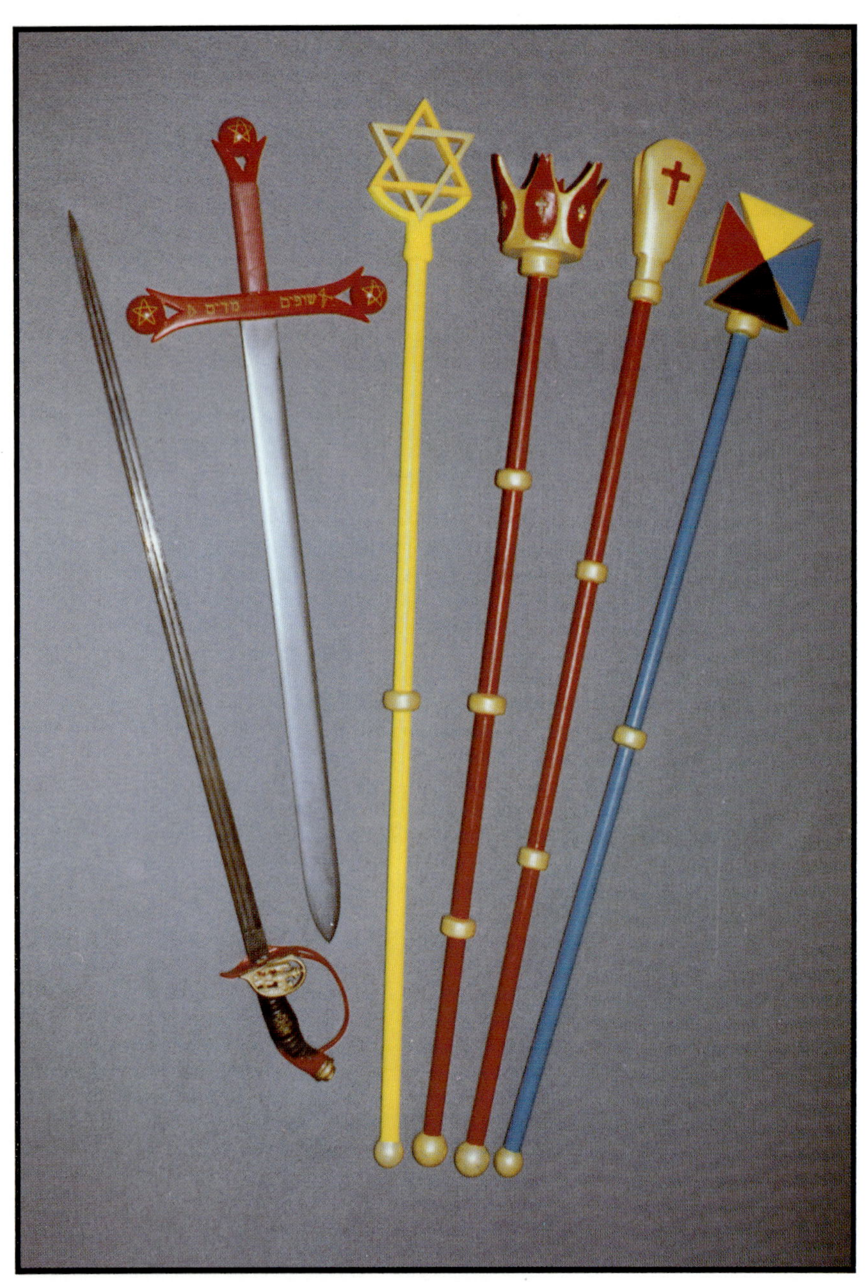

The Outer Order Wands

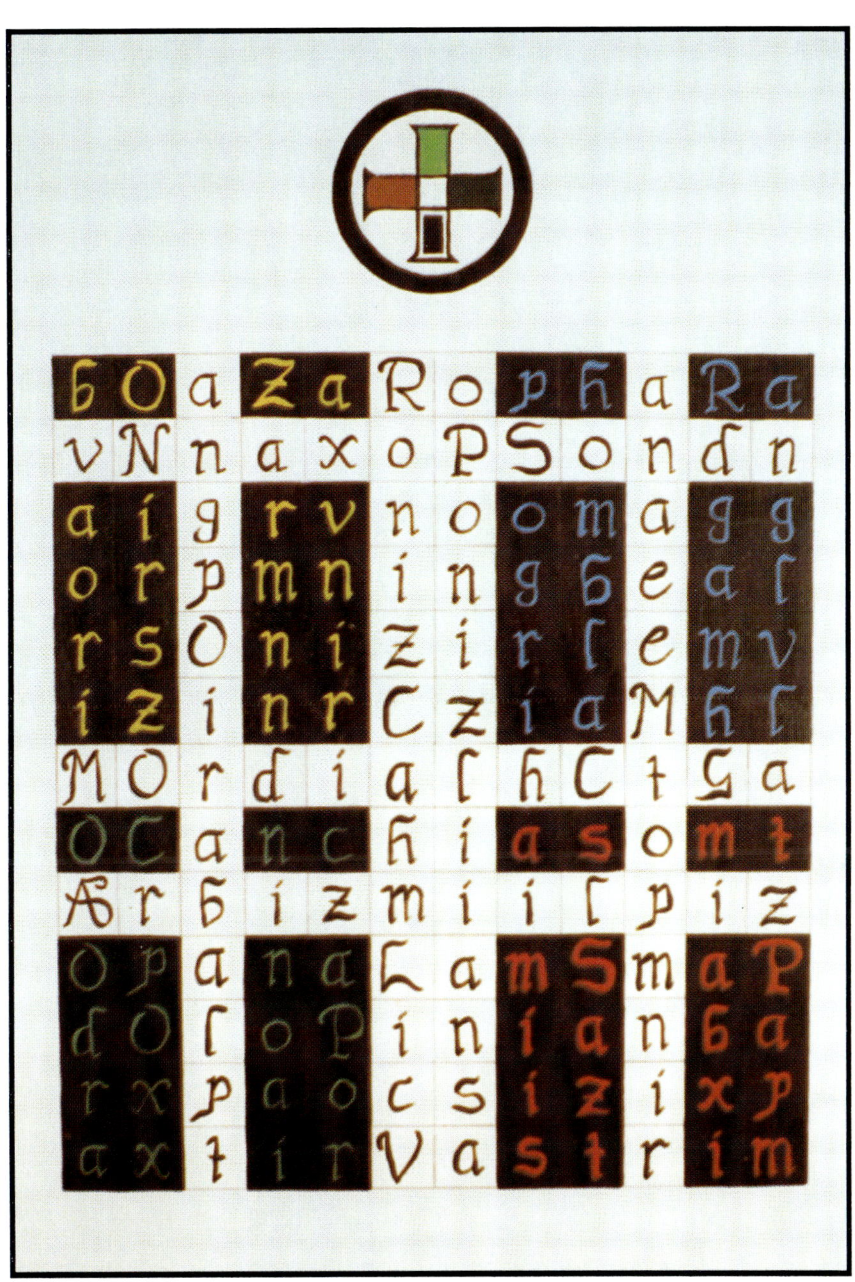

The Enochian Earth Tablet

Crook, Scourge and Crux Ansata

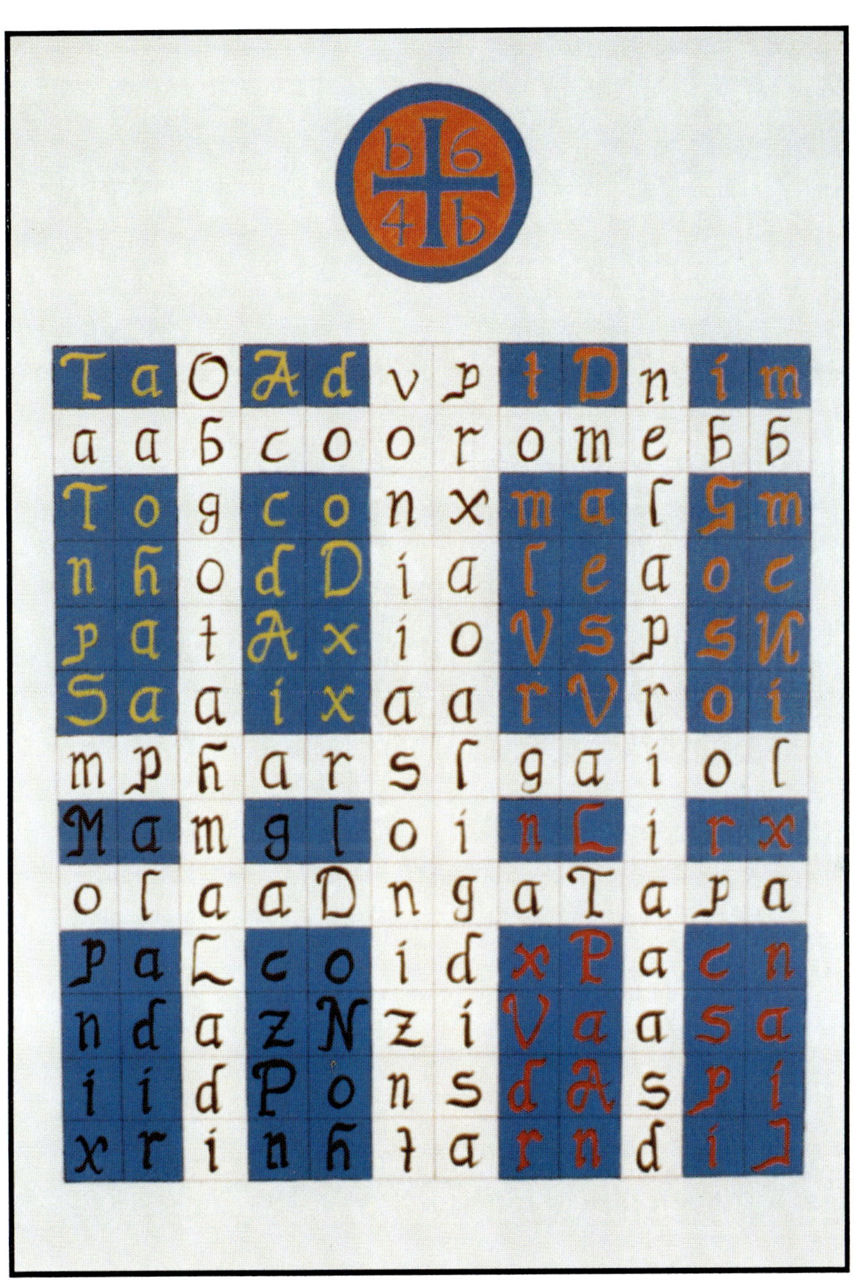

The Enochian Water Tablet

The Four Elemental Implements

The Enochian Fire Tablet

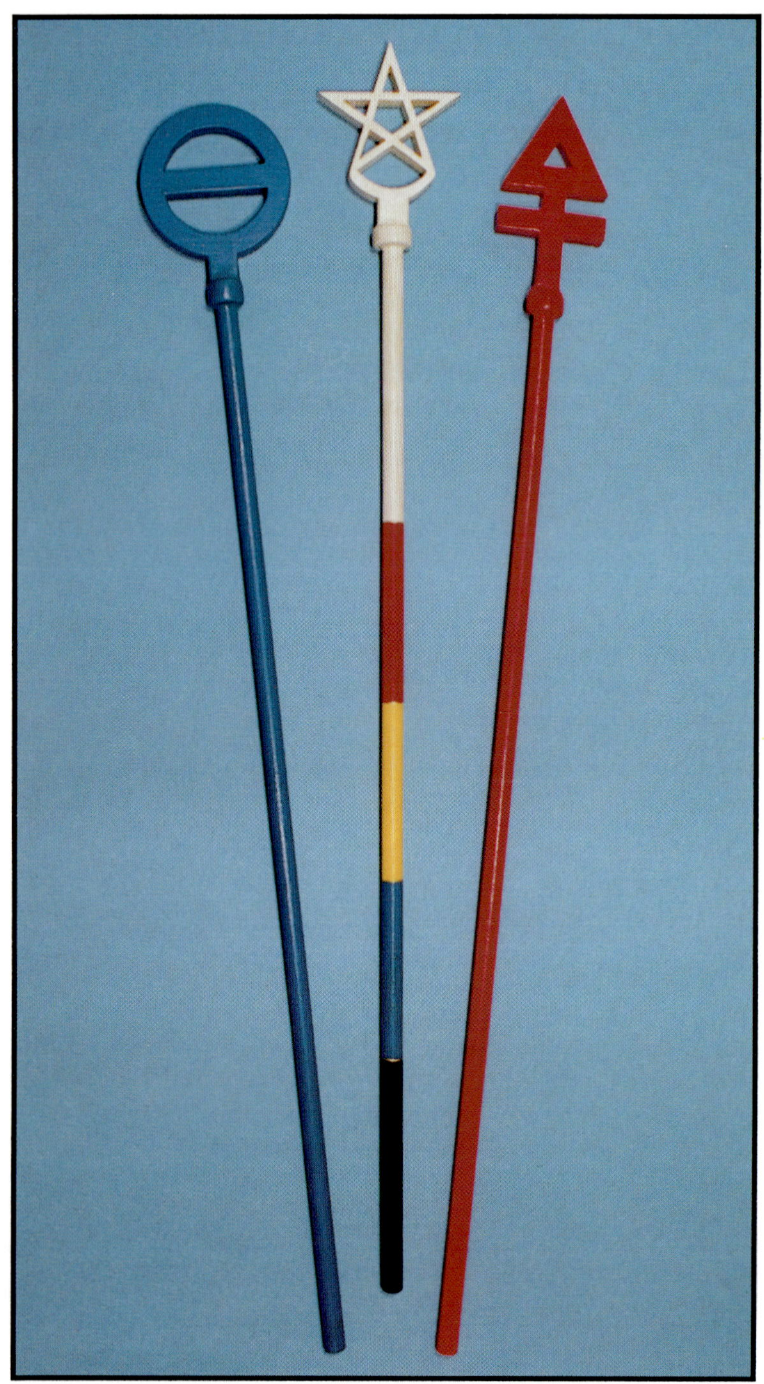

The Portal Wands

The Phoenix Collar and Rose Cross Lamen
of the Chief Adept

The Lamens

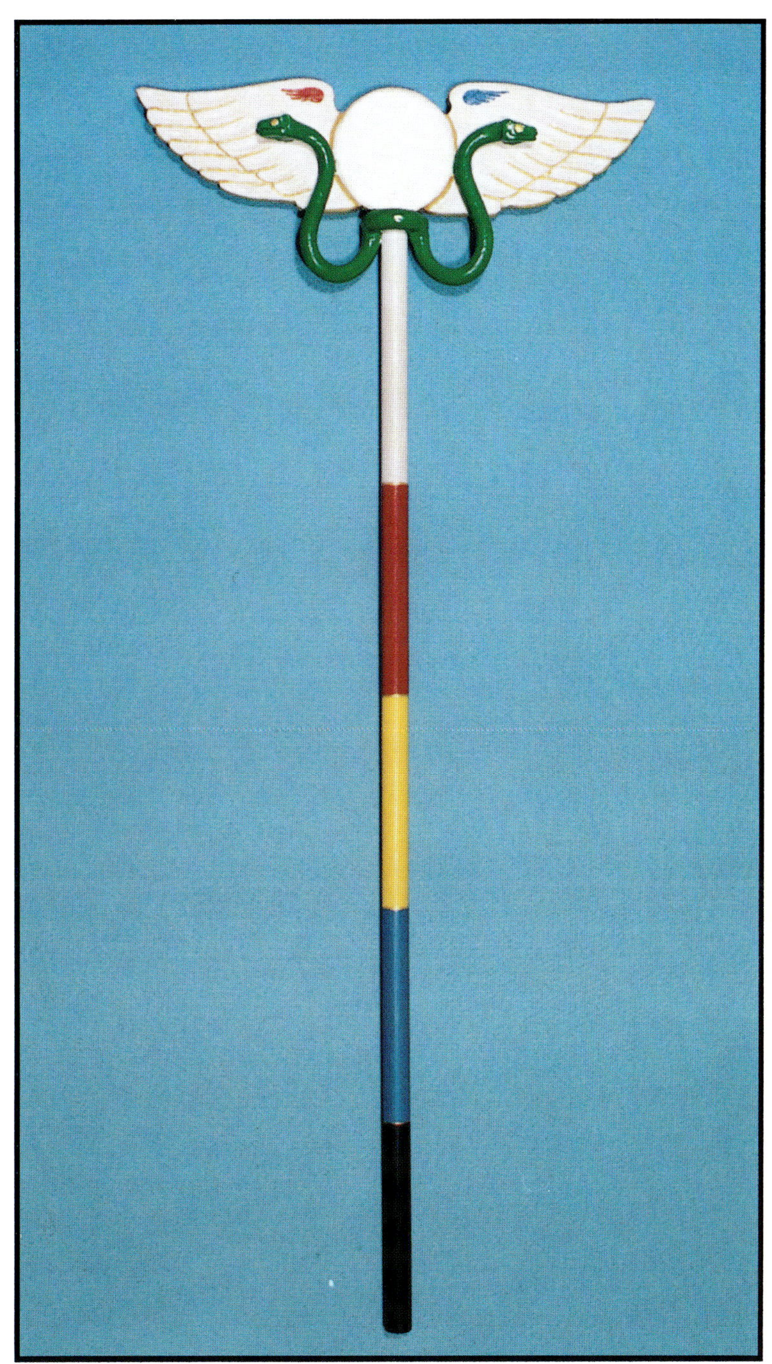

The Chief Adept's Wand

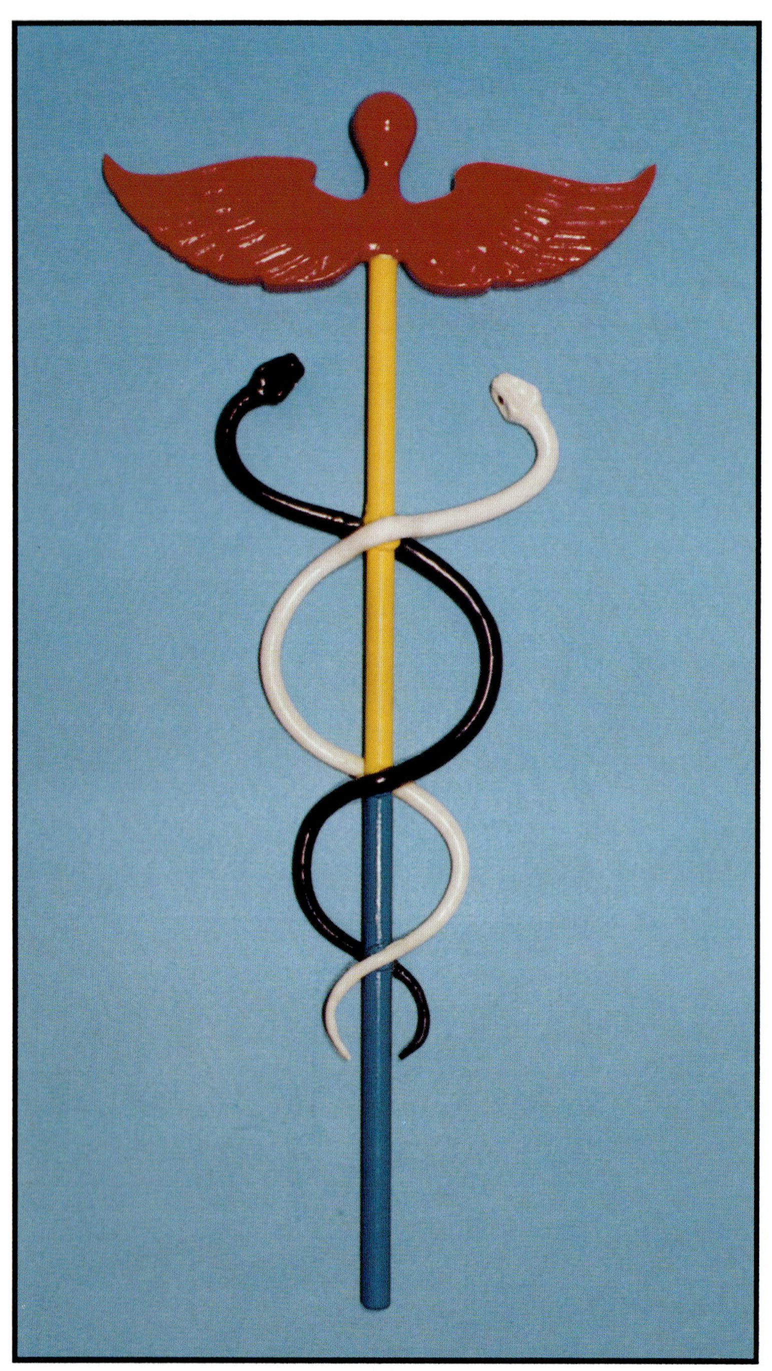

The Caduceus Wand of the Kerux

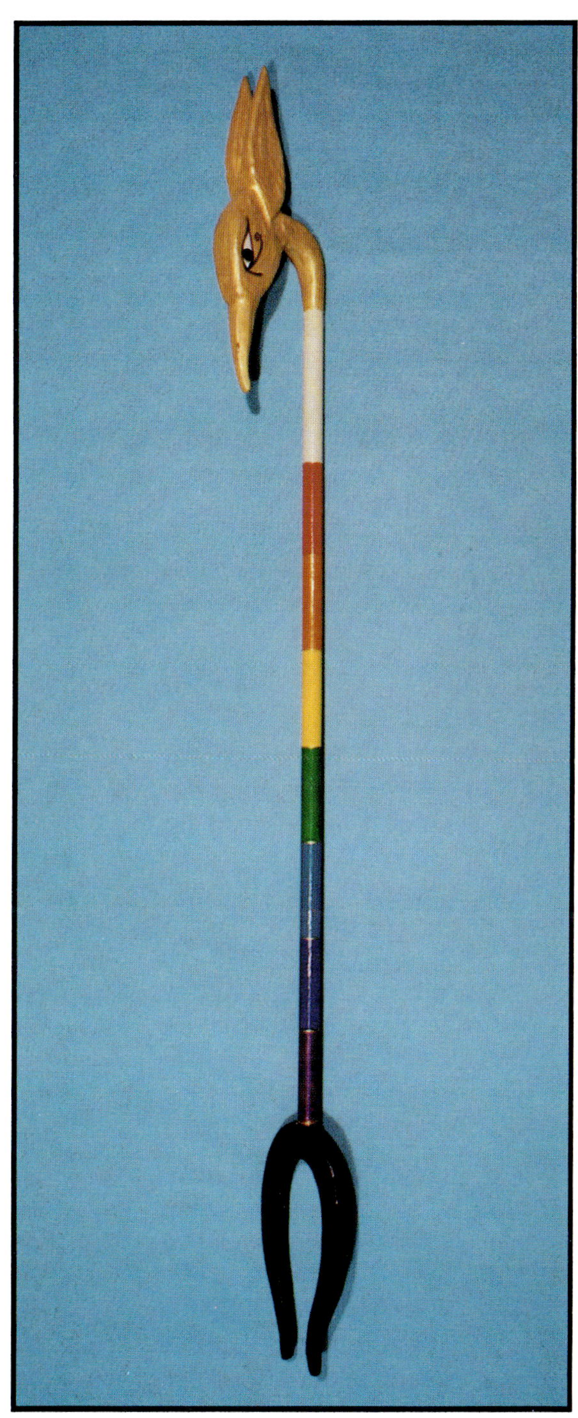

The Phoenix Wand

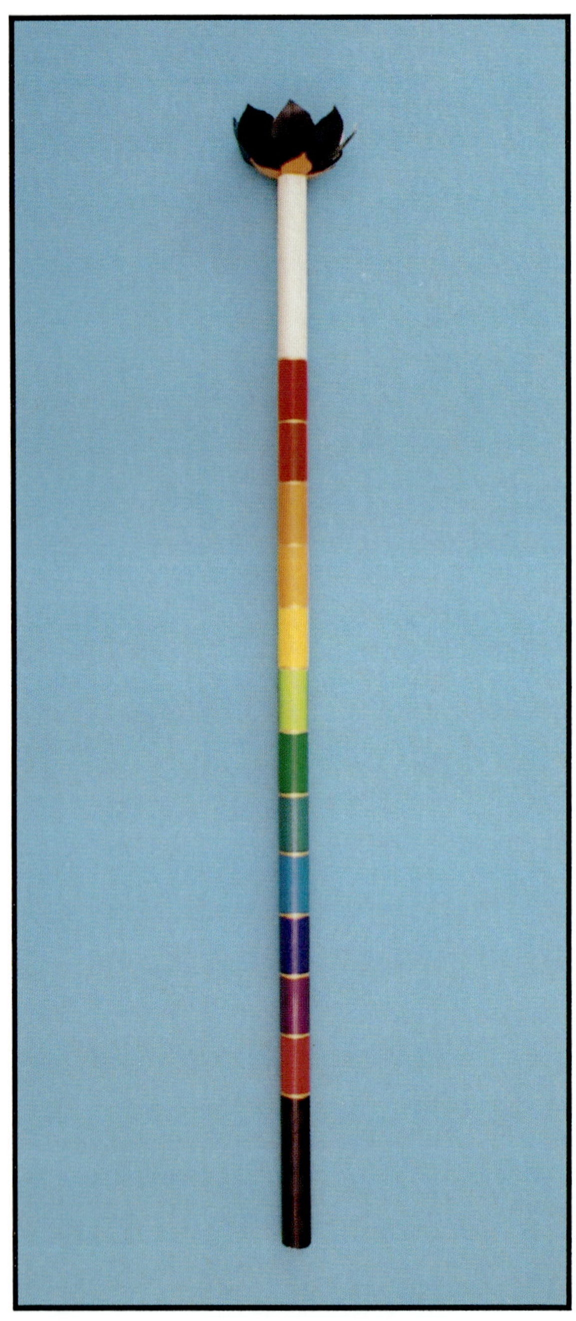

The Lotus Wand

The Enochian Air Tablet

The Ur-uatchti
(Chief Adept's Wand)

Tools Needed

- Scroll saw
- Craft knife with wood carving blade
- Sandpaper (medium and fine grade)
- Artist's brushes (medium to very fine)

Construction

1. Trace the cross portion of the lamen onto the 6" square piece of wood. Trace the four glories separately on the ⅛" basswood. Trace the circle for the rose on the ⅛" basswood. (See Figure 59, page 158.)

2. Cut out all sections of the lamen.

3. Paint the front and sides of the cross with gold paint. Paint the back of the cross and the four glories white. Let dry.

4. Glue the four glories to the cross at the junction of the arms. Let dry. Fill in any gaps with wood putty. Sand with medium sandpaper, apply a coat of gesso, and allow to dry. Sand lightly with fine sandpaper and add another coat if needed. Put the cross aside for the moment.

5. Trace three rows of petals onto the circular rose section. (Be sure to draw the small rose cross in the center of the rose as well.) Using a knife with carving blade, gouge out a slight depression in the center of each rose petal. When finished, the rose section should have a three-dimensional look.

6. Cover the front part of the rose with a coat of gesso. Sand with fine sandpaper. When gesso is dry, paint the front of the rose red. Let dry.

7. Apply glue to the back of the rose and attach to the cross. Paint the small center cross gold. The small circle behind the cross is to remain white. If desired, outline all the petals of the rose (including the red five-petaled rose in the center) with a thin line of black. The small glories behind the five-petaled rose should be green. When dry, cover with a coat of sealant for protection.

Admission Badges of the Portal Grade

The Greek Cross of Five Squares

The *Greek Cross of Five Squares* is the Admission Badge to the "Ritual of the Cross and the Four Elements" in the Portal grade. It symbolizes the equated forces of the four elements ruled by the fifth element of *eth,* or Spirit. In addition, the number five alludes to the powers of the Pentagram; this cross could well be described as a Pentagram in the shape of a cross. It is described in the Portal ceremony as:

> *...a Cross of corrosion, corruption, disintegration and death. Therefore doth it fall in the Paths of Death and the Devil, unless in Hod, the Glory triumpheth over matter and the Corruptible putteth on Incorruption, thus attaining unto the beauty of Tiphareth; unless in Netzach, Death is swallowed up in Victory and the Transformer becometh the Transmuter into Pure Alchemic Gold. 'Except ye be born of Water and the Spirit, ye cannot enter the Kingdom of God.'*[16]

This refers to some very basic alchemic principles. In the science of alchemy, purification arises out of separation, out of the various processes that transpire during the work with separation. Dissolution, also known as separation, is a form of decomposition—a breaking up into component parts. This is a crucial part of alchemic purification. That which is not essential is separated from that which is. That which is pure is freed from the impure. There is a natural and hidden Fire within humanity that brings forth a cleansing process through heat, putrefaction, and distillation—until the pure essence is revealed. Only that which has endured the "trial by Fire" has been purified. Only that which complies with the trial of devotion and love is pure.

This cross is given to the candidate as a symbol of his or her various component "parts." The candidate symbolically examines and scrutinizes the separate parts, which represents the act of decomposition—a necessary step to purification. The different elements must be carefully equilibrated—any imbalance must be sacrificed. (Although we are discussing symbolic ritual acts, these processes must also occur in the psyche of the individual.) Until the initiate has prepared the psyche through separation and purification, he or she cannot receive the mystical eth, the philosophical mercury (Spirit), whereby through knowledge and understanding the lesser is transmuted into the greater. Only then can the true and indissolvible Stone of the Wise be found within as a source of strength and inspiration.

The Greek Cross of Five Squares is designed to be worn by the candidate.

Refer to Figure 60, page 161 for construction diagrams.

Materials Needed

- One 10" x 10" piece of 1/8" thick masonite
- Gesso
- One yard of gold chain (approximately 1/8" thickness)
- Two small brass eye-rings
- Acrylic paint: white, black, red, blue, yellow
- Sealant

Tools Needed

- Jigsaw or scroll saw
- Electric drill with 1/8" bit
- Needle-nose pliers
- Wire cutters
- Sandpaper (all grades)
- Medium artist's brushes

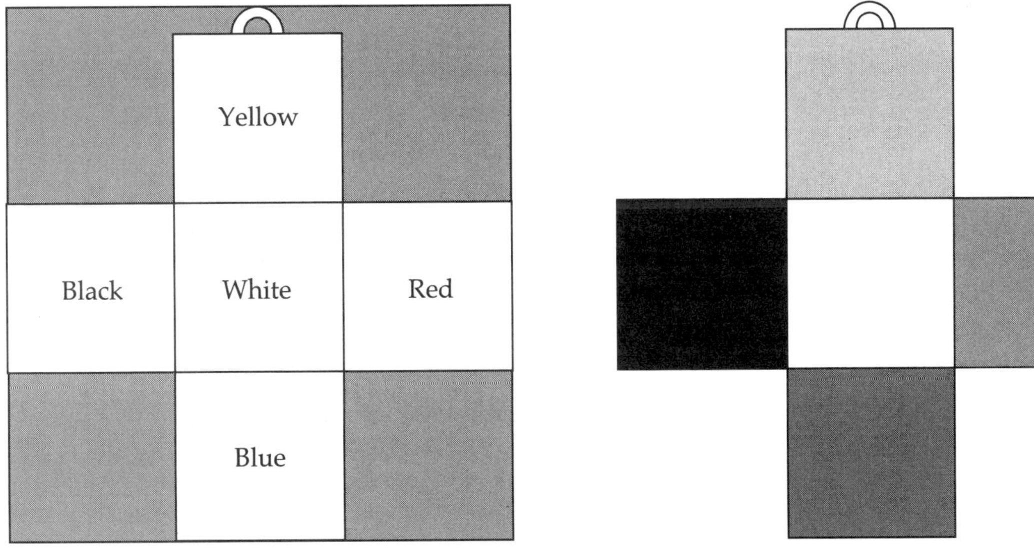

Figure 60: The Greek Cross of Five Squares

Construction

1. Measure out a cross on the masonite that consists of five 3" x 3" squares. The total size of the cross will be 9" x 9". Draw a semicircular "lip" which sticks out about ⅝" from the top square of the cross. (Note: if desired, one could leave the "lip" off the cross entirely and simply glue a piece of hook and loop fastener material to the back of the Admission Badge. The cross could be attached to a collar similar to the kind described in chapter one, page 81.)
2. With the saw, cut out the cross, including the lip, in one piece as shown in the diagram.
3. Using a ⅛" bit, drill a hole into the center of the lip.
4. Sand the edges of the cross smooth. (Begin with course sandpaper and finish with medium sandpaper.) Cover the cross on both sides with gesso. Let dry. Sand lightly with fine sandpaper.

Finishing Steps

5. On the smooth side of the masonite, lightly draw four lines which separate the five squares of the cross. Paint the squares thus:
   - Top square: Yellow
   - Left square: Black
   - Middle square: White
   - Bottom square: Blue
   - Right square: Red
6. When the paint is dry, apply sealant for protection.
7. Using wire cutters, cut off a 3" section of gold chain and stick it through the hole in the lip.
8. Take one of the small brass eye-rings and open it with the needle-nose pliers. Slip both ends of the 3" chain over the opened ends of the eye-ring. Close the eye-ring back up again. You will now have a small closed length of chain attached to the cross.
9. Cut about 3" off the remaining length of chain, leaving a 30" piece. Run this piece through the chain attached to the cross.
10. Take the other eye-ring and attach both ends of the long chain to it as before. The chain is now complete and able to be hung around the neck like a lamen.

The Hiereus' Lamen Admission Badge

The Hiereus' Lamen Badge is the Admission Badge to the "Rite of the Pentagram and the Five Paths" in the Portal grade. This lamen is based on the Hiereus' Lamen in the Neophyte Hall—a triangle within a circle (see chapter one, page 77.) However, the symbolism of this badge is more complex, as indicated by its description in the Portal ceremony:

> *...the Triangle in the Circle is the High symbol of the Holy Trinity, and the first three Sephiroth and of Binah wherein is the Sphere of Saturn, Ruler of the Path Tau....The Lamen in its more special attributions to the Hiereus, has the following meanings. In the circle are the Four Sephiroth, Tiphareth, Netzach, Hod, and Yesod. The first three mark the angles of the Triangle inscribed within, while the side are the Paths of Nun, Ayin and Peh, respectively. In the centre is marked the Letter Samekh indicating the 25th Path.*
>
> *While the wheel revolves, the hub is still. Seek ever then the centre, look from without to within.*[17]

(Note: See *Ritual Use of Magical Tools*, chapter three, "A Guided Visualization for the Portal Grade.") Refer to Figure 61 for construction diagram.

Materials Needed

- 5" x 5" piece of plywood, ¼" thick
- Wood putty
- Gesso
- Paints: yellow, violet, red, orange, green, blue, blue-violet, blue-green, white, and black
- Clear lacquer finish

Tools Needed

- Electric jigsaw or coping saw
- Compass, pencil, and straight edge
- File or rasp
- Artist's brushes (fine and medium sizes)
- Sandpaper (medium and fine)

Figure 61: The Hiereus' Lamen Admission Badge

Construction

Follow steps 1–3 given for the Caduceus Badge in chapter two, page 119.

Finishing Steps

4. Paint the badge as follows :

    - Ground color: Black
    - Tiphareth circle: Yellow
    - Hod circle: Orange
    - Ayin: Blue-violet
    - Peh: Red
    - Triangle and outer circle: White
    - Netzach circle: Green
    - Yesod circle: Violet
    - Nun: Blue-green
    - Samekh: Blue

6. After all the paint has dried, apply a sealant for protection.

The Enochian Tablets

The *Enochian* or *Angelic Tablets,* which include the four Elemental Tablets along with the Tablet of Union, originated from a system of magic that was developed from the ceremonial skrying of Dr. John Dee and Edward Kelly. Beginning in 1582, the Elizabethan magician and his seer continued to uncover the Enochian system over a period of seven years. The two men accumulated a great quantity of work, including an entire language with its own unique alphabet and syntax. This language, known as the "Secret Angelic Language," became known as Enochian because supposedly it was the angelic language revealed to Enoch by the angel Ave. The structure of the Enochian system was based on a cipher of numerological and set permutations of elements arranged on grids of letters known as the Elemental Tablets. From these tablets were derived the names of various elemental powers, angels, beings, and spiritual dominions known as aethyrs.

It was not until MacGregor Mathers incorporated it into the Golden Dawn curriculum 300 years later that the Enochian scheme of magic became a truly effective and powerful system. Enochian is the unifying system of magic that underlies much of the practical work of the Golden Dawn within the higher grades. It combines Qabalah, tarot, geomancy, and astrology, as well as elemental, planetary, and astral work into a unified and comprehensive system. In fact, the Enochian system is so all-encompassing that we will not attempt to describe it in full detail here. We strongly suggest that the reader study the section dealing with Enochian in Regardie's book *The Golden Dawn* (pages 623–696) for more information on the subject.

The Enochian Tablets are four in number, each referring to one of the elements: Earth, Air, Fire, and Water. In addition to these four, there is another smaller tablet, which is called the Tablet of Union, referring to the fifth element of *æther* or Spirit. It is a small tablet of twenty squares, five letters wide and four deep. (See Figure 69 on page 176.) The first line, EXARP, is attributed to Air. HCOMA, the second line, is assigned to Water. NANTA, the third line, alludes to Earth. Finally, the fourth line, BITOM, is attributed to Fire. The function of the tablet, as its name implies, is to unite and bind together the four Elemental Tablets. For purposes of study, the four Elemental Tablets (or Watchtowers) are arranged, as are the elements, in the Pentagram (see Figure 62).

To each tablet are referred innumerable attributions, the principal elementary ones being those of color. Certain squares on each tablet were painted in the color of the element, according to the King Scale, while others were left wholly or partly white. Thus in each tablet there are four principal types of squares (see Figure 63, page 166):

- *Great Cross* of thirty-six squares, lettered in black on white, in the center of the tablet
- *Sephirotic Calvary Crosses*, lettered in black on white, in the four corners of each tablet
- *Kerubic Squares*, which are always in the elemental color of the tablet, and are the four squares immediately above each Sephirotic Cross
- *Servient Squares*, always in the elemental color of the tablet, consist of the sixteen squares of each lesser angle beneath each Sephirotic Cross

The most important item on each Angelic Tablet is the central Great Cross whose shaft descends from top to bottom and divides the tablet from left to right. This cross comprises thirty-six squares and has a double vertical line, which is called *Linea Dei Patris Filiique*, the "Line of God the Father and the Son," and a horizontal line called *Linea Spiritus Sancti*, the "Line of the Holy Spirit." The Linea Spiritus Sancti is always the seventh line or rank of letters from the top, while the two vertical columns of the Linea Dei Patris Filique are always the sixth and seventh columns, counting from either right or left. The Great Cross is the mechanism which divides the tablet…it separates and binds together the four quarters, subelements, or lesser angles as they are called, from one another.

Figure 62: The Pentagram Arrangement of the Enochian Tablets

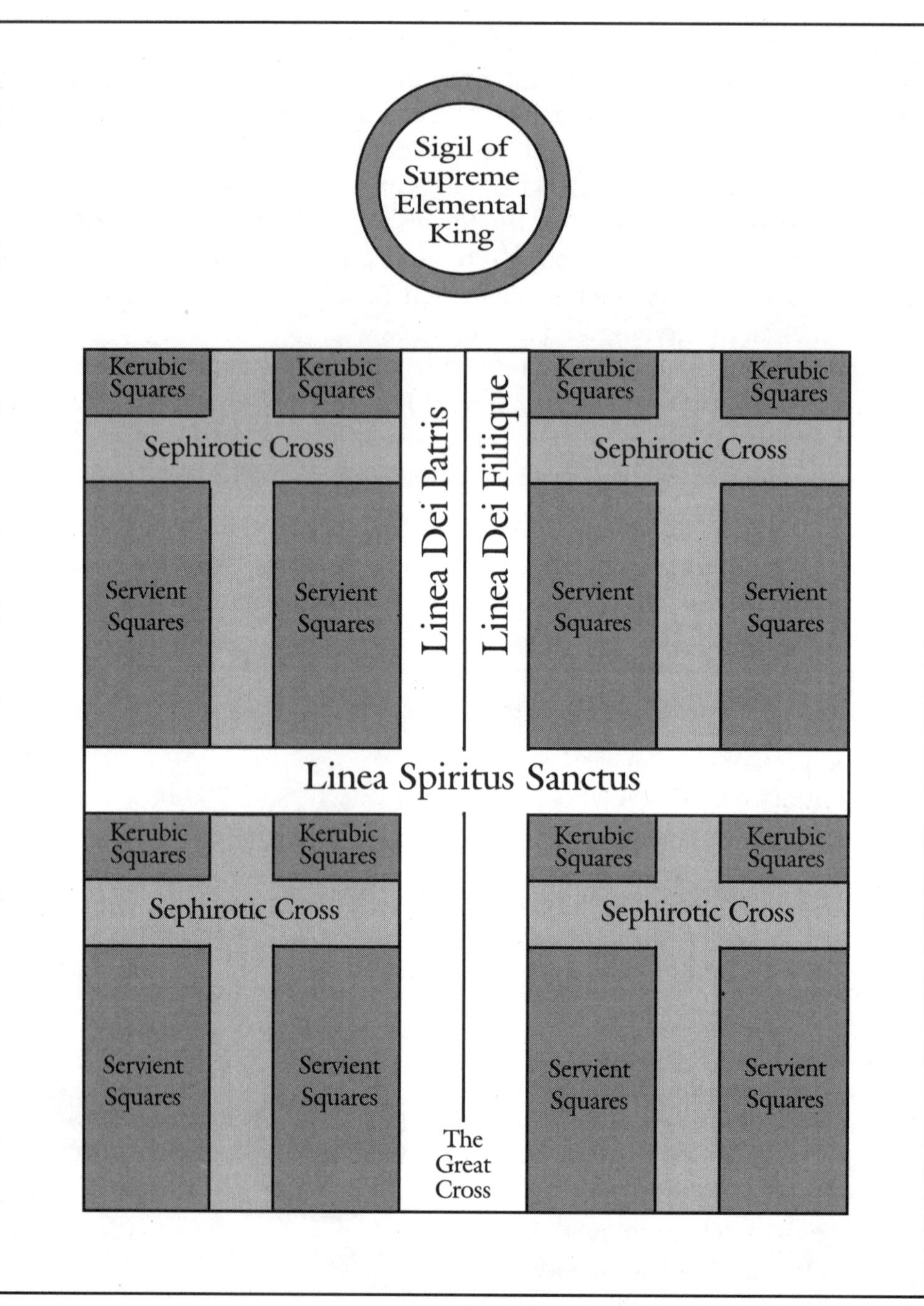

Figure 63: The Basic Enochian Tablet

From this Great Cross of letters, various angelic and divine names are produced, which are of supreme importance. First of all there are the Three Great Secret Holy Names of God which are found in the Linea Spiritus Sancti. This line comprises twelve letters, which are divided into names of three, four, and five letters reading from left to right. Thus in the Air tablet, you will find ORO IBAH AOZPI; in the Water tablet MPH ARSL GAIOL; in the Earth tablet MOR DIAL HCTGA; and in the Fire tablet OIP TEAA PDOCE.

The Three Secret Holy Names of God are the major names of the tablets. These names are conceived to be borne as ensigns on the banners of the Great King of each quarter. The name of the Great King is always a name of eight letters and comprises a spiral or whirl in the center of the Great Cross. The kings of Air, Water, Fire, and Earth are *Bataivah, Raagiosel, Edelperna,* and *Ic Zod Heh Hal.* The king is a very powerful force, and since it initiates the whirl, it is to be invoked with due care.

The next series of important names obtained from the Great Cross are the Six Seniors. Their names begin from the sixth and seventh squares of the Linea Spiritus Sancti, including these squares, and read *outward from the center* along the three lines of the Great Cross to the edge of the tablet. Each is a name of seven letters. The eight-lettered name of the king and the six names of the seniors are invoked by means of the Hexagram. They are attributed to the sun and planets and are on a different and higher plane than the elemental names.

In the center of each lesser angle or quarter will be seen a cross of ten squares. This is called the Sephirotic Calvary Cross. From the letters of this cross are taken two divine names which call forth and control the angels and spirits of the lesser angle, and their names are used in a preliminary invocation when working magically with a square of a lesser angle. From the vertical line of the Sephirotic Cross, reading from above downward, comes a deity name of six letters known as the *Angel of Call*. From the crossbar, reading from left to right, comes a deity name of five letters, the *Angel of Command*. These deities are invoked using the Pentagram and their names must always be read in the directions described previously.

We now come to the colored squares grouped above and below the Sephirotic Cross in each of the four angles. The most important are the four above the crossbar of the Sephirotic Cross—called the *Kerubic Squares*. From these four squares are derived four names of four letters each. Thus, for the top rank of the airy angle of the Fire tablet, we have the letters DO(N)PA which gives us DOPA, OPAD, PADO, ADOP. (Note: The white square in the center belongs to the Sephirotic Cross and is not included in the names derived from the Kerubic squares.) These four names, the names of the four Kerubic angels of the lesser angle, rule the servient squares below the Sephirotic Cross, and of the four, the first is the most powerful as the others are derived therefrom. By prefixing to these four names a letter from the appropriate line of the Tablet of Union, we obtain even more powerful names, archangelic in character. Thus for the Kerubic rank of the Air lesser angle of the Fire tablet (used as our example), the letter "B" of the word "BITOM" on the Tablet of Union is prefixed. This produces BDOPA, BOPAD, BPADO, and BADOP.

The rule is that the first letter of the appropriate line of the Tablet of Union is prefixed only to the names formed from the Kerubic squares. As an example of this method applied to the remaining servient squares, we find:

- "I" is added to the sixteen servient squares of the angle of Air
- "T" is added to the sixteen servient squares of the angle of Water
- "O" is added to the sixteen servient squares of the angle of Earth
- "M" is added to the sixteen servient squares of the angle of Fire

Thus, BITOM will be used entirely on the Fire Tablet and is never used on the other three tablets. The first letter applies to the Kerubic squares of each of the four lesser angles, while the remaining four letters apply to the sixteen servient squares of those angles as shown above. (Thus, in the Air lesser angle of the Fire tablet, the sixteen servient squares will yield a total of sixteen angelic names. The letter "I" can be prefixed to all of them: IOPMN, IPMNO, IMNOP, INOPM, etc.)

The ritual for the consecration of the Four Elemental Weapons gives excellent examples of the archangelic names formed from the Kerubic Squares by the addition of letters from the Tablet of Union.

The reader should note that the Elemental Tablets presented in this book are in accord with the final version revealed to Dee and Kelly by the archangel Raphael on April 20, 1587, and not those described in the Enochian manuscripts presented in Regardie's *The Golden Dawn*. The main difference is that we have avoided the use of "double letter" squares. (See Color Plates 3, 5, 7, and 9 and Figures 64–67, pages 169–172.)

Again the student would be well-advised to seek out further information on this subject.

The Four Elemental Tablets

Materials Needed

- ¾" plywood (pine or birch) in 4' x 8' sheets (you will need ½ of a sheet)
- Wood putty
- Gesso
- Acrylic paints: white, black, red, yellow, blue, green, orange, and violet
- Sealant

r	Z	i	l	a	f	A	y	t	l	p	a
a	r	d	Z	a	i	d	p	a	L	a	m
c	z	o	n	s	a	r	o	Y	a	v	b
T	o	i	T	t	z	o	P	a	c	o	C
S	i	g	a	s	o	m	r	b	z	n	h
f	m	o	n	d	a	T	d	i	a	r	i
o	r	o	i	b	A	h	a	o	z	p	i
t	N	a	b	r	V	i	x	g	a	s	d
O	i	i	i	t	T	p	a	l	O	a	i
A	b	a	m	o	o	o	a	C	v	c	a
N	a	o	c	O	T	t	n	p	r	n	T
o	c	a	n	m	a	g	o	t	r	o	i
S	h	i	a	l	r	a	p	m	z	o	x

Figure 64: The Enochian Tablet of Air

T	a	O	A	d	v	P	t	D	n	i	m
a	a	b	c	o	o	r	o	m	e	b	b
T	o	g	c	o	n	x	m	a	l	G	m
n	h	o	d	D	i	a	l	e	a	o	c
P	a	t	A	x	i	o	V	s	P	s	И
S	a	a	i	x	a	a	r	V	r	o	i
m	P	h	a	r	s	l	g	a	i	o	l
M	a	m	g	l	o	i	n	L	i	r	x
o	l	a	a	D	n	g	a	T	a	P	a
P	a	L	c	o	i	d	x	P	a	c	n
n	d	a	z	N	z	i	V	a	a	s	a
i	i	d	P	o	n	s	d	A	s	P	i
x	r	i	n	h	t	a	r	n	d	i	⅃

Figure 65: The Enochian Tablet of Water

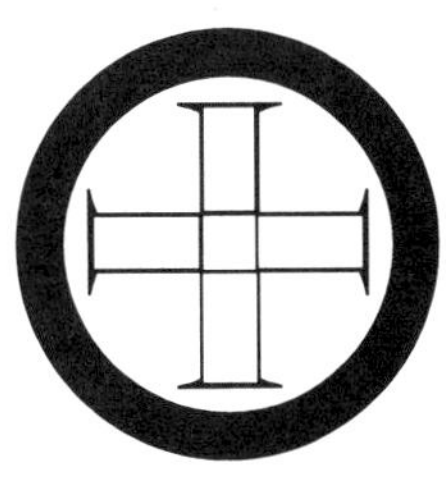

b	O	a	Z	a	R	o	P	h	a	R	a
v	N	n	a	x	o	P	S	o	n	d	n
a	i	g	r	v	n	o	o	m	a	g	g
o	r	P	m	n	i	n	g	b	e	a	l
r	s	O	n	i	z	i	r	l	e	m	v
i	z	i	n	r	C	z	i	a	M	h	l
M	O	r	d	i	a	l	h	C	t	G	a
O	C	a	n	c	h	i	a	s	o	m	t
A	r	b	i	z	m	i	i	l	P	i	z
O	P	a	n	a	L	a	m	S	m	a	P
d	O	l	o	P	i	n	i	a	n	b	a
r	x	P	a	o	c	s	i	z	i	x	P
a	x	t	i	r	V	a	s	t	r	i	m

Figure 66: The Enochian Tablet of Earth

d	o	n	p	a	T	d	a	n	V	a	a
o	l	o	a	G	e	o	o	b	a	v	a
O	P	a	m	n	o	V	G	m	d	n	m
a	p	l	s	T	e	d	e	c	a	o	p
s	c	m	i	o	o	n	A	m	l	o	x
V	a	r	s	G	d	L	b	r	i	a	p
o	i	P	t	e	a	a	p	D	o	c	e
p	s	v	a	c	n	r	Z	i	r	Z	a
S	i	o	d	a	o	i	n	r	z	f	m
d	a	l	t	T	d	n	a	d	i	r	e
d	i	x	o	m	o	n	s	i	o	s	p
O	o	D	p	z	i	A	p	a	n	l	i
r	g	o	a	n	n	q	A	C	r	a	r

Figure 67: The Enochian Tablet of Fire

Tools Needed

- Table saw or circular saw
- Sandpaper (course, medium, and fine)
- Artist's brushes (coarse, medium, and fine)
- Compass

Construction

1. Lay out the half sheet of plywood. Measure off four sections of wood that are 20" x 16". Cut apart all sections with saw.
2. Fill in any gaps with wood putty. Sand all edges smooth (begin with course sandpaper and finish with medium sandpaper). Coat entirely (front, sides, and back) with gesso. Let dry. Sand lightly with fine sandpaper.
3. Take one of the tablets and draw a 12" x 13" square on its front side. (Note: this square is to be 5" from the top edge and 2" from the sides and bottom.)
4. Mark off the 12" x 13" figure completely into 1" squares. (There will be a total of 156 square inches.)
5. At the top of the tablet, where there is a 5" wide white area, find the center and draw a 3" circle using a compass. (Center it between the top edge and the squared-off region.)

Finishing Steps

6. The tablets are to be painted in the King Scale color of the each particular element. The Kerubic and Servient squares of each Elemental Tablet are colored as follows:
   - Fire tablet: Red
   - Air tablet: Yellow
   - Water tablet: Blue
   - Earth tablet: Black
7. The white areas (excluding the borders) will remain white with black letters in all four tablets.
8. Each tablet is divided into four "quarters," which are attributed to the four elements. Thus, on every tablet: the bottom right quarter is attributed to Fire, the top right quarter is assigned to Water, the top left quarter is Air, and the bottom left quarter is Earth. The letters on the colored areas of each tablet (the Kerubic and Servient squares) are to be painted as follows:

Fire Tablet

- Top left: Air—yellow letters on red
- Bottom left: Earth—black letters on red
- Top right: Water—blue letters on red
- Bottom right: Fire—green letters on red

Water Tablet

- Top left: Air—yellow letters on blue
- Bottom left: Earth—black letters on blue
- Top right: Water—orange letters on blue
- Bottom right: Fire—red letters on blue

Air Tablet

- Top left: Air—violet letters on yellow
- Bottom left: Earth—black letters on yellow
- Top right: Water—blue letters on yellow
- Bottom right: Fire—red letters on yellow

Earth Tablet

- Top left: Air—yellow letters on black
- Bottom left: Earth—white letters on black[18]
- Top right: Water—blue letters on black
- Bottom right: Fire—red letters on black

9. All 1" lettered squares should be separated from one another with a thin black line. (Note: This can be painted with acrylic paint, but one needs a steady hand and patience to do it. Another effective way is to use a straight edge and a ballpoint pen with permanent, nonrunning black ink.)

10. The sigils of the Angelic Tablets are to be painted in the upper circle according to Figure 68, page 175:

    - Air: A symbol of a T with four Yods above it
    - Water: A Cross Potent, with two letters (b. b.), a figure 4, and a figure 6 in the angles
    - Earth: A simple Cross Potent in the four colors of Malkuth
    - Fire: A circle with twelve rays

11. When all tablets are painted and dry, apply a coat of sealant.

12. A hook or wire can be attached to the back of each tablet, so that they may be hung on the four walls of the temple. If the walls of the temple are not conducive to hanging objects, tablet stands similar to the banner poles can be constructed and painted in the appropriate elemental colors. (See pages 15–17 for Banner Pole construction.)

The Tablet of Union

Refer to Figure 69, page 176 for construction diagram.

Materials Needed

- ¾" pine or birch plywood (use the leftover piece from the Elemental Tablets)
- Wood putty
- Gesso
- Acrylic paints: white, black, red, yellow, blue
- 6" x 7" piece of white felt material

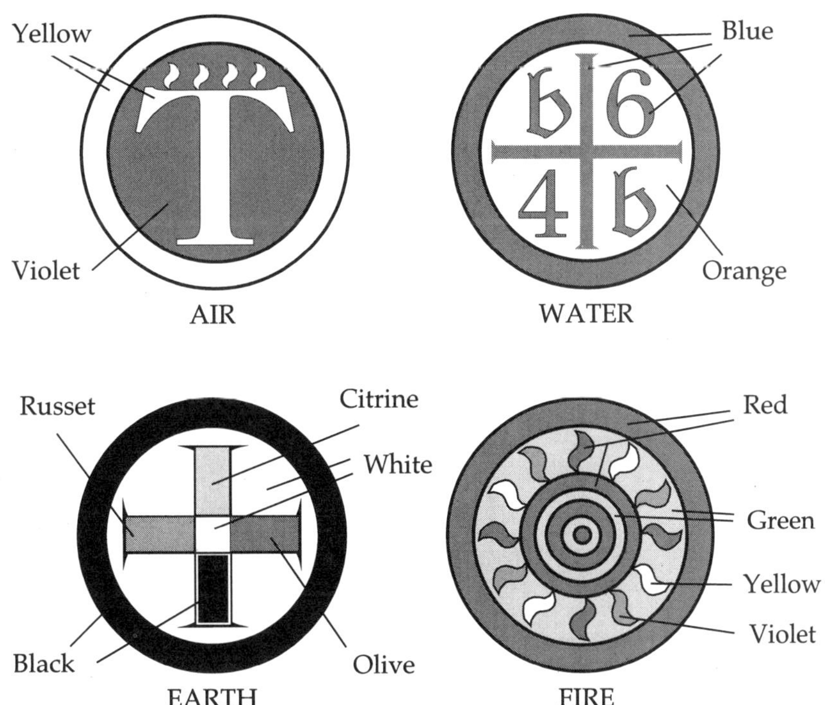

Figure 68: Sigils of the Enochian Tablets

- Fabric glue
- Sealant: clear lacquer finish

Tools Needed

- Table saw or circular saw
- Sandpaper (coarse, medium, and fine)
- Artist's brushes (coarse, medium, and fine)
- Scissors

Construction

1. Measure off a piece of wood that is 7" x 6". Cut out with saw.
2. Fill in any gaps with wood putty. Sand all edges smooth (begin with course sandpaper and finish with medium sandpaper). Coat entirely (front, sides, and back) with gesso. Sand lightly with fine sandpaper. Let dry. Coat front and sides with white paint.
3. On one side of the piece, draw a 5" x 4" square. There will be a 1" white border all around the square. Mark off the 5" x 4" figure completely into 1" squares. (There will be a total of 20 square inches.)

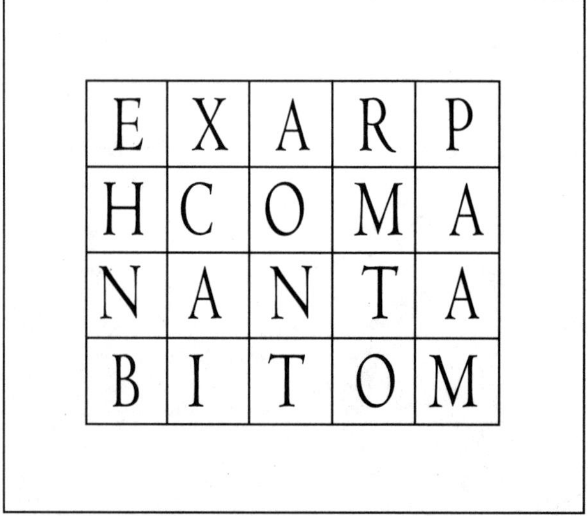

Figure 69: The Tablet of Union

Finishing Steps

4. Take the white felt material and cut out a 7" x 6" square piece. Glue the felt to the back side of the tablet. (This will keep it from scratching the altar.) Pile a few heavy books on the top side of the tablet to insure that the felt is well secured to the wood. Allow to dry.

5. Paint the appropriate letters into the squares as shown in the diagram: Top line—EXARP in yellow letters; second line—HCOMA in blue letters; third line—NANTA in black letters; and for the last line—BITOM in red.

6. All 1" lettered squares should be separated from one another with a thin black line. When all the paint is dry, apply sealant.

Endnotes

1. Regardie, *The Golden Dawn*, 219.
2. Ibid., 203.
3. Ibid., 209.
4. Ibid., 216.
5. In the Qabalistic division of the soul, Hod, Netzach, and Yesod comprise the astral triad of the personality. This is the abode of the waking personality that is normally concerned with worldly affairs, but which can be disciplined into becoming a valuable aid for the higher self.
6. Regardie, *The Golden Dawn*, 215.
7. Ibid., 84.
8. Cirlot, 316–317.
9. Regardie, *The Golden Dawn*, 84.
10. Cirlot, 42.
11. The five points of the Pentagram correspond to the body of a man, with one head, two arms, and two legs. The upright Pentagram, which symbolizes Spirit over matter, is a powerful symbol for good, but when the Pentagram is inverted, it symbolizes matter over Spirit, which is why the inverted Pentagram is considered evil. The Hexagram is the same figure whether inverted or upright. Therefore, it cannot be "turned to evil."
12. This is also one reason why the Earth Pentacle of the Z. A. M. is based on this design.
13. Regardie, *The Golden Dawn*, 205.
14. Cirlot, 68–71.
15. Ibid., 51.
16. Regardie, *The Golden Dawn*, 200.
17. Ibid, 213–214.
18. The discrepancy between the color plate of the Earth Tablet and the description of the Lesser Angle of the Earth Tablet given here is due to a discrepancy in the Enochian Manuscripts themselves. The document titled "The Book of Concourse of the Forces" states that: "The Kerubic and Servient squares on each Tablet are coloured in the elemental colour, with the letters drawn thereon in the complementary colour…"(See Regardie, *The Golden Dawn*, 635.) The manuscript then goes on to say that the letters on the black squares of the Earth quarter of the Earth Tablet are drawn in green. However, the complementary color of black is white, not green. We believe that the letters should be white.

Chapter Four

Implements of the Second Order

The Second Order is not really a part of the Golden Dawn. It is a separate Order, the *Ordo Roseae Rubae et Aureae Crucis*—the "Order of the Red Rose and Golden Cross." This Order, quite distinct from the Golden Dawn, is comprised of adepts who have attained grades ranging from 5=6 and 6=5 to 7=4. The higher grades of 8=3, 9=2, and 10=1 are ascribed to the invisible Third Order and cannot be attained by living persons (although some may claim to hold these high degrees honorarily). To use Regardie's words:

> *...it is impossible for the ordinary individual to understand those (grades) above the grade of Adeptus Minor, and individuals who lay claim openly to such exalted grades, by that very act place a gigantic question mark against the validity of their attainment. He that is exalted is humble.*[1]

It is the duty of the R. R. et A. C. to govern and teach the First Order of the Golden Dawn. The work of ceremonial magic begins upon the initiate's entrance into the Second or Inner Order. The Golden Dawn is strictly a teaching Order, but the R. R. et A. C.

is where the practical applications of magic truly commence. It is in the Second Order that the Initiate learns to construct and consecrate the elemental weapons and perform rituals of high magic.

The Second Order is essentially rooted in the spirit of Rosicrucianism, a spiritual philosophy founded on the life of Christian Rosencreutz, also known as C. R. C., the allegorical founder of the Brotherhood of the Rose Cross. This secretive order of initiates and adepts who studied alchemy, Qabalah, astrology, magic, and Christian mysticism surfaced in Europe around 1614. In 1892, MacGregor Mathers firmly established the ideals of Rosicrucianism into the R. R. et A. C. when he finished the elaborate initiation ceremony into the Adeptus Minor grade. Based on the legend of Christian Rosencreutz, this ritual involves the discovery of his tomb—known as the Vault of the Adepti. This chamber is the primary temple of the Second Order, and no one can be admitted to the R. R. et A. C. without it. No individual can claim to be of a high degree in the Order who has not taken an actual Adeptus Minor initiation performed in a physical vault by a qualified initiator. This chamber is highly charged once every year during the festival of Corpus Christi Day, the one day of the year when the Consecration of the Vault of the Adepti is performed. Corpus Christi means, of course, "the Body of Christ." This Catholic feast day, held in honor of the Eucharist, falls on a different day each year, owing to the fact that it is celebrated a certain number of days after Easter.[2] This tradition, adopted by the Second Order, was undoubtedly started by the early Rosicrucians who referred to it secretively as "Day C." Although some have suggested that the Consecration of the Vault of the Adepti marks the date of the summer solstice, the traditional date of the ceremony is determined by the feast day of Corpus Christi, which can fall anywhere from the end of May to the end of June. In fact, the Order does not ritually observe the solstices, only the equinoxes; the times when day and night are equal in length, alluding once more to the Middle Pillar and the balanced disposition of opposing forces.

The officers of the R. R. et A. C. wear lamens identical to those worn by the Chief Adept in the Portal grade, except that they are suspended by collars in the appropriate colors. The Chief Adept wears a large Rose Cross Lamen analogous to that described in chapter five, but suspended from a collar in the shape of a double-headed phoenix. The collar can be cut from leather and painted, or cut out of fabric and filled with a layer of polyester fiber or similar padding. (See Color Plate 11.)

The ritual clothing of an adept of the Second Order is a white Tau robe, yellow slippers or sandals, and a yellow-and-white striped nemyss. The Inner Order sash has been described in early Order papers as white and in later papers as yellow.[3]

As an initiate is advanced to the higher grades of the Second Order, the sash is ornamented with appropriate symbols.

In the following pages, the ritual implements of the Second Order, especially the wands, will be examined.

Implements of the Second Order

The Chief Adept's Wand: The Ur-uatchti

The *Ur-uatchti* is one of the most powerful and beautiful of all the wands of the Second Order. Outwardly, the Chief Adept's Wand is similar in appearance to that of the Keryx in the Outer Order. However, the symbolism of the Ur-uatchti includes the energies behind the Caduceus Wand and much more. The Chief Adept describes the wand in the Adeptus Minor Ceremony thus:

> *My Wand is surmounted by the Winged Globe, around which the twin Serpents of Egypt twine. It symbolizes the equilibrated force of the Spirit and the Four Elements beneath the everlasting wings of the Holy One.*[4]

This wand is therefore an extension of the Chief Adept's Wand in the Portal, in which the forces of the four elements are crowned and governed by the fifth element of Spirit. In this case, the linear form of spirit (the Pentagram) has been exchanged for the image of the winged globe, a dazzling visual symbol that captures the true essence of Spirit in a manner which speaks to us on a higher level.

The winged globe is one of the most widespread of ancient symbols. It is an emblem of the Sun and the heavens. In Egyptian texts, the Ur-uatchti is associated with Horus, the warrior and a protector god: "From the height of heaven he was able to see his father's enemies, and he chased them in the form of a great winged disk." (See Figure 70.) The text continues;

> *Finally, Horus and his companions went back to Nubia, to the town of Shashertet, where he destroyed the rebels of Uauat, and their ablest soldiers. When this was done Horus*

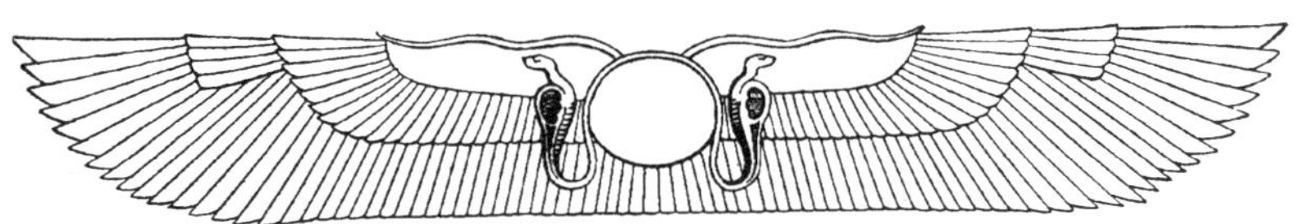

Figure 70: The Winged Disk

changed himself once more into the form of the winged sun-disk with uraei, and took with him the goddesses Nekhebet and Uatchit in the form of two serpents, that they might consume with fire any rebels who still remained. When the gods who were in his boat saw this they said, 'Great indeed is that which Horus hath done by means of his double snake diadem; he hath smitten the enemy who were afraid of him!' And Horus said, 'Henceforth let the double snake diadem of Heru-Behutet be called Ur-uatchti' and it was so. After these things Horus journeyed on in his ship, or boat, and arrived at Apollinopolis Magna (Edfu) and Thoth decreed that he should be called the 'Light-giver, who cometh forth from the horizon.' Hereupon Horus commanded Thoth that the winged sun-disk with uraei should be brought into every sanctuary of all the gods of the lands of the South and of the North, and in Amentet, in order that they might drive away evil from therein. Then Thoth made figures of the winged sun-disk with uraei, and distributed them among the Temples, and sanctuaries, and places wherein there were any gods, and this is what is meant by the winged disks with uraei which are seen over the entrances of the courts of the Temples of all the gods and goddesses of Egypt. The snake goddess on the right hand side of the disk is Nekhebet, and that on the left is Uatchti.[5]

According to Manly Hall, the Ur-uatchti is emblematic of the three persons of the Egyptian Trinity...that the wings, serpents, and solar orb are the insignia of Amoun, Rê, and Osiris.[6] Amoun, one of the oldest of the creator gods in the Egyptian pantheon, is attributed to the Sephirah of Chesed, the sphere symbolically occupied by the Chief Adept. The winged disk also represents matter in a state of sublimination and transfiguration. The wings indicate movement or flight—Spirit in motion. The two serpents allude to the harmony of opposing forces. The colors on the staff refer to the four elements of Fire, Air, Water, and Earth.

The Chief Adept uses the Ur-uatchti in the Inner Order to bring the forces of Spirit and light (L. V. X.) into the temple. The large Ur-uatchti, pictured in Color Plate 4, was used by Israel Regardie to consecrate the Vault of the Adepti at the Georgia temple in 1982. Based on a diagram of the wand shown in Crowley's Equinox, the wand is a full 26" from wing tip to wing tip. (This led Regardie to complain that the wand was simply "too damn big.") In response, a smaller, more manageable wand was constructed using the dimensions given here (see Color Plate 13 and also Figure 71, page 184). The Ur-uatchti can be used in any ritual where the Invocation of Spirit is needed. Because of its affinity with the sphere of Chesed, the Ur-uatchti can be employed whenever the energies of Mercy are needed. It can also be used to invoke or banish the forces of the elements (or those of the Three Mother Letters) with great effect. The protective powers of this wand can be utilized whenever strength and defense is called for (see *Ritual Use of Magical Tools*, chapter four).

Refer to Figure 71 on page 184 for construction diagrams.

Materials Needed

- One ¾" thick dowel approximately 29" long
- ¾" thick piece of soft wood approximately 4" x 14"
- One-pound box of oven-hardening clay
- One ¼" thick dowel or wooden peg 1" long
- One ¾" thick scrap piece of dowel approximately 3" long
- One ¾" thick piece of scrap wood approximately 4" x 8"
- Yellow carpenter's glue
- Wood putty
- Gesso
- Strong bonding glue such as epoxy
- Acrylic paints: red, yellow, blue, green, gold, white iridescent white, and black
- Sealant: clear lacquer finish

Tools Needed

- Jigsaw
- Electric drill with ¼" bit
- Rotary power tool with gouging and carving bits
- Sandpaper (all grades)
- Artist's brushes (large, medium, and fine)
- Cookie sheet (used for baking)

Construction: The Winged Globe

1. With the jigsaw, cut out the winged globe as one piece from the 14" length of wood, as shown in Figure 71, page 184.

2. With a pencil, draw stylized feathers on both sides of both wings. Use the rotary tool to gouge and grind the outline of the feathers, giving them a sculpted look. Sand the wings with course sandpaper until they have a smooth, three-dimensional appearance. Fill in any gaps with wood putty. Sand with medium sandpaper.

3. Find the center of the bottom edge, where the winged globe will be joined to the wand shaft. There drill a hole that is ¼" wide and ½" deep. Drill the same size hole into one end of the 29" long dowel. This will be the top end of the shaft.

The Serpents

4. Take some clay and knead it by hand until it is soft and pliable. Then roll out a 14" long rope of clay. The rope should be no thicker than ½". Add some extra clay to both

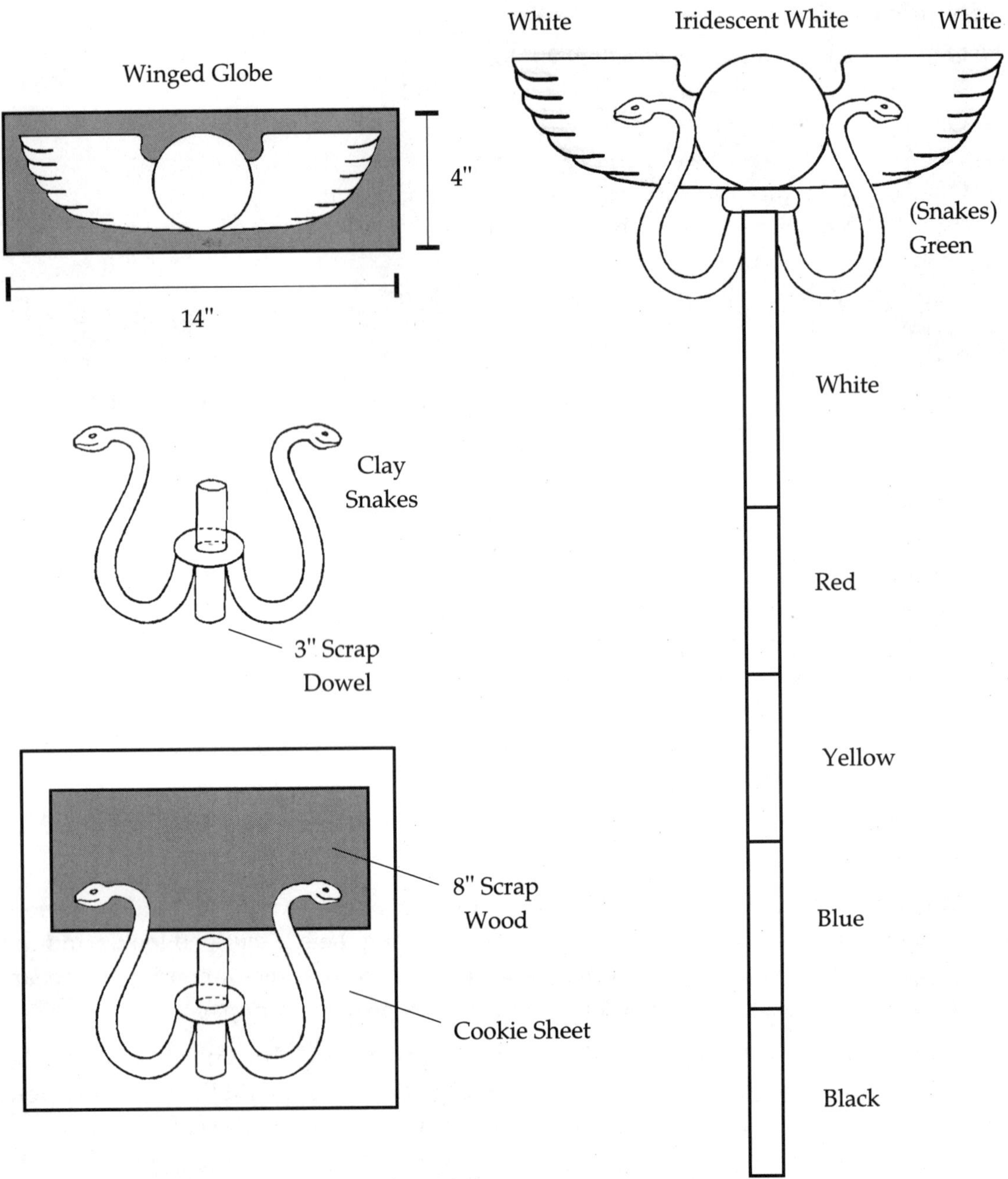

Figure 71: The Ur-uatchti

ends of the rope, and shape them into two diamond-shaped serpent heads. You now have a clay snake with two heads, one at each end. The mouth and eyes of the snakes can be drawn into the clay with a tooth pick or pin. Cut the two-headed snake in half.

5. Roll out another ½" thick rope of clay and shape into a perfect ring that fits over the 3" long piece of scrap dowel. Attach the two serpents firmly to the underside of the clay ring as shown in the diagram.

6. Take the 8" long piece of scrap wood and drape the upper halves of the serpents over it in the position they would occupy if draped over the actual head of the wand. Place the entire assembly (snakes, dowel, and wood) onto a cookie sheet and follow the package directions for baking the clay. (See diagram.) When finished baking, take the cookie sheet out of the oven and let the serpents cool before you touch them.

Finishing Steps

7. Apply a strong epoxy to the inside of the serpent ring. Slide the serpent ring over the top end of the 29" dowel.

8. Pour glue in the hole drilled into the top end of the shaft. Slide the ¼" dowel or wooden peg into the hole firmly, so that half of it sticks out of the end of the shaft. Let dry.

9. Pour glue in the hole drilled into the bottom of the wand head, and slide over the wooden peg sticking out of the top of the shaft. Allow to dry.

10. Sand the wand smooth, especially the shaft. Paint the entire wand with gesso. Allow to dry. Sand the coated wand lightly. Apply a second coat if needed.

11. Paint the winged globe entirely white, but use gold paint to accent the carved lines of the feathers. A coat of iridescent white may be added to the sphere of the globe itself to distinguish it from the wings. Paint the serpents green.

12. With a pencil, mark the shaft of the wand into five sections below the serpent ring. The topmost section will be 6½" in length, while the remaining four will be 5½" long. Of these, the long top portion is to be painted white. The next section will be red. The third section will be blue, and the final part will be black. When all is dry, apply sealant.

The Second Adept's Wand: The Phoenix Wand

In ancient times this scepter was known as the *waas*. It was described as a staff with a forked tail and the head of some animal (𓌀) which was thought to be either a fox, a dog, an ass, or the bennu or phoenix. In paintings this staff was shown being held by both kings and gods. It was a symbol of happiness, abundance, prosperity, and vitality.

According to R. A. Schwaller de Lubicz in his monumental work *The Temple of Man*, the waas scepter was known as "the key of the Nile," and that this symbol was derived from the image of a tree branch with the stem arising from a larger branch, which then divides into two smaller branches. Schwaller continues:

> *It is thus a matter of the rising of the sap (the primordial waters) undergoing the impulse of division, origin of all vegetation. This explanation was later confirmed by one of the waas scepters found in the tomb of Tutankhamun, formed of a natural branch, just as it was cut from the tree and entirely covered in pure gold leaf. We could not better verify the intention of giving a sacred character to this symbol.*[7]

Schwaller goes on to say that the larger branch of the waas staff was symbolically developed into the image of the long snout and ears of a animal, and that the eyes represented small buds on the branch.

In the teachings of the Golden Dawn, the animal head represented on the waas staff was that of the mythical phoenix or Egyptian bennu, a heron-like bird about the size of an eagle, with a long beak and two long ears or feathers on its head. This bird was supposed to have created itself, and to have come into existence from out of the Fire that burned on top of the sacred Persea Tree of Heliopolis. The bennu was essentially a solar bird and was a symbol of the dawning Sun and of the dead Sun-god, Osiris, to whom the animal was sacred and from whose heart it sprang. The bennu represented the birth of the Sun each morning from the dead Sun of yesterday. In addition it became the symbol of the resurrection of humankind, because humanity's spiritual essence was believed to spring forth from the dead physical body. The bennu was thought to be a holy bird that made its appearance once every 500 years. According to Herodotus, the plumage of the phoenix was partly golden and partly red. At the back of its head the phoenix had a peculiar tuft of feathers.[8]

Clement of Alexandria, in the first century C.E., describes the phoenix thus:

> *There is a certain bird which is called a phoenix. This is the only one of its kind and lives five hundred years. And when the time of its dissolution draws near that it must die, it builds itself a nest of frankincense, and myrrh, and other spices, into which, when the time*

is fulfilled, it enters and dies. But as the flesh decays a certain kind of worm is produced, which being nourished by the juices of the dead bird, brings forth feathers. Then, when it has acquired strength, it takes up that nest in which are the bones of its parent, and bearing these it passes from the land of Arabia into Egypt, to the city called Heliopolis. And in open day, flying in the sight of all men, it places them on the altar of the Sun, and having done this, hastens back to its former abode.[9]

Another source says that when the bird's death was near, it would make a nest of sweet-smelling woods and resins, which it would expose to the Sun's rays until it burnt itself to ashes in the Fire. A second phoenix would arise from the marrow of its bones.[10]

Every legend about the bird alludes to periodic destruction and recreation. To the ancient mystics, the phoenix was an appropriate symbol of the immortal human soul, which rises triumphantly from the deceased physical body. In Christian symbolism it signifies the victory of eternal life over death. Medieval Hermeticists considered the bird to be a symbol of alchemical transmutation. In alchemy, the phoenix corresponds to the color red, to the regeneration of universal life, and to the completion of an alchemical process.

The Phoenix Staff or Wand contains all of these ideas. It also represents the sulfur or the active masculine solar principle embodied by the Second Adept who symbolically occupies the position of Geburah. The wand ends in two prongs, which in ancient times (according to some) had a very practical as well as Geburic function; a person walking would sometimes come across a poisonous serpent which could be pinned to the ground with the double-ended staff. Besides the act of saving one from a nasty death, the Phoenix Wand thus represented the triumph of the Sun-god Rê over the evil serpent Apep. (Figure 16, page 40 shows the god Hôôr-Ouêr holding a Phoenix staff.)

In the ceremony of the Adeptus Minor, the Second Adept describes his wand as follows:

Mine is a Wand terminating in the symbol of the Binary, and surmounted by the Tau Cross of Life, or the head of the Phoenix, sacred to Osiris. The Seven colors of the Rainbow between Light and Darkness are attributed to the Planets. It symbolizes Rebirth and Resurrection from Death.[11]

The wand is used in the 5=6 Ceremony to bring into action the powers of life and the vital heat of existence. The shape of the phoenix head suggests a hook, which locks into place over the Ur-uatchti and the Lotus Wand at crucial moments in the ritual.

The Phoenix Wand is a very powerful implement that can be used by an adept whenever the fiery powers of Geburah are called for. It can also be used to invoke, charge, or banish the forces of the seven planets. The fiery nature of this wand gives special strength and authority to any magical operation undertaken. (See *Ritual Use of Magical Tools,* chapter four for a ritual that employs this wand—"The Consecration of a Lunar Talisman," used to enhance one's clairvoyant abilities by inducing dreams and visions.)

See Color Plate 15 and refer to Figure 72 on page 189 for construction diagrams.

Materials Needed

- One ¾" thick dowel approximately 30" long
- One 1½" thick piece of soft wood (pine or bass) approximately 5" x 12"
- One ¾" thick piece of soft wood approximately 5" x 9"
- Two ¼" thick dowels or wooden pegs 1" long
- Yellow carpenter's glue
- Wood putty
- Gesso
- Acrylic paints: gold, white, red, orange, yellow, green, blue, blue-violet, violet, and black
- Sealant: clear lacquer finish

Tools Needed

- Jigsaw
- Electric drill with ¼" bit
- Rotary power tool with gouging and carving bits
- Sandpaper (all grades)
- Artist's brushes (large, medium, and fine)

Construction: The Head of the Phoenix

1. Trace the basic shape of the phoenix head unto the 1½" thick piece of wood. (See Figure 72, page 189. Note: Draw the neck of bird slightly wider than the ¾" width of the shaft.) Cut out the shape with the saw.
2. Make a cut about 4" into the piece of wood that divides the ears or crests of the phoenix into two, as shown in the diagram.
3. Use the rotary tool to "flesh out" the true shape of the animal by rounding its neck and tapering its beak and ears. Generally soften all the rough edges. (Feathers may be implied by carving lines into the face.) Any gaps can be filled with wood putty.
4. Drill a hole ¼" wide and ½" deep into the end of the bird's neck, where the head of the wand will be joined to the shaft.

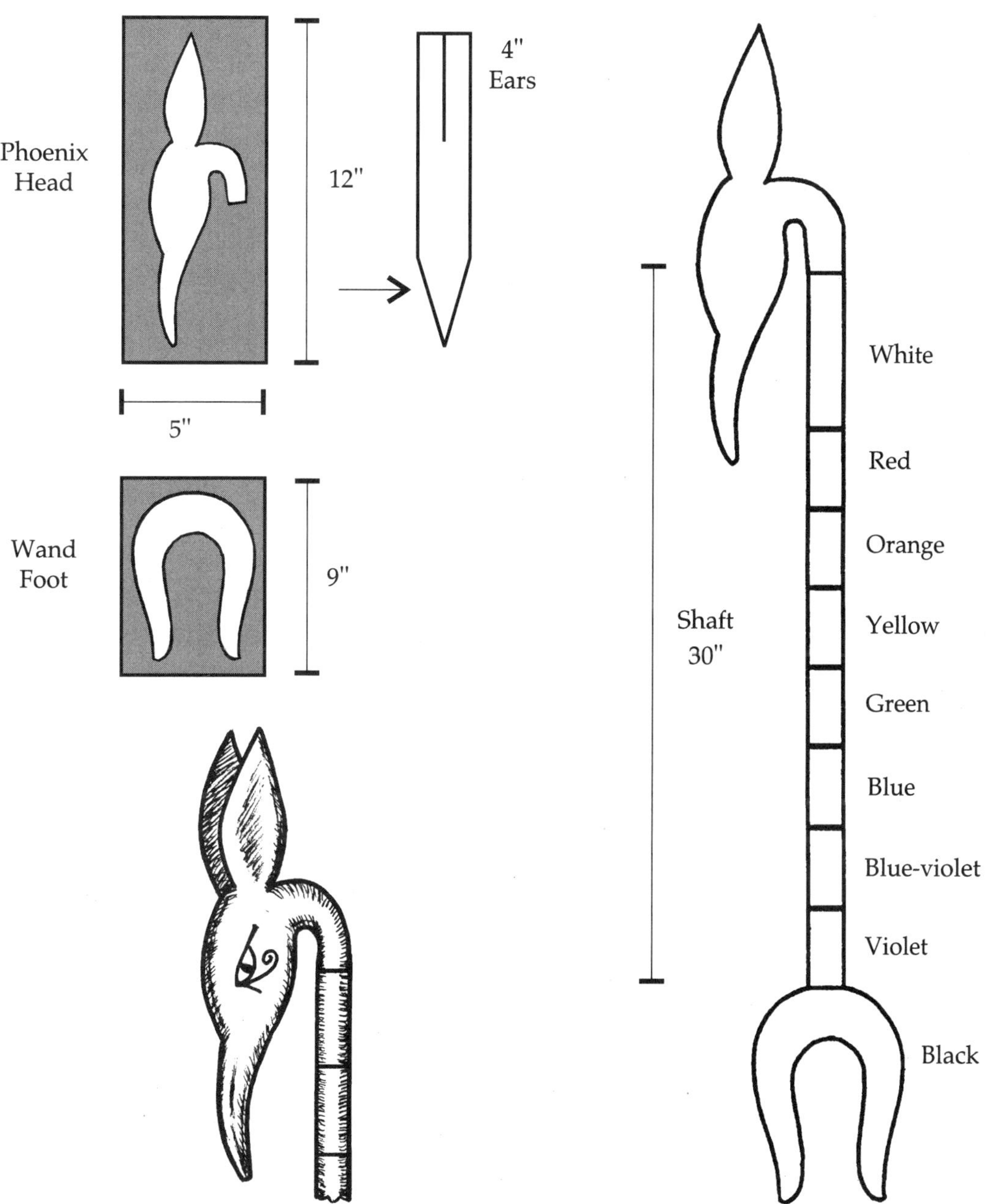

Figure 72: The Phoenix Wand

Construction: The Double-ended Shaft

5. Take the ¾" thick piece of wood (5" x 9") and trace on it the shape of a horseshoe; this will be the "foot" of the wand. (Be sure that the top curve of the foot is the thickest part, about 1½".) Cut out the shape with the saw.
6. Sand all the rough edges smooth. (Begin with course sandpaper and finish with medium sandpaper.) Drill a hole ¼" wide and ½" deep into the top of the horseshoe-shaped foot.
7. Drill the same size hole into both ends of the 30" long dowel shaft.
8. Pour glue into both holes just drilled into the shaft. Attach the two ¼" thick wooden pegs firmly into the glued holes. Allow to dry.

Finishing Steps

9. Pour glue into the holes drilled into both the wand head and the wand foot. Attach these two pieces to the dowel shaft by slipping them over the exposed ends of the wood pegs. Allow to dry.
10. Sand the neck of the phoenix down with course sandpaper until it matches the size of the shaft. Use wood putty to fill in any gaps, then sand the neck with medium sandpaper. (The point of junction between the neck and the shaft should be unnoticeable.) Any gaps where the foot meets the shaft should be filled with putty as well.
11. Cover the wand completely with gesso. Let dry. Sand the shaft lightly with fine sandpaper and apply a second coat if needed.
12. With a pencil, mark the shaft of the wand from the neck to the foot into 8 sections. The topmost section will be the longest—approximately 5½". The remaining seven sections will be about 3½" long.
13. Paint the head and neck of the phoenix gold. Give it Egyptian-style eyes using black and white paint.
14. Paint the long top section below the neck white. The remaining sections are painted as follows in descending order: red, orange, yellow, green, blue, blue-violet, and violet. The foot is to be painted black.
15. After all the paint has dried, apply a coat of sealant to the wand for protection.

The Third Adept's Wand: The Lotus Wand

This wand is identical to that used by the adept in almost all personal magical workings. In the Second Order ceremonies, it is the official wand used by the Third Adept, who personifies the powers of Tiphareth. It symbolizes the development of Creation. The Lotus Wand represents love, while the Phoenix Wand and the Ur-uatchi represent life and light. Instructions on how to make a conventional Lotus Wand are given in chapter five, however, the Lotus Wand of the Third Adept should have a longer shaft than that of a conventional Lotus Wand because in ritual it is used in conjunction with the other wands of the main officers and should be of similar length.

The Crux Ansata: The Ankh Wand

Crux Ansata is Latin for "handle-shaped cross," referring to the ankh. (Figure 87 on page 232 shows the goddess Isis holding an ankh.) The symbolic meaning of the ankh has already been explained at length in the section in chapter one describing the nemyss (page 92). Of primary importance here is the fact that the ankh is a form of the symbol of Venus, the planet whose wall is the door into the Vault of the Adepti (i.e., the Second Order). It is thus the symbolic "key" into the temple of the Inner Order, the "Key of Life," and another form of the Rose and Cross. Venus is the only planet whose sigil embraces all of the Sephiroth on the Tree of Life. Therefore, the wand is painted to represent the force of the ten Sephiroth in nature, divided into a hexad and a tetrad. The oval embraces the first six Sephiroth, and the Tau Cross contains the lower four, answering to the four elements.[12]

The three main officers in the Adeptus Minor ceremony—the Third, Second, and Chief Adept—use their Crux Ansatas to infuse the candidate with the light of L. V. X., causing the Higher Self to descend into his or her Ruach by awakening the Sephiroth of the Middle Pillar in the candidate's Aura. The Crux Ansata can also be used by a magician to charge his or her own sphere of sensation with the forces of the Middle Pillar (see *Ritual Use of Magical Tools,* chapter four). The "Key of Life" is a potent tool for unlocking centers of energy within the adept: creating a pathway for the natural influx of divine light.

Refer to Figure 73 on page 192 for construction diagrams

Materials Needed

- ¾" thick piece of soft wood (pine or bass), 7" x 14"
- Wood putty
- Gesso
- Acrylic paints: white, gray, black, blue, red, yellow, green, orange, violet, and gold
- Sealant: clear lacquer finish

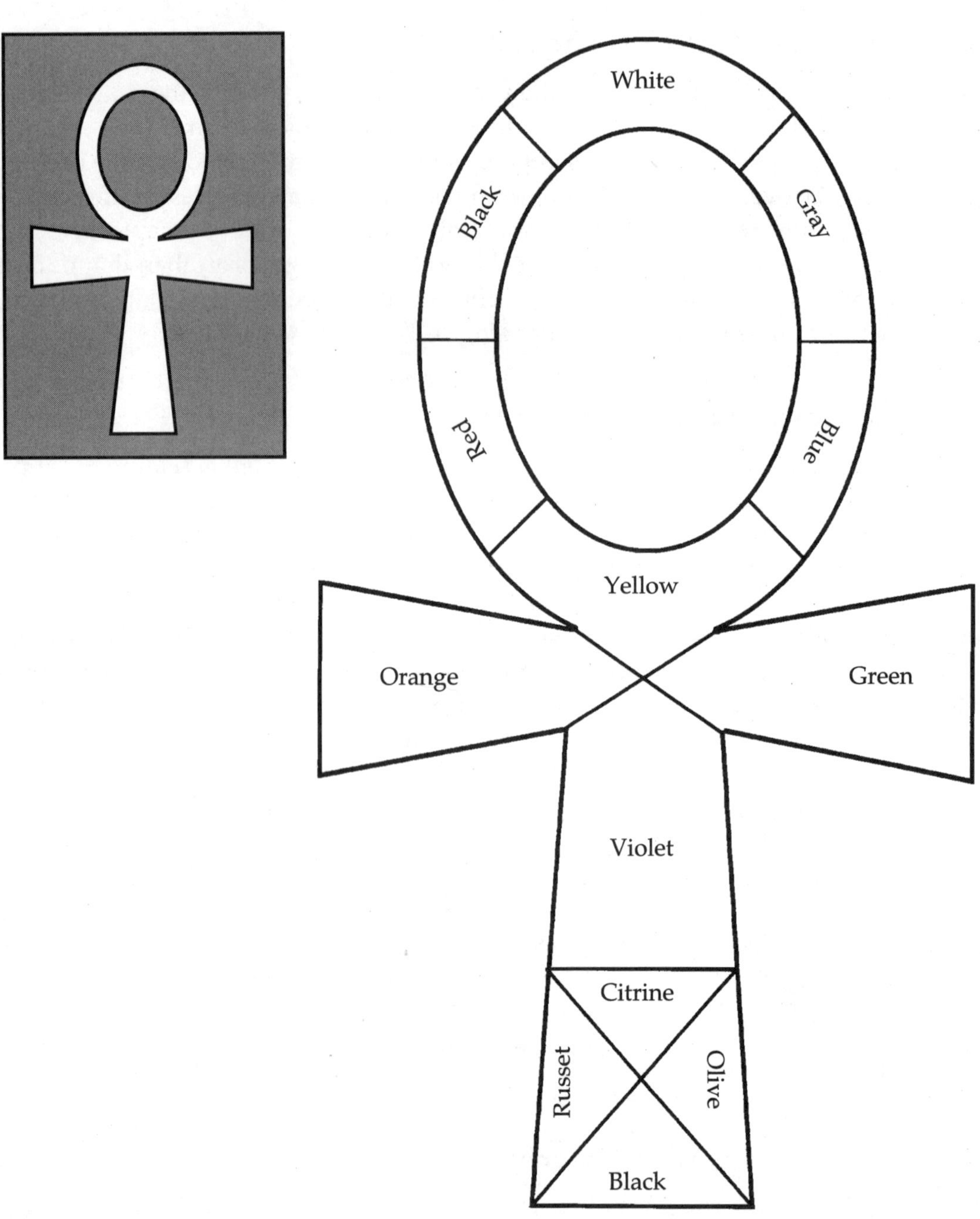

Figure 73: The Crux Ansata

Tools Needed

- Jigsaw
- Electric drill with a bit that is at least ¾"
- Sandpaper (all grades)
- Artist's brushes (medium and fine)

Construction

1. Trace the pattern of the ankh onto the piece of wood, so that the pattern is approximately 7" x 14". (See Figure 73, page 192.) Cut out the outside edge of the ankh with the jigsaw.
2. Into the center of the shaded (waste) area of wood, drill a hole or series of holes large enough to enable the blade of the jigsaw to move unobstructed in the center of this area.
3. Place the saw blade into the hole and cut out the waste area of wood, leaving the true shape of the ankh intact. Sand the ankh smooth.

Finishing Steps

4. Cover the wand entirely with gesso and allow to dry. Sand lightly. Add another coat if needed.
5. Using a pencil and ruler, divide the ankh into ten sections which represent the ten Sephiroth on the Tree of Life. (Note: The bottom section will be subdivided into the four colors of Malkuth.) Mark both sides of the ankh in this manner.
6. Refer to the diagram when painting the wand. Both sides should look identical and must be separated. (Note: You cannot simply paint the sides of the wand all the way around with a given color. This would result in one side of the ankh being painted incorrectly with the Tree of Life in a distorted position. Paint the outside and inside edge of the wand with gold to prevent this.)
7. After all the paint has dried, apply a coat of sealant for protection.

The Crook and Scourge

The *crook* and *scourge* symbolize the opposing concepts of Mercy and Severity. They are the additional implements of the Chief Adept who assumes the godform of Osiris within the tomb. In ancient texts, the waas staff, the *heq-t* scepter or crook, and the *henu* flail or whip were the three symbols of authority and dominion held by Osiris (see Figure 74, page 194). The crook or hooked staff is symbolic of the Mercy of Chesed and the White

Figure 74: The God Osiris with the Phoenix Wand, Crook, and Scourge

Pillar. In Christian symbolism, it is a pastoral attribute, the implement of a shepherd, and a symbol of faith. The crook stands for divine power, communication, and connection. Its suggestive curved shape also implies creative power. In the symbolism of the R. R. et A. C., the crook is painted in the colors of the *Minutum Mundum* diagram. It is divided into the colors symbolic of Kether, Aleph, Chokmah, Taurus, Chesed, Leo, Aries, Tiphareth, Capricorn, and Hod. The implement thus starts in the Supernal realm, leading from Kether to Chokmah via the Eleventh Path (the tarot key of The Fool) and down to Chesed, the seat of Mercy from the Sixteenth Path (the tarot key of The Hierophant), ending at length in the watery sphere of Hod.

The scourge or flail is symbolic of Severity and of the Black Pillar. It, too, is painted in accordance with the Minutum Mundum diagram. It is separated into the colors of Netzach, Scorpio, Tiphareth, Gemini, Binah, Cancer, Geburah, and Mem. The implement symbolically starts in the Fire of Netzach, and crosses the Crook of Mercy. The top of the scourge reaches the sphere of Binah before the flailed ends descend to Geburah and the Twenty-third Path of the Hanged Man.

The Crook of Mercy must be held in the right hand and the Scourge of Severity in the left hand. The arms should then be crossed on the chest and the two implements will be in the proper position to represent the Pillars of Mercy and Severity in the adept's sphere of sensation. According to the Adeptus Minor ceremony, these tools are emblems of eternal opposing forces between which the entire equilibrium of the universe depends. The reconciliation of these forces is the "Key of Life" (the rose and cross, as well as the Crux Ansata) and whose separation is evil and death.[13] The crook and scourge may be employed by an adept in a ceremony to balance and equilibrate the forces of mercy and severity within his or her inner self. They may also be used in a ritual/meditation invoking the godform of Osiris (see *Ritual Use of Magical Tools,* chapter four).

Refer to Figure 75 on page 196 for construction diagrams.

Materials Needed

- One ¾" thick piece of soft wood, 12" x 24"
- Eighteen ½" diameter round wooden beads
- Three ⅜" diameter round wooden beads
- Six 2" long cylindrical wooden beads (all of these beads can be found in most stores which sell hobby and craft supplies)
- Nine ¼" diameter metal beads
- Three 6mm metal bead caps (should be bigger than the hole which runs through the ⅜" wooden beads)
- Three small eye-screws

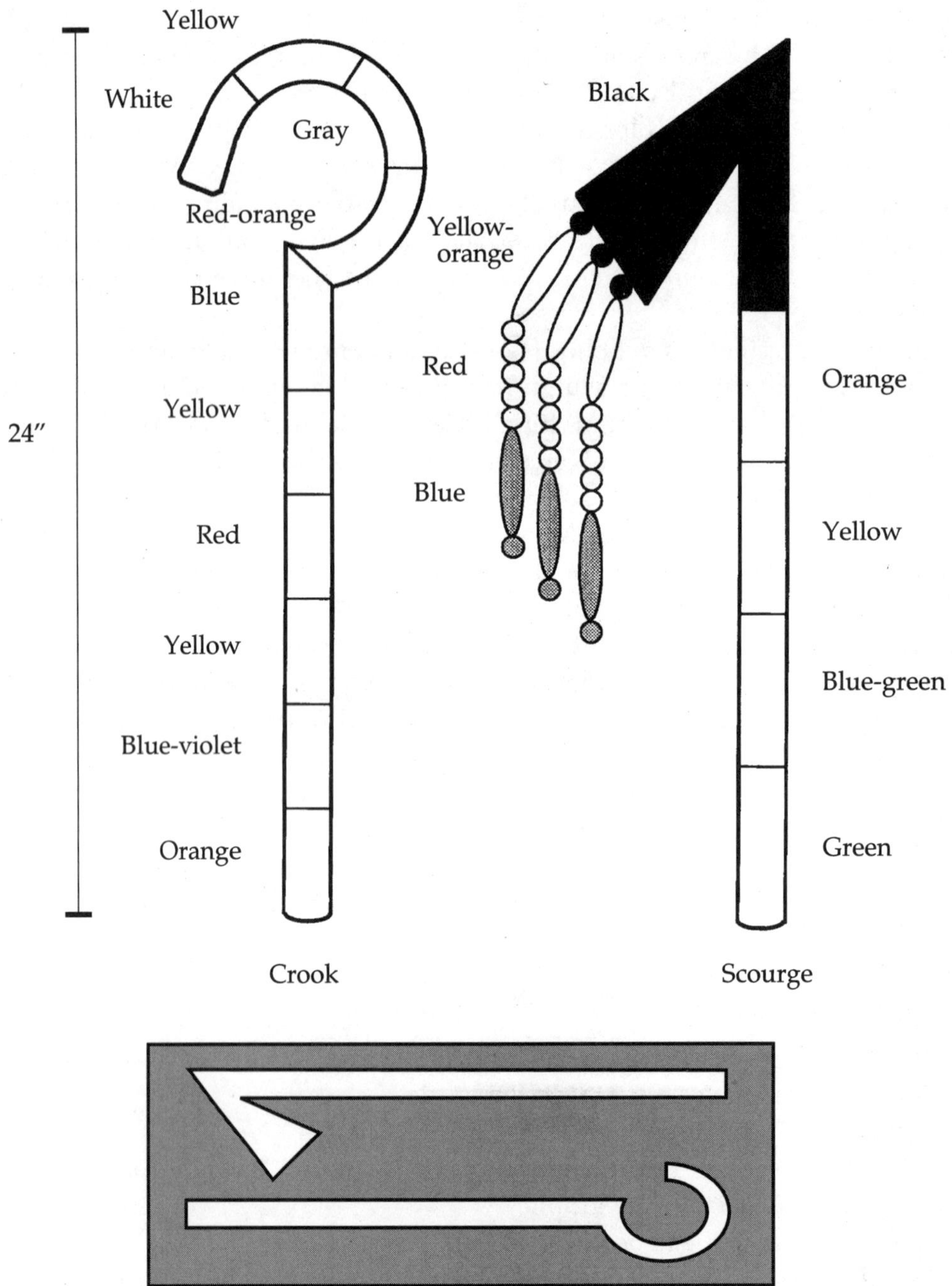

Figure 75: The Crook and Scourge

- Roll of strong but thin wire
- Wood putty
- Gesso
- Acrylic paint: white, yellow, gray, orange, red, blue, blue-violet, green, and black
- Sealant: clear lacquer finish

Tools Needed

- Jigsaw
- Soldering gun (with solder)
- Wire cutters
- Sandpaper (all grades)
- Artist's brushes (medium)

Construction: The Crook

1. On the piece of wood, draw out the basic shapes of both the crook and the scourge. (See Figure 75, page 196) Both implements should be nearly 24" long.

2. Cut out the form of the crook with the jigsaw. Put the remaining piece of wood with the scourge drawn on it aside.

3. Sand the crook form with course, medium and fine sandpaper until smooth. Apply a coat of gesso and allow to dry. Sand lightly with fine sandpaper. Apply another coat if needed.

4. With a pencil, roughly mark off the crook into ten even sections. Starting with the curved end of the crook, paint the sections in descending order as follows:

    - White
    - Yellow
    - Grey
    - Red-orange
    - Blue
    - Yellow
    - Red
    - Yellow
    - Blue-violet
    - Orange

5. After all the paint has dried, apply a sealant for protection.

Construction: The Scourge

6. Cut out the basic shape of the scourge from the wood.

7. Sand the scourge until smooth. Cover entirely with gesso and allow to dry. Sand lightly. Apply another coat if needed.

8. Apply a coat of gesso to all of the wooden beads. Allow to dry.

9. With a pencil, roughly mark off the scourge into five even sections. (The "axe-like" shape of the head will be the longest section.) Paint the sections starting with the "axe," in descending order as follows:

   - Black
   - Orange
   - Yellow
   - Blue-green
   - Green

10. Paint three of the ½" round wooden beads black. Paint the remaining fifteen ½" round beads red. Paint three of the 2" long beads yellow-orange. Paint the remaining three 2" beads blue. Paint the three ⅜" round beads blue.

Finishing Steps

11. Attach the three eye-screws into the end of the "axe head" at even intervals.
12. From the roll of wire, cut off three 16" lengths. Take one of the pieces of wire and run it through one of the eye-screws attached to the scourge. Fold the wire so that it is doubled. (The folded wire will be stronger but its length will now be 8".)
13. String the following number of beads in this order onto the doubled strand of wire: one black bead, one metal bead, one long yellow-orange bead, one metal bead, five red beads, one metal bead, one long blue bead, one small blue bead.
14. Attach the metal bead cap firmly to the two ends of wire sticking out from the last bead. Trim off any excess wire. Use a soldering gun to secure the wire to the bead cap. Attach two more strands of beads to the scourge in the same manner.
15. After all parts of the scourge have been assembled, apply a coat of sealant to protect the paint.

The Cross of Victory

The *Cross of Victory* is a decidedly Rosicrucian implement that is based on the emblem of the rose and the cross. (See Figure 76, page 199). Within this cross, the pagan origins of the symbol, along with its lavish layers of Christian embellishment, are joined in an implement that celebrates the universal spiritual truths. In Christian symbolism, the cross has a two-fold significance. First, it is the symbol of the death of Christ, the Redeemer; secondly, it is the symbol of humility, patience, and the burden of life and self-sacrifice. (It is interesting to note that the emblem can be considered both a symbol of life and of death.)

To the ancients, who deeply considered the astronomical aspect of religion, the cross was a likely symbol of the equinoxes and the solstices, the four times when the Sun was symbolically "crucified" by crossing the line of the ecliptic.[14]

Figure 76: The Rose and the Cross

In most cultures, the Sun also symbolized a divinity who died every night only to be reborn each morning (like Rê, the Egyptian Sun god). Most of the various dying-god myths center around a solar deity who dies and is resurrected.

The shape of the cross suggests the human body, pointing to the mortal side of the immortal solar deity. The cross also suggests the four elements as stated earlier. The Rose of Twenty-five Petals is composed of the five elements of Spirit, Fire, Water, Air, and Earth, divided into their subelements: Spirit of Spirit, Spirit of Fire, Air of Earth, etc. It is the *Pentagrammaton* or "Five-lettered Name" of God. The number twenty-five also alludes to the path of Temperance (Samekh), which leads from Yesod to Tiphareth on the Tree of Life.

The Cross of Victory is a symbol of strength. It alludes to the ultimate goal of an initiate of the mysteries: to understand the nature of the divine by analyzing the elements and subelements that comprise the manifest universe—"for as above, so below." The rose transfixed on the Cross of Victory is multicolored, but the cross itself is painted black. The black cross is a cross of suffering, because the path of an initiate is not an easy one—many tests and trials are to be encountered and overcome. The black cross also refers to putrification, an alchemical process that is necessary to extract the pure gold (essence) from the corruptible matter. This "gold" or divine essence is expressed in the unfolding rose of creation, which is also the dawning light of the Sun of Tiphareth.

Refer to Figure 77 on page 200 for construction diagrams.

Materials Needed

- One ⅞" x ½" piece of basswood, 12" long (model strut found in the model airplane section of most hobby shops)
- One ¼" thick piece of basswood, 3½" x 9"
- One ⅛" thick piece of balsa wood, 3" x 3"
- One piece of black felt

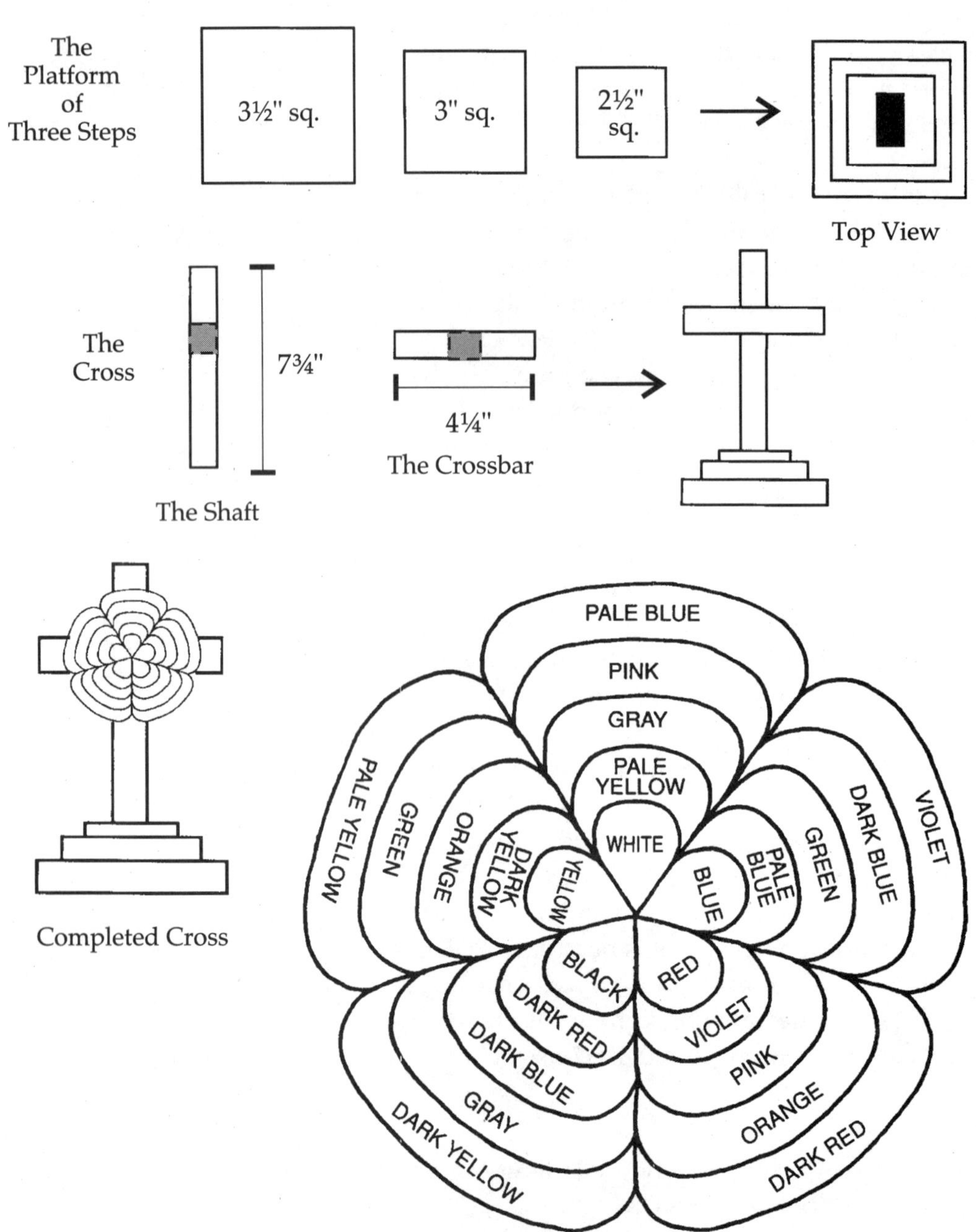

Figure 77: The Cross of Victory

- Yellow carpenter's glue
- Wood putty
- Acrylic paints: black, white, gray, yellow, blue, violet, orange, red, and green
- Sealant: clear lacquer finish

Tools Needed

- Scroll saw
- Small hammer
- Sandpaper (medium and fine grained)
- Artist's brushes (medium and fine)
- Craft knife with carving blade

Construction: The Platform

1. Take the 9" piece of basswood and cut it into 3 pieces: one 3½" square, one 3" square, and one 2½" square piece. (See Figure 77, page 200.) Sand the edges of all three pieces smooth (begin with medium sandpaper and finish with fine sandpaper).
2. Glue all three pieces together, one on top of the other, forming three tiled steps. Allow to dry.
3. Find the center of the smallest (topmost) piece of wood. On it draw a rectangle ⅞" long x ½" wide. Cut out this rectangle using the knife. Cut entirely through the topmost piece of wood and remove the rectangle (waste wood).

Construction: The Cross

4. Take the ⅞" thick piece of basswood (12" long) and cut it into two pieces: one 7¾" long and the other 4¼" long. Sand the ends of both pieces smooth (begin with medium sandpaper and finish with fine sandpaper).
5. Take the longer piece (the shaft) and mark it with two pencil lines: one 1¾" down from the top end, and the other ⅞" down from the first line.
6. Using the scroll saw, make two cuts at the drawn lines halfway into the wood. Use the knife to remove the section of wood that exists between the two cut lines. (Note: You will be left with a piece of wood that resembles a timber from a log cabin—with a gouged out area for another "log" to fit into.)

7. Take the shorter 4¼" piece (the crossbar) and pencil in two lines—both 1⅝" from their respective ends. Cut these lines halfway into the wood as before. Use the knife to remove the wood between the lines, leaving a gouged out area.

8. Slide the two pieces of wood together at the gouged-out areas, forming a perfect Calvary cross. (Check to see if the pieces fit. If the pieces are too tight, sand them until they fit. If they are too loose, the gaps can be filled later with wood putty.) Glue the two sections of the cross together.

The Rose of Twenty-five Petals

9. Take the ⅛" thick piece of balsa wood and draw a 2¾" circle on it. Cut the circle out. Sand the outer edge of the circle smooth.

10. Mark the circle off into five equal sections. Where the pencil lines meet the edge of the circle, make a slight indentation (to indicate the edges of five rose petals). Use the knife to incise the drawn lines.

Finishing Steps

11. Glue the cross into the hole carved into the platform. Glue the rose to the front of the cross where the shaft joins the crossbar.

13. Paint the Cross of Victory entirely with a coat of gesso. Allow to dry. Sand lightly with fine sandpaper.

14. Paint the cross and the platform black. Paint the rose according to the diagram.[15]

The Vault of the Adepti

Kerubic Guardian Plaques

Cirlot, citing Marques-Riviére, says that the "cherubim" (*Kirubi* or *Kherebu*) which stood at the entrance to Assyrian temples were nothing less than gigantic pentacles placed there by the priests as keepers of the threshold—a function which in China was fulfilled by statues of griffins and dragons. He goes on to state that the Egyptian Kerub, a creature with many wings and eyes, was a symbol of vigilance.[16] Their most ancient symbolic form is that of human-headed animals or sphinxes.

The Old Testament describes the Kerubim as they appeared to Ezekiel, surrounding the *Merkabah* or Chariot of God (see Figure 78, page 204):

> *And out of the midst of it there was the likeness of four living creatures, and this is how they looked: they had the likeness of earthling man. And each one had four faces and each had four wings...and as four the likeness of their faces, the four of them had a man's face with a lion's face to the right, and the four of them had a bull's face on the left; the four of them also had an eagle's face...there was one wheel beside the living creatures, by the four faces of each...and their appearance and their structure were just as when a wheel proved to be in the midst of a wheel.* (Ezekiel 1: 4–10).

The symbolism of the Kerubim can be found elsewhere in the Scriptures. When the twelve tribes of Israel encamped in the wilderness, the banners of Judah (the lion), Reuben (the man), Dan (the eagle), and Ephraim (the bull) were placed to mark the four corners of the camp. In Christian symbolism, four of the Apostles became associated with the Kerubim: Mark—the lion; Luke—the ox; John—the eagle; and Matthew—the man.

The Persians had a tradition that four brilliant stars, known as the "Four Royal Stars," marked the four cardinal points. (These stars were found in four constellations of the zodiac, which at that time marked the four seasons.)

These bright Royal Stars were *Regulus*—in Leo, *Aldebaran*—in Taurus, *Antares*—in Scorpius, and *Fomalhaut*—in the Southern Fish (very closely situated to the constellation of Aquarius). These four stars were celebrated throughout Asia. The brilliant star in the constellation of the eagle, *Altair,* has been suggested as the fourth Royal Star instead of Fomalhaut. Thus, as in the vision of Ezekiel, the constellations of the lion, ox, man, and eagle stood in ancient times as the upholders of the firmament and the pillars of heaven. Like sentinels, they seemed to guard the four quarters of the sky. In the Four Royal Stars, the four great decans, or gods who ruled the signs, were believed to dwell.[17]

The Kerubim ultimately constitute the mystical glyph of the completeness of divine wisdom. They are the guardians of the four rivers, which flow down the Tree of Life from the creator. The Kerubim are the Living Powers of Tetragrammaton on the material plane and the Presidents of the Four Elements.[18] They operate through the fixed or Kerubic signs of the zodiac and are symbolized as follows:

Symbols of the Kerubim

Tetragrammaton Letter		**Element**	**Animal Sign**	**Symbol**	
Yod	י	Fire	Lion	Leo	♌
Heh	ה	Water	Eagle	Scorpio	♏ or [eagle glyph]
Vav	ו	Air	Man	Aquarius	♒
Heh final	ה	Earth	Bull	Taurus	♉

Figure 78: The Cherub of Ezekiel

According to Golden Dawn scholar Adam Forrest:

The Angelic Order of the Kerubim, stationed at Yesod on the threshold between Asiyah and the Higher Planes, are Angels of Liminality. Their Work is to govern interaction between the Inner and the Outer Worlds, by serving as Guardians, Heralds, Equilibrators, and Guides.

... At the Fall, the Kerubim were stationed (as illustrated in the emblematic diagram of The Garden of Eden After the Fall) at the liminal Abyss to separate the Supernals from the effects of the Fall; in this role, They are the Tzophe Shamayim, the "Sentinels of the Heavens." In the Temple of Solomon, the Kerubim were depicted on Parokheth, the liminal Veil of the Holy of Holies. They also guarded the liminal Outer entrances to the Temples of Egypt and Mesopotamia.[19]

The Kerubic Guardian Plaques are used to guard the Vault of the Adepti (see Figures 80 and 81, pages 206 and 208.) The circular shape of the plaques can be found in Canaanite sources (see Figure 79). The plaques are described in the Adeptus Minor Ritual thus:

Before the Door of the Tomb, as symbolic Guardians, are the Elemental Tablets, and the Kerubic Emblems, even as before the mystical Gate of Eden stood the watchful Kerubim, and the sword of flame. These Kerubic Emblems be the powers of the Angles of the Tablets. The Circle represents the four Angles of the Tablets bound together in each Tablet through the operation of the all-pervading Spirit, while the Cross within forms with its spokes the Wheels of Ezekiel's Vision; and therefore are the Cross and Circle white to represent the purity of the Divine Spirit. And inasmuch as we do not find the Elements unmixed, but each bound together with each—so that in Air we find not only that which is subtle and tenuous, but also the qualities of heat, moisture, and dryness, bound together in that all-wandering Element; and furthermore also that in Fire, Water and Earth we find that same mixture of Nature—therefore the Four Elements are bound to each Kerubic

Figure 79: A Canaanite Scene

Figure 80: A Kerubic Guardian Plaque

Emblem countercharged with the color of the Element wherein they operate; even as in the Vision of Ezekiel each Kerub had four faces and four wings. Forget not therefore that the Tablets and the Kerubim are the Guardians of the Tomb of the Adepti.[20]

The Kerubim are the angels most often employed in the magical work of the Golden Dawn. Their symbols or images show up several times in the Vault of the Adepti:

... Not surprisingly, as the Angels of Yesod, the Kerubim also occur as an Ennead. The pattern of the Nine is four pairs of Kerubim under the presidency of Gabriel Kerubiel. The Kerubim correspond in this pattern to the ancient Ogdoad of Khmun (Hermopolis) under the presidency of Thoth-Hermes, which has some relation to the oldest and simplest of the Qameoth, the nine-cell Square which now serves as the Qamea of Saturn and Binah.

There are nine occurrences of the Kerubic Tetrad in the symbolism of the Vault of the Adepts: the Kerubim guard the Door of the Vault, they stand upon the Circular Altar, and they watch over the Vault from the top rank of each of the seven Walls.

... The Formula of the 28 Kerubim is a Kerub Tetrad for each of the Seven Planets. The 28 Kerubim are found represented on the walls of the Vault of Christian Rosenkreuz, four in the topmost rank of each of the seven walls. As the Practicus Adeptus Minor learns, these 28 Kerubim may be called forth by the forms of the Lesser Hexagram.

... The Yesodic Kerubim also take on a Tipheretic aspect in relation to the Vault of the Adepts, as the 28 Kerubim on the Walls of the Vault are joined by a further Ogdoad: four outer Kerubim on the Door of the Vault, and four inner Kerubim on the Circular Altar, thus making the Tipheretic Square Number of 36. When this Kerubic Ogdoad reveals the Ennead by being conjoined with Gabriel Kerubiel, the Archangel of the Spirit, from the 36 Kerubim of the Vault the great Tipheretic Solar number of 37 is produced, and confirms the Lunar ability of the Powers of Yesod to reflect the Solar Light of Tiphereth to Malkuth.[21]

The Kerubic plaques could be constructed by an adept and used in conjunction with the Enochian Tablets; each plaque placed in one of the four quarters over its corresponding Elemental Tablet. (Note: The plaques are not to be used in any hall of the First Order, but may be employed in the adept's personal temple.)

A solitary magician may wish to make one Kerubic plaque for personal use, but not all four. If this is the case, the singular plaque should be painted as follows:

- Background behind Lion: Red
- Background behind Eagle: Blue
- Lion: Green
- Eagle: Orange

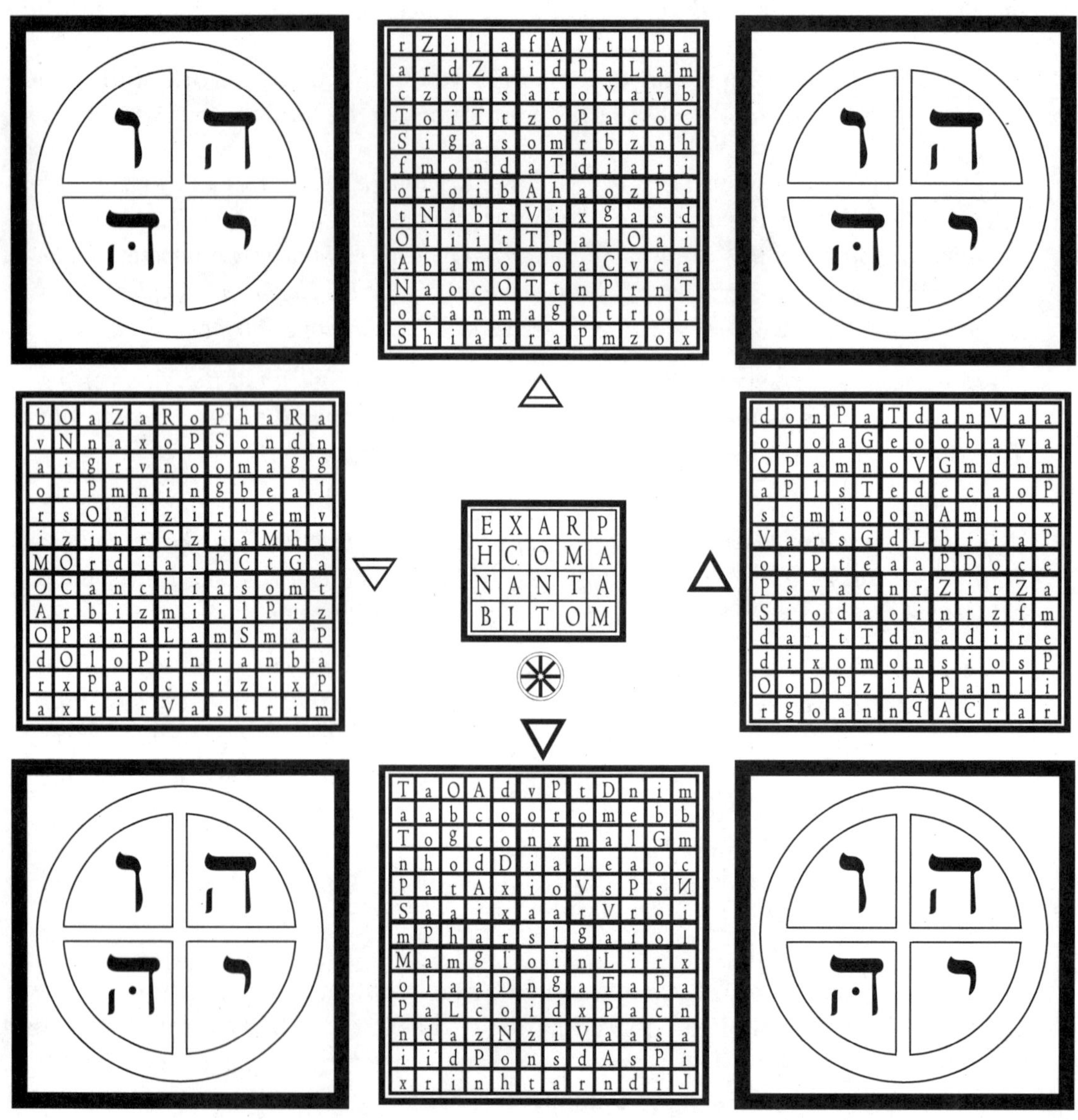

Figure 81: Vault Arrangement of Enochian Tablets and Kerubic Plaques

- Background behind Man: Yellow
- Background behind Bull: Black
- Circle and Cross: White
- Man: Violet
- Bull: White

The singular Kerubic plaque can be placed on the outside entrance to the magician's personal temple. Positioned thus, it can serve to guard the temple room from all unwanted influences. (The letters of the Tetragrammaton may be substituted for the Kerubic faces as they are in Figure 81, page 208.) A ritual charging a single Kerubic plaque is given in *Ritual Use of Magical Tools*, chapter four.

Materials Needed

- One ½" thick piece of plywood approximately 7" x 28"
- Four 10" long strips of balsa wood, ¼" x ¼" thick (model airplane struts—can be found in most hobby shops)
- One ¼" thick piece of balsa wood, 7" x 28"
- Yellow carpenter's glue
- Wood putty
- Gesso
- Acrylic paints: white, black, yellow, violet, blue, orange, red, green
- Sealant: clear lacquer finish

Tools Needed

- Scroll saw
- Electric drill
- Sandpaper (all grades)
- Artist's brushes (medium and fine)

Construction: A Single Plaque

1. Draw a 6" circle on the piece of ½" plywood. Cut out with the scroll saw. Put the wood aside. Draw a 6" circle on the ¼" piece of balsa wood and cut out. Sand the edge with course sandpaper.

2. Trace a smaller circle ½" inside the one just cut out. Drill a hole in the center of this smaller circle, using a drill bit that is wider than your saw blade.

3. Unplug the saw. Detach the blade from the saw and stick it through the hole just drilled. Reattach the saw blade and plug the saw back in. Cut out the inside of the circle (which is waste area) leaving only the 6" diameter outer rim intact. (Note: Don't mutilate the waste area too badly…the Kerubic heads will be drawn on this piece.)

4. Glue the 6" balsa rim to the 6" plywood circle. Allow to dry. Sand the outer part of both circles with medium sandpaper until smooth. Fill in any gaps with wood putty.
5. Take one of the 10" long pieces of balsa wood (model strut) and cut it in half. Take one of the resulting 5" pieces and cut it into two pieces which are 2 ⅜". Glue these three pieces of balsa wood into the center of the plywood circle, forming a perfect equal-armed cross. Where the balsa rim meets each arm of the cross, fill in gaps with wood putty. (Note: You will now have a plaque that is three-dimensional—the four quarters of the piece are lower than the rim and the cross.)
6. Take the balsa wood that is leftover from the circle and draw the heads of the four Kerubim (man, lion, bull, and eagle) on it. Use Figure 80 on page 206 as a pattern for the Kerubim. Cut the four heads out with the scroll saw. (Note: Balsa wood is very soft and the heads can easily be shaped and contoured using fine sandpaper.)
7. Glue the Kerubic heads to the plywood circle, one to the center of each quarter. When all the glue has dried, cover the plaque entirely with a coat of gesso. Allow to dry.
8. Repeat steps 1–7 if a full set of plaques are desired.

Finishing Steps

9. Paint the outer edge of the circle, the rim and the cross white. On the individual plaques, the Kerubim must be painted slightly different:

Air Plaque

- Background color: Yellow
- Lion: Red
- Eagle: Blue
- Man: Violet
- Bull: Black

Water Plaque

- Background color: Blue
- Lion: Red
- Eagle: Orange
- Man: Yellow
- Bull: Black

Earth Plaque

- Background color: Black
- Lion: Red
- Eagle: Blue
- Man: Yellow
- Bull: White

Fire Plaque

- Background color: Red
- Lion: Green
- Eagle: Blue
- Man: Yellow
- Bull: Black

9. Facial detail may be added to all four heads. After all the paint is dry, apply sealant for protection.

A Description of the Vault of the Adepti

The Vault of the Adepti is the powerful ritual chamber of the R. R. et A. C. It is the crowning jewel of all ritual implements in the Western Magical Tradition. No initiation into the Second Order is valid without it. The description of this chamber along with its contents make up some of the most vital portions of the *Fama Fraternitatis* (1614), one of the three most famous Rosicrucian Manifestos.

In the allegory of Christian Rosencreutz, his life and works are recounted, as well as the essential portrayal of his burial chamber. It was this description that MacGregor Mathers brilliantly built on in his creation of the Vault of the Adepti. The unnamed writer of the *Fama* recounts the story of the discovery of the tomb of the founder of the Rosicrucian Fraternity:

Now the true and fundamental relation of the finding out of the high-illuminated man of God, Fra. C. R. C. is this:

... The year following, after (Brother N. N.) had performed his school right, and was minded now to travel, being for that purpose sufficiently provided with Fortunatus' purse he thought (he being a good architect) to alter something of his building and to make it more fit. In such renewing he lighted upon the Memorial Table, which was cast of brasse, and containeth the names of the Brethern, with some few other things. This he would transfer into a more fitting vault, for where or when Brother R. C. died, or in what country he was buried, was by our predecessors concealed and unknown to us. In this table stuck a great naile somewhat strong, so that when it was with force drawn out it took with it an indifferent big stone out of the thin wall or plaistering of the hidden door, upon which was written in great letters—

POST CXX ANNOS PATEBO

with the year of the Lord under it. Therefore we gave God thanks, and let it rest that same night, because first we would overlook our ROTA.—

... In the morning following we opened the door, and there appeared to our sight a vault of seven sides and seven corners, every side five foot broad, and the height of eight foot. Although the Sun never shined in this vault, it was enlightened with another Sun, which had learned this from the Sun, and was situated in the upper part of the center of the ceiling. In the midst, instead of a tomb-stone, was a round altar, covered with a plate of brass, and thereon this engraven—

A. C. R. C. Hoc universi compendium unius mihi sepulchrum feci.

Round about the first circle or brim stood,

Jesus mihi omnia

In the middle were four figures, inclosed in circles, whose circumscription were:

> *1. Nequaquam Vacuum*
> *2. Libertas Evangelii*
> *3. Dei Gloria Intacta*
> *4. Legis Jugum*
>
> *This is all clear and bright, as also the seventh side and the two heptagons.... This vault we parted in three parts, the upper part or ceiling, the wall or side, the ground or floor. Of the upper part you shall understand no more at this time but that it was divided according to the seven sides in the triangle which was in the bright center... Every side or wall is parted into ten squares, every one with their several figures and sentences... The bottom again is parted in the triangle, but because therein described the power and rule of the Inferior Governors, we leave to manifest the same, for fear of the abuse by the evil and ungodly world.... Every side or wall had a door for a chest, wherein there lay divers things, especially our books... (G)enerally all that was done to that end, that if it should happen, after many hundred years, the Fraternity should come to nothing, they might by this only vault be restored again.*
>
> *Now, as we had not yet seen the dead body of our careful and wise Father, we therefore moved the altar aside; then we lifted up a strong plate of brass, and found a fair and worthy body, whole and unconsumed. In his hand he held a parchment called T, the which next unto the Bible is our greatest treasure, which ought not to be delivered unto the censure of the world.*[22]

Under the genius of a magician such as Mathers, this fragment of Rosicrucian knowledge became elucidated in the Ritual of the Adeptus Minor, 5=6 (as published in Regardie's *The Golden Dawn*):

> *Upon more closely examining the Door of the Tomb, you will perceive, even as Frater N.N. and those with him did perceive, that beneath the CXX in the inscription were placed the characters IX thus:*
>
> *POST CXX ANNOS PATEBO*
> *IX*
>
> *...being equivalent to Post Annos Lux Crucis Patebo—At the end of 120 years, I, the Light of the Cross, will disclose myself. For the letters forming LVX are made from the dismembered and conjoined angles of the Cross; and 120 is the product of the numbers from 1 to 5, multiplied in regular progression, which number five is symbolized in the Cross with four extremities and one center point. On the following morning, Frater N. N. and his companions forced open the door and there appeared to their sight a Tomb of Seven*

Sides and Seven Corners. Every side was five feet broad, and eight feet high, even as the same is faithfully represented before you. Although in the Tomb the Sun does not shine, it is lit by the symbolic Rose of our Order in the center of the first heptagonal ceiling. In the midst of the Tomb stands a circular Altar with these devices and descriptions on it:

A. G. R. C. — Ad Gloriam Roseae Crucis
A. C. R. G. — Ad Crucis Rosae Gloriam
Hoc Universal Compendium Unius Mihi Sepulchrum Feci

Unto the Glory of the Rose Cross I have constructed this Tomb for myself as a Compendium of the Universal Unity.

With the next circle is written:

Yeheshua Mihi Omnia—
Yeheshua is all things to me.

In the center are four figures of the Kerubim (colored appropriately) enclosed within circles surrounded by the following four inscriptions and each distinguished by one of the following four inscriptions and each distinguished by one of the letters of the Tetragrammaton:

Yod—Lion—Nequaquam Vacuum—Nowhere a Void.
Heh—Eagle—Libertas Evangelii—Liberty of the Gospel.
Vau—Man—Dei Intacta Gloria—Unsullied Glory of God.
Heh (f)—Ox—Legis Jugum—Yoke of the Law.

and in the midst of all is Shin, the Letter of the Spirit forming thus the Divine Name Yeheshua, from the Tetragrammaton.[23]

The complex scope of the symbolism of the Vault is further described later in the same ritual (see Figure 82 on page 214):

It is divided into three parts—the Ceiling which is white; the Heptagonal Walls of seven Rainbow colors, and the Floor whose prevailing hue is black; thus showing the powers of the Heptad between the Light and the Darkness.

On the ceiling is a triangle enclosing a Rose of 22 petals, within a Heptangle reflected from the Seven Angles of the Wall. The Triangle represents the Three Supernal Sephiroth; the Heptagram, the Lower Seven; the Rose represents the 22 paths of the Serpent of Wisdom. The Floor has upon it also the Symbol of a Triangle enclosed within a Heptagram, bearing the titles of the Averse and Evil Sephiroth of the Qlippoth, the Great Red Dragon of Seven Heads, and the inverted and evil triangle. And thus in the tomb of the Adepti do we tread down the Evil Powers of the Red Dragon and so tread thou upon the evil powers of thy nature. For

Figure 82: Symbolism of the Vault

there is traced within the evil Triangle the rescuing Symbol of the Golden Cross united to the Red Rose of Seven times Seven Petals. As it is written 'He descendeth into Hell.'

But the whiteness above shines the brighter for the Blackness which is beneath, and thus mayest thou comprehend that the evil helpeth forward the Good. And between the Light and the Darkness vibrate the colors of the Rainbow, whose crossed and reflected rays under the Planetary Presidency are shewn forth in these Seven Walls. Remember that thou hast entered by the door of the planet Venus, whose symbol includes the whole Ten Sephiroth of the Tree of Life. Each Wall of the Tomb is said mystically to be in breadth five feet and in height eight feet, thus yielding forty squares, of which ten are marked and salient, representing the Ten Sephiroth in the form of the Tree of Life, acting throughout the Planet. The remaining squares represent the Kerubim and the Eternal Spirit, the Three Alchemic Principles, the Three Elements, the Seven Planets, and the Twelve Signs, all operating in and differentiating the rays of each planet. Note that in all, the Central square alone remains white and unchanged, representing the changeless Essence of the Divine Spirit, thus developing all from the One, through the many under the governance of One.

The colors of the varying squares may be either represented by the color of the Planet and the color of the Force therein mixed together, or by these colors being placed in juxtaposition (not the preferred or most accurate method) or in any other convenient manner; but the foundation of them all is the Minutum Mundum diagram.[24]

Concerning the symbolism of the coffin of Christian Rosencreutz and the diagrams on its surface are described as follows. The lower half of the lid:

Behold the image of the Justified One, crucified on the Infernal Rivers of Daath, and thus rescuing Malkuth from the folds of the Red Dragon.[25]

The upper half of the lid:

And being turned, I saw Seven Golden Light-bearers, and in the midst of the Lightbearers, One like unto the Ben Adam, clothed with a garment down to the feet, and girt with a Golden Girdle. His head and his hair were white as snow, and his eyes as flaming fire; His feet like unto fine brass, as if they burned in a furnace. And his voice as the sound of many waters. And He had in his right hand Seven Stars, and out of his mouth went the Sword of Flame, and his countenance was as the Sun in His Strength.[26]

The diagram of the above biblical passage is based on a woodcut by Albrecht Dürer. (See Figures 83 and 84, pages 216 and 217.) The remainder of the Pastos:

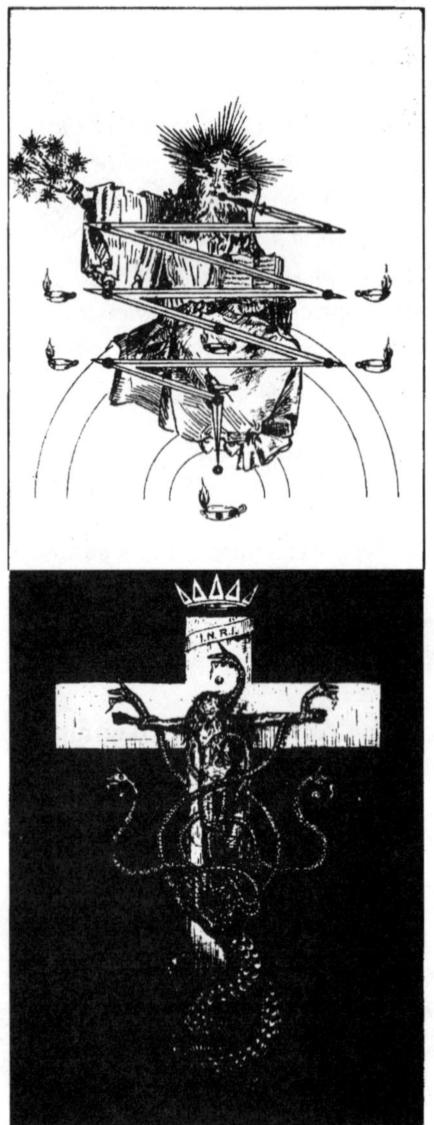

The Lid of the Pastos

White		
Red	Red	
Red-orange		Red
Orange	Orange	
Yellow-orange		
Yellow	Yellow	
Yellow-green		
Green	Green	Yellow
Blue-green	Blue	
Blue		
Blue-violet	Blue-violet	
Violet		Blue
Red-violet	Violet	
Black		

One Side of the Pastos

Figure 83: The Lid of the Pastos / One Side of the Pastos

Figure 84: St. John's Vision of Christ and the Seven Candlesticks (by Albrecht Dürer)

The head of the Pastos is white, charged with a golden Greek Cross and Red Rose of 49 Petals. The foot is black with a white Calvary Cross and Circle placed upon a pedestal of Two Steps. On the sides are depicted the 22 Colors of the Paths, between Light and Darkness.[27]

In a document known as "The Book of the Tomb," the Pastos is further described:

The Pastos which stands under the Circular Altar has no bottom but a hinged lid which can be turned back during the Second Point of the 5=6 Ceremony. The inner surface bears the colors of the Forces. Both the inner and the outer lid of the right side are in the positive scale of colors. To the left, they are in the negative Scale of colors. The head is white inside and out. Outside it bears the Red Rose of 49 petals on a Golden Greek Cross. Inside the 10 colors of the Masculine scale on the Sephiroth in the Tree of Life. The foot is black inside and out. Outside there is a Calvary Cross on three steps with a circle. Inside the 10 children colors in the Sephiroth on the Tree.

The Symbolism of the Seven Sides

(Note: The following is a paper by Wescott, originally published in Regardie's *The Golden Dawn*,[28] reprinted here in its entirety because of its excellent analysis of the symbolism of the Vault Walls. See Figure 85 on page 220.)

Among those characteristics which are truly necessary in the pursuit of magical knowledge and power, there is hardly any one more essential than thoroughness. And there is no failing more common in modern life than superficiality.

There are many who, even in this grade which has been gained by serious study, after being charmed and instructed by the first view of the Vault of Christian Rosencreutz, have made no attempt to study it as a new theme. There are many who have attained many ceremonial admissions and yet know nothing of the emblematic arrangement of the forty squares upon each side.

Some of you do not even know that Venus is, in an astrological sense, misplaced among the sides, and not two in five have been able to tell me why this is so, or what is the basis of the arrangement of the seven colors and forces. Many have told me which element out of the four is missing, and others have told me that the sign Leo occurs twice, but very few can tell me why the two forms of Leo are in different colors in each case, and only a few can tell me without hesitation which Three Sephiroth have no planet attached.

And yet even in the 1=10 grade you are told you must analyze and comprehend that Light or Knowledge, and not only take it on personal authority. Let us then be Adepti in fact, and not only on the surface; let our investigations be more than skin deep. That only which you can demonstrate is really known to you, and that only which is comprehended can fructify and become spiritual progress as distinguished from intellectual gain. Unless you can perceive with the soul as well as see with the eye your progress is but seeming, and you will continue to wander in the wilds of the unhappy.

Let your maxim be *Multum non Multa*—Much rather than many things. And tremble lest the Master find you wanting in those things you allow it to be supposed that you have become proficient in. Hypocrisy does not become the laity; it is a fatal flaw in the character of the occultist. You know it is not only the teacher in this Hall before whom you may be humiliated, but before your higher and divine Genius who can in no wise be deceived by outward seeming, but judgeth you by the heart, in that your spiritual heart is but the reflection of his brightness and the image of Tiphareth, and Tiphareth the reflection of the crowned Wisdom of Kether, and the concealed One.

There are but a couple of pages in the 5=6 Ritual which refer to the symbolism of the seven sides of the Vault. Read them over carefully, and then let us study these things together. First, the seven sides as a group, and then the 40 squares that are on each side.

The seven sides are all alike in size and shape and subdivision, and the forty squares on each side bear the same symbols. But the coloring is varied in the extreme, no two sides are alike in tint, and none of the squares are identical in color excepting the single central upper square of each wall, that square bearing the Wheel of Spirit. The seven walls are under the planetary presidency, one side to each planet. The subsidiary squares represent the coloring of the combined forces of the planet; the symbol of each square is represented by the ground color, while the symbol is in the color contrasted or complementary to that of the ground.

Now these planetary sides are found to be in a special order, neither astronomical nor astrological. The common order of the succession of the planets is that defined by their relative distances from Earth; putting the Sun, however, in the Earth's place in the series—thus: Saturn, Jupiter, Mars, Sun, Venus, Mercury, Moon. Saturn is farthest from the Earth, and the Earth is between Mars and Venus. Beginning with Saturn in the case of the Walls of the Vault, the order is Saturn, Jupiter, Mars, Sun, Mercury, Venus, Moon. Here Mercury and Venus are transposed.

But there is something more than this. For Saturn, the farthest off, is neither the door nor the East, nor anywhere else that is obviously intended. For it is the corner between the South and the Southwest sides. Nor is Luna, at the other end of the scale, in any notable position on the old lines.

There is, then, a new key to their order to be found and used, and such as are very intuitive see it at a glance. The planets are in the order of the Rainbow colors, and in colors because this Adeptus Minor grade is the especial exponent of colors. You Adepti are in the Path of the Chamelion—Hodos Chamelionis. If now you take the planetary colors and affix the planet and arrange them in the order of the solar spectrum and then bend up the series

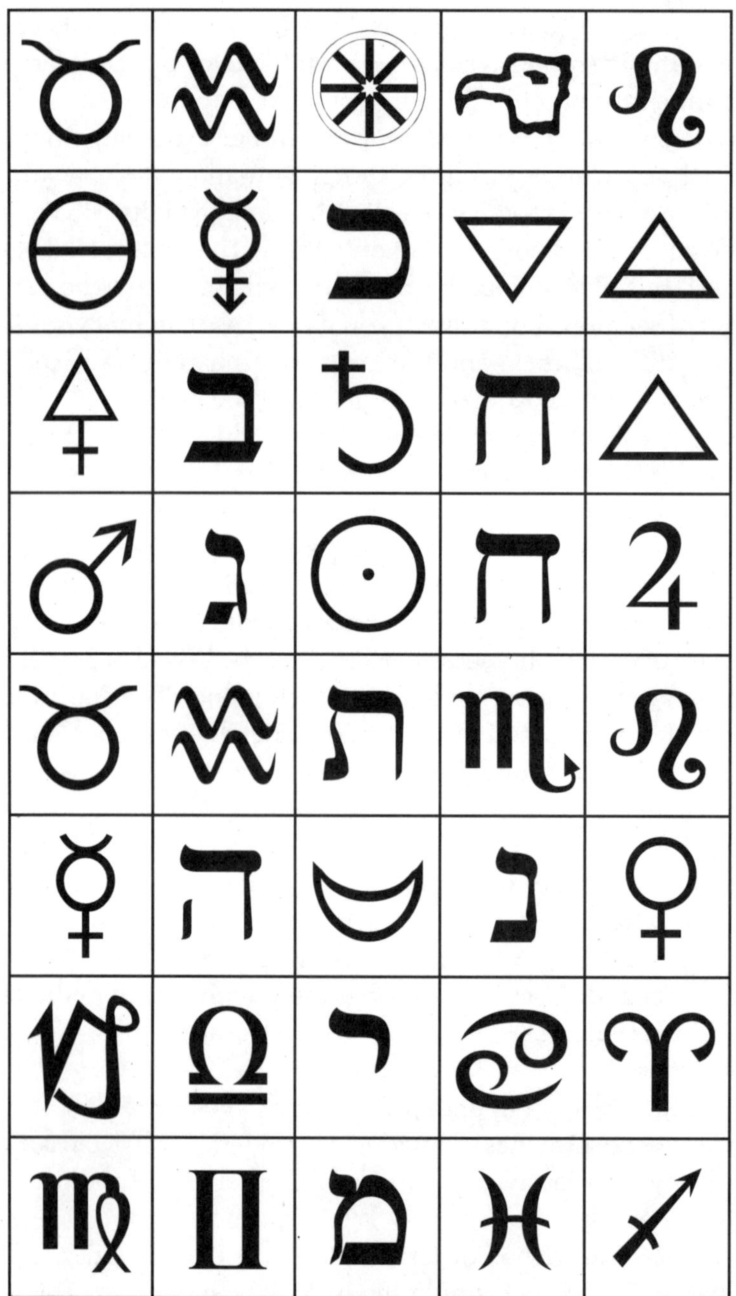

Figure 85: The Wall of the Vault

into a ring and make the chain into a Heptagram, and turn the whole about until you get the two ends of the series to meet at the Eastern point, you will have this mysterium:

Violet—Jupiter	Indigo—Saturn	Blue—Moon
Green—Venus	Yellow—Mercury	Orange—Sun
Red—Mars		

Science teaches, and has rediscovered a great truth, that however valuable the seven colors of the prism may be, there are rays invisible and so not demonstrated here by space. Beyond the red end of the spectrum begins the violet, and these have a great chemical or Yetsiratic force. These forces, ever present and unseen, are represented by the Chief Adept standing erect at the Eastern angle, the most powerful person in the group, and delegate of the Chiefs of the Second Order, and through them of the Mystic Third Order. He it is who has, symbolically, at any rate, passed from death unto life, and holds the Keys of all the creeds. And he it is who may place in our hands the Keys of the locked palace of the King if we are able to make our knocking heard. Representing the East, coming from the East, he faces the Western world, bringing intuition with him; before him lies the symbolic body of our Master C. R. C., our grand exemplar and founder—or at other times, the empty Pastos, from which he has arisen, the Chief Adept.

He has Mars and Geburah at his right hand, and Jupiter and Gedulah at his left hand. He faces Venus in the West, the Evening Star, which represents the entry of the Candidate who has toiled all day until the evening. At even he enters the Western door of the planet Venus, that sole planet unto whose symbol alone all the Sephiroth are conformed. At "evening time there shall be light," the light of mixed colors. So the newly admitted adept comes in contact with the totality of the planetary forces for the first time. A great opportunity opens before him; let him see well that he use it worthily. He enters through the green side of the vault. Green is the color of growth; let him see that he grows.

Upon each side of the vault are forty squares, five vertical series and eight horizontal, the whole being symbolically 5' x 8'. Now the published and printed *Fama Fraternatitas* says these forty feet were divided into ten squares. If you are mathematicians you would know that ten similar squares could not alone be placed in such and area and yet fill it. Ten squares alone to fill a rectangle could only be placed in an area of the shape 5' x 6'. Hence in the *Fama*, ten squares are a blind which we know to represent "Ten squares are marked and salient"—they are the Sephiroth.

Besides the Ten Sephiroth, there are the following: There are the four Kerubim, Three Alchemical Principles, Three Elements, Seven Planets, Twelve Zodiacal Signs, One Wheel of the Spirit—thus 40 in all. The Spirit wheel is on every side and always in the center, and is always depicted unchanged in black upon white.

Upon the sides there are always the four Kerubic emblems—Zodiacal, yet different, for the Eagle replaces Scorpio. (Scorpio has three forms, the Scorpion, the Eagle, and the Snake for the evil aspect.) These Kerubim represent the letters of the name YHVH, and note that they are always arranged in the Hebrew order of the letters. Yod for the Lion, Heh for the Eagle, Vau for the Man, Heh final for the Ox, the Tauric Earth.

Note that these four Zodiacal signs are not in their own colors, but as symbols of the elements have elementary colors. As Zodiacal signs, then, they are found to be compounds of the Elemental and Planetary colors; but they are here as Kerubic emblems compounded of the Elemental color and the Planetary color of the side.

The Three Principles are composed of the color of the Principles, and the color of the Planet of any particular wall. Mercury being fundamentally blue, Sulphur red, and Salt yellow.

The Three Elementals have fundamentally the usual three colors, Fire red, Water blue, Air yellow. Note that Earth is missing.

The Seven planets have their colors as are often stated, and note that each of the seven is set beside its appropriate Sephirah, so that there are three Sephiroth which have no Planet: Kether, Chokmah, and Malkuth.

The twelve Zodiacal Signs are the lower portion of the sides of the vertical column. The central one has none of the twelve; they are allotted between the four remaining columns. Further note that they are only three ranks, the 5th, 7th, and 8th; none are in the 6th rank from above.

This arrangement then shows: Four Triplicities and three Quaternaries. Observe well the arrangement; it is complex but not confused.

1. Kerubic Fixed. Shining Rank.
2. Cardinal Fiery. Solar Rank.
3. Common (mutable) Airy. Subtle Rank.

From above down, or in columns these are: Earthy Signs. Airy Signs. Watery Signs. Fiery Signs.

Rank 5. The Kerubic line shows the signs in the order of Tetragrammaton read in Hebrew.

Rank 7. The cardinal line shows the signs from the right in order of astronomical sequence of the solar course; vernal equinox, summer solstice, autumnal equinox, winter solstice.

Rank 8. The common line shows the Signs again in a different position. Here the earliest in the year is Gemini on the left of Mem, and passing left to Virgo, you then go round to extreme right to Sagittarius, pass centerwards to Pisces close to Malkuth. The coloring of each square is dual—a ground color, and the color of the emblem. The ground color is a compound of the color of the Planet of the side tinting the color of the Force to which the Square is allotted.

Each side has the Square of its own planet in its own unmixed color, and with this exception all the colored grounds are compound. The emblem color is always complimentary to the ground color.

The ritual of the Adeptus Minor gives the definite colors of each planet and sign which are to be used in this system. There are other allotments of color to each of these symbols and forces, but these are retained as mysteries yet to be evolved and revealed when you have become familiar with the present simple and elementary system.

—"The Symbolism of the Seven Sides"
by G. H. Frater N. O. M. (Dr. W. W. Westcott)

All of the preceding information concerning the Vault, though it barely scratches the surface, should be more than enough to show the utter complexity and marvelous ingenuity that went into its creation. A complete analysis of the construction methods, symbolism, and use of the Vault would require reams of information that would make this book impossibly long. There is also the danger of misusing such a powerful ritual chamber where banishings are forbidden. The possibility for disaster is great if a person unwittingly invokes some unwanted energy into this highly consecrated space and cannot get rid of it unless he or she completely clears the chamber by banishing—rendering it a magical void. Therefore we will not go into detail about the construction of a Vault, but we will share a few insights brought about through experience. It is likely that some of the Vaults from the early days of the Order were painted on large sheets of canvas, intended to be more or less portable. Moina Mathers (Soror Vestigia Nulla Retrorsum) was responsible for painting the elaborate designs of the Vault at Isis-Urania in London and possibly another at Ahathoor in Paris. Moina's preferred technique was a combination of oil paint and collage on canvas. It is possible that the walls of some Vaults were done in this manner.

When the Golden Dawn was revived in the United States in the late 1970s,[29] it was decided that a more sturdy Vault was called for. This involved the construction of a room out of wood and plaster, not only ensuring that the angles of the heptagon would be absolutely correct, but also that the room would be a virtual soundproof chamber; blocking out all outside noises while at the same time enhancing all spoken vibrations. When Regardie consecrated this Vault on Corpus Christi, June 26, 1982 and initiated two people into the grade of 5=6, he ensured that a valid initiatory branch of the original Order was established. (See Figure 86, page 224.) The old house containing the Vault was altered to ensure that its inner chamber could not be discovered by accident. The parlor

Figure 86: Israel Regardie in the Vault of the Adepti

was completely sealed off from the rest of the house, as if the room never existed. Entrance to the chamber was gained only through a small door cut into the back wall of a closet, which led to the antechamber or portal of the Vault.[30]

A small door was constructed in the Venus wall of the Vault to be the main entrance into the Tomb. The solar wall of the Vault was, in fact, a huge door that swung open into what remained of the hidden parlor. Both of these doors were made to appear invisible to anyone inside the chamber. A small coffin was purchased at a local funeral parlor and painted in the appropriate colors to serve as the pastos of C. R. C., i.e., the Chief Adept. (This later proved to be too heavy and awkward and has since been replaced by a pastos that is light and easily transported by a single person.)

The building of a Vault in such a manner is obviously a feat of carpentry that the average magician studying on his or her own is not likely to undertake. However, a single Vault wall can be reproduced in miniature for study and meditation. This diminutive wall has proven to be an effective tool for Adepts who do not have consistent access to a proper Vault. (Note: The colors on the miniature are the pure colors of the symbols, unmixed with planetary colors.)

The Miniature Vault Wall

Materials Needed

- 10" x 16" piece of wood, canvas board, or masonite
- Gesso
- Acrylic paints: red, orange, yellow, green, blue, blue-violet, violet, red-violet, black, and white
- Clear lacquer finish

Tools Needed

- Straight edge
- Artist's brushes (various sizes)

Construction

1. Cover the board with a coat of gesso and allow to dry.
2. Mark the surface of the board off into 2" squares (five squares wide and eight squares high—a total of forty).
3. Trace the symbols onto the board according to the diagram of the Vault Wall (see Figure 85, page 220). Paint the symbols as follows:

	Ground Color	**Charge Color**
Squares:		
Spirit	White	Black
Kerubic:		
Leo	Red	Green
Scorpio	Blue	Orange
Aquarius	Yellow	Violet
Taurus	Black	White
Sephiroth:		
Kether	White	Black
Chokmah	Gray	Pale gray
Binah	Black	White
Chesed	Blue	Orange
Geburah	Red	Green
Tiphareth	Yellow	Violet
Netzach	Green	Red
Hod	Orange	Blue
Yesod	Violet	Yellow
Malkuth	Citrine, russet, black, olive	White
Elements:		
Fire	Red	Green
Water	Blue	Orange
Air	Yellow	Violet
Alchemic Principles:		
Sulfur	Pale red (pink)	Dark green
Mercury	Pale yellow	Dark violet
Salt	Pale blue	Dark orange
Planets:		
Saturn	Blue-violet	Yellow-orange
Jupiter	Violet	Yellow
Mars	Red	Green
Sol	Orange	Blue
Venus	Green	Red
Mercury	Yellow	Violet
Luna	Blue	Orange

Zodiacal Signs:

Aries	Red	Green
Taurus	Red-orange	Blue-green
Gemini	Orange	Blue
Cancer	Yellow-orange	Blue-violet
Leo	Yellow	Violet
Virgo	Yellow-green	Red-violet
Libra	Green	Red
Scorpio	Blue-green	Red-orange
Sagittarius	Blue	Orange
Capricorn	Blue-violet	Yellow-orange
Aquarius	Violet	Yellow
Pisces	Red-violet	Yellow-green

5. After all the paint is dry, cover with a coat of clear lacquer for protection.

Endnotes

1. Regardie, *The Golden Dawn*, 21.
2. The Feast of Corpus Christi of the Western Christian Church the Presence of the body (corpus) of Jesus Christ in the Eucharist. A movable holiday, it is observed on the Thursday (or, in some nations, the Sunday) after Trinity Sunday. In the fifteenth century, it became the principal feast of the church, where mystery and miracle plays were a prominent feature of the celebration.
3. It is probable that what seems to be described as two different sashes is, in fact, one sash that is white trimmed and ornamented with yellow.
4. Regardie, *The Golden Dawn*, 224.
5. Budge, *Gods of the Egyptians*, Vol. 1, 483.
6. Hall, *The Secret Teachings of All Ages*, xlix.
7. Schwaller de Lubicz, *The Temple of Man*, Volume Two, 1001. Schwaller includes a drawing of a simple tree branch, which, when inverted, displays the exact shape of the *waas* scepter. According to Schwaller, the waas was an important symbol associated with the city of Thebes and the god Amun. The godform of Amun has a significant role in the Adeptus Minor Ritual of the Golden Dawn.
8. Herodotus, *Histories*, 146.
9. Hall quoting Clement.
10. Cirlot, 253.
11. Regardie, *The Golden Dawn*, 224.
12. Ibid.
13. Ibid., 236–237.
14. "In Herschel's ground plan of the universe in human form...our solar system is located at the heart of the Divine Man of the skies. Hence, the catastrophe in our solar system, by which the ecliptic was sundered from the celestial equator, was a rapture or piercing of the heart of the Divine Man. The ecliptic and equator no longer coinciding, they formed a cross upon which the Divine Man was transfixed in space. This idea was familiar to the Hindus and to Plato." (Manly P. Hall, *The Secret Teachings of All Ages*, color plate 181, text accompanying illustration.)
15. If desired, an image of the Resurrected One can be attached to the front of the cross—not the bloodied and suffering Christ portrayed in many images, but Christ the King: strong, calm, and ascended into the higher.
16. Cirlot, 45.
17. Olcott, 234.
18. Regardie, *The Golden Dawn*, 61.
19. "This Holy Invisible Companionship," by Adam Forrest, published in *The Golden Dawn Journal, Book Two: Qabalah: Theory and Practice*, Cicero and Cicero, 198–199.
20. Regardie, *The Golden Dawn*, 233. In the original GD, many temples used the letters of the Tetragrammaton in place of the faces of the Kerubim for these plaques. (We prefer the full Kerubic faces.) Whether one decides to create the Kerubic faces as given here or simply paint the Hebrew letters of YHVH in their place (or combine the letters with the faces), the color scheme listed here should be adhered to.
21. "This Holy Invisible Companionship," by Adam Forrest, published in *The Golden Dawn Journal, Book Two: Qabalah: Theory and Practice*, Cicero and Cicero, 203–204.

22. Excerpt from *The Fama Fraternitatis, or A Discovery of the Fraternity of the most laudable Order of Rosy Cross,* first published in 1614. This excerpt is from the 1652 English Translation of Eugenius Philalethes (Thomas Vaughan).
23. Regardie, *The Golden Dawn,* 233–235.
24. Ibid., 242–246
25. Ibid., 239.
26. Ibid.
27. Ibid., 246.
28. Ibid., 266–269.
29. See the foreword to *Ritual Use of Magical Tools* by Adam P. Forrest.
30. As a note of interest, a reproduction of a painting titled "A Man in Armor" by Rembrandt, hung on the outside door of this closet. The same weekend that Regardie consecrated the Vault, we discovered in a book called *A Christian Rosenkreutz Anthology,* that this same painting was said to represent none other than Christian Rosenkreutz himself.

CHAPTER FIVE

The Adept's Personal Temple

For a proper magical working in the tradition of the Golden Dawn, the adept will need many of the items mentioned in the preceding chapters. These include the Banners of the East and West, the pillars, the cross and triangle, an iset, the Enochian Tablets, the altars (black or white depending on the working), a cup of water, and a censer of incense. Traditionally, an oil lamp burned above the altar of the Theurgist is a sign of the radiant presence of the divine. However, we have never relished the thought of hot, flammable liquid being suspended in the air over the magician's work space, so we recommend simply placing a white candle on the altar. Also needed are the white Tau robe, yellow sash, and the yellow-and-white striped nemyss, which are the ritual garb of the Second Order. All of these items make up the core of the adept's personal temple, where the magician does his or her personal and most powerful ritual work—outside of and apart from group temple work.

In the Golden Dawn system, the Neophyte Adeptus Minor can only become a fully trained initiating Hierophant by undertaking a prescribed curriculum of study. A series of tests must be passed before the Neophyte Adept can claim the title of Zelator Adeptus

Figure 87: The Goddess Isis with Lotus Wand and Ankh

Minor (Z. A. M.), the lowest grade which may hold the office of Hierophant. Included within this work is the construction and consecration of the Elemental Weapons or Implements. These implements are specialized tools for gaining access to and working with the spirits of the four elements. The Adept must also construct a Lotus Wand, which is to be carried at all Second Order functions, along with the Rose Cross Lamen, the personal emblem of both the Adept and the Order to which he or she belongs. In addition, a personal Magical Sword is needed.

To obtain real force implanted in any magical weapon by consecration, the Adept is required to be healthy, pure, strong in mind, free from anxiety, and apart from disturbances. He or she is required to have mastered the details of the ceremony and to be familiar with the proper pentagrams and other symbols.

The Primary Implements

The Lotus Wand

The most important aid in ritual magic is, and always will be, the magic wand.[1]

The Lotus Wand is based on the *Wadj* or Papyrus Scepter of the ancient Egyptians. Used as an amulet, it was intended to give its owner increased vigor and youth. Made from mother of emerald or light blue porcelain, the Wadj was said to represent the power of the goddess Isis. (See Figure 87, page 232.)

The Lotus Wand is for general use in magical working. It is carried by the Z. A. M. at all meetings of the Second Order at which the initiate has the right to be present. It is to be made by the Adept unassisted and to be consecrated by him or her alone. It is not to be touched by any other person, and kept wrapped in white silk of linen, free from external influences other than Adept's own on the human plane.

The ten upper and inner petals refer to the purity of the ten Sephiroth. The middle eight refer to the counter-charged natural and spiritual forces of Air and Fire. The lowest and outer eight refer to the powers of Earth and Water. The center and amber portion refers to the spiritual Sun, while the outer calyx of four orange sepals shows the action of the Sun on the life of things by differentiation.

As a general rule, the white end of the wand is used to invoke and the black end to banish. The white end may be used to banish by tracing a banishing symbol against an evil and opposing force, which has resisted other efforts. By this is meant that by whatever band you are holding the wand, whether white for spiritual things, by black for mundane, by blue for

Sagittarius, or by red for the fiery triplicity, you are, when invoking, to direct the white extremity to the quarter desired. When banishing, point the black end to that quarter.

The wand is never to be inverted, so that where very material forces are concerned, the black end may be the most suitable for invocation, but with the greatest caution.

In working on the plane of the zodiac, hold the wand by the portion you refer to between the thumb and two fingers.

If a planetary working be required, hold the wand by the portion representing the day or night house of the planet, or else by the sign in which the planet is at the time.

Planet		**House**	**Sign**	**Band**
♄	Saturn	Day house[2]	Aquarius	Violet band
		Night house	Capricorn	Blue-violet
♃	Jupiter	Day house	Sagittarius	Blue band
		Night house	Pisces	Red-violet band
♂	Mars	Day house	Aries	Red band
		Night house	Scorpio	Blue-green band
♀	Venus	Day house	Libra	Green band
		Night house	Taurus	Red-orange band
☿	Mercury	Day house	Gemini	Orange band
		Night house	Virgo	Yellow-green band
☉	Sol	In Leo only		Yellow band
☽	Luna	In Cancer only		Yellow-orange band

For example, if Venus is the planet referred to, use Libra in the day and Taurus at night.

Should the working be with the elements, one of the signs of the triplicity of the elements should be held according to the nature of the element you are intending to invoke. (*Fire triplicity:* Aries, Leo, Sagittarius. *Water triplicity:* Cancer, Scorpio, Pisces. *Air triplicity:* Gemini, Libra, Aquarius. *Earth triplicity:* Taurus, Virgo, Capricorn.) Bear in mind that the Kerubic sign is the most powerful action of the element in the triplicity.

Hold the wand by the white portion for all divine and spiritual matters or for the Sephirotic influences, and for the process of rising in the planes. Hold the black part only for material and mundane matters.

The Lotus Flower is not to be touched in working, but in Sephirotic and spiritual things, the flower is to be inclined toward the forehead; to rise in the planes, the orange-colored center is to be fully directed to the forehead.[3]

The Golden Dawn's traditional ritual for "The Consecration of the Lotus Wand" is given in *Ritual Use of Magical Tools*, chapter five. An additional ritual for the use of the Lotus Wand is also given.

See Color Plate 16 and refer to Figure 88 on page 236 for construction diagrams.

Materials Needed

- One ¾" dowel anywhere from 24" to 40" in length (the wand described here has a shaft length of 26")
- One square foot of copper or tin sheet metal
- One brass locknut—also called a hanger bolt (a plain brass screw may be substituted)
- Cider vinegar
- Masking tape
- Gesso
- Acrylic paints: red, orange, yellow, green, blue, blue-violet, violet, red-violet, black, and white
- Sealant: clear lacquer finish

Tools Needed

- Electric drill
- Tin snips or metal shears
- Small vise
- Artist's brushes (large, medium, and fine)
- Emery cloth
- Fine sandpaper
- File
- Pliers
- One index card

Construction: The Flower

1. Wash the copper or tin sheet metal with cider vinegar. Rough-up the surface of the metal on both sides of all sections with emery cloth to enable the paint to stick to it.

2. Cover one side of the metal with masking tape. (Lay strip after strip of masking tape over the metal until it is completely covered.)

3. With a pencil, draw out the four sections of the Lotus flower (as shown in Figure 88, page 236) on the masking tape covering the sheet metal. The largest section (eight petals) should be approximately 4¼" in diameter. The second largest (eight petals)

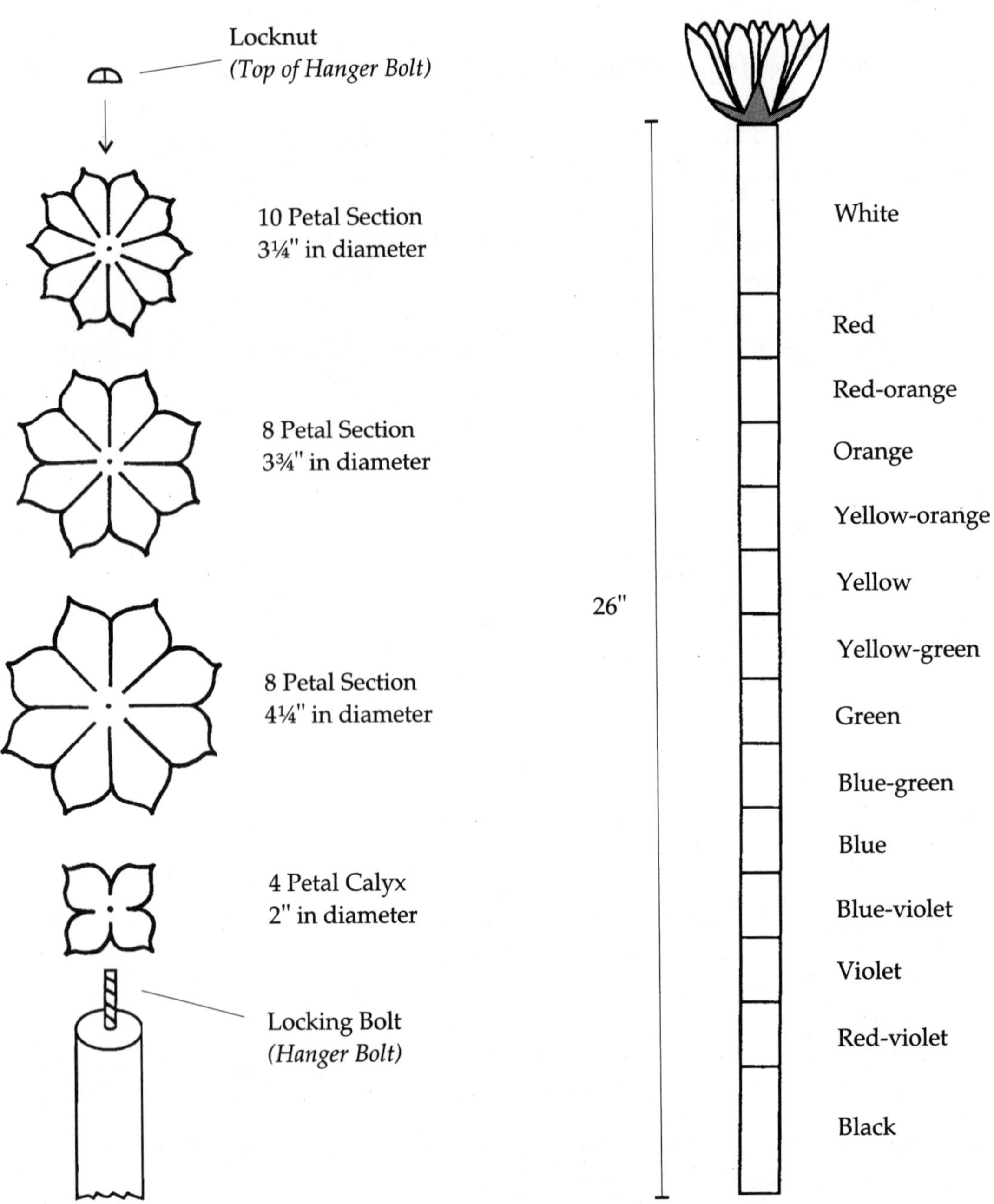

Figure 88: The Lotus Wand

should be approximately 3¾" across. The ten-petaled section should be about 3¼" across. The small, four-sepaled calyx is only 2" in diameter.

4. Cut out the four sections of the Lotus Flower and file the edges so they are smooth.
5. Drill a hole in the center of each section of the flower. (Use a drill bit that is the same size as the shaft of the locknut or screw used to hold the assemblage together.)
6. Using the pliers, bend the pieces so that they turn inward slightly, like an opening flower. Cover each petal with a piece of cloth first, to avoid marking the metal.
7. Cover both sides of all sections with a white primer coat. Let dry.
8. Paint the ten-petaled piece white on both sides. Paint the two eight-petaled pieces white on one side (inside) and olive on the other (outside). Olive is created from mixing green with violet. The calyx is orange on both sides. (Note: Acrylic paint is theoretically not supposed to stick to metal, but if the pieces have been thoroughly washed with cider vinegar, then rubbed with emery cloth, you should have no difficulty, although it will take at least three coats of paint. We have created numerous Lotus Wands in this manner and have never experienced a problem.)
9. On the olive-colored outside of the large eight-petaled piece, paint a pattern of five veins in black on each petal. Spray or brush on sealant for protection. Let dry.

Construction: The Shaft

10. Drill a hole in one end of the dowel which is to be the top. (Use a bit that matches the size of the shaft of the locknut or screw that will hold the assemblage together.)
11. Cover the dowel with a coat of gesso. Let dry and sand with fine sandpaper. Repeat if necessary.
12. Measure down 4½" from the top of the dowel. Mark with a pencil. Pencil in twelve more marks, going down the shaft from the first measurement at intervals of 1½". The measurement from the last pencil mark to the end of the wand will be 3½".
13. Using an index card as a straight edge by wrapping it around the dowel at the place of the first pencil mark, draw a line completely around the shaft. Do this at all penciled measurements leading down the dowel.
14. Paint each section of the dowel as shown in the diagram using the acrylic paints listed.[3] (You may wish to paint a thin gold line between each band of color or use thin pinstriping to separate the bands with an attractive golden line.) Let the paint dry completely. Spray or brush on sealant for protection. Let dry.

Figure 89: The Front of the Rose Cross Lamen

Finishing Steps

15. Assemble all the pieces of the Lotus as follows: The ten-petaled piece is placed inside the smaller of the two eight-petaled pieces. This is in turn placed inside the large eight-petaled piece. The calyx is placed under the others, between the larger petaled section and the top of the shaft. (Washers can be placed between the pieces to separate them.)

16. Attach the screw portion of the brass locknut into the hole drilled in the top of the shaft. Place the assembled Lotus Flower over the end of the screw; the threaded top of the screw should stick out from the end of the shaft. Place the locknut over the exposed end of the screw and turn until it locks into place. The Lotus should now be firmly attached to the wand. (The advantage in using a brass locknut as opposed to a regular brass screw is that it looks like the center of a flower, rather than the head of a screw. Oven-hardening clay can be added to a regular nut to make it look more attractive.)

The Rose Cross Lamen

The Rose Cross Lamen is to be made by each Adept alone, consecrated—never touched by any other person—and wrapped in white silk or linen when not in use. The motto of the owner is painted on the reverse side, and it is to be worn suspended from a yellow collarette at all meetings of Adepts.

This lamen is a complete synthesis of the masculine, positive, or rainbow scale of color attributions, which is also called "the Scale of the King." (See Color Plate 11 and Figure 89, page 238.)

The four arms of the cross belong to the four elements and are colored accordingly. The white portion belongs to the Holy Spirit and the planets.

The twenty-two petals of the rose refer to the twenty-two paths on the Tree of Life. It is the cross in Tiphareth, the receptacle and the center of the forces of the Sephiroth and the paths.

The extreme center of the rose is white, the reflected spiritual brightness of Kether, bearing on it the Red Rose of Five Petals and the Golden Cross of Six Squares; four green rays issue from around the angles of the cross, from which the Second Order takes its name. They are the symbols of the Receiving Force.

On the white portion of the lamen, below the rose, is placed the Hexagram with the planets in the order which is the key of the Supreme Ritual of Hexagram.

Around the pentagrams, one placed on each elemental colored arm, are drawn the symbols of the spirit and the four elements, in the order which is the key to the Supreme Ritual of the Pentagram. On each of the floriated ends (the arms) of the cross are arranged the three alchemical principles of sulfur, salt, and mercury, but in a different order for each elemental arm, and as showing their different operation within the different elements.

The uppermost arm of the cross, allotted to Air, displays the yellow color of Tiphareth. In it the flowing, philosophic, mercurial nature is most potent and without hindrance to its mobility; hence the ever moving nature of Air. Its sulphurous side is drawn from the part of Fire, hence its luminous and electrical qualities. Its saline side is from Water, whence result clouds and rain from the action of the solar forces.

The lowest arm of the cross, attributed to Earth, is of the four colors of Malkuth, the Earth being of the nature of a container and receiver of the other influences. The citrine section answers to its airy part, the olive to the watery section, the russet to the fiery portion,

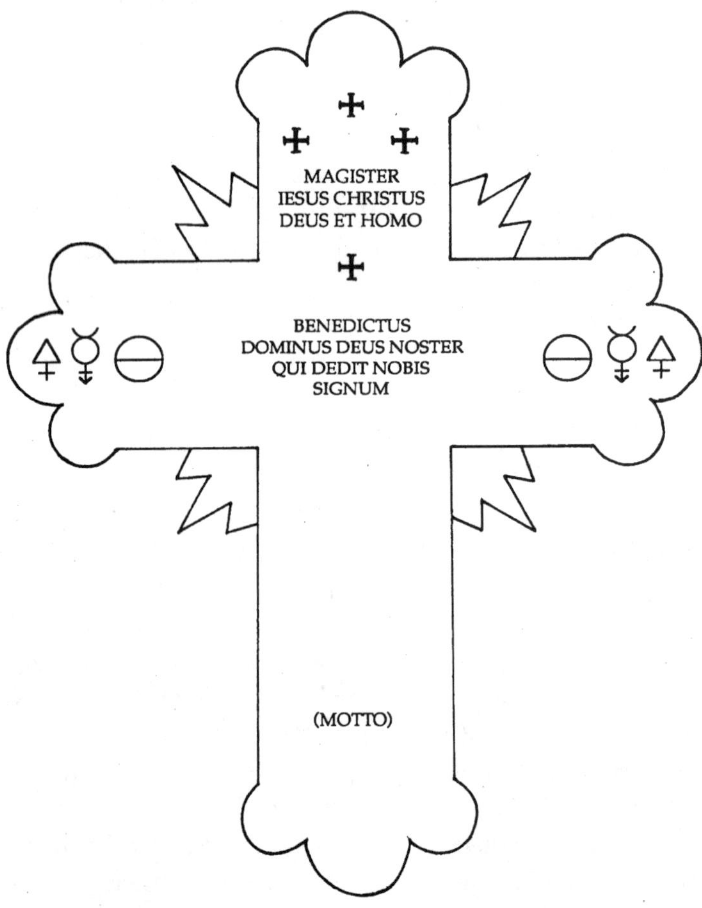

Figure 90: The Back of the Rose Cross Lamen

and the black to the lowest part, Earth. In the earthy section, the mercurial nature is also most potent, but hindered by the compound nature, whence its faculty becomes germinative rather than mobile, while the sulfur and the salt are respectively from the sides of Water and Fire, which almost neutralize their natural operation and bring about the fixedness and immobility of Earth.

The arm assigned to Fire is of the red color of Geburah, and in it the sulphurous nature is chief, whence its powers of heat and burning. The salt is from the side of Earth, whence the necessity for a constant substantial pabulum whereon to act. The mercury is from the side of Air, whence the leaping, lambent motion of flame, especially when acted upon by wind.

The extremity attributed to Water is of the blue color of Chesed, and in it the saline side is chief as exemplified in the salt water of the ocean, to which all waters go; and from whence also is derived the nature of always preserving the horizontal line. The mercurial part is from Earth, whence the weight and force of its flux and reflux. Its sulfuric part is from the Air, whence the effect of waves and storms, so that the disposition of these three principles forms the key of their alchemic operation in the elements.

The white rays issuing from behind the rose at the inner angles between the arms of the cross are the rays of the divine light, issuing and coruscating from the reflected light of Kether in its center; and the letters and symbols on them refer to the analysis of the Key Word of an Adeptus Minor, *I. N. R. I.* by which the opening of the Vault is accomplished.

The Twelve Simple Letters of the Hebrew Alphabet are assigned to the twelve outer petals, which follow the order of the signs of the zodiac. Uppermost is Heh, the letter of Aries, followed by Vav, Zayin, Cheth, Teth, Yod, while the letter of Libra, which is Lamed, is lowermost. The ascending letters are Nun, Samekh, Ayin, Tzaddi, and Qoph.

The Seven Double Letters of the middle row are assigned to the planets in the order of their exaltations, the planets being wanderers; the stars are fixed with respect to the Earth. These letters are Peh, Resh, Beth, with Daleth exactly over Libra, followed by Gimel, Tau, and Kaph.[5]

The Three Mother Letters are allotted to the elements and are so arranged that the petal of Air is beneath the arm of the cross allotted to Air, while those of Fire and Water are on counterchanged sides, so that the forces of the arms of the cross should not override the planetary and zodiacal forces in the rose, which might otherwise be the case if the petal of Fire were placed on the same side as the arm of Fire and that of Water on the side of Water.[6]

The rose is also a glyph of the entire manifest universe. This symbol when properly painted should resemble a perfect color wheel. Any error in the pigments will be readily apparent to an artist. The Hermetic Order of the Golden Dawn developed a method of drawing sigils from the rose in which a name was transliterated into its Hebrew letters. A continuous line is drawn from one Hebrew letter to the next. Sigils drawn from the rose are more practical to use than those drawn from traditional Qameas or Magical Squares.

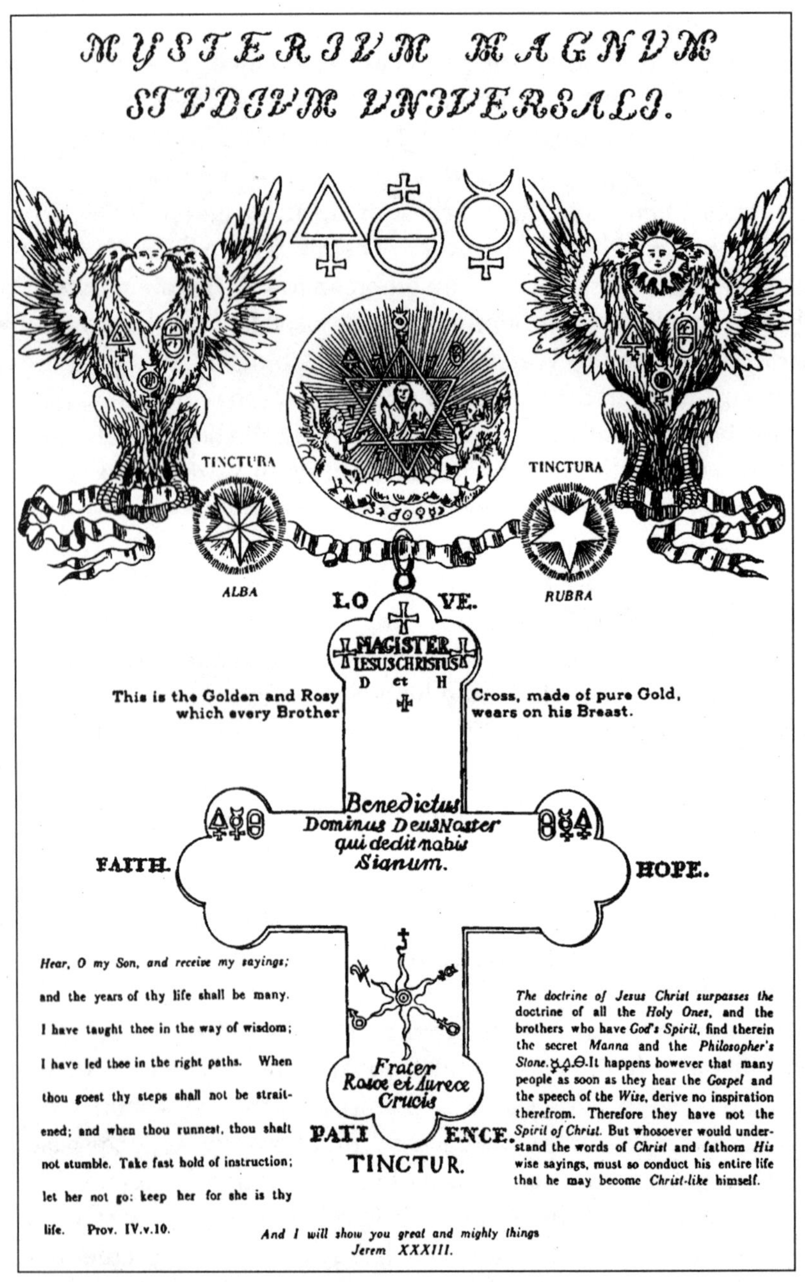

Figure 91: The Great Cross of the Rosicrucians

The back of the cross bears the following inscription in Latin: "The Master Jesus Christ, God and Man." It falls between four Maltese crosses, which represent the four pyramids of the elements opened out. This inscription is placed at the uppermost part because therein is affirmed a descent of the divine force into Tiphareth, which is the central point between supernals and the lower Sephiroth. (See Figure 90, page 240. Compare this with the Great Cross of the Rosicrucians from "The Secret Symbols of the Rosicrucians" [1785], shown in Figure 91, page 242.)

At the lowest part is written the motto or magical name of the magician who has attained to the grade of Zelator Adeptus Minor, because therein is the affirmation of the symbolic elevation of the human into the divine. But this is impossible without the assistance of the divine spirit from Kether, whence the space above Malkuth is white on the front of the cross, white being the symbol of the spiritual rescued from the material.

In the center of the cross's back side, between the symbols of the alchemical principles, of which the outermost is sulfur, the purgatorial Fire of suffering and self-sacrifice, is written in Latin, "Blessed be the Lord our God who hath given us the Symbol Signum." This is a word of six letters, representing the six creative periods in the universe.[7]

Many magicians make this lamen out of heavy cardboard which is then painted in the appropriate colors. However, we have always preferred lamens with a sculptured, three-dimensional appearance. The Rose Cross Lamen described here has the feel and solidity of a truly powerful magical implement. The colors must be clear and brilliant. If they are not, the symbol is useless either as a symbol or insignium. This is another reason why the acrylic colors listed in the introduction (page xxx) should be used.

The Golden Dawn's traditional ritual for "The Consecration of the Rose Cross" is given in *Ritual Use of Magical Tools*, chapter five. An additional ritual for the use of the lamen is also given.

Refer to Figure 89 on page 238 and Figure 90 on page 240 for construction diagrams.

Materials Needed

- One 6" square piece of pine, bass, or plywood, ½" or ⅜" thick
- One small piece of ⅛" thick basswood
- Yellow carpenter's glue
- Wood putty
- Gesso
- Acrylic paints: red, orange, yellow, green, blue, blue-violet, violet, red-violet, black, white, and gold
- Sealant: clear lacquer finish

Tools Needed

- Jigsaw or scroll saw
- Craft knife with wood carving blade
- Sandpaper (medium and fine)
- Artist's brushes (medium to very fine)

Construction

1. Trace the cross portion of the lamen onto the 6" square piece of pine or plywood. Make it the same size as the cross shown in Figure 89, page 238. Trace the four glories separately on the ⅛" basswood. Trace the circle for the rose on the ⅛" basswood.

2. Cut out all sections of the lamen.

3. Glue the four glories to the cross at the junction of the arms. Let dry. Fill in any gaps with wood putty. Sand with medium and fine sandpaper. Apply a coat of gesso and allow to dry. Sand lightly with fine sandpaper and add another coat if needed.

4. Trace three rows of petals onto the circular rose section. (Be sure to draw the small rose cross in the center as well.)

5. Using the knife with carving blade, gouge out a slight depression in the center of each rose petal. (When finished, the rose section should have a three-dimensional look.)

6. Cover the front part of the rose with a coat of gesso. Let dry. Apply glue to the back of the rose and attach to the cross. Allow to dry.

Finishing Steps

7. Paint the Rose Cross in the following colors:

   The Arms
   - Right arm: Blue with orange symbols
   - Left arm: Red with green symbols
   - Top arm: Yellow with violet symbols
   - Bottom arm: Upper half–white with black symbols; lower half–citrine, olive, russet, and black with white symbols

   The Center of the Rose
   - Gold cross with green glories and a red rose of five petals in the center
   - Background circle of white

The Petals of the Rose

א	Aleph	Yellow ground, violet letter
ב	Beth	Yellow ground, violet letter
ג	Gimel	Blue ground, orange letter
ד	Daleth	Green ground, red letter
ה	Heh	Red ground, green letter
ו	Vav	Red-orange ground, blue-green letter
ז	Zayin	Orange ground, blue letter
ח	Cheth	Yellow-orange ground, blue-violet letter
ט	Teth	Yellow ground, violet letter
י	Yod	Yellow-green ground, red-violet letter
כ	Kaph	Violet ground, yellow letter
ל	Lamed	Green ground, red letter
מ	Mem	Blue ground, orange letter
נ	Nun	Blue-green ground, red-orange letter
ס	Samekh	Blue ground, orange letter
ע	Ayin	Blue-violet ground, yellow-orange letter
פ	Peh	Red ground, green letter
צ	Tzaddi	Violet ground, yellow letter
ק	Qoph	Red-violet ground, yellow-green letter
ר	Resh	Orange ground, blue letter
ש	Shin	Red ground, green letter
ת	Tau	Blue-violet ground, yellow-orange letter

8. The back of the cross, as well as the four glories, are to be painted white with black letters. The sides of the lamen may be painted either gold or the colors of the arms.

9. Once the painted Rose Cross Lamen is dry, apply a coat of sealant for protection. When completely dry, a small piece of hook and loop fastener material can be glued to the back of the cross, which will attach to a yellow collar similar to the one described in chapter one, pages 81–83.

The Magic Sword

The Magic Sword of the Z. A. M. is to be used in all cases where great force and strength are to be used and are required, but principally for banishing and for defense against evil forces. For this reason it attributed to the Geburah and of Mars, whose names and forces are to be invoked at its consecration, which should take place in the day and hour of Mars, or else during the course of the Fiery Tattwa.[8]

Any convenient sword may be adapted to this use, but the handle, hilt, and guard must be such as to offer surfaces for inscriptions. The sword should be of medium length and weight. (See Figure 92.)

The motto of the Adept should be engraved on it, or painted on the hilt in letters of green, in addition to the appropriate mystic sigils and names. The hilt, pommel, and guard are to be colored red. The blade should be clean and bright. Pentagrams should be painted on salient portions, because this is the lineal figure of Geburah. The divine and angelic names related to Geburah are then to be added in green, and also their sigils drawn from the rose. The sword must be consecrated in due form.

Here again let the Zelator Adeptus Minor remember their obligation to never use the knowledge of practical magic for purposes of evil, and let the Adept be well assured that if evil magic is performed, notwithstanding the sacred pledge, the evil that the magician endeavors to bring about will react on him or herself. The magician will experience that very thing that he or she has endeavored to bring about for another.[9]

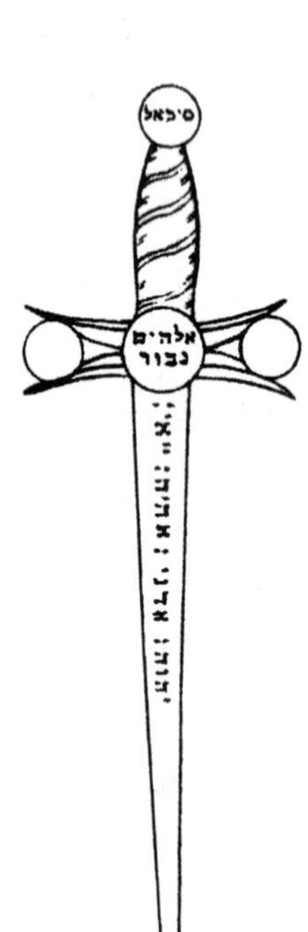

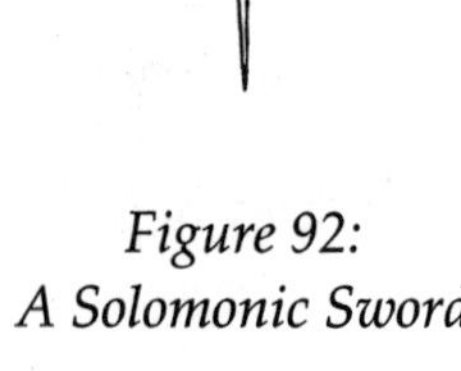

Figure 92:
A Solomonic Sword

The sword is to be used with great respect only for banishings, protection, and certain rituals (such as consecrations and evocations), where the force of Geburah is needed to bar and to threaten.

The Golden Dawn's traditional ritual for "The Consecration of the Magic Sword" is given in *Ritual Use of Magical Tools*, chapter five. An additional ritual for the use of the sword is also given.

Refer to Figure 93 on page 248 for construction diagrams.

Materials Needed

- One 1½" wide piece of flat steel, 4' long and ⅛" thick
- One ¾" thick piece of pine or basswood approximately 6" x 9"
- Three 1½" wooden balls
- Masking tape
- Strong epoxy
- Yellow carpenter's glue
- Smooth piece of red leather
- Gesso
- Acrylic paint: red, green
- Clear butyrate lacquer

Tools Needed

- Vise
- Jigsaw or hacksaw with metal cutting blade
- Electric drill with ⅛" bit
- Electric grinder (or drill with grinding wheel)
- Coarse and fine emery cloth
- File
- Sandpaper (coarse, medium, and fine)
- Craft knife
- Artist's brushes (medium to fine)

Construction: The Blade

1. Secure the flat steel in a vice. Using a jigsaw or hacksaw, cut one end of the piece of steel into a shank that is ¼" wide and 4" long. (See Figure 93, page 248.)

2. Using a grinding wheel with course emery cloth, grind the other end of the steel down until both edges taper down to a point. Grind both edges of the blade as well (the edges do not have to be extremely sharp). Use a finer emery cloth for smoothing the steel where you have ground it down. Polish the blade and remove any rust spots. Apply a coat of clear butyrate lacquer to protect the steel and prevent rusting. Put aside to dry fully.

Construction: The Hilt

3. Take the ¾" piece of wood and draw the pattern for the two pieces which comprise the handle: the guard and the grip. The guard should be 9" long and 1" wide at the center. (The double tips should flare out 2" tip to tip on either end.) The grip will be 6" long and 1" wide at the middle. Only one end has double tips which flare out 2".

4. Cut the two pieces out with the jigsaw.

5. Use coarse sandpaper to sand down all six tips on the ends of the two pieces until they are tapered points. (The guard of the sword is based on two crescents placed back-to-back.)

6. Find the center of the top of the guard (on the ¾" side—NOT the 1" front.) Mark with a pencil. Mark the center of the bottom as well. (This will be the side that butts up against the top of the blade.)

7. Secure the guard in a vise. Using a ⅛" bit, drill a hole through the mark you have drawn. You should now have a guard piece with a hole that runs through the center

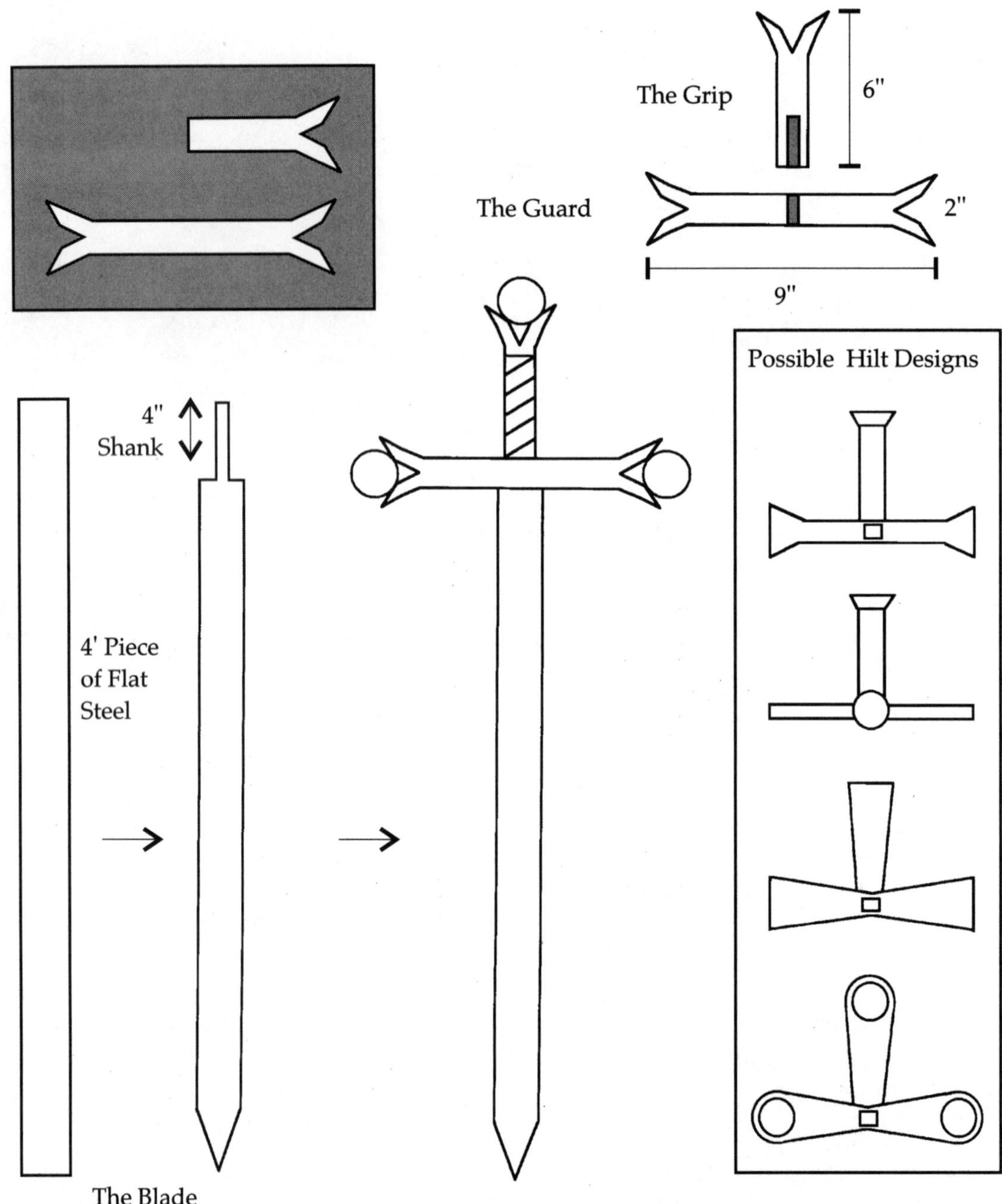

Figure 93: The Magic Sword

from top to bottom. Drill two holes close together in a straight line lengthwise from this hole in order to widen the original hole. (The extended hole should be wide enough to run the shank of the blade through it.) Use a small file inside the widened hole to even it out. Sand the entire piece with fine sandpaper.

8. Secure the grip in the vise. Find the center of the end which has no tips. Drill a straight ⅛" hole into the end which is 4" deep. Drill a couple more holes as before to widen the original hole in order to fit the blade shank. Sand the entire piece with medium and fine sandpaper.
9. Assemble the blade, guard, and grip to see if all pieces fit well and are not crooked. Make adjustments if necessary. Then fill the holes of both handle pieces with a strong epoxy. Attach the shank of the blade through the guard piece and into the grip. Hold pieces firmly until the epoxy sets. Allow to dry fully.
10. Take one of the wooden balls and epoxy it into place between one set of double tips on the handle. Repeat with the other two wooden balls. Allow to dry.

Finishing Steps

11. Cover the top end of the steel blade with masking tape to protect it while painting the handle.
12. Apply a coat of gesso to the handle. Let dry. Sand with fine sandpaper. Apply another coat if needed. (Leave about 4" of the grip unpainted from the guard to just below the double tips—this part will be covered by leather.)
13. Paint the gesso-covered areas, including the wooden balls, with acrylic red paint. Allow to dry. A second coat may be needed.
14. Cut the piece of red leather into a long strip 1¼" wide. Apply carpenter's glue to the unpainted area of the grip. Wrap the leather in an even spiral around the grip. Trim off excess leather with the craft knife. Allow to dry.
15. Paint pentagrams on both sides of the wooden balls in green. Also paint in green the Hebrew names and sigils shown in Figure 94 on page 250, on all sides of the guard:
    - God name: Elohim Gibor (ALHIM GBOR) אלהים גבור
    - Archangel: Kamael (KMAL) כמאל
    - Angels: Seraphim (ShRPhIM) רפים
    - Planet: Mars, Madim (MDIM) מדים
    - Planetary angel: Zamael (ZMAL) זמאל

- Planetary Intelligence: Graphiel (GRAPhIAL) גראפיאל
- Plantary spirit: Bartzabel (BRTzBAL) ברצבאל
- Motto: Magician's Magical Name

16. After all the paint has dried, coat the handle with a clear lacquer finish for protection. Let dry. Remove masking tape from blade.

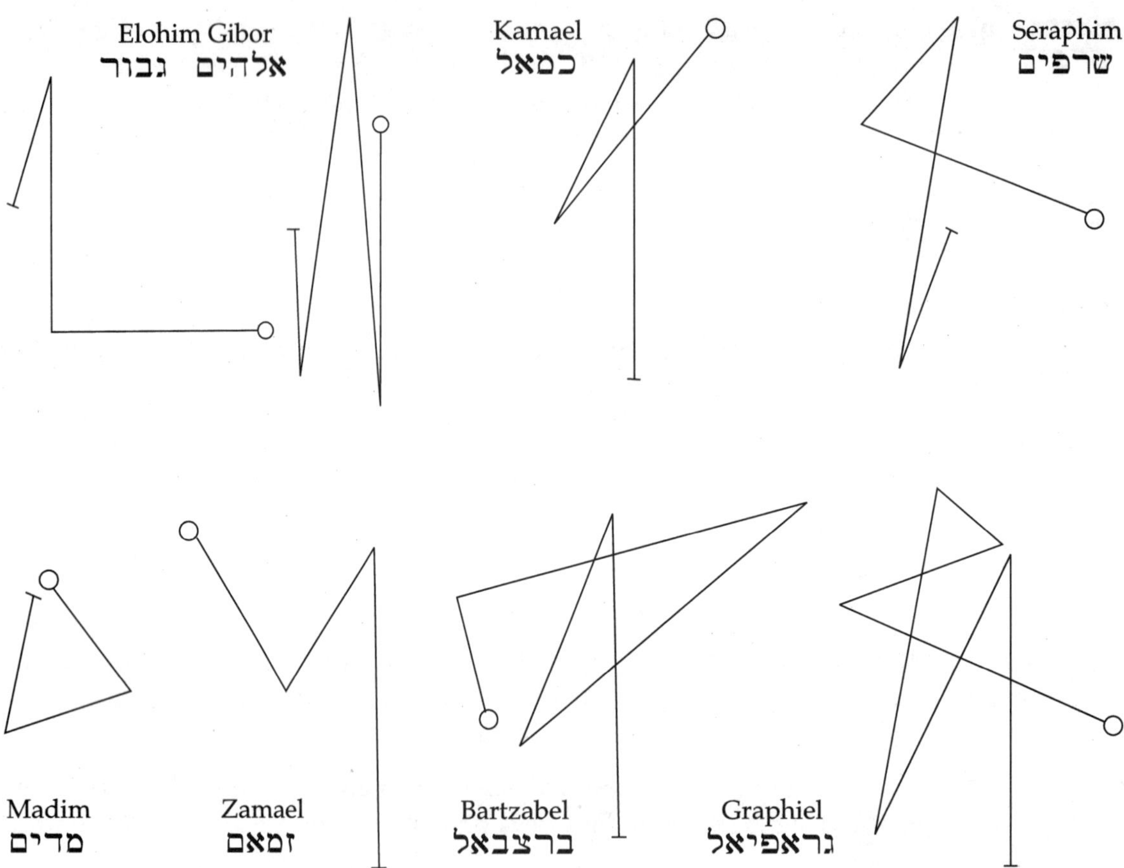

Figure 94: Sigils and Hebrew Names for the Magic Sword

The Four Elemental Weapons

The *Four Elemental Weapons* or tools are the Earth Pentacle, the Air Dagger, the Water Cup, and the Fire Wand. (See Color Plate 8.) They are the tarot symbols of the letters of the divine name YHVH, and of the elements, and have a certain bond and sympathy between them. So even if only one is to be used, the others should also be present. Therefore, let the Z. A. M. remember that when one works with these forces he or she is, as it were, dealing with the forces of the letters of the divine name.

Each implement must be consecrated, and when this has been done, no one else should touch it.[10]

The Earth Pentacle

The word *pentacle* or *pantacle* is derived from the Latin word *pentaculum,* which is said by some to mean "small painting." Eliphas Levi described the pentacle as being similar to a talisman: "We have defined a Pantacle as a synthetic character resuming the entire magical doctrine in one of its special conceptions. It is therefore the full expression of a completed thought or will: it is the signature of a spirit." Levi goes on to say that "a Pantacle is the perfect summary of a mind.... (It) serves to focus all intellectual force into a glance, a recollection, a touch. It is, so to speak, a starting-point for the efficient projection of will."[11] Pentacles were usually circular and painted or engraved with symbolism appropriate to the magical work at hand. Magical grimoires are filled with pentacles ornamented with various forms of symbolism. (See Figure 95.)[12]

The pentacle can be said to represent a *container* for the magical forces inscribed on it. It is used to encircle these forces and bring them into physical (earthly) manifestation.

The Earth Pentacle of the Golden Dawn is used by the adept in all magical workings pertaining to the nature of Earth, and is under the presidency of the Hebrew letter Heh Final, and of the "Pentacle of the Tarot." The Zelator Adeptus Minor uses it in rituals where the spirits of the element of Earth are invoked.[13]

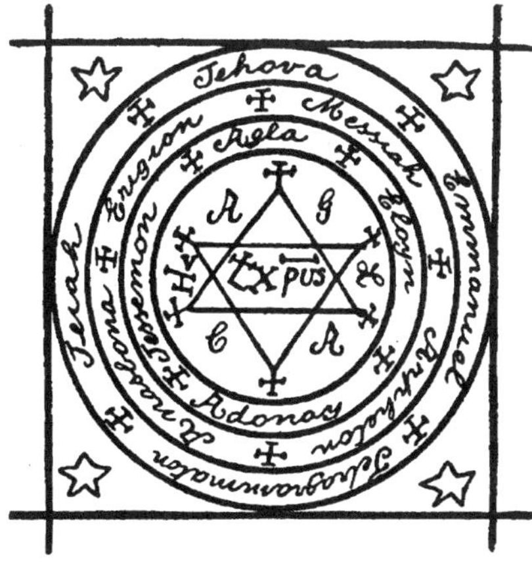

Figure 95: Grand Pentacle of Solomon

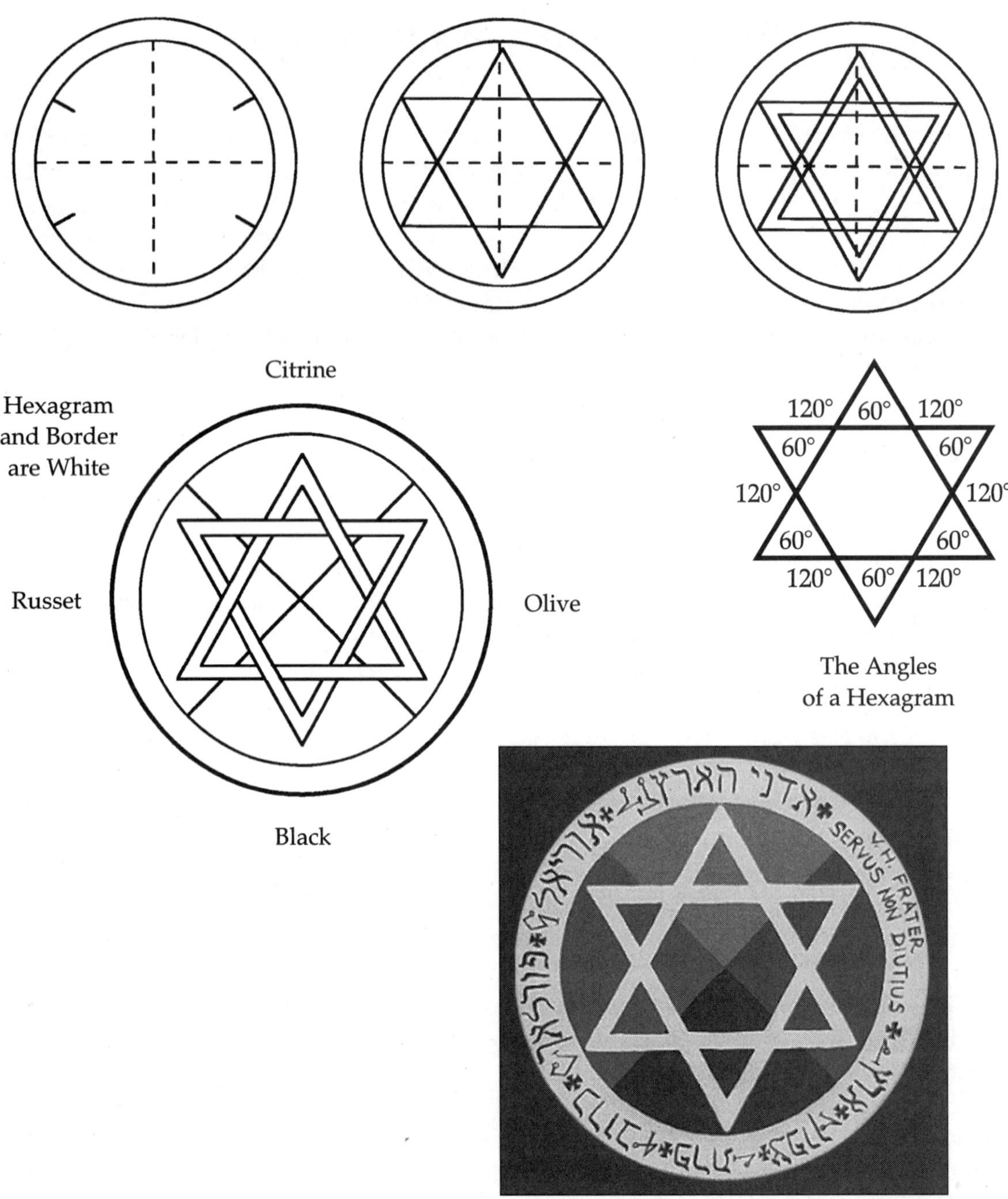

Figure 96: The Earth Pentacle

The four quarters of the pentacle are painted in the Briah (Queen Scale) colors of Malkuth, alluding to the sub-quarters or sub-elements that exist within the make-up of the tenth Sephirah. The citrine quarter is the airy part of Earth, formed from the mixture of orange and green (Hod and Netzach). Russet is the fiery part of Earth, formed from the mixture of orange and violet (Hod and Yesod). Olive is the watery part of Earth, created from combining green and violet (Netzach and Yesod). Black is coarse, Earth of Earth, a combination of all the colors grounding in Malkuth.[14]

The white edge and border of the pentacle allude to the necessity of spirit which must ever guide the actions of matter. The white Hexagram is a symbol of the divine union of opposites, the marriage of Fire and Water. It represents perfection, harmony, and reconciliation. Here it symbolizes the divine spirit equilibriating and binding together all four elements of Malkuth.

The Golden Dawn's traditional ritual for "The Consecration of the Pentacle" is given in *Ritual Use of Magical Tools*, chapter five. An additional ritual for the use of the Earth Pentacle is also given.

Refer to Figure 96 on page 252 for construction diagrams.

Materials Needed

- 5" x 5" piece of soft wood (pine or bass), ½" thick
- Wood putty
- Gesso
- Acrylic paint: white, black, orange, green, violet
- Sealant: clear lacquer finish

Tools Needed

- Electric jigsaw or coping saw
- Compass, pencil, and straightedge
- Protractor
- Artist's brushes (fine and medium sizes)
- File or rasp
- Sandpaper (course, medium, and fine)

Construction

1. Using the compass, draw a 4½" or 5" circle on the piece of wood. Cut out circle with saw.
2. If disk has jagged edges, file them smooth. Sand with course and medium sandpaper. If there are any gaps or holes, fill them with wood putty.

3. Sand the disk with fine sandpaper until it is smooth. Paint entire disk with gesso. Let dry. Sand. Apply a second coat, if needed, and let dry and sand again.

Drawing the Hexagram

4. Find the center hole created by the compass point and draw a second, smaller circle ½" inside the edge of the disk. (See Figure 96, page 252.) Lightly draw a cross from the center of the circle, dividing it into four equal portions.
5. Divide the circle into six equal parts beginning at the intersection of the top of the circle and the vertical line of the cross. Place the protractor on the vertical line of the cross and measure off 60 degrees and 120 degrees to the left and right of the vertical line. Mark these four angles with a pencil. You should now have six pencil marks as shown in the diagram. Draw lines to connect these points, forming the Hexagram.

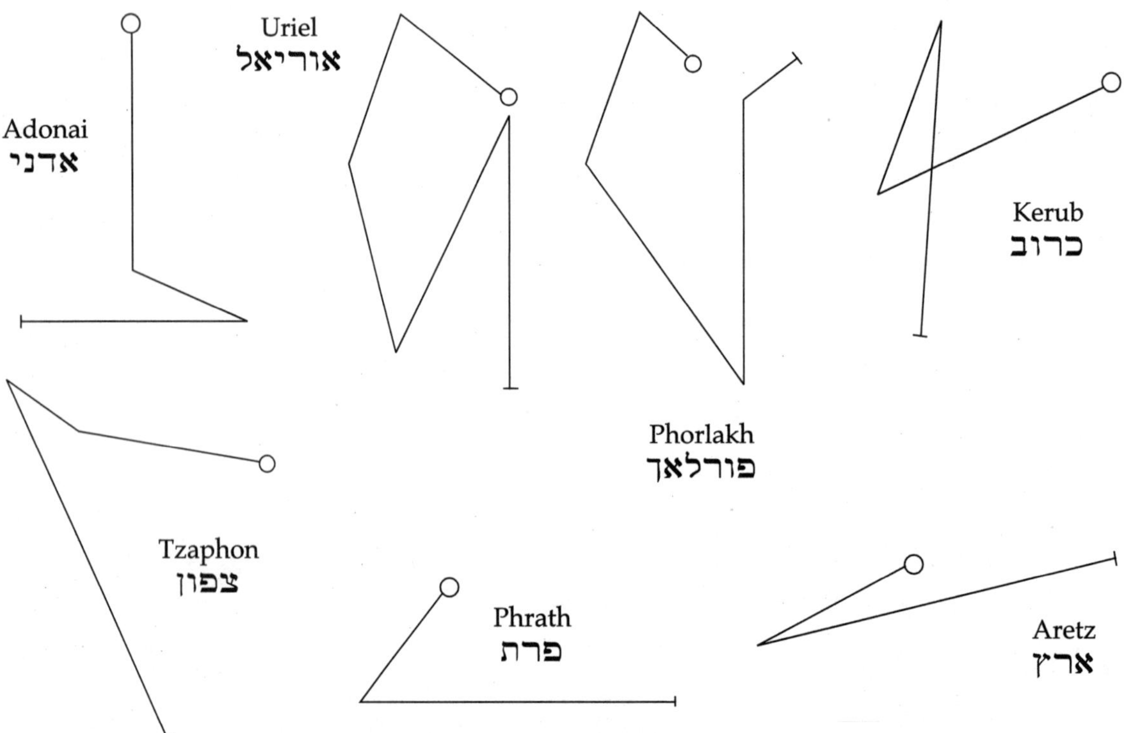

Figure 97: Sigils and Hebrew Names for the Earth Pentacle

6. Draw a second set of lines approximately ¼" inside the first. Divide the quarters created by the cross in half, thus creating a second diagonal cross, which is to be painted in the Queen Scale colors of Malkuth.
7. Repeat steps 4–6 on the other side of the disk. (Try to align the hexagrams to matching positions on both sides.)

Applying the Colors

8. Using the medium and small artist's brushes, paint the pentacle, one side at a time, as follows:
    - Edge and border: White
    - Top quarter: Citrine—a mixture of orange & green
    - Left quarter: Russet—a mixture of orange & violet
    - Right quarter: Olive—a mixture of green & violet
    - Bottom quarter: Black
    - Hexagram: White
9. Allow the paint to dry thoroughly.

Finishing Steps: The Inscriptions

10. Lightly trace with a pencil two circular guidelines on the white outer band. (These can be removed later with a kneaded eraser.) Within these guidelines trace the necessary inscriptions in Hebrew followed by the appropriate sigils (see Figure 97, page 254).
    - God name: Adonai (ADNI)[15] אדני
    - Archangel: Uriel (AURIAL) אוריאל
    - Angel: Phorlakh (PhORLAK) פורלאך
    - Ruler: Kerub (KRUB) כרוב
    - River of Paradise: Phrath (PhRTh) פרת
    - Cardinal point: Tzaphon (TzPhON) צפון (North)
    - Element: Aretz (ARTz) ארץ (Earth)
    - Motto: Magician's Magical Name

    Using a fine-tipped brush, paint all these inscriptions, in black, on both sides of the pentacle. Allow to dry.
11. Spray or brush on a sealant to protect the finished pentacle.

The Air Dagger

The *Air Dagger* is to be used by the Adept in all magical workings of the element of Air, and under the presidency of the Hebrew letter Vav and the "Sword of the Tarot."

There should be no confusion between the Magic Sword and the Air Dagger. The Magic Sword is under Geburah and is for strength and defense. The Air Dagger is attributed to elemental Air and the letter Vav of YHVH. It is to be used with the three other Elemental Implements. The Magic Sword and the Air Dagger belong to different planes and any substitution of one for the other is harmful. In addition, the Air Dagger of the Z. A. M. is not to be used in rituals that call for a plain dagger, such as the Lesser Banishing Ritual of the Pentagram. For this ritual, a dagger of no special design is required.[16]

The handle of the Air Dagger is yellow, the color assigned to elemental Air. The dagger can be likened to the tip of the spear, cast through the air to hit its target.[17]

The Golden Dawn's traditional ceremony for "The Consecration of the Air Dagger" is given in *Ritual Use of Magical Tools,* chapter five. An additional ritual for the use of Air Dagger is also given.

For this implement the most important thing is that the handle be wide enough to paint the appropriate names and sigils on. However, if such a dagger is not forthcoming, it is possible to rework a short-handled dagger to the needed specifications.

Refer to Figure 98 on page 258.

Materials Needed

- Metal-handled dagger with a 4" to 6" long blade
- One can of primer paint (gray or white)
- Enamel or acrylic paint: yellow and violet
- Sealant: clear lacquer finish

Tools Needed

- Emery cloth
- Sandpaper (course and fine)
- Masking tape
- Artist's brushes (fine and medium sizes)

Construction

1. Cover the blade with masking tape.
2. Use emery cloth or course sandpaper on the handle of the dagger to "rough up" the surface of the metal (enough to hold the primer coat of paint).

3. Spray the handle with a primer coat of paint. Allow to dry thoroughly. Sand lightly with fine sandpaper.
4. Paint the handle with several coats of yellow paint. (If you use enamel paint, be certain that the color of the paint approximates that of the acrylic paint described in the introduction on page xxx.)
5. Allow the dagger to dry thoroughly overnight before removing the masking tape.

Finishing Steps: The Inscriptions

6. Pencil in and then paint the following names in Hebrew along with their sigils on the handle of the Air Dagger. Use acrylic violet paint for these names. (Note: In this case, the yellow is the "ground" color, while the violet is the "charge.") The names and sigils to be painted on the handle of the Air Dagger are as follows (see also Figure 98, page 258):
   - Divine name: YHVH (YHVH)[18] יהוה
   - Archangel: Raphael (RPhAL) רפאל
   - Angel: Chassan (ChShN) חשן
   - Ruler: Aral (ARAL)[19] אראל
   - River of Paradise: Hiddekel (HDQL) הדקל
   - Cardinal point: Mizrach (MZRCh) מזרח (East)
   - Element: Ruach (RUCh) רוח (Air)
   - Motto: Magician's Magical Name

   Let the paint dry. Then spray or brush on a sealant for protection of the paint.

Alternative Methods for Creating the Handle

One way of extending the handle of the dagger to a more appropriate size and shape is to use oven-hardening clay. Simply mold the clay over the handle into the desired shape and bake it in the oven following the directions for hardening the clay. (The Air Dagger with the T-shaped handle pictured in Color Plate 8 was constructed in this fashion.)

Another way to extend the handle is to remove the blade entirely from the old handle and mount it on a new one. Many inexpensive daggers are sold in flea markets for anywhere between $4 to $15. These daggers usually have a wooden grip between a brass guard and pommel. Secure the wooden shaft of the dagger in a pair of vice grips. Then take another pair of vise-grips or pliers and unscrew the brass pommel until it comes off. All the parts of the handle should come off once the pommel is removed, although you may require a hammer to loosen the various parts. All that will remain is the dagger blade

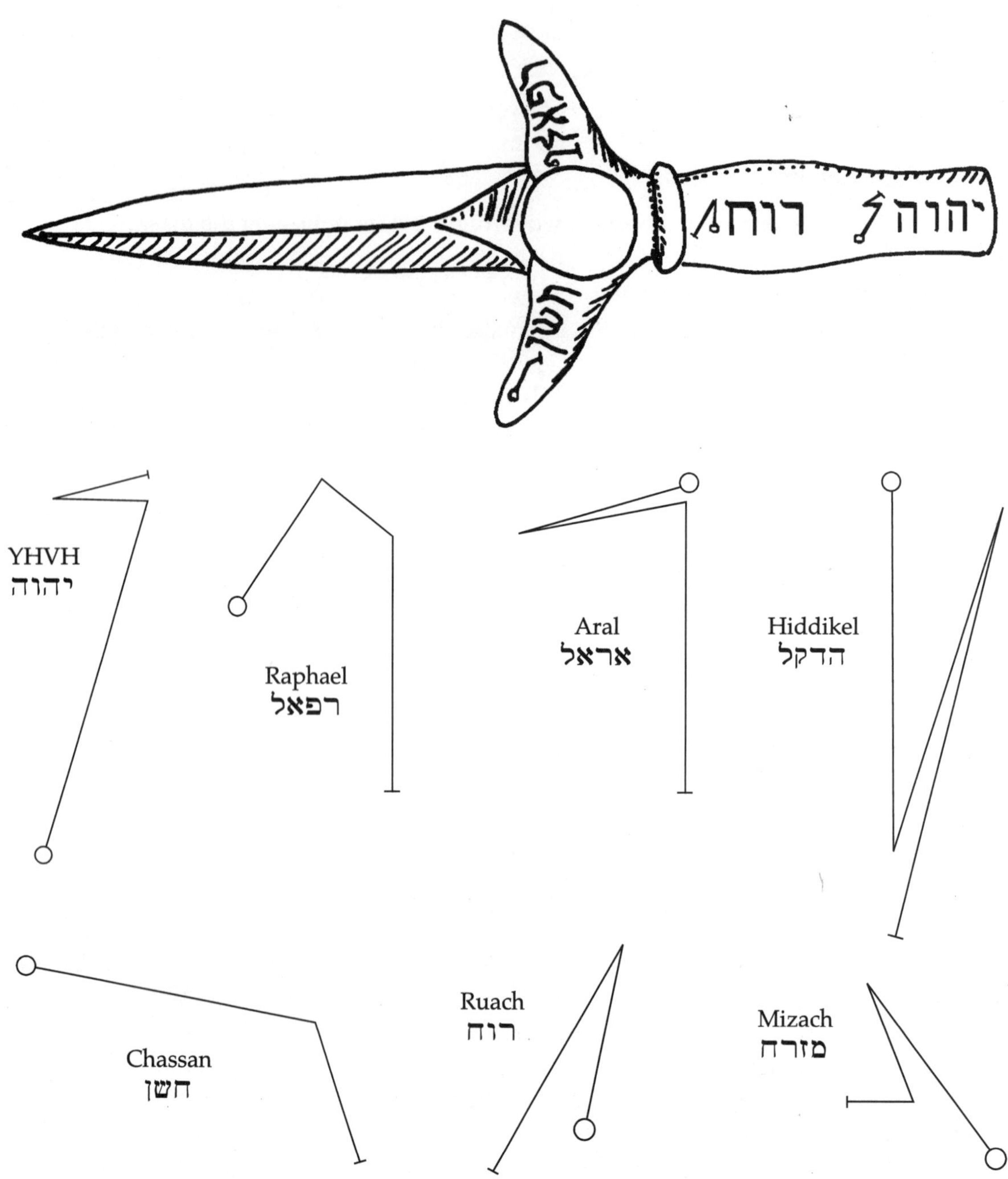

Figure 98: Sigils and Hebrew Names for the Air Dagger

with a metal shank sticking out the back. This entire operation should take no more than five minutes. A wooden handle like that of the Magic Sword (only smaller in scale) can then be constructed and attached to the dagger blade.

The Water Cup

The Water Cup is used by the Zelator Adeptus Minor in all magical workings pertaining to the nature of elemental Water, and under the presidency of the Hebrew letter Heh and the "Cup of the Tarot."

This cup should not be confused with a separate chalice required for the Repast of the Four Elements. A plain chalice of this sort is symbolic of the heart center of Osiris and of Tiphareth. The elaborate Water Cup of the Z. A. M. is to be used in rituals involving the elements.

Since the design of the Water Cup presented below is based on the Cup of Stolistes, as referred to in the Practicus grade, it partakes of the same symbolism. (Refer to the Stolistes Cup Admission Badge of the Grade of 3=8 in chapter two.)

The Water Cup of the Z. A. M. is one implement whose construction seems to vary with the ingenuity of the magician making it. The Golden Dawn instructions suggest that any glass cup with a stem can be used, and paper petals attached.[20] Although this method is the least satisfying, it appears to have been the most common method used to create the cup. In our time there seem to be a large number of Magicians who are also talented artists and craftspeople. Some have produced highly creative elemental weapons, which no doubt would have made nineteenth-century magicians envious. One of the most beautiful implements we've seen is the traditional Water Cup formed from melted or slumped stained glass.

Many magicians have a way of finding a metal, ceramic or wooden cup that will work nicely for the elemental tool. The top of the cup should flare outward like a crocus flower, a design which was often used in ancient Egyptian cups (see Figure 99, page 260). One of the wooden Water Cups shown was made from a single piece of wood cut out on a lathe.

The type of cup that we have found most satisfactory for this implement is based on the Cup of Stolistes as described in the 3=8 grade of Practicus. (See Color Plate 8). This form of the cup is not as difficult to make as it might first appear.

The Golden Dawn's traditional ritual for "The Consecration of the Water Cup" is given in *Ritual Use of Magical Tools*, chapter five. An additional ritual for the use of the Water Cup is also given.

Refer to Figure 100 on page 262 for construction diagrams.

Egyptian Lotus Cups

A Stained Glass Water Cup

Wooden Water Cups

Figure 99: Egyptian Lotus Cups and Water Cups

Materials Needed

- Plain wooden bowl, such as a sugar bowl, approximately 3½" wide and 3" high
- One 8" square piece of basswood, ¼" thick
- One 3" square piece of basswood, ¾" thick
- One 1½" wooden ball
- Quick-setting epoxy
- Grout or plaster of Paris
- Wood putty
- Gesso
- Acrylic paints: blue and orange
- Spar urethane for waterproofing

Tools Needed

- Scroll saw or coping saw
- Rotary power tool with carving wheel and gouging bit
- Sandpaper (coarse, medium, and and fine)
- Small chisel
- Artist's brushes (medium and fine)

Construction: The Bowl (Crescent)

1. Remove any varnish or finish from the bowl with paint remover.
2. If the bottom of the bowl is too shallow, cut a small circular piece of the ¾" basswood to fit just over the bottom side of the bowl. Make one side of it concave with the rotary tool.
3. Glue the concave side to the bottom of the bowl. Let dry. Sand the added-on piece of wood with coarse sandpaper until it is rounded enough to look like the natural base of the bowl.
4. Take the bowl and gouge out the bottom of it to form a concave area that will fit snugly against the wooden ball.
5. With the rotary tool and carving wheel, carve eight equal petals onto the bowl so that the petals look as if they are raised off the surface of the vessel. (You may instead opt for gluing on petals that have been cut out of poster board or cardboard.)

Construction: The Triangular Base

6. Take the ¼" thick basswood and cut out three triangles which are 3¾" wide at the base and 3" high. (Note: The base needs to be wider than the height for support.)

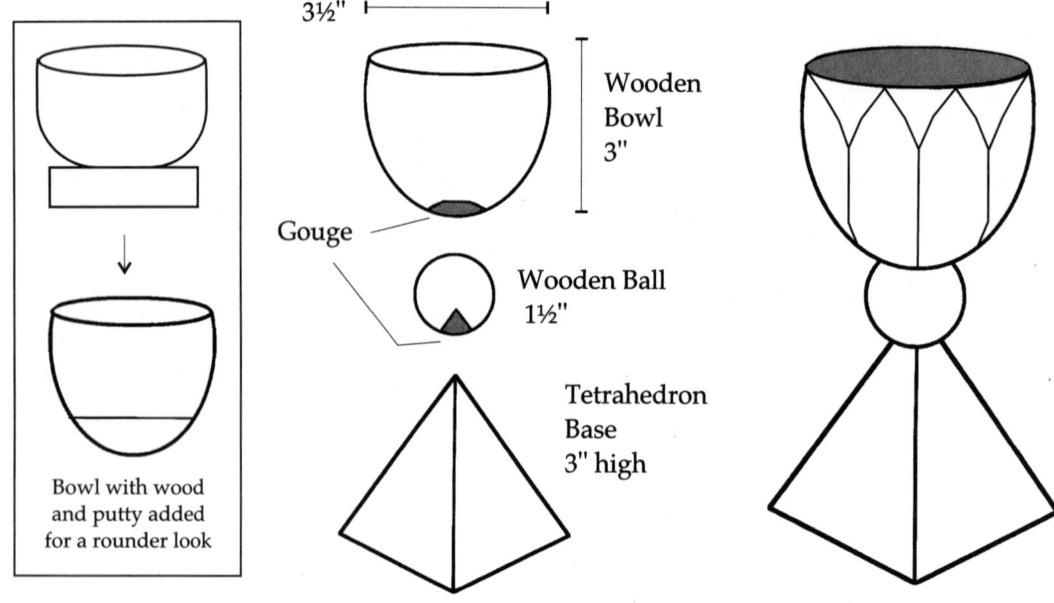

Figure 100: Construction of the Water Cup

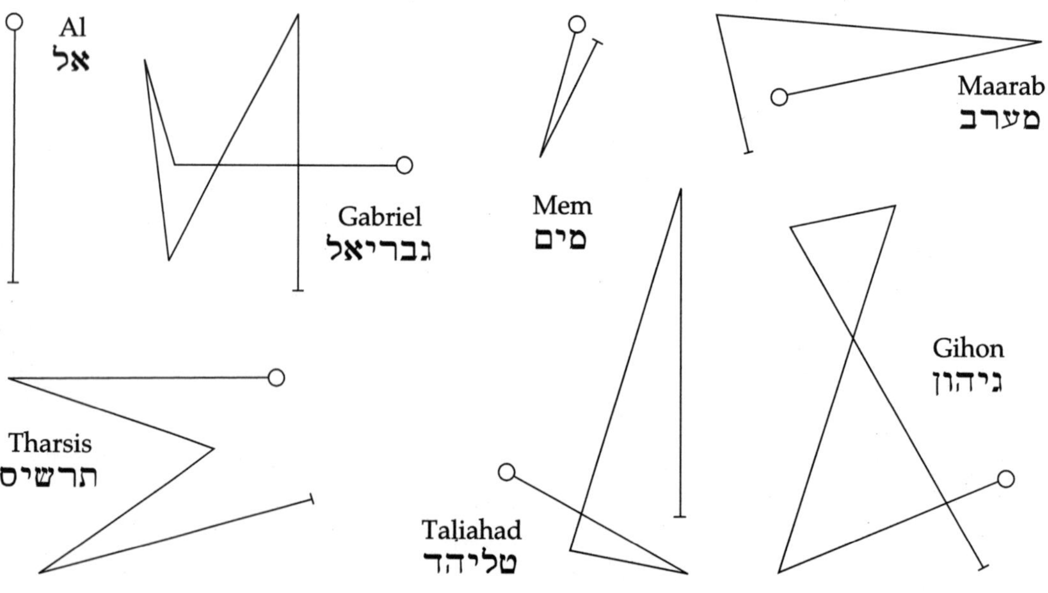

Figure 101: Sigils and Hebrew Names for the Water Cup

7. On one side of all three triangles, sand the two edges (not the base) at an angle inward, giving you two mitered edges on the same side of each triangle.

8. Glue the mitered edges of all three triangles together to form a three-sided pyramid. (The mitered edges on the inside of the pyramid will insure that the figure will have three perfect seams.) Let the glue dry. Fill any gaps with wood putty. Sand with medium sandpaper.

Construction: The Ball (Circle)

9. In the bottom of the wooden ball, chisel out a triangular hole that will fit snugly over the apex of the pyramid base.

10. Using a quick-setting epoxy, glue the ball onto the top of the pyramid. Be sure it is centered. Allow glue to harden.

11. Glue the bowl to the top of the ball. Be sure it is centered (walk around the implement to check its straightness—the pyramidal base often causes optical illusions of bending). Hold the bowl in place until the epoxy sets. Allow glue to harden.

12. Turn the cup upside down and fill the pyramidal base with grout or plaster of Paris. This gives the bottom of the cup weight, to help balance the unusual design of the implement. Let dry.

Finishing Steps

13. Paint the entire cup, inside and out, with gesso. Let dry. Sand lightly with fine sandpaper until smooth. Add a second coat if needed.

14. Paint the petals of the cup with acrylic blue. The ball, base, and inside of the cup can be of a lighter blue. The edges of the petals, the Hebrew names, and sigils should be painted in orange. The inscriptions for the Water Cup are as follows (see also Figure 101, page 262):

    - Divine name: EL (AL)[21] אל
    - Archangel: Gabriel (GBRIAL) גבריאל
    - Angel: Taliahad (TLIHD) טליהד
    - Ruler: Tharsis (ThRShIS) תרשים
    - River of Paradise: Gihon (GIHON) גיהון
    - Cardinal point: Maarab (MAaRB) מערב (West)
    - Element: Mem (MIM) מים (Water)
    - Motto: Magician's Magical Name

15. After all the paint has dried, cover the entire cup with spar urethane to protect and water-proof the cup. Make certain that the inside of the cup is well coated. Allow to dry thoroughly.

Alternative Methods for Creating the Water Cup

Metal cups or goblets made out of brass or pewter are easy to find in many department stores or flea markets. If a metal cup is used, smooth the surface to be painted with an emery cloths. The petals can be etched in using an electric cutting tool with a fine bit. Files and emery cloth with varying coarseness made be used. Apply masking tape over all areas of the cup except the petals. Then spray the petals with a metal primer coat. Let the primer dry, then paint the petals with a brilliant enamel blue.

Eight petals cut out of leather could easily be glued on to a brass, pewter, or wooden cup with a sturdy, general-purpose craft glue. (The petals may be cut to fit precisely, or they may overlap each other.) This is perhaps the easiest way to create a Water Cup that has the added advantage of being very sturdy—it will not break if dropped.

If a suitable wooden cup is found, take off any varnish with a paint remover. The lines of the petals can be carved into the surface of the cup using a rotary tool and gouging bit. The entire cup should be painted with a prime coat of gesso and allowed to dry before being painted with acrylic paint.

The Fire Wand

The Fire Wand of the Z. A. M. is used in all magical workings pertaining to the nature of elemental Fire and is under the presidency of the Hebrew letter Yod and of the "Wand of the Tarot." It should not be used in anything other than a ritual which involves the elements.[22]

The shape of the wand is phallic—a cone mounted on a shaft. Cirlot states that the symbolism of the cone may be derived from the association of the circle with the triangle or pyramid.[23] Some writers have stated that it is a solar symbol. In any event, the flaming Yods painted around the cone firmly establishes its Father/Fire energy. Since the Hebrew letter Yod also represents a sperm, the inseminating qualities of Fire are also stressed on this implement.[24]

The Fire Wand is the most challenging of all the Elemental Weapons to construct. The problem it presents is that a magnetic wire must run through its center, end to end. The Golden Dawn manuscripts suggest making the wand out of bamboo cane, which has a natural hollow running through it. Some Fire Wands are cut entirely on a lathe. Nowadays, it is possible to find a drill bit which is slender and 12" in length. Of course, drilling a hole straight through the center of a 10" long dowel is a feat worthy of a master craftsman and we don't usually recommend it. The dowel could be cut into three sections to make drilling easier, but it is still difficult. The wooden Fire Wand presented later in this chapter is a far easier alternative.

However, the easiest way to create a Fire Wand that we've yet encountered is explained in the next section.

The Golden Dawn's traditional ritual for "The Consecration of the Fire Wand" is given in *Ritual Use of Magical Tools*, chapter five. An additional ritual for the use of the Fire Wand is also given.

An Easy-to-Make Fire Wand

Refer to Figure 102 on page 266.

Materials Needed

- ¾" wide PVC hollow tubing, 12" long (PVC pipe is a sturdy white plastic pipe that can be purchased at a home building supply store)
- One sturdy wire clothes hanger, (approximately 1/16" in diameter) straightened out, then cut with a wire cutter to 18" long (this will allow approximately 1" excess to cut after insertion)
- One conical-shaped hard plastic Christmas tree ornament (approximately 4" long)
- Can of Foam Plus, an expanding foam sealant (make sure it has the trigger straw)
- Good general-purpose craft glue
- 7" of double-stick ½" foam tape (this will allow approximately 1" excess)
- One sheet of artist's drawing paper
- Two round white plastic chair protector caps, 1" in diameter
- Acrylic paints: red, yellow, green, and white
- Sealant: clear lacquer spray

Tools Needed

- Ruler and craft knife
- Wire cutters
- Scissors
- Drill and 1/16" drill bit, plus another bit slightly smaller than the size of the base of the cone
- Small hacksaw with fine blade (not necessary if PVC is cut at time of purchase)
- Strong magnet
- Fine pointed and a broad-shaped artist's brush
- Pencil

Construction

1. Cut the PVC tubing to a length of 12" with a fine-toothed hacksaw, or have it cut to size at the time of purchase.
2. Remove the aluminum hanging portion of the Christmas ornament and discard.
3. Drill a 1⁄16" hole in the center of the base and tip of the plastic ornament (the holes should be big enough to run the hanger wire through both ends).
4. Drill a 1⁄16" hole in the center of the bottom plastic chair cap (the hole should be big enough to run the hanger wire through). Drill a hole in the top chair cap making the hole large enough so the bottom of the cone fits securely into the chair cap.
5. Magnetize the wire by repeatedly moving a strong magnet across it in one direction only. Test its magnetism by using the tip of the wire to pick up a pin. The end which attracts the pin will be the end that sticks out of the cone-shaped head of the wand.
6. Paint the parts prior to assembly using the broad paint brush:
   - Paint the rod with red acrylic paint
   - Paint the chair caps with bright yellow paint
   - Paint the cone with alternating red and yellow swirling stripes
7. Apply glue to the inside of the bottom chair cap. Fit the cap over one end of the PVC pipe. (This will become the bottom of the wand.)
8. Feed the magnetized wire (with magnetized end in first) through the cap, leaving 1⁄16" exposed, and then the PVC tubing, with the remainder of the wire to extend beyond the tubing.

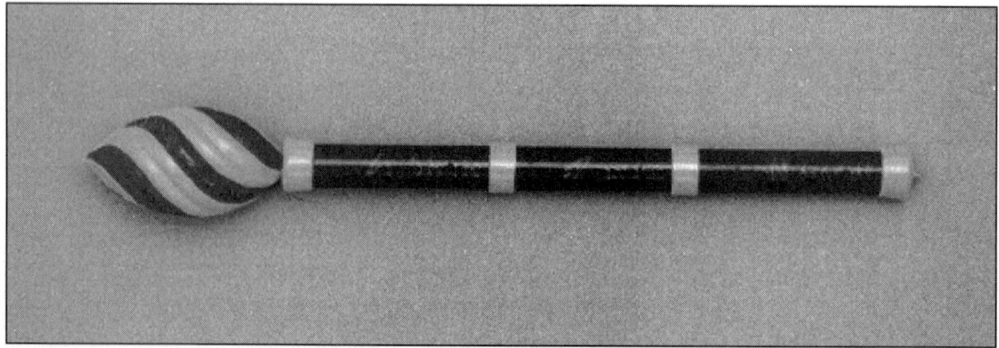

Figure 102: A Simple Fire Wand

9. Spray the inside of the PVC pipe with the foam filler making sure that the wire is centered inside the rod. The foam will expand and, when dry, will allow the wire to be secured and centered. (Follow the instructions on the foam filler can for safety and other instructions.)
10. Apply a small amount of glue to the inside of the top chair cap and secure to the top part of the wand making sure that the wire feeds through the center of the cap.
11. Apply a small amount of glue to the bottom of the plastic ornament and force it through the plastic chair cap to make a secure fit. Make sure the wire feeds through the conical ornament with the remainder of the wire exposed.
12. Trim the excess wire with wire cutters, leaving approximately 1⁄16" exposed at the tip of the wand.
13. Allow the glue and foam to dry.
14. Lay all of the 7" of double-stick foam tape on a surface that the tape can be lifted up from later (glass works great.) Peel off the foam tape protector, and cover the top side of the foam tape with the artist's paper. Using a craft knife, trim the paper to fit the width of the tape. Apply bright yellow paint to the paper and to the sides of the foam tape.
15. Measure around the rod and mark the foam tape with a pencil. With a straight edge and craft knife cut two pieces. Apply the two pieces of foam tape around the wand shaft at intervals of approximately 3⅝" (it should be evenly spaced between the two chair caps).

Finishing Steps

16. Paint the following inscriptions on the red parts of the wand, the cone and shaft, in green. (See Figure 103, page 268.) When all paint is dry, spray on sealant.
    - Divine name: Elohim (ALHIM)[25] אלהים
    - Archangel: Michael (MIKAL) מיכאל
    - Aangel: Ariel (ARIAL)[26] אריאל
    - Ruler: Seraph (ShRPh) שרף
    - River of Paradise: Pison (PIShON) פישון
    - Cardinal point: Darom (DROM) דרום (South)
    - Element: Ash (ASh) אש (Fire)
    - Motto: Magician's Magical Name

—Instructions for an Easy-to-Make Fire Wand contributed by Bill and Judi Genaw

A Wooden Fire Wand

Refer to Figure 104, page 270 for construction diagrams.

Materials Needed

- One ¾" dowel, 12" long
- One 1⁄16" diameter steel wire, 15¾" long
- One 2" x 3" piece of soft wood (pine or bass)
- Epoxy
- Yellow carpenter's glue
- Gesso
- Acrylic paints: red, yellow, green
- Wood putty
- 1" x 3" piece of leather, approximately ⅛" or more in thickness
- Sealant: clear lacquer finish

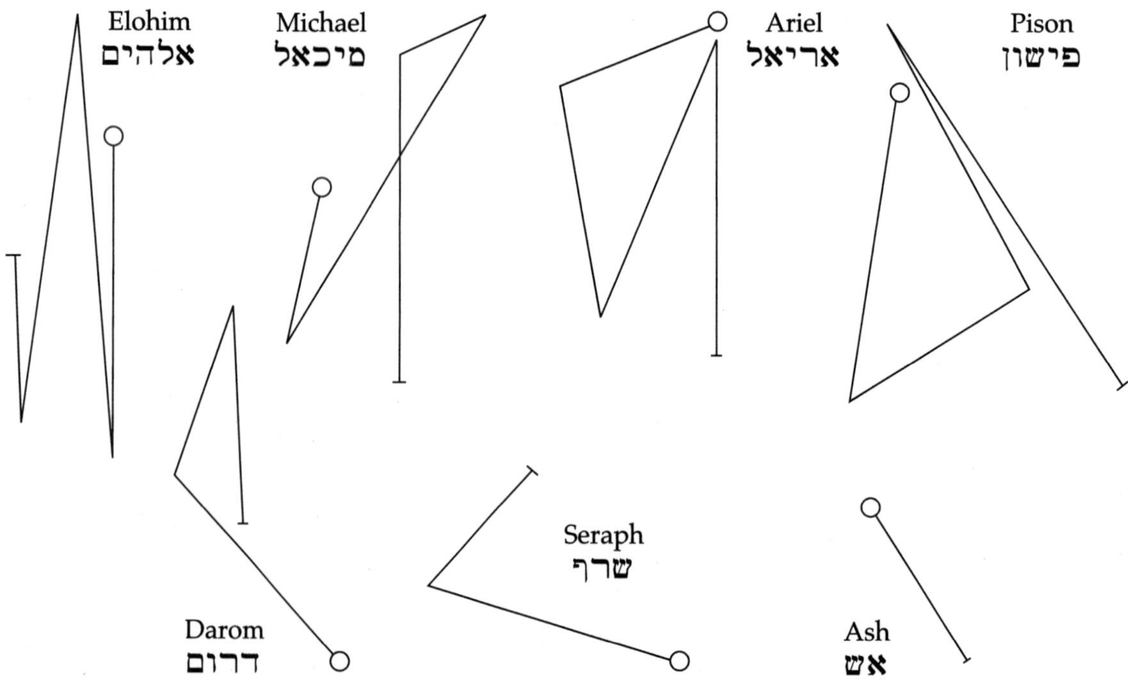

Figure 103: Sigils and Hebrew Names for the Fire Wand

Tools Needed

- Table saw
- Two pieces of wood (long enough to guide the dowel during cutting)
- Vise
- Electric drill with ¾" bit
- Straight edge and craft knife
- Strong magnet
- File or rasp
- Artist's brushes
- Sandpaper (course, medium, and fine)

Construction: The Shaft

1. Set up the table saw so that only ⅜" of the blade is exposed. Set up the protective fence of the saw so that it is ⅜" away from the blade.

2. THIS IS IMPORTANT: Use the two pieces of wood to guide the dowel through the saw—never get your hands close to the saw blade. Use one piece to push the dowel from the bottom end lengthwise over the blade slowly. Use the other piece of wood to hold the dowel (from the side) against the fence to guide it. DO NOT RUSH! Safety is the most important consideration here. You can always buy another dowel if your first effort is not satisfactory.

3. Using the wood pieces, push the dowel lengthwise across the saw blade. The end result should be a dowel with a ⅜" deep cut running its entire length.

Construction: The Cone

4. Reset the table saw so that the blade protrudes 1". Take the 2" x 3" long piece of soft wood and run it across the blade lengthwise using the two pieces of wood to guide it as before. You will end up with a piece of wood that has a 1" cut running through its 3" length.

5. Secure the piece of wood in a vice. At the exact center point of one end (easily found by the cut just made), drill a shallow hole approximately ⅛" deep using a ¾" drill bit. (The end of the shaft will later fit snugly into this slight depression.)

6. With the wood still in the vice, shape its top end into the desired cone-shape using a rasp or file and course sandpaper. Then turn the piece around so that you can round off the bottom of the cone.

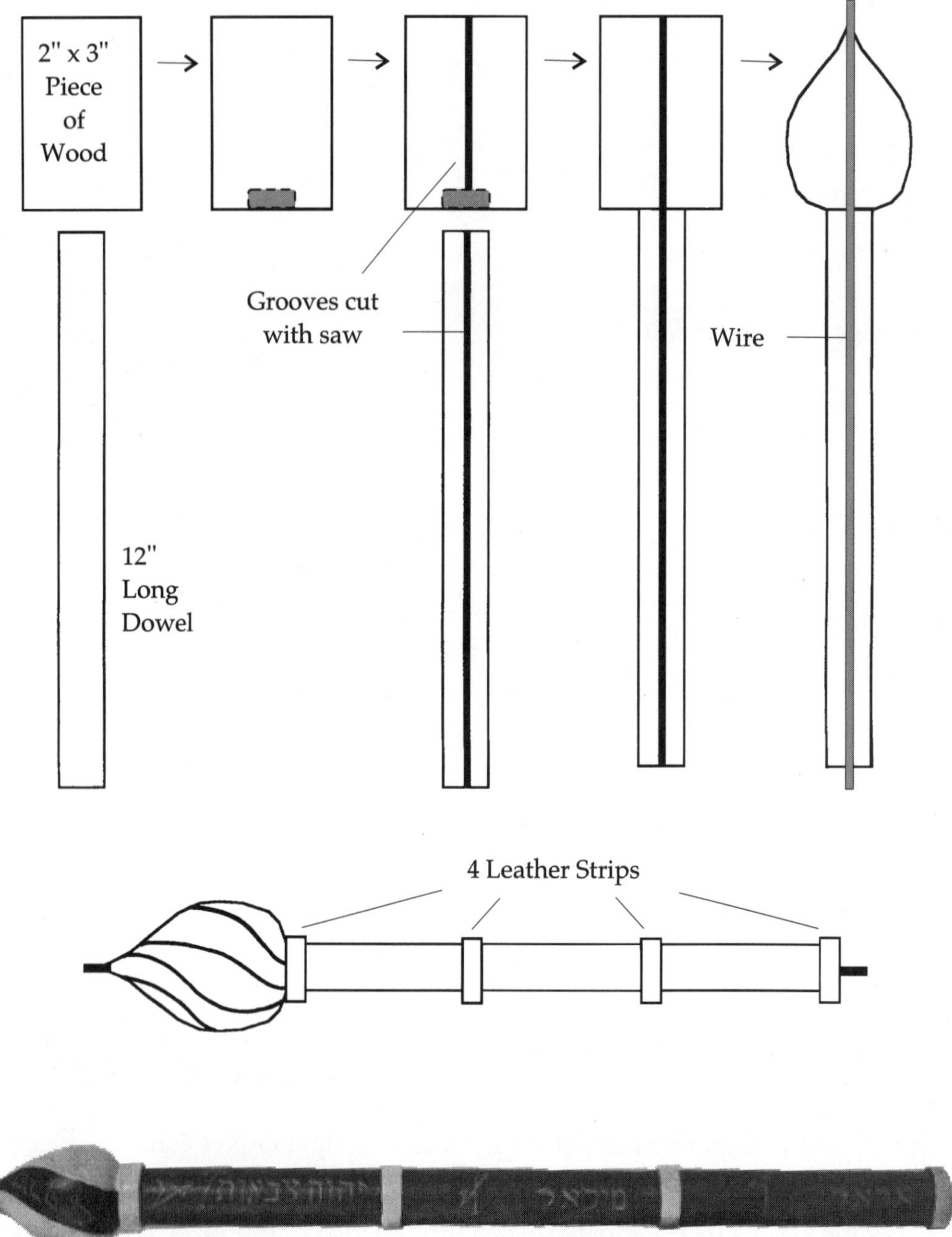

Figure 104: Construction of the Wooden Fire Wand

Construction: The Wire

7. Take the wire and repeatedly move a strong magnet across it in one direction only. When the wire is effectively magnetized, it should be able to pick up a pin. The end which attracts the pin will be the end that sticks out of the cone-shaped head of the wand.

8. Apply glue to one end of the shaft and secure into the ¾" hole drilled into the bottom of the cone. Make sure that the grooves cut into both pieces are perfectly aligned. Let dry completely.

9. Place the wire into the groove of the shaft and cone so that the magnetized end of wire sticks out about 1⁄16" from the point of the cone. The wire should also stick out 1⁄16" from the bottom of the shaft.

10. Fill in the groove with wood putty. Let dry, then sand smooth with medium sandpaper so that the wand appears never to have been cut at all.

Construction: The Bands

11. Take the piece of leather and cut it into four strips 3" long and ¼" wide, using a straight edge and a craft knife.

12. Glue the underside of each strip and wrap around the wand shaft at intervals of approximately 3⅝". (Trim off excess leather with the knife.) One strip will be directly under the cone, two will be in the central area of the shaft, and the fourth will be placed at the very bottom of the shaft.

13. Fill in gaps with wood putty and let dry. Sand lightly with fine sandpaper if needed. Cover the entire wand with gesso and let dry. Sand with fine sandpaper, and add a second coat if needed.

Finishing Steps

14. Draw three wavy, flame-shaped Yods at even lengths around the cone. Paint these Yods and the four bands in yellow.

15. Paint the remaining part of the cone and the shaft with red. Paint the inscriptions listed in Step 16 on page 267 in green on the red parts of the wand's cone and shaft.. (See Figure 103, page 268.) When all the paint is dry, spray or brush on sealant.

A Carrying Case for the Adept's Magical Tools

The adept might want to construct a box or carrying case for his or her Elemental Weapons. A wooden box or sturdy suitcase large enough to hold the four Elemental Weapons (in addition to the Lotus Wand and Rose Cross Lamen if desired) can be used for this purpose. Obtain two pieces of styrofoam or foam rubber large enough to fit snuggly inside the box or suitcase (the pieces should fit one on top of the other, like a top and bottom). The result will be a sturdy, attractive carrying case that will protect the adept's magical tools.

Materials Needed

- Suitcase
- Styrofoam or foam rubber
- Red velvet cloth
- Good general-purpose craft glue

Tools Needed

- Ruler and craft knife
- Scissors

Construction

1. Carve or cut depressions into the bottom piece of styrofoam or foam rubber that are in the shapes of the implements, so that the implements will slide easily into them.
2. Cut similar depressions into the top piece of foam, so that both pieces, with the implements between them, fit together precisely, but not so tightly that it is difficult to remove the implements from either piece.
3. Cover both pieces of foam with a nice piece of red velvet or similar cloth and glue into place.
4. Finally, when you are satisfied with the way that the implements and the foam pieces with the cloth covering fit together, glue the bottom piece of foam into the bottom of the box or suitcase.
5. Glue the top piece of foam into the top of the top or suitcase. The box or suitcase can be decorated on the outside with appropriate symbolism, if desired, or left plain.

Endnotes

1. Bardon, *The Practice of Magical Evocation*, 35. (In ancient Egypt, apotropaic wands carved from ivory, as well as various staffs and rods, were the primary tools of the magician.) Bardon goes on to state that: "Above all, the magic wand is the symbol of the will, the power and the strength by which the magician maintains his influence on the sphere for which he has made and charged it. A magician will not have just one wand for his practice, but he will make several wands depending on what he intends to do or attain." This is also true of the Golden Dawn magician, who is required to make a Lotus Wand, a Fire Wand, etc.
2. In Regardie's *The Golden Dawn*, page 302, the zodiacal signs given for the Day House and the Night House of Saturn were mistakenly transposed. Here they are listed correctly.
3. Regardie, *The Golden Dawn*, 302–303.
4. Some authors have mistakenly listed the color of the Leo (Teth) band as lemon yellow or greenish-yellow. The true color for this band is pure yellow as given on a standard color wheel. This is also true for the Teth petal on the Rose Cross Lamen.
5. In all editions of Regardie's *The Golden Dawn*, the Hebrew letters Tau and Kaph are shown incorrectly transposed on the second ring of petals. In the accompanying diagram of the Rose Cross Lamen shown here, these letters are shown in their proper positions.
6. Regardie, *The Golden Dawn*, 310–311.
7. Ibid., 311–312.
8. Tattva is a Sanskrit word meaning "quality." The five main tattvas (Prithivi, Vayu, Apas, Tejas, and Akasa), correspond to the five elements of Earth, Air, Water, Fire, and Spirit. To find the Course of a Tattwa, note the time of sunrise. Akasha always begins with sunrise and lasts 24 minutes, followed by Vayu—24 minutes, Tejas—24 minutes, Apas—24 minutes, and Prithivi—24 minutes.
9. Regardie, *The Golden Dawn*, 317.
10. Ibid., 320.
11. Levi, *Transcendental Magic*, 254, 272.
12. *Clavicula Salomonis* or *The Key of Solomon the King, The Secret Grimoire of Turiel, The Grimoirium Verum, The Grimoire of Honorius,* and *The Fourth Book of Occult Philosophy* are just a few of the magical grimoires dating from the sixteenth and seventeenth centuries which show a wide variety of pentacle designs.
13. Regardie, *The Golden Dawn*, 322.
14. The colors of Malkuth in the Queen Scale have perplexed many people. Oftentimes, citrine has been depicted in many books as being nearly yellow. However, orange mixed with green will rarely yield the color yellow.
15. There has been a lot of confusion regarding the divine Hebrew names that are to be painted on the Four Elemental Weapons. According to Wang's *The Secret Temple*, the names are to be as follows: Earth Pentacle—Adonai ha-Aretz, Air Dagger—Shaddai El Chai, Water Cup—Elohim Tzabaoth, and Fire Wand—YHVH Tzabaoth. These are the divine names given in Outer Order grade ceremonies relating to the Sephiroth of Malkuth, Yesod, Hod, and Netzach, which also have elemental associations. However, the correct names are given in the consecration rituals of these implements (see Regardie, *The Golden Dawn*, 324). They are: Earth Pentacle—Adonai, Air Dagger—YHVH, Water Cup—El, and Fire Wand—Elohim. These are the same Hebrew names given in the SIRP and they relate to the Sephiroth of Malkuth, Tiphareth, Chesed, and Geburah. (Kathleen Raine's book *Yeats, The Tarot and the Golden Dawn*, shows a picture of William Bulter Yeats' Earth Pentacle inscribed with the divine name *Adonai*.

16. *The Key of Solomon* (96–97) describes a black-hilted knife that was to be used for "making the circle" and striking "terror and fear into the Spirits"—(a banishing in the Golden Dawn tradition)—and a separate white-hilted knife for "all necessary Operations of the Art, except the Circles." (This would include invoking the Spirits.) The Key also describes the Magic Sword as a weapon used primarily for "strength and defense in all Magical Operations, against all mine Enemies, visible and invisible....a Protection in all adversities."
17. Regardie, *The Golden Dawn*, 322.
18. See Endnote 15.
19. Golden Dawn magicians have traditionally listed Ariel as the ruler of elemental Air and Aral as the Angel of Fire. But according to Adam Forrest in his article "Mysteria Geomantica" published in *The Golden Dawn Journal: Book One: Divination:* "...the correct name of the Angel of Elemental Fire is *Ariel* ("the Lion of God"), not Aral. An error in Agrippa was long preserved in the Order, in which the two names Ariel and Aral were swapped. This long-lived confusion was only made possible because the four Præfects of the Elements have generally not been recognized as the names of Orders of Angels. Seraph, Cherub, Tharsis, and Aral (more properly Erel) are simply the singular forms of Seraphim, Kerubim, Tarshishim, and Erelim." We have adopted these corrections here. However, if the magician feels more comfortable using the traditional Golden Dawn attributions of these names, then he or she should do so.
20. Regardie, *The Golden Dawn*, 320–322.
21. See Endnote 15.
22. Ibid., 320.
23. Cirlot, 61. (As a note of interest, wooden cones or eggs that are approximately the right size, can be found in many craft supply stores. Sometimes they can even be found cut in half lengthwise.)
24. The wand is primarily an implement of the will. (See Endnote 1.) In the teachings of the Golden Dawn, the wand is naturally aligned with the element of Fire through the associations of will, primary force, masculinity, the Qabalistic world of Atziluth, and the Hebrew letter Yod. There has been a lot of unnecessary confusion concerning the proper elemental attributions of the wand and the dagger. In the book *Techniques of High Magic,* which was based largely on the teachings of the Golden Dawn, Francis King and Stephen Skinner made the statement that the Order's own attributions of these implements incorporated a "blind," and that the proper elemental attribution of the dagger was Fire, while the wand was affiliated with Air. A couple of authors from another esoteric tradition have jumped on this notion with the statement that these attributions were "a deliberate blind perpetuated by the early Golden Dawn, which has unfortunately not yet died a natural death." Our position on the matter is this: if other spiritual traditions wish to use different elemental associations for these implements, for whatever reason—that's perfectly alright. But the Golden Dawn system employs the wand for Fire in accordance with the Order teachings stated above. To suggest that the founding Adepts of the original Golden Dawn—the only practicing magicians who studied, created, and *used* these particular tools—were deliberately trying to blind themselves with misinformation, is totally absurd.
25. See Endnote 15.
26. See Endnote 19.

CHAPTER SIX

Non-traditional Implements

On occasion, new implements have been designed by Inner Order members for the purpose of introducing to Outer Order members the practical techniques of ceremonial magic. The creation of such tools was inspired by recent additions to the curriculum of the Golden Dawn. Previously, ritual work was not begun by the student until he or she had advanced to the Second Order. However, in recognition of the fact that the wide availability of occult material in various publications had caused students to be better prepared to begin practical work, the modern incarnation of the Golden Dawn has incorporated some practical ritual techniques and implements into the curriculum of the Outer Order. The Outer Wand of Double Power is an example of this kind of implement.

Other implements described in this chapter are new tools which have been created for use in rituals based on the traditional ceremonial techniques of the Golden Dawn. Many more such implements can be devised by the creative magician.

The Outer Wand of Double Power

The Outer Wand of Double Power is a simple wand employed in the basic Golden Dawn techniques of invoking and banishing (see *Ritual Use of Magical Tools,* chapter six).

Materials Needed

- One ¾" thick wooden dowel approximately 20" long
- Gesso
- Acrylic paint: white and black
- Sealant: clear lacquer finish

Tools Needed

- Sandpaper (fine grained)
- Artist's brushes (medium)
- Masking tape

Construction

1. Cover the dowel with a coat of gesso. Allow to dry. Sand lightly until smooth. Apply a second coat if needed.
2. Mark the dowel into two sections, each 10" in length. (See Figure 105.) Paint half of the wand black and the other half white. (Use masking tape to paint a straight line separating the two halves of the wand.)
3. When all the paint is dry, apply a coat of sealant for protection.[1]

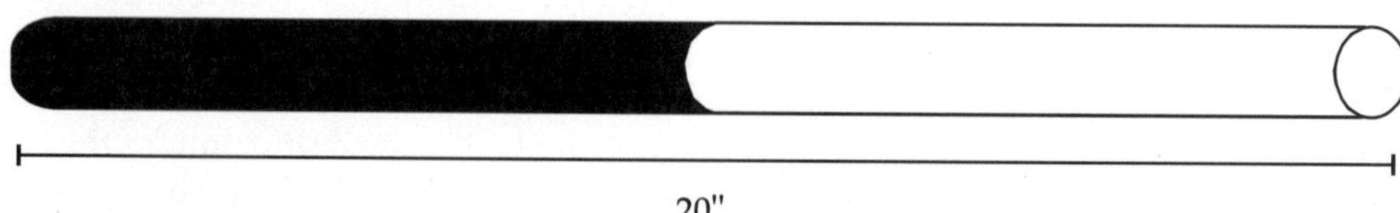

Figure 105: The Outer Wand of Double Power

The Rose Cross Wand

The Rose Cross Wand was designed specifically for use in the traditional Rose Cross Ritual of the Second Order. The symbolism of the Rose and Cross was previously described in chapter five, on page 239.

The Rose Cross is one of the emblems associated with the sixth Sephirah of Tiphareth, the sphere of beauty and equilibrium. The color of the head of the wand denotes the illumination of L. V. X., the divine light of the cross. The cross stands upon a single golden ring, which alludes to Tiphareth. The shaft of the wand is divided into the colors of Tiphareth in each of the Four Worlds of the Qabalah in descending order: *Tiphareth in Atziluth*—pink, *Tiphareth in Briah*—yellow, *Tiphareth in Yetzirah*—salmon, *Tiphareth in Assiah*—yellow-orange. Grasping the wand by any of these four bands in performance of the Rose Cross Ritual, or a meditation on Tiphareth, can help the magician explore the sixth Sephirah in these specific Qabalistic Worlds. (See *Ritual Use of Magical Tools,* chapter six for "The Ritual of the Rose Cross.")

Refer to Figure 106 on page 278 for construction diagrams.

Materials Needed

- One ¾" thick dowel between 20" to 24" in length
- One ¾" thick piece of pine or basswood, approximately 6" x 6"
- One ¼" wooden dowel or peg 1" in length
- Wood putty
- Gesso
- Acrylic paints: white, gold, red, yellow, orange
- Sealant: clear lacquer finish

Tools Needed

- Scroll saw or coping saw
- Electric drill with ¼" and ¾" bits
- Sandpaper (coarse, medium, and fine)
- Index card
- Artist's brushes (large, medium, and fine)

Construction: The Rose Cross Head

1. Draw the circled cross shown in Figure 106, page 278, on the 6" x 6" piece of wood. (The shaft of the cross will be 6" in length, while the arms will be 4".) With the saw, cut out the outer shape of the circled cross.

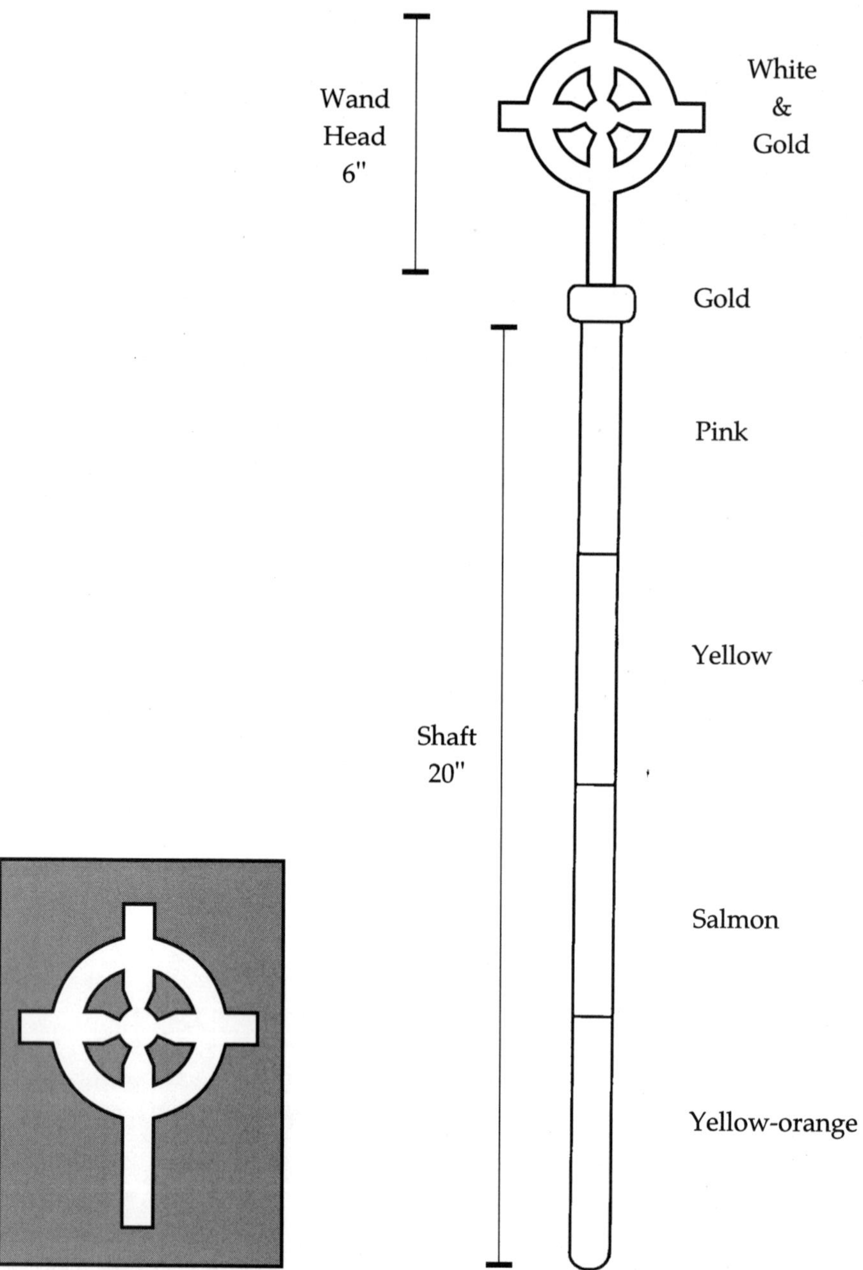

Figure 106: The Rose Cross Wand

2. Drill four holes, one inside each of the shaded (negative space) areas of the wand head. (Remember: It is important to use a drill bit that is wider than your saw blade.)

3. With your saw unplugged, detach the blade from the saw. Stick the blade through one of the holes you have drilled and reattach the blade to the saw. Plug the saw back in and begin cutting out the shaded area of wood. Repeat this process for all four drilled holes until all the waste area of wood has been cut out.

4. Drill a hole ½" deep and ¼" wide in the center of the bottom of the wand head.

Construction: The Shaft

5. From a leftover piece of the ¾" thick pine wood, draw one 1½" circle. Cut it out. In the center, drill a ¾" diameter hole. You will end up with a donut-shaped ring of wood.

6. Take the long dowel (shaft) and drill a hole ½" deep and ¼" in diameter into one end.

7. Glue the 1" wooden peg into the hole you have just drilled so that half of the peg is embedded into the end of the dowel and half of it sticks out. Apply glue to the inside of the ring. Slide it over the top end of the shaft. (If the ring is too tight, sand inside its center hole with course sandpaper.)

8. Pour some glue into the hole you drilled into the bottom end of the wand head and attach to the wand shaft. Let dry.

Finishing Steps

9. Fill in any gaps with wood putty. Sand the entire surface of the wand with medium sandpaper so that it is smooth.

10. With a paint brush, cover the wand with a coat of gesso. Allow to dry.

11. Sand the painted surface (especially the shaft) lightly with fine sandpaper until smooth. Apply a second coat if needed.

12. Measure and mark the shaft into four equal sections. Use an index card wrapped around the shaft to draw a straight line around the dowel. Paint the wand as follows:
    - Cross: White front and back with gold sides[2]
    - Ring: Gold
    - Top quarter of shaft: Rose pink (mixture of red and white)
    - Second quarter of shaft: Yellow
    - Third quarter: Salmon (mix pink and yellow)
    - Bottom quarter: Yellow-orange

13. Paint or spray on a sealant to protect the painted wand. Allow to dry.

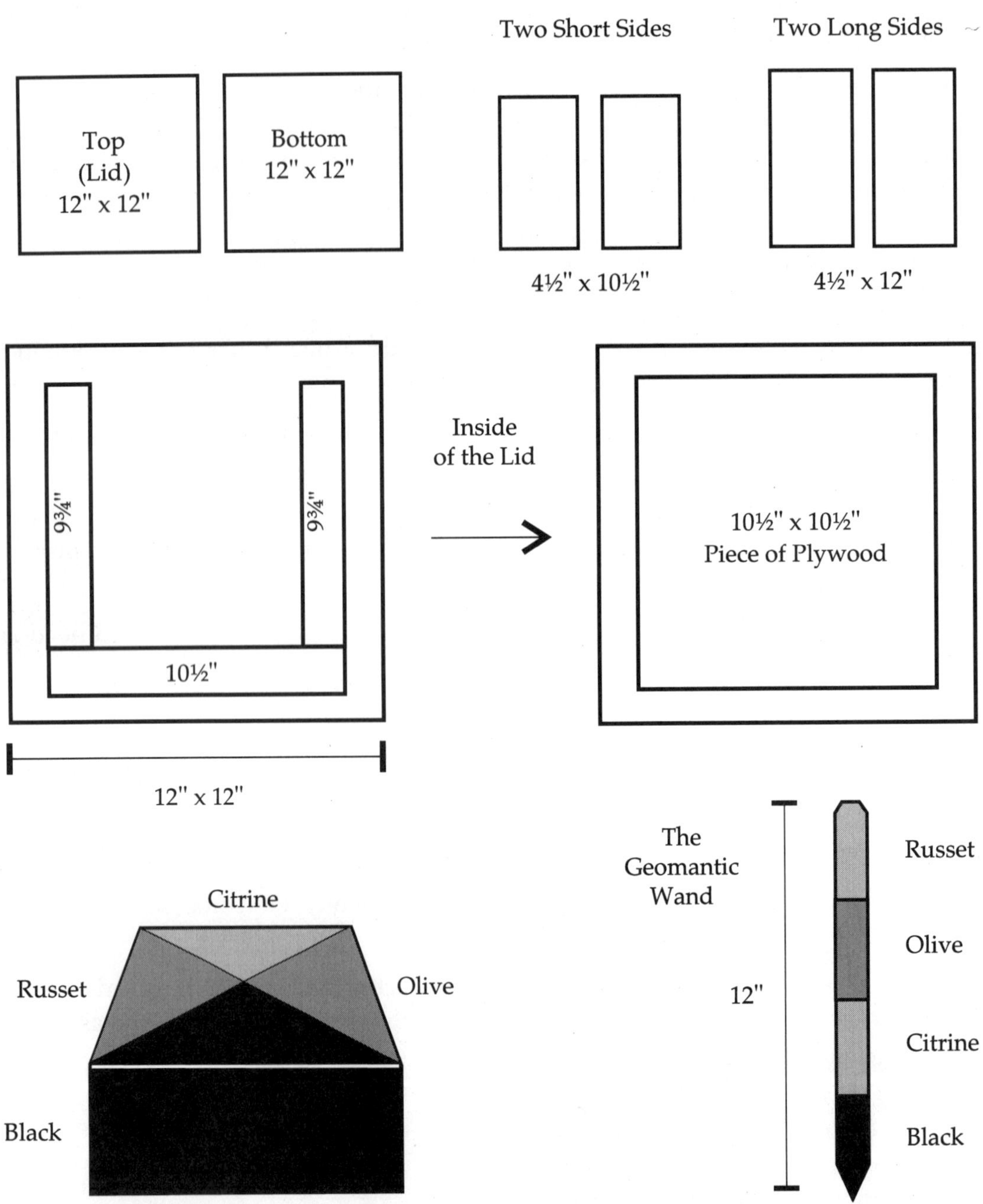

Figure 107: The Geomantic Box

The Geomantic Box

Geomancy is an ancient form of divination associated with the element of Earth. It was originally performed by poking holes into dirt or sand to obtain different symbols and figures. These geomantic figures were then used to obtain answers to particular questions. Although nowadays this procedure can be done entirely using pen and paper, there is an advantage to using earth in that it helps to formulate the magical link between the diviner and the planetary Genius summoned.

The Golden Dawn made the study of geomancy a part of its curriculum, along with the tarot, astrology, and the tattvas. The art of Geomancy is described in Israel Regardie's *The Golden Dawn*, but his discussion is limited in that most of the tables list only a narrow set of fixed responses to proposed questions (for instance: evil, good, medium, sometimes evil). These stock answers are not well suited to accommodate the types of questions the modern geomancer asks. However, by reading between the lines of furnished answers and consulting a good book on astrology, the outcome of the divination may be accurately determined for any questions.

Since it isn't always convenient to step outside and poke holes in the ground to obtain an answer to a question, a box can be made to hold consecrated soil, and a geomantic divination can be done at your convenience. A special wand can also be constructed for use with the Geomantic Box.[3]

See *Ritual Use of Magical Tools*, chapter six, for instruction on how to perform geomantic divinations using the box and wand described here.

Refer to Figure 107 on page 280 and Figure 108 on page 282 for construction diagrams.

Materials Needed

- One piece of ¾" thick plywood, approximately 1' x 4'
- One ¼" thick piece of plywood, 10½" square
- One ¼" thick dowel, approximately 12" long
- One ¾" x ½" piece of basswood (model strut), at least 31" long
- Wood glue
- Wood putty
- 1½" long finishing nails
- Gesso
- Acrylic paints: black, white, violet, orange, and green
- Sealant: clear lacquer finish

Geomantic Figure	Zodiacal Attribution	Name of Figure	Ruling Planet	Sigil of Genius	Ruler (Genius)	Geomantic Figure	Zodiacal Attribution	Name of Figure	Ruling Planet	Sigil of Genius	Ruler (Genius)
	♈	Puer	♂		Bartzabel		♎	Puella	♀		Kedemel
	♉	Amissio	♀		Kedemel		♏	Rubeus	♂		Bartzabel
	♊	Albus	☿		Taphthartharath		♐	Acquisitio	♃		Hismael
	♋	Populus	☽		Chasmodai		♑	Carcer	♄		Zazel
	♋	Via	☽		Chasmodai		♒	Tristitia	♄		Zazel
	♌	Fortuna Major	☉		Sorath		♓	Laetitia	♃		Hismael
	♌	Fortuna Minor	☉		Sorath		☊	Caput Draconis	♀ ♃		Hismael & Kedemel
	♍	Conjunctio	☿		Taphthartharath		☋	Cauda Draconis	♂ ♄		Zazel & Bartzabel

Figure 108: The Geomantic Figures and Their Genii

Tools Needed

- Table saw or jigsaw
- Hammer
- Nail punch
- Sandpaper (course, medium, and fine)
- Artist's brushes

Construction: The Box

1. Cut the ¾" plywood into six pieces as follows:

    - Top: One 12" x 12" piece
    - Bottom: One 12" x 12" piece
    - Two short sides: Both pieces 4½" x 10½"
    - Two long sides: Both pieces 4½" x 12"

2. Nail the four side pieces together, end to end, as in Figure 107, page 280. The 12" long piece will be directly opposite its twin, with the shorter pieces separating them. Be sure to apply glue to the edges before nailing. Glue and nail the bottom piece to the four side pieces. Fill in any gaps with wood putty and sand smooth with course and medium sandpaper.

Construction: The Lid

3. Take the ¾" x ½" model strut and cut it into three pieces: one 10½" long piece and two 9¾" long pieces.

4. Glue these three pieces onto the inside of the lid piece, so that they are all ¾" from the edge on three sides.

5. Nail the ¼" thick piece of plywood to the inside of the lid over the three pieces of wood. The lid should fit snugly in place over the box. If it is too tight, sand the inside pieces of the lid with course sandpaper.

Finishing Steps

6. Cover the box with a coat of gesso. Allow to dry, then sand lightly with fine sandpaper.

7. Mark the top of the box into four sections, corner to corner. Paint the sections in the appropriate Malkuth colors: citrine, olive, russet and black. Paint the sides of the box accordingly. Paint the bottom and inside of the box black.

8. Paint the underside of the lid white. On this white field, paint in black a list of the geomantic figures and sigils shown in Figure 108, page 282. This diagram will be a handy reference in an actual divination. (Sigils associated with the element of Earth can also be painted on the inside of the lid. See the sigils of the Earth Pentacle in chapter five, Figure 96, page 254.)

The Geomantic Wand

9. Take the 12" long slender dowel and sharpen one end of it. Measure the wand off into four equal sections. Paint the wand either black or in the four colors of Malkuth in the following order: russet, olive, citrine, and black. (The pointed end should be black.) The wand can be stored in the hollow space inside the lid of Geomantic Divination Box under the ¼" plywood.
10. Apply a coat of sealant to the box, inside and out. Apply sealant to the wand as well.
11. The box should be filled with dry black earth. Sand does not yield the best results. The soil can be taken from a special or sacred place to help reinforce a strong spiritual bond between the earth and the geomancer. The wand is used to poke holes into the consecrated soil. Once the box is completed and filled with earth, it should be consecrated. (See *Ritual Use of Magical Tools*, chapter six.)

The Spirit Wand

The Hebrew letter Shin, when painted white, represents the fifth element of Spirit. (When red, it becomes the Shin of Fire.) This letter has the numerical value of 300, which has the same Qabalistic value as Ruach Elohim, a Hebrew phrase meaning "the Spirit of God." Shin consists of three Yods, or flaming tongues of light. The letter symbolizes the highest aspirations of the soul, and indeed, the three Yods seem to point toward the omnipresence of the Supernal triad.

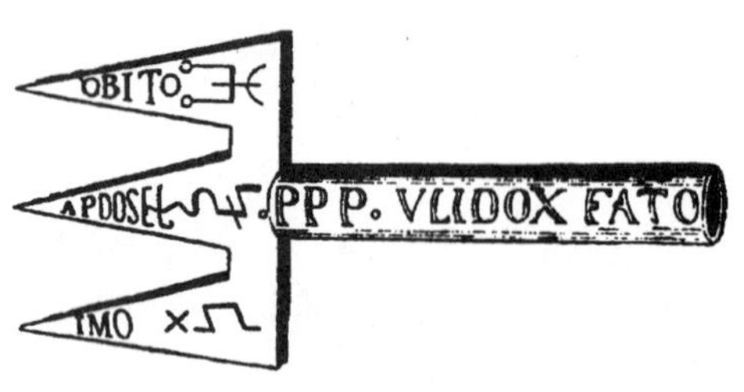

Figure 109: The Trident

According to Levi, Paracelsus replaced the magic wand of the magician with the trident, a figure which expressed "the synthesis of the triad in the monad, thus completing the sacred tetrad."[4] (See Figure 109.)

The Spirit Wand is divided into five sections, one for each letter of the *Pentagrammaton*, the five-lettered name of *Yeheshuah* (יהשוה),

and the five elements. (See Figure 110, page 286.) The colors on the shaft represent the five subelements of *eth*:

- White—Spirit of Spirit
- Pale yellow—Air of Spirit
- Gray—Earth of Spirit
- Pink—Fire of Spirit
- Pale blue—Water of Spirit

Refer to Figure 110, page 286 for construction diagrams.

Materials Needed

- One ¾" thick dowel between 20" to 24" long
- One ¾" thick piece of pine or basswood, approximately 6" x 6"
- One ¼" wooden dowel or peg 1" long
- Wood putty
- Gesso
- Acrylic paints: white, gray, red, yellow, blue
- Sealant: clear lacquer finish

Tools Needed

- Scroll saw
- Electric drill with ¼" and ¾" bits
- Sandpaper (coarse, medium, and fine)
- Index card
- Artist's brushes (large, medium, and fine)

Construction: The Head

1. Draw the Hebrew letter Shin, shown in Figure 110, on the 6" x 6" piece of wood. (The letter should be no more than 4" x 4".) With the saw, cut out the shape of the letter.
2. Drill a hole ½" deep and ¼" wide in the center of the bottom of the letter.

Construction: The Shaft

3. From a leftover piece of the ¾" thick pine wood, draw one 1½" circle. Cut it out. In the center, drill a ¾" diameter hole. You will end up with a donut-shaped ring of wood.
4. Take the long dowel (shaft) and drill a hole ½" deep and ¼" in diameter into one end of it. Glue the 1" wooden peg into the hole you have just drilled so that half of the peg is embedded into the end of the dowel and half of it sticks out.

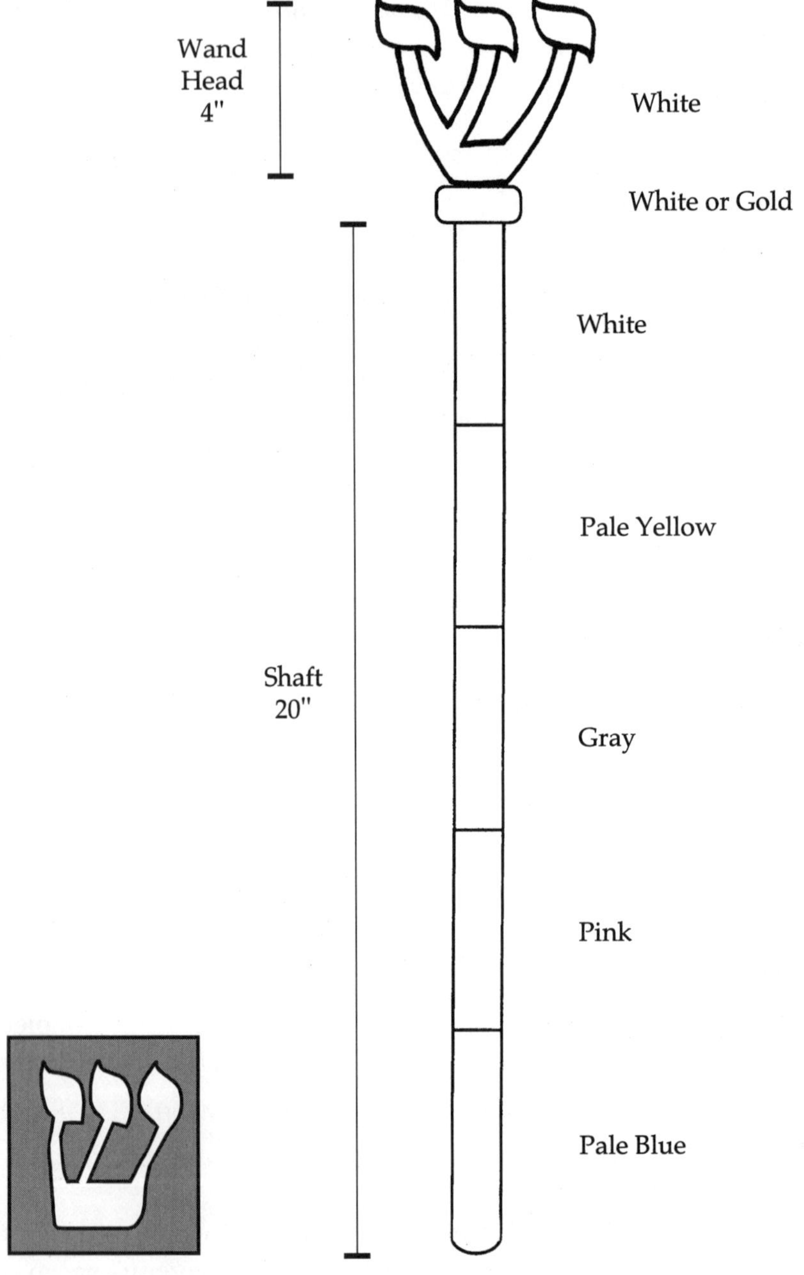

Figure 110: The Spirit Wand

5. Apply glue to the inside of the ring. Slide it over the top end of the shaft. (If the ring is too tight, sand inside its center hole.) Pour some glue into the hole you drilled into the bottom end of the wand head and attach the Shin to the wand shaft. Let dry.

Finishing Steps

6. Fill in any gaps with wood putty. Sand the entire surface of the wand so that it is smooth. With a paint brush, cover the wand with a coat of gesso. Allow to dry.
7. Sand the painted surface (especially the shaft) lightly until smooth. Apply a second coat if needed.
8. Measure and mark the shaft into five equal sections. Use an index card wrapped around the shaft as a guide to draw a straight line around the dowel. Paint the wand as follows:
   - Wand head: White
   - Ring: White
   - Upper (first) section of the shaft: White
   - Second section: Pale yellow (yellow and white)
   - Third section: Gray
   - Fourth section: Pink (red and white)
   - Fifth section: Pale blue (blue and white)
9. Paint or spray on a sealant to protect the painted wand. Allow to dry.

   (Note: An alternative version of the Spirit Wand could be made utilizing the Spirit Wheel ⊛ as the wand head in place of the Shin.)

The Sephirotic Wand

This wand is adapted from the Lotus Wand, which is grasped by the white band to invoke any of the Sephiroth. The Sephirotic Wands are each naturally aligned by their geometric heads to a particular Sephirah. (See Figure 111, page 289.) The shafts are divided into the color scales of the Four Worlds of the Qabalah: Atziluth, Briah, Yetzirah, and Assiah. For example, the Binah Wand with the triangular head has its shaft divided into the colors of: *Binah in Atziluth* (red), *Binah in Briah* (black), *Binah in Yetzirah* (dark brown), and *Binah in Assiah* (gray-flecked pink). The head of the wand is always white. These wands can be used in a ritual/meditation to invoke and explore the energies of a particular Sephirah in any of the Four Worlds (see *Ritual Use of Magical Tools*, chapter six, for a ritual of this type.)

(Note: An ambitious magician could make a series of wands allotted to the twenty-two paths of the tarot, using the same methods given here. The head of such a wand would be fashioned in the shape of one of the twenty-two letters of the Hebrew alphabet—Teth for the path of "Strength," Mem for "The Hanged Man," and so forth. The shaft would likewise be divided into four sections and painted as the path colors in the four color scales. See Regardie's *The Golden Dawn*, page 99, for a complete list of these color scales.)

Materials Needed

- One ¾" thick dowel between 20" to 24" long
- One ¾" thick piece of pine or basswood, approximately 8" x 8"
- One ¼" wooden dowel or peg 1" long
- Wood putty
- Gesso
- Acrylic paints: white, iridescent white, black, gray, red, yellow, blue, green, orange, violet, blue-violet, and red-violet
- Sealant: clear lacquer finish

Tools Needed

- Scroll saw
- Electric drill with ¼" and ¾" bits
- Sandpaper (coarse, medium, and fine)
- An index card
- Artist's brushes (large, medium, and fine)

Construction: The Head

1. Draw the geometric designs shown in Figure 111, page 289, on the 8" x 8" piece of wood. (The wand head should be no more than 4" x 4".)
2. With the saw, cut out the shape of the letter. (Follow steps 3–4 on page 73 for cutting out the shaded or waste areas of wood. For the more complex designs such as the enneangle and dekangle, you might wish to cut out just the outside shape of the form and simply paint the shaded/waste areas with a neutral gray or black.)
3. Drill a hole ½" deep and ¼" wide in the center of the bottom of the wand head.

Construction: The Shaft

4. Follow steps 3–5 as given for the construction of the Spirit Wand on pages 285–287.)

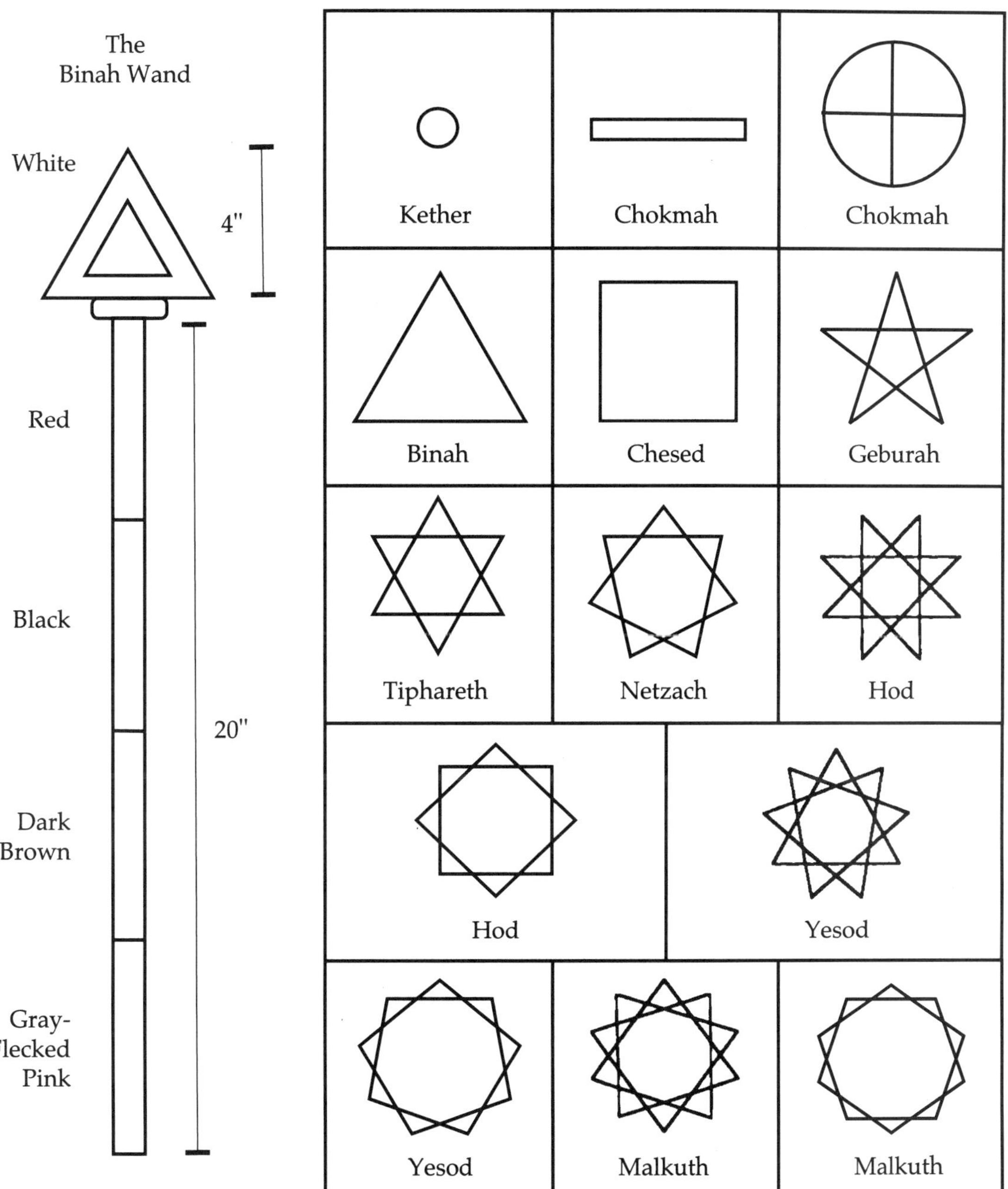

Figure 111: The Sephirotic Wand

Finishing Steps

5. Fill in any gaps with wood putty. Sand the entire surface of the wand with course and medium sandpaper until it is smooth.
6. With a paint brush, cover the wand with a coat of gesso. Allow to dry. Sand the painted surface (especially the shaft) lightly with fine sandpaper until smooth. Apply a second coat, if needed.
7. Measure and mark the shaft into four equal sections. (Use an index card wrapped around the shaft as a guide to draw a straight line around the dowel.)
8. Paint the wand as follows, depending on which Sephirah the wand is attributed to:

   Kether: *The point and ring*—iridescent white. *The top section*—iridescent white. *The second section*—white brilliance (white covered by a coat of iridescent white.) *The third section*—white brilliance. *The bottom section*—white-flecked gold.

   Chokmah: *The line and ring (or cross in circle and ring)*—white. *The first section*—soft blue (blue mixed with a small amount of white). *The second section*—gray. *The third section*—bluish Mother-of-Pearl (blue mixed with iridescent white). *The bottom section*—white-flecked red, blue, and yellow.

   Binah: *The triangle and ring*—white. *The first section*—red. *The second section*—black. *The third section*—dark brown (red and black mixed). *The final section*—gray-flecked pink.

   Chesed: *The square and ring*—white. *The first section*—violet. *The second section*—blue. *The third section*—deep violet (violet and blue mixed). *The final section*—deep blue-flecked yellow.

   Geburah: *The Pentagram and ring*—white. *The first section*—orange. *The second section*—red. *The third section*—red-orange. *The final section*—red-flecked black.

   Tiphareth: *The Hexagram and ring*—white. *The first section*—pink. *The second section*—yellow. *The third section*—salmon (pink and yellow mixed). *The final section*—yellow-orange.

   Netzach: *The heptagram and ring*—white. *The first section*—yellow-orange. *The second section*—green. *The third section*—yellow-green. *The final section*—olive-flecked gold.

   Hod: *The octagram and ring*—white. *The first section*—violet. *The second section*—orange. *The third section*—russet. *The final section*—yellow-brown flecked white.

   Yesod: *The enneagram and ring*—white. *The first section*—blue-violet. *The second section*—violet. *The third section*—dark violet (violet mixed with a touch of black). *The final section*—citrine-flecked blue.

Malkuth: *The enneagram and ring*—white. *The first section*—yellow. *The second section*—citrine, russet, olive, black. *The third section*—citrine, russet, olive, black-flecked gold. *The final section*—black-rayed yellow.

9. Paint or spray on a sealant to protect the painted wand. Allow to dry.

The Tarot Divination Wand

This wand is used to charge and give added strength to any divination using the Tarot. The wand is small enough to carry anywhere along with a deck of Tarot cards. The wand should be painted in the King Scale colors of the five elements. The sigils of the four Qabalistic Words ornament each section of the Wand.

See *Ritual Use of Magical Tools,* chapter six for an invocation using this wand.

Refer to Figure 112 on page 292 for construction diagrams.

Materials Needed

- One ⅜" dowel approximately 6" to 8" long
- Gesso
- Acrylic paints: white, black, red, blue, yellow, green, orange, and violet
- Sealant: clear lacquer finish

Tools Needed

- Sandpaper (fine grained)
- Artist's brushes

Construction

1. Cover the dowel with a coat of gesso. Let dry. Sand lightly with fine sandpaper.
2. Divide the shaft into five sections, one long section and four shorter sections. Paint the longest section white. This is the top of the wand. Paint the shorter sections in descending order as follows: red, blue, yellow and black.

Finishing Steps

3. On the white end, paint the symbol of a wheel with twelve spokes in black. (You may wish to paint the wheel on the very tip of the wand.) Also on the white band, paint the sigil of the angel HRU, the word ROTA, and your own magical motto.

4. On the red band, paint the letters and sigil of the word ATZILUTH אצילות in green.
5. On the blue band, paint the letters and sigil of the word BRIAH בריאה in orange.
6. On the yellow section, paint the letters and sigil of YETZIRAH יצירה in violet.
7. On the black band, paint the letters and sigil of the word ASSIAH עשיה in white.
8. Apply a coat of sealant for protection.

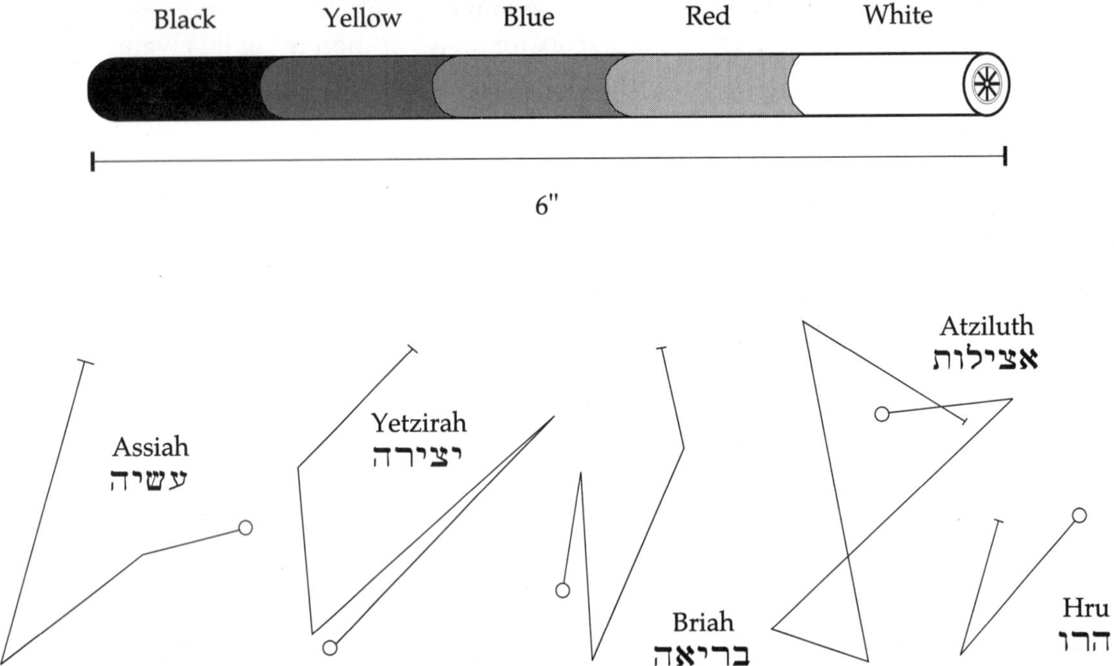

Figure 112: The Tarot Wand / Sigils and Hebrew Names

Endnotes

1. For a more elaborate wand, crystals could be set into each end of the wand, attached by glue or by copper wire wrapped around the bottom of the crystal and the tip of the wand. A single strand of wire could be placed to run along the length of the wand, connecting the crystals.
2. You may decide to paint the crosses all gold with a red circle.
3. Regardie suggested making these implements in *The Golden Dawn*, page 539. The design of the Geomancy Box presented here was provided by Bill Allen.
2. Levi, 226.

Glossary

Abba: Hebrew for "father." Often used to describe Chokmah.

Achad: Hebrew for "unity."

Acquisitio: Latin for "gain." A geomantic tetragram (∵) affiliated with the planet Jupiter and the zodiacal sign of Sagittarius.

Adept: An initiate who has reached a certain high level of attainment. In the Golden Dawn, a member of the Second Order.

Adeptus Minor: The "lesser adept." The first grade of the Golden Dawn's Inner Order, the R. R. et A. C. The adept grades comprise the Third Degree.

Admission Badge: A symbol that is given to a candidate at his or her initiation to ensure entrance into the temple.

Adnakhiel: The archangel of Sagittarius. Often mistakenly spelled *Advachiel*.

Adonai: Hebrew word for "lord," intoned in the south in the LBRP, and with the pentagram of Earth in the SIRP. Divine name associated with the Earth Pentacle.

Adonai ha-Aretz: Hebrew phrase for "lord of earth." Divine name associated with Malkuth.

Agla: Hebrew notariqon or acronym for the phrase *Atah Gebur Le-Olahm Adonai* or "Thou art Great forever, my Lord." Intoned in the north in the LBRP and with the Passive Spirit Pentagrams in the SIRP.

Ahaphi: The ape-headed Son of Horus who is stationed in the northwest and associated with Earth.

Ahathôôr: A great Egytpian goddess. In the Neophyte Hall, the human-headed Kerub of the east. The Kerub of Air.

Aima: Hebrew for "mother." In Qabalah it is "the bright, fertile mother," a title of Binah.

Aima Elohim: Hebrew for "Mother of the gods."

Air: One of the four magical elements. Air is said to be a combination of the qualities of heat and moisture. Air is considered active, masculine, intellectual, ethereal, abstract, and communicative. (See *Elements*.)

Air Dagger: One of the four Elemental Weapons or implements of the Adept. Used to invoke or banish the element of Air.

Aja: A Hindu name for Aries.

Akasha: Derived from a Sanskrit word meaning "to shine." The tattva associated with the element of Spirit, depicted as a black egg.

Akashic Record: The idea that all of the experiences and memories of every living being are contained in the substance of the ether.

Al (or *El*): Divine name of Chesed intoned in the west in the SIRP and associated with the Pentagram of Water. Divine Hebrew name associated with the Water Cup.

Al-Hamal: "The sheep." An Arabic name for Aries.

Albus: Latin for "white." A geomantic tetragram (⁝⁚) affiliated with the planet Mercury and the zodiacal sign of Gemini.

Alchemy: A process of transformation, discipline, and purification. There are two types of alchemy which often overlap. Practical, laboratory, or outer alchemy is concerned with transforming a base material into a higher and more purified substance, such as the turning of lead into gold or the extraction of a medicinal substance from a plant in order to create a healing elixir. Spiritual, theoretical, or inner alchemy is concerned with the transformation of the human soul from a state of baseness to one of spiritual enlightenment. Alchemical texts are often full of allegory and mythological symbolism.

Aleph: Hebrew for "ox." A Hebrew letter (א) with the English equivalent of "a" and the value of 1.

Ama: Hebrew for "mother." In Qabalah it is "the dark, sterile mother," a title of Binah.

Ambriel: The archangel of Gemini.

Amen: A notariqon or acronym for the Hebrew phrase *Adonai Melekh Na'amon,* meaning "Lord, faithful King." Its implied meaning is "so be it," or "so mote it be."

Amenet: Egyptian name for "west." The direction belonging to the Underworld.

Amissio: Latin for "loss." A geomantic tetragram (⁘) affiliated with the planet Venus and the zodiacal sign of Taurus.

Amnitziel: The archangel of Pisces.

Amru: A Syrian name for Aries.

Amset: The man-headed Son of Horus who is stationed in the northeast and associated with Air.

Angel: An entity within the divine hierarchy. A pure and high spirit of unmixed good in office and operation. Angels are anthropomorphic symbols of what we consider to be good or holy. Angels and archangels are considered specific aspects of God, each with a particular purpose and jurisdiction. The names of Qabalistic angels usually end in the suffixes "el" or "yah," which are divine names of God, indicating that the angels themselves are "of God." The word angel is derived from the Greek word *angelos* meaning "messenger."

Angelic host: A group or multitude of angels.

Ankh: Egyptian symbol of Eternal Life ☥.

Anoup empeIebet: Coptic for "Anubis of the East." The godform of the Keryx.

Anoup emp Emenet: Coptic for "Anubis of the West." The godform of the Phylax. (See *Ophooui.*)

Anup: The Egyptian god Anubis.

Aral (also *Arel* or *Erel*)**:** Ruling spirit of the element of Air. (Traditionally assigned to Fire.) One of the Aralim or Erelim. (See *Erelim.*)

Ararita: A notariqon or acronym used in Hexagram rituals. The word is formed from the first letters of the sentence: *Achad Rosh Achdotho Rosh Ichudo Temurahzo Achad,* which means, "One is His beginning, One is His individuality, His permutation is One." It affirms that the ultimate divinity is unitary in nature.

Archangel: A powerful angel who governs large groups or hosts of lesser angels. (See *Angel.*) According to some, archangels have free will, whereas angels do not.

Ariel: Hebrew for "Lion of God." An angel associated with the element of Fire, and sometimes with the element of Air.

Ariete: The Italian name for Aries.

Aretz: Hebrew word for "earth."

Arrit: The antechamber to the Egyptian underworld.

Ashim: Hebrew for "the Souls of Fire." The angelic host of Malkuth.

Asmodel: The archangel of Taurus.

Asshur: Hebrew for "straightforward, level, harmonious." One of the twelve tribes of Israel that is affiliated with the sign of Libra.

Assiah (also *Olam Assiah*): The fourth of four Qabalistic worlds or stages of manifestation. Assiah is the dense world of action and matter. It is attributed to Malkuth and the element of Earth.

Assumption of Godforms: A magical technique wherein the adept identifies him or herself with a particular deity by "assuming its form." The archetypal image of the deity is created on the astral by focused visualization, vibration of the deity's name, the tracing of its sigil, etc. The magician then steps into this astral image and wears it like a garment or mask, continuing to strengthen the image with focused concentration. This is performed in order to create a vehicle for that particular aspect of the divine that the magician is working with. (See *Godform.*)

Astral: From the Greek word *astrum* or "star."

Astral Plane: An intermediate and invisible level of reality between the physical plane and higher, more divine realms. It is the common boundary between the individual and noumenal reality. A nonphysical level of existence which is the basis of the physical plane. The astral plane has several "layers" of density and vibrational rate. The upper astral lies close to the angelic realms, while the lower astral is the world of dreams and phantasms.

Astrology: An ancient science that examines the action of celestial bodies on all living beings, nonliving objects, and earthly conditions, as well as their reactions to such influences. Whereas modern astronomy is considered an objective science of stellar distances, masses, and speeds, astrology is considered a subjective and intuitive science which not only deals with the astronomical delineation of horoscopes, but is also looked upon as a philosophy which helps explain the spiritual essence of life.

Atah: Hebrew word meaning "Thou art." Used in the Qabalistic Cross.

Atziluth (also *Olam Atziluth*): The first of four Qabalistic worlds or stages of manifestation. Atziluth is the divine world of archetypes. It is attributed to Kether and the element of Fire.

Augoeides: "The Higher Genius." A Greek term for the Holy Guardian Angel.

Aura: A shell or layer of astral substance which surrounds and permeates the physical body. Also called the Sphere of Sensation. (See *Subtle Body.*)

Auramoouth: Coptic form of the Egyptian goddess Mut. The godform of the Stolistes.

Ave: The great angel who was said to have revealed the angelic language to Enoch.

Ayin: Hebrew for "eye." A Hebrew letter (ע) with the English equivalent of "aa" or a nasal "o," with the value of 70.

Banishing: A ritual designed to get rid of unwanted spiritual energies. Banishings are usually a prelude to more complex rituals.

Banners of the East and West: In the Golden Dawn, they are the primary symbols of Light and Darkness that are used respectively by the Hierophant and the Hiereus.

Bara: A Persian name for Aries.

Barkhiel: Hebrew for "Lightning of God." The Archangel of Scorpio.

Bartzabel: The Spirit of Mars. In geomancy, Bartzabel is the ruler or genius associated with the tetragrams of Puer, Rubeus, and Cauda Draconis.

Bataivah: Enochian king of Air.

Belier: The French name for Aries.

Beni Elohim: Hebrew for "Sons of the Gods," or "Children of the Gods." The angelic host of Hod.

Benjamin: Hebrew for "son of the right hand, son of fortune." One of the twelve tribes of Israel that is affiliated with the sign of Sagittarius.

Beth: Hebrew for "house." A Hebrew letter (ב) with the English equivalent of "b" and "v" and the value of 2.

Binah: Hebrew word for "understanding," referring to the third Sephirah on the Tree of Life.

Bitom: Enochian name for the spirit of fire, taken from the Tablet of Union.

Boaz: The left-hand or black pillar of King Solomon's Temple. The feminine Pillar of Severity on the Tree of Life. Together the Pillars of Boaz and Jachin symbolize the polarized forces of night and day, strength and mercy, active and passive. Boaz is represented by the black pillar in the Hall of the Neophytes. (See *Jachin; Pillar of Severity*.)

Body of Light: The astral body, or etheric double. (See *Subtle Body*.) Often used to describe a ritually constructed vehicle for astral traveling.

BRH: The Lesser Banishing Ritual of the Hexagram.

Briah (also *Olam Briah*): The third of four Qabalistic worlds consisting of Chokmah and Binah. Briah is the World of Creation and the realm of archangels. It is attributed to the element of Water.

Caduceus: The winged, serpent-entwined wand of Hermes. In the Golden Dawn, the Caduceus Wand is carried by the Keryx.

Cancellaria: A female Cancellarius.

Cancellarius: Latin word meaning "chancellor" or "high official." Keeper of records. One of the Three Chief Officers in the Neophyte Hall.

Candidate: A prospective initiate.

Caput Draconis: Latin for "the dragon's head." A geomantic tetragram (⁝) affiliated with the northern node of the Moon and the element of Earth.

Carcer: Latin for "prison." A geomantic tetragram (⁝) affiliated with the planet Saturn and the zodiacal sign of Capricorn.

Cauda Draconis: Latin for "the dragon's tail." A geomantic tetragram (⁝) affiliated with the southern node of the Moon and the element of Fire.

Chasmodai: The Spirit of Luna. In geomancy, Chasmodai is the ruler or genius associated with the tetragrams of Populus and Via.

Chassan: An angel associated with the element of Air.

Chesed: Hebrew word for "mercy," referring to the fourth Sephirah on the Tree of Life. Also called *Gedulah,* which means "greatness, magnificence."

Cheth: Hebrew for "fence." A Hebrew letter (ח) with the English equivalent of "ch" and the value of 8.

Chiah: In Qabalah, the part of the soul located in Chokmah. It is described as the life-force, divine will, and source of action.

Chokmah: Hebrew word for "wisdom," referring to the second Sephirah on the Tree of Life.

Christian Rosencreutz: The allegorical founder of the Brotherhood of the Rose Cross. Sometimes referred to as C. R. C. (See *Rosicrucianism.*)

Circumambulate: To walk around in a circle, especially as part of a ritual.

Color Scales: Four lists of various colors that are assigned to the letters of the Tetragrammaton and the four Qabalistic Worlds: the King Scale (Yod, Atziluth), the Queen Scale (Heh, Briah), the Prince Scale (Vav, Yetzirah), and the Princess Scale (Heh Final, Assiah).

Comananu: The name of an Enochian governor.

Conjunctio: Latin for "conjunction." A geomantic tetragram (⁘) affiliated with the planet Mercury and the zodiacal sign of Virgo.

Consecrate: To make sacred. A ritual dedication of a person or object to a specific purpose. In the Golden Dawn, the officer known as the Dadouchos consecrates with a censer of incense.

Crook and Scourge: Implements of authority associated with the Egyptian god Osiris. They are used by the Chief Adept in the R. R. et A. C. to represent Mercy and Severity.

Cross and Triangle: The primary symbols of the Hermetic Order of the Golden Dawn.

Cross of Victory: A small black Calvary Cross ornamented with a rose of twenty-five petals. An implement used in the R. R. et A. C.

Crux Ansata: Latin for "handle-shaped cross." The Ankh Wand. (See *Ankh.*)

Crux Gammata: Latin for "Gammadion Cross." So called because it can be constructed from four Greek gammas (Γ). The Fylfot Cross 卐.

Daath: Hebrew word for "knowledge." The so-called "Invisible Sephirah" on the Tree of Life, Daath is not really a Sephirah, but rather a conjunction of the energies of Chokmah and Binah. It can be likened to a passageway across the Abyss.

Daleth: Hebrew for "door." A Hebrew letter (ד) with the English equivalent of "d" and the value of 4.

Darom: Hebrew for "south."

Deity: A god or goddess. A spiritual being embodying one or several aspects of divine essence. Divinity.

Deosil: In a clockwise or sunwise direction. The usual direction of movement in a ceremony. (See *Widdershins.*)

Dexter: In geomancy, the term used for "clockwise."

Divination: Based on the Latin word *divinatio* which means "the faculty of foreseeing." The word comes from the Latin term for "divine power" or "of the gods." Divination is the art of uncovering the divine meaning behind chance events. In the Golden Dawn, it is used as a tool for psychic well-being and spiritual growth. There are various methods of divination, including cartomancy (reading tarot cards) and geomancy (earth divination).

Divine Name: A name associated with a deity or an aspect of God that is vibrated or intoned during ritual.

Divine Self: Our true, pure, transcendent self which contains a spark of divinity.

Diviner: One who performs a divination.

Dadouche: A female Dadouchos.

Dadouchos: Greek word meaning "torch bearer." An officer in the Neophyte Hall who performs consecrations.

Dan: Hebrew for "judge, righteous judgment, advocate." One of the twelve tribes of Israel that is affiliated with the sign of Scorpio.

Djed: The backbone of Osiris.

Djehoti: The Egyptian god Thoth. Often written as *Tehuti.*

Dominus Liminis: Latin for "Lord of the Portal." A Portal initiate.

Earth: One of the four magical elements. Earth is said to be a combination of the qualities of cold and dryness. It is considered passive, feminine, solid, physical, stable, slow-moving, and grounded. (See *Elements.*)

Earth Pentacle: One of the Elemental weapons or implements of the Adept. Used to invoke or banish the element of Earth.

Edelperna: Enochian king of Fire.

Eheieh: Hebrew word meaning "I am." Divine name associated with Kether.

Eidolon: An image of an ideal.

El: Hebrew word meaning "god." Divine name associated with Chesed. (See *Al.*)

Elements: In magic there are four basic elements (fire, water, air, and earth) which are regarded as realms, kingdoms, or divisions of nature. They are the basic modes of existence and action, and the building blocks of everything in the universe. A fifth element, Spirit, is said to bind together and govern the lesser four. In the Mystic Repast of the Neophyte Ceremony, the rose, fire, chalice of wine, and bread and salt are symbols of the elements.

Elementals: Spirits belonging to the nature of the elements, having hierarchies similar to those of angels and archangels. An elemental spirit is said to be composed of only one elemental essence.

Elemental Tablets: Four charts stemming from the Enochian skryings of John Dee and Edward Kelly. They contain several rows of letters and are assigned to the four elements of Fire, Water, Air, and Earth. The names of numerous angels, archangels, and spiritual entities are derived from the letters on these charts. The Elemental Tablets play an important role in the Outer Order ceremonies of the Golden Dawn and are used in the higher magical workings of the Second Order. The four tablets are said to be bound together and ruled by the Tablet of Union. (See *Enochian; Tablet of Union.*)

Elemental Weapons: The four personal implements of an Adept used in ceremonial magic and associated with the elements. They include the Fire Wand, the Water Cup, the Air Dagger, and the Earth Pentacle.

Elexarpeh: The name of an Enochian governor.

Eloah: Hebrew for "god, goddess." Often seen as the feminine aspect of deity, just as *Yah* is seen as the masculine aspect of deity. The password of the Practicus grade, having a numerical value of 36.

Elohim: Hebrew word meaning "god(s)."

Elohim Gibor: A Hebrew phrase meaning "Almighty God." A divine name associated with Geburah.

Elohim Tzabaoth: Hebrew phrase meaning "God of Armies." Divine name associated with Hod.

Enochian: A genuine language and a system of magic that was discovered by Dr. John Dee (1527–1608), who was a magician, philosopher, astrologer, and advisor to Queen Elizabeth, and his assistant Edward Kelly. The Enochian system was received through the crystal skryings of Kelly, under Dee's supervision. The system was described as the "language of the angels" or the "language of Enoch," and came to be called the Angelic or

Enochian language (Enochian is pronounced "Eh-NO-kee-an," not "Eh-NAH-kee-an, because the prophet Enoch's name in Hebrew was spelled *Heh, Nun, Vav, Kaph* הנוך. The letter Vav is pronounced as a long "o," and when the name of Enoch was tranliterated into Greek, the Vav was replaced by the letter *omega*—also pronounced as a long "o.") Enochian magic is a complex system of elemental and spiritual hierarchies, which was further developed by the Golden Dawn.

Ephraim: Hebrew for "doubly fruitful." One of the twelve tribes of Israel that is affiliated with the sign of Taurus.

Erelim: Hebrew for "the thrones." The angelic host of Binah.

Êse: Coptic form of the Egyptian goddess Isis. The godform of the Praemonstrator.

Eth: A word used to indicate essence or spirit, the fifth element.

Evil Triad: In the Neophtye Hall, an entity symbolized by a devouring beast. An unbalanced force that is put down by the Hierophant in the Hall of Judgment. The unblanced portion of the human psyche that the initiate must strive to balance.

Evocation: A ritual designed to manifest or "evoke" a spiritual entity from the invisible realms into the magician's field of awareness. Sometimes called "summoning spirits."

Exarp: Enochian name for the spirit of air, taken from the Tablet of Union.

Fama Fraternitatis: The first of three famous and mysterious Rosicrucian Manifestos, the *Fama* first appeared in the German town of Kassel in 1614, and initiated interest in the Rosicrucian movement—a movement which focused on the spiritual evolution of humanity, and employed the tools of both religion and science, including the study of Alchemy, Hermetics, and Qabalah. The *Fama* is the story of the mythical founder of this movement—Christian Rosencreutz. It was translated into English in 1652 by Thomas Vaughan. MacGregor Mathers drew heavily on the legend of Christian Rosencreutz's life and the discovery of his tomb as portrayed in the *Fama* when he wrote the Golden Dawn's Adeptus Minor Ritual. (See *Christian Rosencreutz, Rosicrucianism.*)

Fire: One of the four magical elements. Fire is said to be a combination of the qualities of heat and dryness. It is considered active, masculine, spontaneous, quick, initiating, vitalizing, and energetic. (See *Elements.*)

Fire Wand: One of the Elemental Weapons or implements of the Adept. Used to invoke or banish the element of Fire.

Flaming Sword: The image of a crooked sword or lightning bolt that links the ten Sephiroth of the Tree of Life. It represents the manifestation of the universe by the natural succession of the ten divine emanations.

Flashing Colors: Colors that are directly opposite each other on an artist's color wheel. Also called complementary colors.

Formula of the Magic of Light: The practical magic of the Golden Dawn as classified under the five letters of the Pentagrammaton—YHShVH (יהשוה). Evocations and invocations fall under the category of the Hebrew letter Yod and the element of Fire. Consecrations of Talismans and the production of natural phenomena are classified under the second letter Heh and the element of Water. All works of spiritual development and transformations are attributed to the letter Shin and the element of Spirit. All works of divination are assigned to the letter Vav and the element of Air. All works of alchemy are classified under the final letter Heh and the element of Earth. (See *Pentagrammaton*.)

Fortuna Major: Latin for "greater fortune." A geomantic tetragram (⁝) affiliated with the Sun, the zodiacal sign of Leo, and the element of Air.

Fortuna Minor: Latin for "lesser fortune." A geomantic tetragram (⁝) affiliated with the Sun and the zodiacal sign of Leo.

Four-fold Breath: A method of rhythmic breathing used prior to mediation and ritual. (Breath in to the count of four, hold the breath to the count of four, exhale to the count of four, keep the lungs empty to the count of four.)

Four Worlds of the Qabalah: A four-fold division of the Tree of Life which separates the Tree into four levels of manifestation. The highest level is the most abstract and ethereal, while the lowest level is the most dense. They include *Atziluth, Briah, Yetzirah,* and *Assiah.*

Fylfot Cross: An equilateral cross with arms bent at right angles. 卐 Also called the swastika, Crux Gammata, Hammer of Thor, and Hermetic Cross. (See *Crux Gammata.*)

Gabriel: Hebrew for "Strength of God." Hebrew archangel of elemental Water, invoked in the LBRP and the SIRP. Also the name of the archangel of Yesod and the Moon.

Gad: Hebrew for "good fortune, abundance." One of the twelve tribes of Israel that is affiliated with the sign of Aries.

Geburah (or *Gevurah*)**:** Hebrew word for "power." Often referred to as "severity," Geburah is the fifth Sephirah on the Tree of Life.

Gedulah: Hebrew for "greatness, magnificence." A title of Chesed.

Genius: A ruling or protective spirit. The plural form is *genii.*

Geomancy: An ancient form of divination associated with the element of Earth, which utilizes astrological correspondences.

Gihon: The second river of Eden which flows into Chesed and is assigned to the element of Water.

Gimel: Hebrew for "camel." Letter of the Hebrew alphabet (ג) with the sound of "g" and the value of 3.

Gnomes: The elemental beings of Earth. (See *Elemental.*)

Godform: An archetypal image of a god or goddess that is constructed by visualization on the astral plane. (See *Assumption of Godforms.*)

Godhead: The universal and divine essence which is the source of all.

Graphrith: Hebrew for "sulfur."

Great Work: A term borrowed from alchemy's *magnum opus*. Refers to the path of human spiritual evolution, growth, and illumination, which is the goal of ceremonial magic.

Guph (also *G'uph*)**:** The lowest part of the soul, centered in Malkuth. A low level of subconscious intelligence that is closely tied to the physical body.

Hamaliel: The archangel of Virgo.

Hanael: The archangel of Capricorn.

Hap-Ouêr: In the Neophyte Hall, the bulled-headed Kerub of the north. The Kerub of Earth.

Harparkrat: Also called Harpocrates. Horus the child. The Egyptian god of silence.

Hcoma: Enochian name for the spirit of water, taken from the Tablet of Union.

Hegemon: Greek word meaning "guide." A main officer in the Neophyte Hall, who guides the candidate around the temple.

Hegemone: A female Hegemon.

Heh: Hebrew for "window." A Hebrew letter (ה) with the English equivalent of "h" and the value of 5.

"Hekas, Hekas, este Bebeloi": A magical phrase originally uttered at the Eleusinian Mysteries which means "far, far away be the profane." In the Golden Dawn, this phrase is used to indicate that a ritual is about to begin.

Henu: The Egyptian term for the flail or scourge (See *Crook and Scourge.*)

Heq-t: The Egyptian term for the crook. (See *Crook and Scourge.*)

Hermes Trismegistus, or "Hermes the Thrice-Great": The Greek god Hermes and the Egyptian god Thoth merged into one figure who was said to be the first and greatest magician. Hermes Trismegistus was reputed to be an ancient Egyptian priest and magician who was credited with writing forty-two books collectively known as the Hermetic literature. These books, including the *Emerald Tablet* and the *Divine Pymander,* describe the creation of the universe, the soul of humanity, and the way to achieve spiritual rebirth.

Hermetic: Of, or relating to, Hermes Trismegistus or the works ascribed to him. Having to do with the occult sciences, especially alchemy, astrology, and magic that are derived from Western sources (Hebrew, Egyptian, and Greek).

Hexagram: A geometric figure which has six points, formed from two interlocking triangles. The two triangles correspond to opposing forces of fire and water. The Hexagram shows these rival energies balanced and in harmony with each other. Also called the "Star of David" and the "Star of the Macrocosm." It is also a symbol of the perfected human being, and signifies the Hermetic principle of "as above, so below." In the Golden Dawn, Hexagram rituals are used to invoke or banish planetary forces.

HGA: Holy Guardian Angel. (See *Higher Self.*)

Hiddikel: The third river of Eden which flows into Tiphareth and is assigned to the element of Air.

Hiereia: A female Hiereus.

Hiereus: Greek word meaning "priest." A main officer in the Neophyte Hall who bars and threatens the candidate.

Hierophant: Greek word meaning "initiating priest." The primary, initiating officer in the Outer Order of the Golden Dawn.

Hieropantissa: A female Hierophant.

Higher Self: A personification of the transcendent spiritual self that is said to reside in Tiphareth and mediate between the Divine Self and the Lower Personality. Sometimes referred to as the Holy Guardian Angel, the Lower Genius, and the Augoeides.

Hismael: The spirit of the planet Jupiter. In geomancy, Hismael is the ruler or genius associated with the tetragrams of Acquisitio, Laetitia, and Caput Draconis.

Hod: Hebrew word for "splendor," referring to the eighth Sephirah on the Tree of Life.

Hodos Chamelionis: The mystic title of the Adeptus Minor which means "path of the chameleon."

Hôôr: Coptic form of the Egyptian god Hor or Horus.

Hôôr Ouêr: Coptic form of the Egyptian god Hor Wer or Haroueris "Horus the Elder."

Hôôr pekhroti: Coptic form of the Egyptian god Harparkrat or "Horus the Child."

HRU: The archangel who is said to be set over the Tarot.

IAO: The supreme God of the Gnostics, equivalent to the Tetragrammaton of the Hebrews. In the Golden Dawn, the letters of the name IAO are used to represent Isis, Apophis, and Osiris, or the cycle of life, death, and rebirth.

Iczodhehal: Enochian king of Earth.

Imperator: Latin word meaning "leader, commander." The lawgiver. One of the three Chief Officers in the Neophyte Hall.

Imperatrix: A female Imperator.

Initiate: Implies a "new beginning." A person who has undergone initiation into a magical group. The act of initiating a new member into a magical group.

Initiation: A ceremony, ritual, test, or period of instruction with which a new member is admitted to an organization or level of attainment.

I. N. R. I.: An important acronym in both orthodox religion and in magic. The initials of a Latin phrase once placed by the Romans at the top of the Cross, which stood for *Jesus Nazarenus Rex Judecorum*, or "Jesus of Nazareth, King of the Jews." Medieval alchemists theorized that it meant *Igne Natura Renovatur Integra* or "the whole of nature is renewed by fire," or *Igne Nitrum Raris Invenitum*—"shining is rarely found in fire." Masonic author J. S. M. Ward attributed the initials to the first letters of certain Hebrew words used to describe the four elements (**I**/Yam/Water; **N**/Nour/Fire; **R**/Ruach/Air; **I**/Yebeshah/ Earth). I. N. R. I. is known as the "Keyword" and is used in the Golden Dawn's Inner Order to describe the cycle of the seasons, the equinoxes and solstices, as well as the cycles of birth, death, and rebirth (**I**/Yod/Virgo; **N**/Nun/Scorpio; **R**/Resh/the Sun; **I**/Yod/Virgo).

Invocation: A ritual or portion of a ritual designed to establish communication with a higher spiritual entity. The magician allows a higher being to use his physical body as a vehicle for communication with the physical world. A potent prayer used to invoke a deity.

Invoke: To call a spiritual entity or force into the temple.

Iophiel: Hebrew for "the Beauty of God." The Intelligence of Jupiter.

Iset: Isis. Egyptian for "Throne."

Issachar: Hebrew for "he will bring reward." One of the twelve tribes of Israel that is affiliated with the sign of Cancer.

Jachin: The right-hand or white pillar of King Solomon's Temple. The masculine Pillar of Mercy on the Tree of Life. Together the Pillars of Boaz and Jachin symbolize the polarized forces of night and day, strength and mercy, active and passive. Jachin is represented by the White Pillar in the Hall of the Neophytes. (See *Boaz; Pillar of Mercy*.)

Judah: Hebrew for "praise YHVH" or "praise Yah." One of the twelve tribes of Israel that is affiliated with the sign of Leo.

Kabehsonef: The eagle-headed Son of Horus who is stationed in the southwest and associated with Water.

Kabiri: Deities from the Samothracian Mysteries. They are referred to in the Practicus Ceremony. (See *Samothracian Mysteries*.)

Kaph: Hebrew for "palm of the hand." A Hebrew letter (כ) with the English equivalent of "k" and the value of 20.

Kaph Cheth: The password of the Philosophus grade, which means "power." Its numerical value is 28, the mystic number of the Philosophus grade.

Kassiel: Hebrew for "Speed of God." The archangel of the planet Saturn.

Kedemel (or Qedemel): The Spirit of Venus. In Geomancy, Kedemel is the ruler or genius associated with the tetragrams of Amissio, Puella, and Caput Draconis.

Kerub: A ruling spirit associated with elemental Earth. Also, the singular of *Kerubim*.

Kerubim: The "strong ones." The angelic host of Yesod.

Kerykissa: A female Keryx.

Keryx (or *Kerux*)**:** Greek word meaning "herald." An officer in the Neophyte Hall, who leads circumambulations and gives announcements.

Kether: Hebrew word for "crown," referring to the first Sephirah on the Tree of Life.

Keyword: (See *I. N. R. I.*)

Khabs am Pekht: (See *Konx om Pax*.)

Khorsia: Hebrew for "throne." A title of Binah.

Konx om Pax: A Greek-based magical phrase used in the Eleusinian Mysteries. Used by the Golden Dawn to mean "Light in Extension." An Egyptian version of the phrase is *Khabs am Pekht*. (See *Light in Extension*.)

Kuzi: A Turkish name for Aries.

Laetitia: Latin for "joy." A geomantic tetragram (⁘) affiliated with the planet Jupiter and the zodiacal sign of Pisces.

Lamed: Hebrew for "ox-goad." A Hebrew letter (ל) with the English equivalent of "l" and the value of 30.

Lamen: A symbol suspended from a collar and worn on the chest.

LBRP: Lesser Banishing Ritual of the Pentagram. A basic Golden Dawn ritual which cleanses the temple or ritual space of unwanted energies.

Le-Olahm, Amen: Hebrew phrase meaning "the World forever, unto the Ages." A phrase used in the Qabalistic Cross. (See *Amen*.)

Levannah: The Hebrew name for the Moon.

License to Depart: Granting a spiritual entity permission to leave the temple or circle after the work of magic has been completed.

Light in Extension: Signifies "Light rushing out in One Ray." The divine light extending itself into manifestation.

Lotus Wand: The primary implement of an Adept. It is used to invoke or banish all manner of energies. The primary wand of the Third Adept of the R. R. et A. C.

LVX: The Latin word for "light." In the Second Order of the Golden Dawn it implies "the Light of the Cross," since the letters L, V, and X are all portions of one type or another of the cross. These letters are attributed to primary Egyptian gods and to certain grade signs as follows: **L** = Isis Mourning; **V** = Apophis and Typhon; and **X** = Osiris Risen. (These are known as the LVX Signs and they are the grade signs of the Adeptus Minor. Along with the sign of Osiris slain, they present the cycles of life, death, and rebirth inherent in the seasons—the Equinoxes and the Solstices.)

Maa Kheru: Egyptian for "true of voice."

Maarab: Hebrew for "west."

Maat (or Mêet): Egyptian goddess of justice and truth.

Madim: The Hebrew name for the planet Mars.

Magic: The art of causing change to occur in one's environment and one's consciousness. Willpower, imagination, intention, and the use of symbols and correspondences play a major role in this art. (See *Theurgy.*)

Malka be Tarshisim ve-ad Ruachoth Schechalim: A virtually untranslatable name of the Intelligence of Luna. According to author David Godwin, the best translation of the phrase is "Queen of the Chrysolites and the Eternal Spirits of the Lions."

Malkuth: Hebrew word for "kingdom," referring to the tenth Sephirah on the Tree of Life.

Maltese Cross: A cross formed from four triangles. This symbol crowns the Praemonstrator's Wand.

Manasseh: Hebrew for "who makes to forget." One of the twelve tribes of Israel that is affiliated with the sign of Gemini.

Mantle: A cloak or outer garment worn over a robe.

Matet Boat: The ship of the Egyptian god Rê which travels through the sky during the day.

Meditation: The act of quieting the mind in order to "listen" to the inner communications from the Higher Self.

Melach: Hebrew for "salt."

Melakh: Hebrew for "messenger," meaning an angel.

Melchidael: Hebrew for "Fullness of God." The archangel of Aries.

Melekim: Hebrew for "the Kings." The angelic host of Tiphareth.

Mem: Hebrew for "water." A Hebrew letter (מ) with the English equivalent of "m" and the value of 40.

Mem Heh: The password of the grade of Theoricus, *Mah* is the secret name of Yetzirah, the world of formation. Its numerical value is forty-five, which is the mystic number of the grade of Zelator.

Mesha: A Hindu name for Aries.

Michael: The name of the Hebrew archangel of Hod. Also the name of the archangel of Fire invoked in the LBRP and the SIRP.

Middle Pillar: The central pillar on the Tree of Life. The *Exercise of the Middle Pillar* is a Golden Dawn technique for awakening the Sephiroth or Galgalim of the Middle Pillar within the magician's sphere of sensation. (See *Pillar of Mildness.*)

Minutum Mundum: Latin for "small universe." It refers to a diagram of the Tree of Life that shows the Sephiroth in the Queen Scale of color and the Navitoth in the King Scale of color.

Mizrach: Hebrew for "east."

Motto: A special, magical name or phrase chosen by the magician for use in a magical lodge. A magical name is taken on in order to disassociate oneself from the mundane world for the duration of the magical work. Many magicians choose mottos that have personal spiritual significance for them. Golden Dawn mottos are typically in Latin and Hebrew.

Multans: A medieval Anglo-Norman name for Aries.

Muriel: The archangel of Cancer. The name comes from the Greek "myrrh."

Mystic Repast: A partaking of the elements. Similar to the Christian Eucharist.

Nahar: Hebrew for "never failing waters." The primary river of Eden flowing from the Supernals. In Daath Nahar was divided into four heads: Hiddikel, Gihon, Pison, and Phrath.

Nanta: Enochian name for the spirit of earth, taken from the Tablet of Union.

Naphthali: Hebrew for "my wrestling" or "wrestling of God." One of the twelve tribes of Israel that is affiliated with the sign of Virgo

Navitoth: The twenty-two paths that connect the Sephiroth on the Tree of Life.

Nebethô: Coptic form of the Egyptian goddess Nephthys.

Nemyss: A type of ancient Egyptian headdress worn by Golden Dawn magicians.

Neophyte: Comes from the Greek word *neophytos* or "newly planted." A beginner. The Neophtye grade is the first initiation into the Golden Dawn. It is symbolized by the number 0 within a circle and the number 0 within a square. A person who has been admitted into the grade of Neophyte. A temple that is arranged for a Neophyte initiation is called the Neophyte Hall.

Neophyte Signs: (See *Projection Sign* and *Sign of Silence*.)

Nephesh: In Qabalah, the part of the soul located in Yesod, which is described as the Lower Self or Lower Unconscious. Contains primal instincts, fundamental drives, and animal vitality. Sometimes called the etheric double or the astral body.

Neshamah: In Qabalah, the highest part of the soul. The Greater Neshamah encompasses Kether, Chokmah, and Binah. The highest aspirations of the soul. The Neshamah proper, or intuitive soul, is found in Binah.

Netzach: Hebrew word for "victory," referring to the seventh Sephirah on the Tree of Life.

Nun: Hebrew for "fish." A Hebrew letter (נ) with the English equivalent of "n" and the value of 50.

Nun Heh: The password of the grade of Zelator, said to mean "ornament." Its numerical value is fifty-five, which is the mystic number of the grade of Zelator.

Occult: From the Latin word *occuiere,* meaning "to cover up." Hidden or secret. Occult wisdom signifies secret wisdom. Wisdom that is kept secret so as not to be profaned. Wisdom or knowledge that is not known to the masses.

Opening by Watchtower: A ritual created by Israel Regardie based on the SIRP and the ceremony of the Consecration of the Vault of the Adepti. It is used to invoke the elements and set up a consecrated space as a prelude to the main ritual.

Opening of the Key: A complex method for reading the tarot used in the Second Order of the Golden Dawn. It utilizes five consecutive tarot spreads in a single reading.

Ophanim: Hebrew for "wheels." The angelic host of Chokmah.

Ophooui: Coptic for the Egyptian god Opowet. The godform of the Phylax. (See *Anoup emp Emenet.*)

Ousiri: Coptic form of thc Egyptian god Osir or Osiris. The godform of the Hierophant.

Paroketh: A boundary that exists between Tiphareth and the four lowest Sephiroth on the Tree of Life. Often called "the Veil."

Pastos: The coffin or sarcophagus of Christian Rosencreutz.

Peh: Hebrew for "mouth." A Hebrew letter (פ) with the English equivalent of "p" and "ph" and the value of 80.

Pentagram: A geometric figure based on the pentangle, which has five lines and five "points." Figures based on the pentangle include the pentagram and the pentagon. The pentagram or five-pointed star is attributed to the five elements of Fire, Water, Air, Earth, and Spirit. Sometimes called the "Blazing Star," "wizard's foot," the "Star of the Magi," and the "Star of the Microcosm." Also called the *pentalpha* because it can be constructed out of five Greek alphas.

Pentagrammaton: A Greek word which means "five-lettered name." Refers to the Hebrew name of YHShVH (יהשוה)—Yeheshuah or the Hebrew name of Jesus, which is the Tetragrammaton, YHVH, with the letter Shin placed in the center of the name.

Periclinus de Faustus: The mystic title of the Zelator which means "Wanderer in the Wilderness." The feminine form is *Pericline de Faustus.*

Pharos Illuminans: The mystic title of the Philosophus which means "Illuminated Tower of Light."

Philosopher's Stone: The Stone of the Wise. An alchemical symbol of the transmutation of humanity's lower nature into a higher, more purified spiritual state. True spiritual attainment and illumination. In practical alchemy, the Stone signifies the manufacturing of gold from a base metal. In spiritual alchemy, it is the transmutation of the Lower into the Higher. (See *Alchemy*.)

Philosophus: Comes from a Greek word which means "lover of wisdom." The Philosophus grade is the fifth initiation into the Golden Dawn, and the last of the four elemental grades which comprise the First Degree of the Order. It is associated with the element of Fire and the seventh Sephirah of Netzach. It is symbolized by the number four within a circle and the number seven within a square. A person who has been admitted into the grade of Philosophus. The plural form is *Philosophi.*

Phoenix Wand: The primary wand of the Second Adept of the R. R. et A. C.

Phorlakh: An angel associated with the element of Earth.

Phrath: Euphrates. The fourth river of Eden which flows into Malkuth and is assigned to the element of Earth.

Phylakissa: A female Phylax.

Phylax: Greek word meaning "sentinel." An officer who guards the Neophyte Hall.

Pillar of Mercy: The right-hand pillar on the Tree of Life, comprised of the Sephiroth of Chokmah, Chesed, and Netzach. The White Pillar. (See *Jachin*.)

Pillar of Mildness: Also called the Middle Pillar or the Pillar of Equilibrium. The central pillar on the Tree of Life comprised of the Sephiroth of Kether, Daath, Tiphareth, Yesod, and Malkuth. (See *Middle Pillar*.)

Pillar of Severity: The left-hand pillar on the Tree of Life, comprised of the Sephiroth of Binah, Geburah, and Hod. The Black Pillar. (See *Boaz*.)

Pison: The first river of Eden which flows into Geburah and is assigned to the element of Fire.

Populus: Latin for "people." A geomantic tetragram (⁞⁞) affiliated with the Moon and the zodiacal sign of Cancer.

Poraios de Rejectis: The mystic title of the Theoricus which means "Brought from among the Rejected."

Portal Grade: The intermediate grade between the First and Second Orders of the Golden Dawn. The Second Degree of the Order.

Portal Signs: *The Opening of the Veil* and *The Closing of the Veil.*

Practicus: The fourth initiation into the Golden Dawn, and the third of the four elemental grades which comprise the First Degree of the Order. The name practicus indicates that the initiate is beginning to put theory into practice. It is associated with the element of Water and the eighth Sephirah of Hod. It is symbolized by the number three within a circle and the number eight within a square. A person who has been admitted into the grade of Practicus. The plural form is *Practici.*

Praemonstrator: Latin word meaning "guide" and "one who prophesies." The teacher. One of the Three Chief Officers in the Neophyte Hall.

Praemonstratrix: A female Praemonstrator.

"Procul O Procul Eta Profani": Latin for "Far, far from this place be the profane." (See *Hekas! Hekas! Este Bebeloi."*)

Projection Sign: Also called the *Projecting Sign* and the *Sign of Horus.* One of the two Neophtye Signs of the Golden Dawn.

Protection Sign: Also called *Protecting Sign,* the *Sign of Silence,* and the *Sign of Harpocrates.* One of the Neophtye Signs of the Golden Dawn.

Psyche: The Greek word for "soul." The mind functioning as the center of thought, emotion, and behavior and consciously or unconsciously adjusting or mediating the body's responses to the social and physical environment.

Puella: Latin for "girl." A geomantic tetragram (⁛) affiliated with the planet Venus and the zodiacal sign of Libra.

Puer: Latin for "boy." A geomantic tetragram (⁘) affiliated with the planet Mars and the zodiacal sign of Aries.

Qabalah: Hebrew word meaning "tradition." It is derived from the root word *qibel,* meaning "to receive." This refers to the ancient custom of handing down esoteric knowledge by oral transmission. What the word Qabalah encompasses is an entire body of ancient Hebrew mystical principles that are the cornerstone and focus of the Western Esoteric Tradition.

Qabalistic Cross (or QC): A short ritual that is incorporated into the LBRP. The Qabalistic Cross forms an equilibrated cross of light in the magician's sphere of sensation.

Qamea (or *Kamea*): Comes from a Hebrew root word meaning "talisman." A Qamea or Magical Square is a diagram showing a series of numbers arranged so as to yield the same number total whether the numbers are added up horizontally by rows, vertically by columns, or diagonally. The number of the sum of each column of figures and the total sum of all the numbers on the square are numbers that are especially attributed to a particular planet. The Magical Squares or Qameoth (plural) are essentially planetary talismans.

Qlippoth: A Hebrew word meaning "shells." Chaotic and unbalanced forces or entities. Evil demons. Negative opposites of the harmonious Sephiroth. Singular form is *Qlippah*.

Qoph: Hebrew for "back of the head." A Hebrew letter (ק) with the English equivalent of "q" and the value of 100.

Querent: One who asks a question in a divination.

Quintessence: The "fifth essence." Refers to spirit, which is sometimes referred to as the fifth element. That which binds together and governs the four elements of Fire, Water, Air, and Earth.

Raagiosel: Enochian king of Water.

Raphael: Hebrew for "Healer of God." The name of the archangel of Tiphareth, also the name of the archangel of elemental Air, invoked in the LBRP and the SIRP.

Raziel: The archangel of Chokmah.

Resh: Hebrew for "head." A Hebrew letter (ר) with the English equivalent of "r" and the value of 200.

Reuben: Hebrew for "behold a son, vision of the son." One of the twelve tribes of Israel that is affiliated with the sign of Aquarius.

Rising on the Planes: A method of astral work that developed out of the Golden Dawn's technique of Traveling in the Spirit Vision. This is a purely spiritual process that uses the Qabalistic Tree of Life. The magician's consciousness is placed within the astral body, which ascends the various levels of the Tree.

Rose Cross: A key symbol of the Golden Dawn's Second Order. It is based on the Rosicrucian symbolism of the Red Rose and the Cross of Gold. The Rose Cross Lamen is worn by Adepts. The Ritual of the Rose Cross is a Second Order ritual for calming and balancing energies. (See *Lamen*.)

Rosicrucianism: A mystical and philosophical movement which emerged in the seventeenth century and spawned several secret organizations or orders concerned with the study of religious mysticism, alchemy, Qabalah, and professing esoteric spiritual beliefs.

The symbolism of Rosicrucianism is primarily Christian and the Rosicrucian path emphasizes the way of transformation through the Christ impulse. (See *Christian Rosencruetz.*)

Rota: Latin for "wheel." Often used as an anagram for the word "taro" or "tarot."

R. R. et A. C.: Initials for the *Rosae Rubeae et Aureae Crucis* or "the Red Rose and the Golden Cross." The name of the Golden Dawn's Second or Inner Order.

Ruach: Hebrew word for "breath," "air," and "spirit." The middle part of the Qabalistic soul representing the mind and reasoning powers.

Ruach Elohim: Hebrew phrase for "Spirit of God." Personified by the feminine figure of the Shekinah.

Rubeus: Latin for "red." A geomantic tetragram (⁘) affiliated with the planet Mars and the zodiacal sign of Scorpio.

Sachiel: Hebrew for "covering of God." The archangel of the planet Jupiter.

Salamanders: Elemental beings associated with Fire. (See *Elementals.*)

Samekh: Hebrew for "prop." A Hebrew letter (ס) with the English equivalent of "s" and the value of 60.

Samothracian Mysteries: Named for the Greek island of Samothrace. Said to be the oldest of the Greek Mystery religions. (See *Kabiri.*)

Sandalphon: The archangel of Malkuth and the left-hand Kerub of the Tree of Life..

Sash: A long band of cloth worn over the shoulders as a symbol of rank or grade.

SBRP: The Supreme Banishing Ritual of the Pentagram.

Scepter of Power: The Hierophant's Wand.

Scepter of Wisdom: The Hegemon's Wand.

Sektet Boat: The ship of the Egyptian god Rê which traveled through the Underworld at night.

Sepher Yetzirah: Hebrew phrase meaning "Book of Formation." The name of one of the oldest of the Qabalistic texts. It was circulated in varying oral forms until around 100 B.C.E. to about C.E. 200, when it was standardized. The text describes the formation of the universe by comparing it with the creation of the twenty-two letters of the Hebrew alphabet. A brief tract from the Hebrew text written in 1642 by Joannes Stephanus Rittangelius, called "The Thirty-two Paths of Wisdom," was later added to the *Sepher Yetzirah.*

Sephirah: (See *Sephiroth.*)

Sephiroth: Hebrew word meaning "numbers, spheres, emanations." Refers to the ten divine states or god-energies depicted on the Qabalistic Tree of Life. The singular form is *Sephirah.*

Seraph: The ruling spirit of the element of Fire. Also, the singular form of *Seraphim.*

Seraphim: Hebrew for "the Flaming Ones." The angelic host of Geburah.

Serpent of Wisdom: An image of a serpent entwined around the Tree of Life, which represents the ascending order of the twenty-two Navitoth on the Tree of Life. It represents the reflux current of energy aspiring to reach its divine source.

Shabbathai: Hebrew for "the seventh." The Hebrew name of the planet Saturn.

Shaddai El Chai: Hebrew phrase meaning "Almighty Living God." Divine name of Yesod.

Shekinah: The divine or visible presence of God. A title of Malkuth, as the lower reflection of Binah, personified as a radiant goddess.

Shemesh: Hebrew name for the Sun, adapted from *Shamash,* the name of the Sumerian Sun god.

Shin: Hebrew for "tooth." A Hebrew letter (ח) with the English equivalent of "sh" and "s" and the value of 300.

Sigil: A seal, sign, or signature. A symbol used to represent a spiritual force, such as an angel, archangel, or a divine name of God. Any name or word can be made into a sigil.

Simeon: Hebrew for "hearing, obeying." One of the twelve tribes of Israel that is affiliated with the sign of Pisces.

Simulacrum: An image used in sympathetic magic that is considered to be the magical double of the object that it represents.

Sinister: In geomancy, the term used for "counterclockwise."

SIRP: The Supreme Invoking Ritual of the Pentagram. An Inner Order ritual for invoking elemental energies.

Solve et Coagula: Latin phrase meaning "dissolve and coagulate." Alchemical axiom which points to the practice of reducing a solid to a liquid and back to a solid again. Used as a metaphor for the practice of psychotherapy and self-integration.

Sorath: The Spirit of Sol, the Sun. In geomancy, Sorath is the ruler or genius associated with the tetragrams of Fortuna Major and Fortuna Minor.

Sphere of Sensation: The aura.

Squilling: In geomancy, the method used for producing the random generation of tetragrams.

Stolistes: Greek word meaning "preparer." An officer in the Neophyte Hall who is in charge of all regalia and purifications.

Subtle Body: The psychophysical circuitry of a human being through which the life force flows. Energy blueprint for the physical body. Sometimes called the astral body, etheric double, or body of light.

Supernal: Celestial or heavenly. In Qabalah, it refers to the three highest Sephiroth on the Tree of Life, which are often called the Supernal triad.

Sylphs: Elemental beings associated with Air. (See *Elementals*.)

Tabard: A tunic or capelike garment worn by a knight over armor and ornamented with his heraldic emblems. In the Golden Dawn it is sometimes used in place of a cloak.

Tabitom: The name of an Enochian governor.

Tablet of Union: The Enochian Tablet of spirit which binds together and governs the other four Elemental Tablets. Painted on the tablet are Enochian divine names including: *Exarp*—for Air, *Hcoma*—for Water, *Nanta*—for Earth, and *Bitom*—for Fire.

Taliahad: An angel associated with the element of Water.

Talisman: An object which is charged or consecrated toward the achieving of a specific end. A talisman is a magical object that has been charged with a force that it is intended to represent. Usually intended to draw something to the magician.

Taphthartharath: The Spirit of the planet Mercury. In geomancy, Taphthartharath is the ruler or genius associated with the tetragrams of Albus and Conjunctio.

Tarot: A system of divination that employs a set of seventy-eight cards separated into two main divisions—the Major and Minor Arcana. The Major Arcana includes twenty-two trump cards and the Minor Arcana includes sixteen court cards and forty numbered cards.

Tattva: Sanskrit word meaning "quality." The five main tattvas (Prithivi, Vayu, Apas, Tejas, and Akasa) correspond to the five elements of Earth, Air, Water, Fire, and Spirit.

Tau: Hebrew for "cross." A Hebrew letter (ת) with the English equivalent of "t" and "th" and the value of 400.

Tau Robe: A long-sleeved magician's robe that is shaped like the letter "T" (with arms extended out).

Teli: A Hebrew name for Aries.

Teth: Hebrew for "serpent." A Hebrew letter (ט) with the English equivalent of "t" and the value of 9.

Tetragram: A divine word or name composed of four letters. Also refers to a geomantic figure composed of four lines. There are sixteen tetragrams used in geomancy.

Tetragrammaton: A Greek word meaning "four-lettered name." Refers to the highest divine Hebrew name of God, YHVH (יהוה).

Tetrahedron: A polyhedron with four faces (three sides plus the base which is the fourth side). The Solid Triangle or Pyramid of Flame.

Tharsis: The ruling spirit of the element of Water.

Thaumaturgy: Greek word meaning "miracle-working." Magic used to create changes in the material world.

Thaum-Esh-Neith: Coptic form of the Egyptian goddess Neit or Neith.

Tharpesh: In the Neophyte Hall, the lion-headed Kerub of the south. The Kerub of Fire.

Theoricus: Comes from the Greek word for "beholder," "onlooker" or "student." The Theoricus grade is the third initiation into the Golden Dawn, and the second of the four elemental grades which comprise the First Degree of the Order. It is associated with the element of Air and the ninth Sephirah of Yesod. It is symbolized by the number two within a circle and the number nine within a square. A person who has been admitted into the grade of Theoricus. The plural form is *Theorici.*

Theurgy: Greek word meaning "God-working." Magic used for personal growth, spiritual evolution, and for becoming closer to the Divine. The type of magic advocated by the Golden Dawn. A magician is also known as a Theurgist or "God-worker."

Thirty-Two Paths of Wisdom: The ten Sephiroth and the twenty-two paths that connect them.

Thmê: Coptic form of the Egyptian goddess Maat or Mêet. The godform of the Hegemon.

Thôouth: Coptic form of the Egyptian god Djehoti or Thoth. Godform of the Cancellarius.

Thought-form: A mental image created and solidified in astral substance by willpower and visualization.

Thoum Moou: In the Neophyte Hall, the eagle-headed Kerub of the west. The Kerub of Water.

Three Alchemic Principles: Three fundamental substances in alchemy that are said to exist in all things. They are sulfur, mercury, and salt, which relate to the ideas of soul, spirit, and body. These substances are not to be confused with ordinary substances of the same name.

Tiphareth: Hebrew word for "beauty," referring to the sixth Sephirah on the Tree of Life.

Toouamaautef: The jackel-headed Son of Horus who is stationed in the southeast and associated with Fire.

Tree of Life (in Hebrew *Etz ha-Chayim*): A glyph or symbol that is central to the Qabalah. It is a symmetrical drawing of ten circles or spheres known collectively as Sephiroth, arranged in a certain manner with twenty-two connecting paths running between the spheres. It is considered a blueprint for understanding all things and relationships in the universe, including the essence of God and the soul of humanity. (See *Qabalah; Sephiroth.*)

Tristitia: Latin for "sorrow." A geomantic tetragram (⁘) affiliated with the planet Saturn and the zodiacal sign of Aquarius.

Tuat: The Egyptian Underworld.

Tzaddi: Hebrew for "fish-hook." A Hebrew letter (צ) with the English equivalent of "tz" and the value of 90.

Tzaphon: Hebrew for "north."

Tzaphqiel: Hebrew for "beholder of God." The archangel of Binah.

Undines: Elemental beings associated with Water. (See *Elementals.*)

Uriel (or **Auriel**): Hebrew for "Light of God." Archangel of elemental Earth, invoked in the LBRP and the SIRP.

Urim and Thummin: Part of the breastplate of the ancient Hebrew High Priest. The singular form of the word *Thummim* is *Thom*, meaning "perfection, completion." The singular form of the word *Urim* is *Ur*, meaning "light."

Vault of the Adepti: The ritual chamber of the Second Order.

Vav: Hebrew for "nail." A Hebrew letter (ו) with the English equivalent of "o," "u," and "v" and the value of 6.

Verkhiel: The archangel of Leo.

Via: Latin for "way." A geomantic tetragram (⁞) affiliated with the Moon, the zodiacal sign of Cancer, and the element of Water.

Vibratory Formula: A method by which divine names and words are intoned forcefully and with authority in a "vibration." Properly performed, the vibration should be felt throughout the entire body, and imagined to be vibrated throughout the universe.

Waas: The Egyptian term for the Phoenix Wand. (See *Phoenix Wand.*)

Wadj: The Egyptian term for the Papyrus Scepter or Lotus Wand. (See *Lotus Wand.*)

Water: One of the four magical elements. Water is said to be a combination of the qualities of cold and moisture. It is considered passive, feminine, receptive, sustaining, subconscious, creative, fluidic, and generative. (See *Elements.*)

Water Cup: One of the Elemental weapons or implements of the Adept. Used to invoke or banish the element of Water.

Western Esoteric Tradition: Hermeticism. (See *Hermetic.*)

Widder: A German name for Aries.

Widdershins: The anticlockwise direction, against the sun. (See *deosil.*)

Yah: Divine Hebrew name associated with Chokmah.

Yechidah: In Qabalah, the highest part of the soul located in Kether. It is described as the true Divine Self. The purest form of consciousness.

Yeheshuah: Hebrew name for Jesus. A divine name associated with the five elements. Referred to as the Pentagrammaton. (See *Pentagrammaton.*)

Yesod: Hebrew word for "foundation," referring to the ninth Sephirah on the Tree of Life.

Yetzirah: The third of four Qabalistic Worlds or stages of manifestation. It is known as the World of Formation and is the realm of angels. It is attributed to the spheres of Chesed, Geburah, Tiphareth, Netzach, Hod, and Yesod. It is attributed to the element of Air. (See *Four Worlds of the Qabalah.*)

YHVH: Four letters, Yod Heh Vav Heh or YHVH (יהוה), which stand for the highest Hebrew name for God, whose real name is considered unknown and unpronounceable. These letters are also attributed to the four elements of Fire, Water, Air, and Earth. Often referred to as the Tetragrammaton. (See *Tetragrammaton.*)

YHVH Eloah ve-Daath: Divine Hebrew name of Tiphareth meaning "Lord, God of Knowledge."

YHVH Elohim: Divine Hebrew name of Binah, meaning "the Lord, God." Also associated with Daath in the Exercise of the Middle Pillar.

Yesod: Hebrew word for "foundation," referring to the ninth Sephirah on the Tree of Life.

Yod: Hebrew for "hand." A Hebrew letter (י) with the English equivalent of "y" and "i" and the value of 10.

Z.A.M.: Zelator Adeptus Minor.

Zayin: Hebrew for "sword." A Hebrew letter (ז) with the English equivalent of "z" and the value of 7.

Zauir Anpin: Hebrew for "short-faced." In Qabalah, it refers to the son or offspring of Aima and Abba. Attributed to the Sephiroth of Chesed, Geburah, Tiphareth, Netzach, Hod, and Yesod, but especially referred to Tiphareth. Also called *Microprosopus* or the "Lesser Countenance."

Zazel: The spirit of Saturn. In geomancy, Zazel is the ruler or genius associated with the tetragrams of Carcer, Tristitia, and Cauda Draconis.

Zebulun: Hebrew for "dwelling, habitation." One of the twelve tribes of Israel that is affiliated with the sign of Capricorn.

Zelator: Comes from the Greek word for "zealot." The Zelator grade is the second initiation into the Golden Dawn, and the first of the four elemental grades which comprise the First Degree of the Order. It is associated with the element of Earth and the tenth Sephirah of Malkuth. It is symbolized by the number one within a circle and the number ten within a square. A person who has been admitted into the grade of Zelator.

Zuriel: Hebrew for "My Rock is God." The archangel of Libra.

Bibliography

"A Brother of the Fraternity." *Secret Symbols of the Rosicrucians of the 16th and 17th Centuries.* Kila, MT: Kessinger Publishing Co.

Ashcroft-Nowicki, Dolores. *The Shining Paths.* Wellingborough, Northamptonshire: The Aquarian Press, 1983.

Bardon, Franz. *The Practice of Magical Evocation.* West Germany: Dieter Rüggeberg, 1975.

Budge, E. A. Wallis. *Egyptian Magic.* New York: Dover Publications, Inc., 1971.

———. *The Gods of the Egyptians, Vol. 1 & 2.* New York: Dover Publications, Inc., 1969.

———. *The Book of the Dead.* London: Routledge & Kegan Paul Ltd., 1969.

Burckhardt, Titus. *Alchemy.* Great Britain: Element Books, 1987.

Case, Paul Foster. *The Book of Tokens.* 10th ed. Los Angeles: Builders of the Adytum, 1983.

Cicero, Chic, and Sandra Tabatha Cicero. *Ritual Use of Magical Tools.* St. Paul, MN: Llewellyn Publications, 2000.

———. *Secrets of a Golden Dawn Temple.* St. Paul, MN: Llewellyn Publications, 1992.

———. *Self-Initiation into the Golden Dawn Tradition.* St. Paul, MN: Llewellyn Publications, 1992.

Cirlot, J. E. *A Dictionary of Symbols.* 2nd ed. New York: Philosophical Library, 1983.

Colquhoun, Ithell. *Sword of Wisdom.* New York: G. P. Putnam's Sons, 1975.

Crowley, Aleister. *777.* York Beach, ME: Samuel Weiser, Inc., 1973.

Divine Pymander of Hermes Mercurius Trismegistus. Des Plaines, IL: Yogi Publication Society, date unknown.

Fame and Confession of the Fraternity of the R: C:. Privately printed for the S. R. I. A. Great Britain, 1997.

Forrest, Adam P. "Mysteria Geomantica: Teachings on the Art of Geomancy." *The Golden Dawn Journal: Book One: Divination.* Edited by Chic & S. Tabatha Cicero. St. Paul, MN: Llewellyn Publications, 1994.

———. "This Holy Invisible Companionship." *The Golden Dawn Journal: Book Two: Qabalah: Theory and Magic.* Edited by Chic and S. Tabatha Cicero. St. Paul, MN: Llewellyn Publications, 1994.

Fortune, Dion. *The Mystical Qabalah.* New York: Ibis Books, 1981.

Gilbert, R. A. *The Golden Dawn Companion.* Wellingborough, Northamptonshire: The Aquarian Press, 1986.

———. *The Sorcerer and His Apprentice.* Wellingborough, Northamptonshire: The Aquarian Press, 1983.

Godwin, David. *Godwin's Cabalistic Encyclopedia.* 2nd ed. St. Paul, MN: Llewellyn Publications, 1989.

Gray, William G. *The Ladder of Lights.* York Beach, ME: Samuel Weiser, Inc., 1981.

Hall, Manly P. *The Secret Teachings of All Ages.* Los Angeles: The Philosophical Research Society, Inc., 1977.

Herodotus. *Histories.* Great Britain: Wordsworth Editions Ltd., 1996.

Inman, Thomas. *Ancient Pagan and Modern Christian Symbolism.* Kila, MT: Kessinger Publishing Co.

James, Geoffrey. *The Enochian Evocation of Dr. John Dee.* Gillette, NJ: Heptangle Books, 1984.

King, Francis and Stephen Skinner. *Techniques of High Magic.* Rochester, VT: Destiny Books, 1991.

Knight, Gareth. *A Practical Guide to Qabalistic Symbolism.* New York: Samuel Weiser, Inc., 1983.

Kraig, Donald Michael. *Modern Magick.* St. Paul, MN: Llewellyn Publications, 1988.

Levi, Eliphas. *Transcendental Magic.* York Beach, ME: Samuel Weiser, Inc., 1995.

Mathers, S. Liddell MacGregor Mathers. *The Key of Solomon the King.* York Beach, ME: Samuel Weiser, Inc., 1984.

McLean, Adam. *The Alchemical Mandala.* Grand Rapids, MI: Phanes Press, 1989.

Olcott, William Tyler. *Star Lore of All Ages.* New York: G. P. Putnam's Sons / The Knickerbocker Press, 1911.

Parachemy, Journal of Hermetic Arts and Sciences. Summer 1979, Vol. VII, Number 3.

———. Summer 1977, Vol. V, Number 3.

Raine, Kathleen. *Yeats, The Tarot and the Golden Dawn.* Dublin: The Dolmen Press, 1976.

Regardie, Israel. *Ceremonial Magic.* Wellingborough, Northamptonshire: The Aquarian Press, 1982.

———. *The Complete Golden Dawn System of Magic.* Phoenix, AZ: Falcon Press, 1984.

———. *Foundations of Practical Magic.* 2nd ed. Wellingborough, Northamptonshire: The Aquarian Press, 1983.

———. *The Golden Dawn.* 4th ed. St. Paul, MN: Llewellyn Publications, 1982.

———. *The Middle Pillar.* 3rd ed. St. Paul, MN: Llewellyn Publications, 1998.

———. *The Tree of Life.* York Beach, ME: Samuel Weiser, Inc., 1972.

Schwaller de Lubicz, R. A. *The Temple of Man, Vol. 1 & 2.* Rochester, VT: Inner Traditions International, 1998.

Stanley, Thomas. *The Chaldaean Oracles.* Gillette, NJ: Heptangle Books, 1989.

Stebbing, Lionel. *A Dictionary of the Occult Sciences.* London: Emerson Press, date unknown.

Torrens, R. G. *The Secret Rituals of the Golden Dawn.* New York: Samuel Weiser, Inc., 1973.

Waite, Arthur Edward. *The Book of Black Magic.* York Beach, ME: Samuel Weiser, Inc., 1983.

Wang, Robert. *The Qabalistic Tarot.* York Beach, ME: Samuel Weiser, Inc., 1983.

———. *The Secret Temple.* New York: Samuel Weiser, Inc., 1980.

Figure 113: Israel Regardie with Chic Cicero in 1984

Index

A

B

C

D

G

H

M

N

Q

R

S

Y

Z

REACH FOR THE MOON

Llewellyn publishes hundreds of books on your favorite subjects! To get these exciting books, including the ones on the following pages, check your local bookstore or order them directly from Llewellyn.

ORDER BY PHONE

- Call toll-free within the U.S. and Canada, 1-800-THE MOON
- In Minnesota, call (651) 291-1970
- We accept VISA, MasterCard, and American Express

ORDER BY MAIL

- Send the full price of your order (MN residents add 7% sales tax) in U.S. funds, plus postage & handling to:

Llewellyn Worldwide
P.O. Box 64383, Dept. K142-2
St. Paul, MN 55164–0383, U.S.A.

POSTAGE & HANDLING

(For the U.S., Canada, and Mexico)

- $4.00 for orders $15.00 and under
- $5.00 for orders over $15.00
- No charge for orders over $100.00

We ship UPS in the continental United States. We ship standard mail to P.O. boxes. Orders shipped to Alaska, Hawaii, The Virgin Islands, and Puerto Rico are sent first-class mail. Orders shipped to Canada and Mexico are sent surface mail.

International orders: Airmail—add freight equal to price of each book to the total price of order, plus $5.00 for each non-book item (audio tapes, etc.).

Surface mail—Add $1.00 per item.

Allow 2 weeks for delivery on all orders.
Postage and handling rates subject to change.

DISCOUNTS

We offer a 20% discount to group leaders or agents. You must order a minimum of 5 copies of the same book to get our special quantity price.

FREE CATALOG

Get a free copy of our color catalog, *New Worlds of Mind and Spirit*. Subscribe for just $10.00 in the United States and Canada ($30.00 overseas, airmail). Many bookstores carry *New Worlds*—ask for it!

Visit our web site at www.llewellyn.com for more information.

Experiencing the Kabbalah

A Simple Guide to Spiritual Wholeness

Chic Cicero and Sandra Tabatha Cicero

The mystical Kabbalah is one of the best esoteric systems ever devised for providing an interactive spirituality. It shows us the origin of the entire cosmos, the eternal mind of God, and the spiritual development of humankind. It can even help to bring out our latent psychic gifts. It is a precise mystical system that describes universal laws and how to utilize spiritual principles in everyday life.

While the Kabbalah has long been a central pillar of Western magic, many beginners are intimidated by its complexity. *Experiencing the Kabbalah* is a beginner's guide to the subject, which emphasizes learning the concepts through personal hands-on experience. The simple exercises and ritual drama engage your personal creativity and imagination while forming the basis of a personal daily practice for increasing your own psychic abilities.

1-56718-138-4, 5$^{3}/_{16}$ x 8, 240 pp., illus., softcover **$9.95**

Prices are subject to change.

1-800 THE MOON

The Golden Dawn

The Original Account of the Teachings, Rites & Ceremonies of the Hermetic Order

Israel Regardie

Complete in one volume with further revision, expansion, and additional notes by Regardie, Cris Monnastre, and others. Expanded with an index of more than 100 pages!

Originally published in four bulky volumes of some 1,200 pages, this 6th Revised and Enlarged Edition has been entirely reset in modern, less space-consuming type, in half the pages (while retaining the original pagination in marginal notation for reference) for greater ease and use.

Corrections of typographical errors perpetuated in the original and subsequent editions have been made, with further revision and additional text and notes by noted scholars and by actual practitioners of the Golden Dawn system of Magick, with an Introduction by the only student ever accepted for personal training by Regardie.

Also included are Initiation Ceremonies, important rituals for consecration and invocation, methods of meditation and magical working based on the Enochian Tablets, studies in the Tarot, and the system of Qabalistic Correspondences that unite the World's religions and magical traditions into a comprehensive and practical whole.

This volume is designed as a study and practice curriculum suited to both group and private practice. Meditation upon, and following with the Active Imagination, the Initiation Ceremonies are fully experiential without need of participation in group or lodge. A very complete reference encyclopedia of Western Magick.

0–87542–663–8, 840 pp., 6 x 9, illus., softcover **$29.95**

Prices are subject to change.

1-800 THE MOON